DAVID MATTHEW
KENNEDY

DAVID MATTHEW
KENNEDY
BANKER, STATESMAN, CHURCHMAN

MARTIN BERKELEY HICKMAN

Volume 1 in Monograph Series of the
David M. Kennedy Center for International Studies
Brigham Young University
Provo, Utah

Published by Deseret Book Company
in cooperation with the
David M. Kennedy Center for International Studies

First printing September 1987

Library of Congress Cataloging-in-Publication Data

Hickman, Martin Berkeley, 1925–
    David Matthew Kennedy: banker, statesman, churchman.

    Bibliography: p.
    Includes index.
    1. Kennedy, David Matthew, 1905– . 2. Bankers—
United States—Biography. 3. Statesmen—United States—
Biography. 4. Church of Jesus Christ of Latter-day
Saints—Biography. I. Title.
HG2463.K46H53   1987   332.1'092'4 [B]   87-19898
ISBN 0-87579-093-3

CONTENTS

PREFACE

Members of the cabinet of the president of the United States take precedence in the cabinet according to the date their department was created. When David Matthew Kennedy took his place in the cabinet as Secretary of the Treasury, he stood second only to the Secretary of State. He retained his cabinet position after he left Treasury to become ambassador-at-large, and thus under State Department protocol ranked second only to the Secretary of State. No other native of Utah or member of The Church of Jesus Christ of Latter-day Saints has held a higher position in the United States government or in the American diplomatic service.

But David Kennedy's achievements are not limited to his government service. He has not had just one career, but three. For a decade before he became Secretary of the Treasury, he was chairman and chief executive officer of Continental Illinois Bank and Trust Company. Under his leadership Continental was transformed from a conservative institution serving corporate customers in the Midwest into one of the largest commercial banks in the world with branches in Africa, Asia, Europe, and South America. Then late in life he began a third career as special representative of the First Presidency of The Church of Jesus Christ of Latter-day Saints. That demanding assignment drew on the experience he gained as a banker and statesman. But unlike his previous positions, his call as special representative involved neither profit nor power, but a commitment to his deepest religious convictions.

I have tried to create a context for those careers that would give readers a clear picture of the challenges Kennedy faced in each of them. That task required discussion of the Federal Reserve system, the role of commercial banks in the American economy, inflation, the politics of Japanese-American textile trade, and the international monetary system. In presenting those issues I have tried to strike a balance between oversimplification and unnecessary detail. Although those topics are all highly technical, there seemed no way to do justice to Kennedy's contributions without creating a meaningful framework for them.

At one time I planned to entitle this biography *David M. Kennedy: A Mormon Life*. Despite the change in title, one of my goals remained to examine Kennedy's professional career within the context of his Mormon heritage, including his longstanding active involvement in church affairs as a member of the church's lay clergy. I have aspired to weave his religious faith into the biography both as motivation and result. This is a book about a believer by a believer; consequently I have not feigned objectivity in an effort to distance myself from Kennedy's religious experience. At the same time, I have aspired to integrate Kennedy's commitment to the Church into the biography in such a way that readers who did not share that commitment would grasp its importance in understanding his motivations, character, and life-style.

I began this project at the invitation of Spencer J. Palmer, then director of the David M. Kennedy Center for International Studies, and Jae R. Ballif, provost and vice-president of Brigham Young University. I am grateful to them for their support and encouragement over the past four years. The work could not have been completed without the assistance of three outstanding research assistants: Greg Johnson, who began the project with me and who supervised arranging the Kennedy Papers in a computerized filing system for easy and rapid retrieval; Dale Lyman, whose research on the Treasury years was particularly helpful; and Grant Paul Skabelund, whose eye for detail has assured that names, dates, and other factual references in the text and citations in the footnotes are accurate and precise. He was also responsible for assuring that all changes in the text were properly made, a task he managed with patience and skill.

Dan Miller prepared a helpful memorandum on the legal issues in the merger of Continental with City National Bank. Gordon Irving, who skillfully supervises the oral history program in the Historical Department of The Church of Jesus Christ of Latter-day Saints, made David Kennedy's oral history available to me. He also made useful suggestions during the course of my research that opened new avenues of investigation. I would be ungrateful if I did not recognize the wholehearted support of Joyce Penrod and Clara Thomas, my administrative assistant and my secretary, during the time I served as dean of the College of Family, Home, and Social Sciences at BYU.

Marilyn Webb, Manager of the Faculty Support Center in the college, supervised the transcription of the numerous interviews and processed the initial drafts of the book.

I am grateful to many members of David Kennedy's family and to his associates in church, business, and government who generously shared their experiences and comments in interviews. Their names are listed in the sources, beginning on page 367.

Eleanor Knowles, executive editor at Deseret Book, has overseen the production of the book at every step. She has also reminded me that the length of a biography is not the best test of its quality. Kent Ware, design director at Deseret Book, is responsible for the design of the cover and the text. Kelly Nielsen, cartographic technician in the Geography Department at BYU, designed the map showing the areas where David Kennedy spent his youth.

Randall Jones and Frank Fox, friends and colleagues, have read all or part of the manuscript and have saved me from errors and sharpened my prose. Spencer Condie read the chapter on the church years and made several insightful comments. Howard Christy, senior editor of Scholarly Publications at Brigham Young University, read the entire manuscript with care, insight, and rigor. His suggestions have made it a stronger book, and for that I am grateful. A word of appreciation is due for Louise Williams, assistant editor, Scholarly Publications, for making her computer system available during the editing process.

Finally, I am grateful for the advice of Spencer Palmer, who has read every draft of the manuscript and whose faith in the project never wavered. And, of course, the book could not have been completed without the full cooperation of David and Lenora Kennedy and their four daughters, Marilyn, Barbara, Carol, and Patricia. In addition to the oral history, David and Lenora graciously consented to ten interviews and provided letters and documents relating to family affairs. Each of their daughters enriched my understanding of their father by sharing with me their unique perspective of his character and achievements.

Lastly and most importantly, I am grateful for the sustaining presence of my wife, JoAnn. Not only has she believed in me and in the project, but she has read every word of the book, with less concern for my ego than with improving my work. She nursed me through a heart attack that delayed work on the book for three months and has fended off demands on my time that would have slowed my progress. There are debts that can never be repaid, but can only be acknowledged. I am grateful for the chance to acknowledge my debt to her that I cannot repay.

The advice and support I have received have contributed substantially to whatever merit there is in this book. Any failures or errors are my sole responsibility.

NOTE OF EXPLANATION

The frequency with which I have had to refer to The Church of Jesus Christ of Latter-day Saints has led me to use "the Church," or Mormon church, rather than the full name.

For those not familiar with some of the terms used in connection with the Church, a brief explanation is in order. The Church is led by a president, who has two counselors; these three men constitute the First Presidency, one of the two governing bodies of the Church. The other is the Quorum (or Council) of the Twelve Apostles. Operational responsibility is vested in the Presiding Bishop and his two counselors and in the Quorum of the Seventy. These four bodies—the First Presidency, the Quorum of the Twelve, the Presiding Bishopric, and the Quorum of the Seventy—constitute the General Authorities of the Church. Geographically, the Church is divided into stakes and wards. Each stake is headed by a president with two counselors, assisted by a high council of twelve. Wards, which are subdivisions of stakes, are presided over by a bishop with two counselors. The Church has a lay clergy, so that stake and ward officers are rotated in office and continue their occupations while they serve in ecclesiastical positions. Where there are not enough members to organize a stake, the affairs of the Church in a specified geographical area are administered by a mission president. Within the missions are branches, each headed by a president and counselors.

1

RANDOLPH:
BOYHOOD YEARS

The Bear River, which has its origin in the Uinta Mountains of northeastern Utah, cuts its way northward through the mountains of northern Utah and southern Idaho to what is now Soda Springs, Idaho, before turning sharply southward to Cache Valley, Utah. From there it meanders through Box Elder Valley until it empties into the Great Salt Lake. When the river leaves the Uintas, it enters a valley approximately forty miles long and four miles wide. To the east are the Crawford Mountains, which rise sharply from the valley floor, six thousand feet above sea level, to Mount Rex at a height of nine thousand feet. To the west, the Wasatch Mountains rise more gently to a crest dividing the valley from the rest of Utah. The Bear River Valley, as it became known to the first settlers, is a harsh land with long winters and short summers.

Indians had long known the valley as a fertile hunting ground for deer, elk, antelope, sage hens, and bear, and fish were plentiful in the Bear River and in the streams that feed it. They knew also that winters in the valley were severe and the summers all too short. Had they understood what was required to make the valley a useful site for the white man's agriculture, they would have advised the first settlers to seek homesteads elsewhere. But they were not consulted when the first Mormon settlers from St. Charles, Idaho, arrived in the spring of 1870. St. Charles and a number of other settlements were established along the shores of Bear Lake, northeast of the Bear River Valley and separated from it by the Wasatch Mountains, in 1864 under the leadership of Charles C. Rich, a member of the Quorum of the Twelve Apostles of The Church of Jesus Christ of Latter-day Saints (commonly called the Mormon Church).[1] When the first settlers left St. Charles to make the short but difficult trip over the mountains to the Bear River Valley, they were already seasoned veterans in the process of creating new settlements. On March 14, 1870, Randolph Stewart led his small group of settlers to the north end of the valley, to a stream later known as Big Creek. They made camp on a knoll and began to search for a likely site for a town.

The Mormon settlement pattern called for settlers to live in villages and towns rather than on their farms outside the community. Hence, Stewart and his companions, under the direction of Charles C. Rich, who arrived a week later, began to lay out a town site, which would be called Randolph in honor of Stewart. That first year they laid out claims to lots in the town, dug wells, and planted crops. Most of the settlers intended to spend the winter outside the valley and return in the spring, but twenty-six of the original group stayed all winter, living in tents and a few rough-hewn huts. In June 1871, Brigham Young, president of the Church, took advantage of the Union Pacific Railroad, which passed through the south end of the valley, to visit the settlement and organize a ward of the Church, with Stewart as the first bishop. Creation of the ward reflected the settlers' determination to make Randolph their permanent home regardless of ensuing hardships.

Some four years after the founding of Randolph, a young Scotsman who had been working in the coal mines in Almy, Wyoming, came to the area to find land on which to settle his family. John Kennedy, Jr., together with his brother, James, had emigrated from Scotland in 1870, leaving behind their parents and nine other children. The two older sons had been sent ahead to prepare the way for the rest of the family, whose decision to leave Scotland had its roots in their conversion to The Church of Jesus Christ of Latter-day Saints.[2] The message that the Mormon missionaries had brought to the Kennedy family in their humble home in Kilmarnock,

2

Ayrshire, was that a prophet, Joseph Smith, had been called of God to restore the pure gospel of Jesus Christ. They announced that the Church of Jesus Christ had been established in America and that converts should leave their homes in the Old World to assist in the building of it. Thus, the two brothers immigrated to the United States in search of a new life that promised spiritual as well as economic rewards. They would not only add strength to the ranks of the Saints who had preceded them to the headquarters of the Church in the West, but they also hoped to find the possibility of owning land, a dream beyond their reach in Scotland.

In 1870 the two brothers left Scotland on the steamship *Colorado* for the United States. Arriving without enough money to make the trip west, they sought work in the coal mines of Pennsylvania. When they had enough money saved, they left the coal mines of Pennsylvania for those of Almy. Coal mining was not what had brought them to America, however; they wanted land that they could call their own. But first they had to earn enough money to bring the rest of the family to America, and then save enough to buy land. The family was reunited in 1872, when John, Sr., accompanied by his wife, Elizabeth, and the nine other children, finally came to America. Two years later the family purchased land three miles south of Randolph among the banks of Big Creek, 160 acres that stretched from the Bear River into the foothills of the Wasatch Mountains. The older sons continued to work in the mines in the winter, for in those first years they could not make a living from the ranch. As they married, the Kennedys, a close-knit family, built homes near one another, and inevitably the community that grew up around those homes was called Kennedyville. That name eventually disappeared and was replaced by Argyle, a name that recalled the Scottish origins of its settlers.

When John, Jr., took up his homestead in Rich County, he was already a married man with a family. Soon after his arrival in Almy he had married Hannah Simpson, and three children were born to them before they saved enough money to buy the land that they hoped would take John out of the coal mines forever.

3

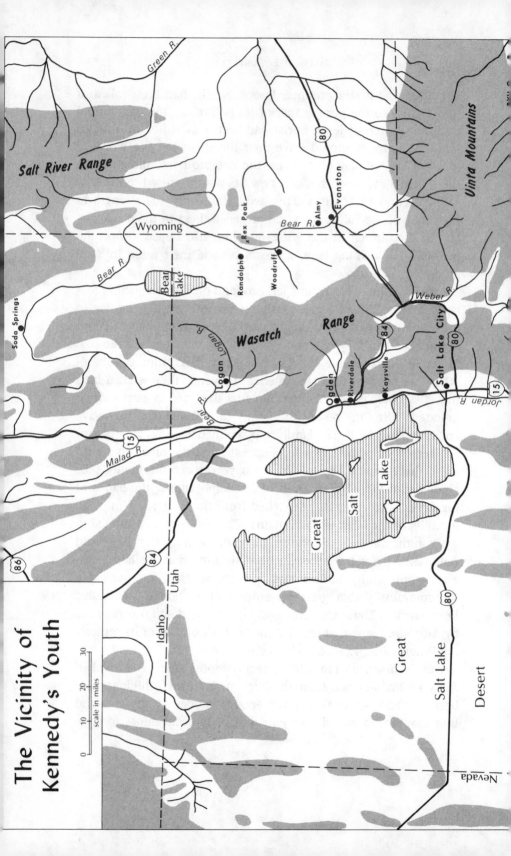

The Vicinity of Kennedy's Youth

scale in miles
0 10 20 30

Salt River Range

Green R.

80
Evanston
Almy
× Rex Peak
Bear R.
Wyoming
Randolph
Woodruff
Bear R.
Bear
Lake
Soda Springs
Weber R.
84
Salt Lake City
80
15
Wasatch   Range
Logan R.
Logan
Ogden
Riverdale
Kaysville
Jordan R.
Bear R.
15
Malad R.
Great   Salt   Lake
86
84
Idaho
Utah
80
Great

Salt Lake

Desert

Nevada

Uinta Mountains

Ultimately, they would have a family of sixteen children; in addition, they would raise the daughter of John's sister, who died soon after her daughter's birth. Their first home in Argyle had just one room for John and Hannah and their first five children. In the winter of 1879–80 the roof of the cabin caught fire, and though no one was hurt, the family needed a new home. John decided that it was a good time not only to repair the roof but also to provide more room for his family. With the help of his brothers, he built a log home with three rooms and a kitchen. That house remained home for John and Hannah until her death in 1901.

John remained the dominant figure in the Kennedy family for the rest of his life. He settled family disputes and administered justice in what he thought were the best interests of the family. On one occasion he told his son George, "Your brother Joe needs help. I understand he owes you nineteen hundred dollars and he can't pay that; it is too much of a burden for him. I want you to just forget and forgive that." George's wife was incensed that her husband would forgive a debt that large when they needed money. However, George's response was brief: "Because my father asked me to." Joe recognized the sacrifice that George made for him, and his appreciation for George's gesture strengthened their already strong ties.

John not only was respected by his family but also enjoyed the trust of the community. He served two terms as a county commissioner, one term in the Utah state legislature, and as a justice of the peace in Rich County. His prominence in the community was also reflected in his call to positions of leadership in the Church. The families living in Argyle originally attended church in Randolph, but because of the difficulty of getting to church, particularly in the winter, the Kennedyville Branch was organized in 1893. In 1895 the branch was reorganized into the Argyle Ward by the Bear Lake Stake presidency, and John, Jr., was called to be the bishop by Heber J. Grant, a member of the Church's Quorum of the Twelve Apostles.

For the next twenty-seven years John was the spiritual leader of the Argyle Ward. He spoke in sacrament meeting (the weekly worship service), counseled his flock to avoid the sins of the world, bore his testimony of the restoration of the gospel through Joseph Smith, and blessed the members of the ward. As bishop, John held the ward together for those twenty-seven years. Eventually, as families moved away from Argyle, the number of ward members decreased until it was decided to combine the Argyle Ward with the Randolph Ward. On February 9, 1913, the eighteen ward members present at sacrament meeting voted unanimously to support that proposal.

The third child of John and Hannah, and the last to be born before the family moved from Almy to Argyle, was named George at his birth on December 4, 1874. George learned early in his youth to shoulder his share of the ranch chores. He gained a reputation for being a hard worker, a reputation that would last through his life.[3] As his younger brothers became old enough to assume their share of the work, George began to seek work with the other ranchers in the valley, including Peter Johnson, who had joined the Church with his mother in Denmark. The two of them immigrated to the United States in 1862 and joined a handcart company for the trip to Utah. Peter married Matilda Brown in April 1873, and the next spring they moved to Rich County, where he purchased land adjoining that of John Kennedy, Jr. By the time George went to work on the Johnson ranch, Peter was one of the most successful ranchers in Rich County, with a large herd of sheep that summered in the valley and wintered on the Utah-Nevada border.

While George was working for Peter, he began to court Peter's oldest daughter, Katherine (Katie), whom he had known since she was a child, and who was now an attractive young woman. After a short courtship they were married on August 30, 1896; he was twenty-one and she was not yet eighteen. Though Katie did not have the opportunity of schooling beyond the limited education the one-room school in Argyle provided, she came from a family that prized education. In the years after her marriage, her father would lease his ranch to George and his own son, Will, and take his family to Logan so the younger children could attend Utah State Agricultural College. Despite leaving her father's home before she could share in that opportunity, Katie developed a deep love for literature, particularly poetry. She knew the Scottish poets, not only because she was surrounded by Scots in Argyle but also because her mother was Scottish and the rhymes of the Ayrshire brogue came naturally to her. She also knew the works of Gray, Pope, and Keats among the English poets and Longfellow among the Americans, and as her children became old enough to share her enthusiasm, she would read to them from her favorite poets.

No sooner had George and Katie exchanged marriage vows than they went to work for twenty-five dollars a month and board and room on a ranch owned by John W. Dykins. Dykins must have been a tough taskmaster, for when George's brother James filled in for George that winter, he complained that Dykins drove him like a slave from morning to night. Katie worked only until their oldest son, Lorenzo George (L. G.), was born in the first year of their marriage. Two years later Karl joined the family, and a third son, Melvin, was born in 1902. After their marriage George worked at various ranches in the valley, but by 1904 he, with his brother Will and Katie's brothers, Will and Peter, Jr., purchased a large herd of sheep from Peter, Sr. In the summer they could graze the sheep in the Wasatch Mountains west of Argyle, but because

George Kennedy

of the severe winters in the Bear River Valley, they had to move the sheep to a winter range on the Salt Lake desert. This meant that from October to April they were separated from their families, but for George the separation was the price he had to pay to accumulate enough capital to get a ranch of his own. The first step toward that goal was taken when he, in partnership with his brothers-in-law, was able to lease the ranch of Peter, Sr., after the Johnson family moved to Logan. The conflicts that often mar family relationships when family members are in business together never threatened the close friendship George enjoyed with Katie's brothers, particularly Will. Will Johnson, he was later to write, was his "main chum," and so he remained for the rest of their lives.

George and Katie's marriage was based not only on their love, but also on their shared commitment to the Church. Although George's father was bishop of the Argyle Ward for twenty-seven years, his children, particularly the boys, were not noted for their piety. Honest, hard-working men who struggled to wrench a living from the land, they were out on the Wasatch range with their sheep and cattle in the summer, and they each took their turn staying with the sheep on the winter range on the Salt Lake desert. In such circumstances, weekly attendance at Sabbath meetings was neglected more often than not, as were some of the central rites of the Church.[4] George was noted in the family as being the most ardent in his religious faith, and Katie joined him in that faith. They took part in church activities and served in church callings, he as a ward officer and she in the Relief Society, the women's auxiliary organization. They made public confessions of their commitment to the Church as they shared their testimonies in the monthly fast meetings, and, in an era when attendance at weekly sacrament meeting was remarkably low, they were regular attenders.

In 1905, with three young boys, ages nine, seven, and three, to care for, and the prospect of owning their own ranch in the offing, George and Katie awaited the birth of their fourth child. On July 21 George and his brothers were stacking hay in the barn not far from the Kennedys' two-room log house. Katie, uncomfortable because of the summer heat, could hear the sounds of the derrick and the squeak of the pulley as load after load of hay was moved from the wagon to the barn. That afternoon her birth pains began. Though this was her fourth child and the midwife, Sarah Cornia, was experienced, Katie anxiously thought of all the things that could go wrong in the birth of her baby. Her fears disappeared when she held a healthy baby boy in her arms. She and George named him David Matthew. Later she would tell David that she loved him at first sight despite his "red face and long nose, which was as long as Mrs. Cornia's nose."

The world into which David Kennedy was born was in the twilight of an era dominated by the British Empire. With the defeat of Napoleon at Waterloo in 1815, Britain had become the arbitrator of European, and hence world, politics. British statesmen used their economic and military power to assure that the sun never set on the British Empire. In 1905 the world was at peace. Even the most pessimistic seers did not foresee the savage trench warfare of World War I that would ravage France and Belgium for four years, result in the death of millions of soldiers on both sides, bring a Communist government to power in Russia, undermine the economic base of the British Empire, force the abdication of the German emperor, involve the United States in a European war, and permanently change the nature of world politics.

In the United States, there were increasing doubts about the benefits of the rapid industrialization following the Civil War. Theodore Roosevelt was challenging the power of the trusts and offering the nation "A Square Deal." The "Muckrakers" were exposing the excesses of large corporations and the corruption of big-city bosses. Henry Ford was exploring ways to make automobiles cheap enough for the American worker, Orville and Wilbur Wright excited the imagination of the nation with their successful flights at Kitty Hawk, and Thomas Edison had already given the nation the electric light and was hard at work perfecting his motion picture projectors and recording devices. Though historians would later date the end of the frontier at 1890, homesteaders continued the westward thrust of the nation and immigrants continued to seek a better life in the new world.

9

In 1905, the year David Kennedy was born, Utah had been a state only nine years. The long, drawn-out struggle for statehood ended when Wilford Woodruff, president of The Church of Jesus Christ of Latter-day Saints, announced in 1890 that the Mormons were no longer practicing plural marriage. Converts to the Church, albeit in decreasing numbers, were still coming to Utah from northern Europe and other parts of the United States. Fortunes were being made in mining as the Wasatch and Oquirrh mountains gave up their gold, silver, copper, zinc, and lead to the lucky and adventurous. Even those who clung to the land prospered, for farm income almost doubled in the same period. In 1905, after sixty years of relative isolation, Utah was becoming integrated into the national economic, social, and political life of America. In Gustive Larson's telling phrase, Utah was "Americanized" in order to achieve statehood, and the process continued apace in the twentieth century.

Rich County with its county seat, Randolph, was in many ways in Utah but not of Utah. The county was separated from the rest of the state by the Wasatch Mountains on the west and the Uinta Mountains on the south. The major economic center was Evanston, Wyoming, a mining town located on the Union Pacific Railroad thirty miles southeast of Randolph. Hence, economically and geographically it was part of Wyoming, but culturally and politically it was a part of Utah and the Mormon cultural sphere. It was settled as part of the Mormon colonization effort, and it remained predominately a Mormon settlement. Politically, it mirrored the rest of Utah, for the county voted Republican in the 1904 election and the Republican party dominated political life in the county through the decade and beyond.

Randolph, in the year of David's birth, had a population of over five hundred. The 1900 census shows a population of 571 living in town, but probably another 150 to 200 lived on farms near town and did not appear in the statistics. Randolph was still very much a frontier community; though telephone service came to the community in 1898, it did not have electric lights until 1917. Merchandise was freighted thirty miles over primitive roads by horse and wagon from the railhead at Evanston. Much of the news from the outside world came from the Church-owned

*Katherine Johnson Kennedy, mother of
David M. Kennedy, and her sister,
Elizabeth Kennedy Johnson*

Deseret News, published in Salt Lake City. Local papers such as the
Round-up and the *Rich County News*, also carried a surprising
amount of state, national, and international news, in addition to
chronicling the events of Rich County.

The *Rich County News*, published from 1907 to 1928, mirrored everyday life in Randolph. Dr. Matthew S. Reay, who became
a legend as a country doctor, let subscribers know they could reach
him day and night by Bell Phone; the Spencer brothers, who owned
the general merchandise store, advertised their summer sale of
men's and women's clothing; and the Jensen and Holland's Candy
& Cigar Stand, operated in conjunction with the Pool and Amusement Hall, notified customers that it was the agent for the Evanston
Steam Laundry. It was in the pages of the *News* that Joshua Eldredge
announced "Our Spring Goods Are 'IN,' nuf sed"; ranchers were
warned that horse "gyps" were about, and they could protect themselves by buying a copy of "Horse Secrets" for only $1.25; and
women were promised health and happiness if they would take
Lydia Pinkham's Vegetable Compound, or Dr. Pierce's Favorite Pre-
scription, which guaranteed to make weak women strong and sick
women well. The local news column notified subscribers of visitors to Randolph, business and pleasure trips taken by its citizens,
parties and dances being held, progress on local construction
projects, and reports of church and community functions. Leaders
of the Young Ladies' Mutual Improvement Association sponsored
by the Randolph Ward incurred the ire of the publisher of the
News when they sent away to Evanston for handbills advertising

their annual party. "Not that we care one iota, but we take it that our services being unworthy of their work when it is for cash," the editor fumed, ". . . hereafter we can look for the Evanston paper, where they have their other work done, to make all their free announcements."

David's birth marked the beginning of Katie's own struggle with poor health, for she was crippled by chronic arthritis that finally made it too difficult for her to care for the family. The Smock family, from whom George bought a ranch in January 1906, was moving to Oregon, and they convinced Katie and George that a doctor near to where they were moving had successfully treated people with arthritis. Katie was reluctant to leave the family, but when her brother Will and his wife, Elizabeth (who was George's sister) said that they would look after David, she finally agreed to go to Oregon. She spent the next year away from her family, so for the first year of his life David lived with his aunt, whom he would always call his second mother.

The world of David Kennedy's boyhood, bounded by Rich County, became an intrinsic part of his self-identity. The center of that world was the extended Kennedy and Johnson families of grandparents, parents, brothers, uncles, aunts, and cousins. David's understanding of his world began with the families' memories embodied in accounts of the difficulties they faced and the sacrifices they made in wrenching the land from the wilderness. He relived in those family stories the dirty, backbreaking toil required to clear the land of sagebrush, the struggle to bring water to the land by building the Kennedy ditch (still in use) that tapped the water of Big Creek, the winters spent in the mines of Almy to finance the purchase and development of the land, and the final realization of the dream that had led his grandfather Kennedy from the mines of Scotland to become a leading rancher in Rich County. David's awareness of family ties was sharpened by intermarriage in the two families, the lease of his grandfather's ranch by his father and his uncle, the involvement of his two grandfathers in the Bank of Randolph, his grandfather Kennedy's influence as the spiritual leader of the Argyle Ward, and his boyhood friendship with his cousins on both sides, all of which contributed to a sense of family-identity that remained strong throughout his life.

On the surface the Randolph of David's childhood was a homogeneous Mormon community. Church-sponsored dramas, dances, and socials were the principal diversions from the routine of daily life. Church leaders figured prominently in holiday celebrations, the Church provided the impetus and support for the first school, and in many respects it was difficult to separate church and civic concerns. But those surface impressions, while not entirely wrong, conceal a good deal of diversity. Mormons were expected to follow the advice of their church leaders and eschew liquor and tobacco, but as early as 1872, the town fathers received two requests for licenses to sell liquor. Church influence was also attenuated by the rigors of ranch life, which required that many of the men spend long periods of time away from home tending the sheep and cattle. Living in those isolated circumstances, church dietary rules and careful observance of ordinances and rituals were often neglected. And there were deeper conflicts. In 1890 a newly elected school board sued to have the Church evicted from the building the two organizations shared. "Two of our trustees have got quite 'Liberal' of late," a contemporary account alleged, "and so want to take the house from the rightful owners and give it to the school district without any remuneration whatever, and in addition ask for $500 attorney fees, etc."[5]

In a small town like Randolph, it was inevitable that David would become aware of these differences and conflicts, for they existed within his own extended family. He began to develop at an early age, therefore, the ability to distinguish between those values on which the family and community were united and those that divided them. Sensing more than fully understanding those differences, he learned to respect, and often to love, those who did not share all his values, and this incipient tolerance, when it was fully developed, would include not only the diversity of Randolph but also the far more complex and extensive diversity of peoples and cultures far removed from the mountain valleys of Utah.

The Kennedys lived in Randolph year-round until 1912, when David was seven. That summer they moved to Kaysville, twenty

13

The George Kennedy family: David (front), Katherine, Melvin, Lorenzo George (L. G.), Karl, and George. Inset: Ivan, who was born later

miles north of Salt Lake City, where winters were milder. But they returned to Randolph each summer, and David attended school there during the year 1914–15. In October 1912, George sold the Smock ranch and, in partnership with his brother Joseph, bought a larger ranch—known as the Crawford ranch—of some eight hundred acres about seven miles from Randolph. The partnership lasted just over a year, when George bought Joseph's share. Before this move, George had built a home in Randolph, where the family had lived during the winter months.[6]

The Crawford ranch was the ranch of David's boyhood memories, and it was there that he first began to help in the harvest of hay for winter feed. The hardest job, stacking the hay as it was lifted onto the stack by the derrick, went to David's oldest brother, L. G. His father and his brother Karl ran the mowing machines. David's job was to drive the horses that ran the derrick. It was hot dusty work, but David thought it was better to run the derrick than to be up on the stack feverishly wielding a pitchfork to arrange

14

each load of hay so that the stack would rise evenly to its required height.

By the time he was nine, David was promoted to the mowing machine. He was, however, too short of limb to reach the pedals that raised and lowered the cutting bar. L. G., an accomplished blacksmith, lowered the seat so David could reach the pedals, so with instructions from his father to jump off in the event of a runaway, David began his career as a hay mower. When a thunderstorm arose on the first day, his team of mules, Trigger and Greely, bolted across the field. David could not rein them in, so, remembering his father's advice, he jumped off the mower. The mules finally ran into a fence, which brought them to a halt, but the mowing machine was so badly damaged that not even L. G.'s skills were sufficient to repair it, and the mowing had to wait for two days until new parts were brought from Evanston.

Haying and other work around the ranch were in David's eyes boring chores, but the roundup, the real work of the ranch, had romantic appeal for the youth. When he became old enough to work on the ranch, he began begging his father to be taken on the roundup. Each year his father had a different excuse: David was too young, the work was too difficult, it wouldn't be fair to the other riders to expect them to do their work and look after him at the same time. Finally, when he was ten, David broke down his father's resistance. George sent his young son off on his first roundup mounted on Clover with instructions that if he became lost, he was to let the horse have his head and Clover would bring him back to the ranch. Although George let David believe that he was on his own, he asked another rancher, Milton J. "Melt" Hatch, to keep an eye on the boy. George, wise in the ways of cowboys, cautioned David that around the campfire they would tell him tall tales to frighten him and seek to play jokes on him.

David learned that the roundup was hard work with some challenges he had not anticipated. The first day he set off with a canteen of water and a can of pear preserves for lunch. His job was to help "Melt" round up cattle in the ravines that cut down the mountainside. The day was hot, he was thirsty, and he soon exhausted the water in his canteen, so it was with relief that he found a small spring. He tried to drink even though the spring was defouled by the cattle, but he had to give up because the muddy water was undrinkable. There was nothing to do but drive the cattle on through the heat of the afternoon to the roundup camp at Split Rock, where there was a clear flowing spring. When they arrived at the spring, both boy and horse gulped the water so fast that "Melt" pulled them away before they made themselves sick.

The world of ranch work into which David plunged at an early age was more than just work, it was part of his education. Farmers and ranchers in the rural America of the early twentieth century transmitted their skills and knowledge by having their sons work alongside them. From their fathers, sons learned more than the skills; they learned the satisfaction of a job well done and the courage to persevere in the face of adversity. Working alongside his father, David also learned the importance of concentrated and sustained effort even though that effort sometimes resulted in disappointment, as when the price of beef brought little reward for the family's hard work. For the rest of his life he understood that the achievement of any goal depends far more on effort than it does on fate or luck.

David's education in ranching was similar to that of other boys in Randolph, but for him there was another facet to his education for life that was unique. Katie's poor health meant that she needed help with household chores she would ordinarily have done herself. The older boys, L. G., Karl, and Melvin, were needed in the fields, so it often fell to David to stay behind with his mother. His first assignment was to tend the children of a woman George hired to help Katie. It was a task he hated, and often his charges bore the brunt of his frustration. He tried to appease one of them by pulling her in a wagon, only to find out that every time he stopped, she started to cry. He began locking her in the shed until one day she got into the wagon grease, getting it all over herself and everything else in the shed. Finally in his frustration, David spanked her. That was the last straw; her mother told Katie that things had gone far enough and it was time that David be punished, which she inteded to do by throwing him in the canal. Katie in her own anger agreed, and into the canal David went. To their dismay they discovered that the water was deeper than they expected, and he nearly drowned. After that experience Katie announced that in the future she would discipline David.

As David grew older, he assumed even greater responsibility for household chores. Katie was able to do most of the cooking, but the heavy work, such as scrubbing floors, washing, and churning the butter, had to be done by someone else. For David those hours spent with his mother were lessons in courage. Despite her pain and her inability to get around, she maintained an active interest in her church work and pursued her love of literature. She also began to write poetry, and hardly a birthday or an anniversary went by without family or friends receiving a poem from Katie. She taught David that it was in his power to determine his own destiny—a destiny, Katie repeatedly told him, that must include a church mission and an education. If David learned diligence and hard work from the Kennedys, his desire to go on a mission and to get an education were a legacy from the Johnsons. His grandfather Johnson sent most of his children to Logan to attend the Utah Agricultural College and later bought a home in Logan. His Uncle William was the first and only missionary called from the Argyle Ward. Katie wanted these opportunities for all of her sons, but only David was to realize her vision.

David's boyhood in Randolph was a mirror in which he saw himself for the rest of his life. It was in Randolph that he first learned that aping the ways of the world was apt to bring misery. One cold December day his father's hired men, out feeding the cattle, asked David if he would drive the team while they pitched the hay from either side of the wagon. David noticed that one of the men was chewing tobacco and thought he would like to try some, so he made a deal: yes, he said, he would drive the team if they would give him a chew of tobacco. It was a bargain David lived to regret, for one of the men, thinking to have some fun at David's expense, took hold of David's bib overalls and shook him so hard that he swallowed the tobacco cud. He became violently ill with a high fever, and when the men confessed to George what they had done, David was taken the seven miles from the ranch to

Randolph to have his stomach pumped by Dr. Reay. The nauseating taste of that tobacco came rushing back to David years later when at a dinner party the flavor of the sauce on the meat resurrected that experience and he had to leave the table.

It was in Randolph that he had his most memorable fist fight and unwillingly got involved in a horse race that resulted in a broken leg. The fight was stopped by David's older brother Karl when it became obvious that David was overmatched. "You should have known better," he told David. "That kid is older and stronger than you even though he is not much bigger than you." Karl's most

*Melvin and
David Kennedy*

telling advice was that in the future David should talk instead of fight, because he was a much better talker than a fighter. The horse race began as Melvin and David were riding home on their favorite horse, Pearl. Some older boys riding behind them decided to race, and as they came alongside Melvin and David, Pearl bolted into a run. The other racers ran down the roadway, but Melvin and David, astride Pearl, were forced off the road. Suddenly the canal loomed ahead. The horses on the road crossed on a bridge, but Pearl with a mighty leap jumped the canal. The boys, riding bareback, had nothing to hold on to, and as Pearl hit the ground they fell off. Melvin was knocked unconscious and David's leg was broken. Since Melvin seemed to be the most seriously hurt, he received immediate attention, while David suffered with his broken leg. But that pain was soon forgotten when the doctor finally set his leg. David's screams reached all the way to the barn, where Katie had taken refuge so that she would not have to witness his ordeal.

David's discomfort while his broken leg healed was assuaged by a gift from his grandfather Johnson. While recuperating, the boy developed a passionate longing for a pair of red cowboy boots and pestered his father to go to Evanston to get some. But Evanston was thirty miles away, and George, who considered the boots a passing fancy of a youngster feeling sorry for himself, paid little heed to David's repeated importunings. Finally David asked his mother to help him write to his grandfather Johnson in Logan. Off went the letter, and back by return mail came a beautiful pair of red boots. David put a boot on his good leg and lay in bed enjoying its shiny glow.

Randolph was also the scene of David's first business deal. George had a herd of sheep, and each spring at lambing time, some ewes would die while giving birth. Ordinarily the sheepherders would dispose of the motherless lambs because they had no way of taking care of them, but David and Melvin were allowed to care for those lambs, feeding them first with a nipple and then gradually teaching them to drink from a bucket. Each year they added a few lambs to their flock; the rams would be slaughtered for meat, but they would keep the ewes for breeding. Then Melvin, a natural mechanic, decided he wanted to try to build an airplane, but he had no money for parts. When his father refused to finance his scheme, he approached David for a loan of ten dollars. David, who thought that the loan was really a subsidy in disguise, declined, so Melvin offered to sell his half of the herd for the ten dollars. That proposal seemed more attractive to David, and the deal was struck. But although he kept the herd for several years, the profits he envisioned when he wrote his first check for ten dollars, drawn on the Bank of Randolph, never entered his pocket. In the agricultural depression of 1921, with cash scarce, he gave the sheep to his father to raise money to pay the taxes on the ranch.

Although David would spend his teenage years in Ogden and Riverdale, thirty-five miles north of Salt Lake City, home was always Randolph: the family, the ranch, the fishing and hunting trips that came after the last load of hay was stacked each season (three- to five-day trips that were planned all summer and relived all winter), the campfires with cowboys spinning tall tales, the one-room school in Argyle where J. Clyde Brewer was the principal and only teacher, the school in Randolph and frequent scoldings by Principal Hial Lee Bradford for playing at school after class when he should have been home, visits to Eldredge's store that usually ended with Joshua Eldredge giving him a generous portion of candy for his penny and telling him what a fine boy he was, the Christmas program when he had to stand on a chair to recite "The Old Striped Stocking" because otherwise he was too small to be seen, the one-cylinder Reo his father purchased in Evanston (one of the first cars in Randolph), the ward where his grandfather Kennedy presided each week and where David first heard his father and mother bear testimony of their faith, the winters when canals froze solid and L. G. and Karl would pull him along between them as they skated to school, the near disaster when his dog "Bob" prevented him from wading into a slough by barking and grabbing at his pants until his father came to rescue him, and the nights spent sleeping in the hayloft. These were the memories that made the town of Randolph David Kennedy's spiritual and emotional home.

2

THE MATURING YEARS –
AND LENORA

The summer of 1912 marked a significant turning point in David's boyhood. Katie's continued poor health and her desire for her sons to have a better education than Randolph could provide prompted a decision to move to Kaysville, Utah, for the winter. Thereafter, David would spend most summers on the ranch, but all his schooling, except for a brief return to Randolph for the 1914–15 school year, would be in Kaysville, Ogden, or Riverdale, southwest of Ogden.

The family rented a house in Kaysville, and two or three times a week George and Katie drove the fifteen miles to Ogden in their Overland car to see Katie's doctor. Although the doctor continued to hold out hope that she would eventually recover, her health was a constant concern. If the move to Kaysville did not bring an immediate improvement in Katie's health, the boys' schooling opportunities widened. David began to be aware of the outside world when his fifth-grade class studied the lives of the presidents. He recorded in his diary: "Our president now is Woodrow Wilson and I believe he is pretty good." In the spring of 1916 he developed kidney trouble, and he frequently missed school to go to Ogden with his parents for medical treatment.

At the end of the school year in May 1916, Katie's doctor recommended that she remain in Ogden for the summer. George

21

needed the older boys on the ranch, so it fell to David, who was a month shy of his eleventh birthday, to stay with his mother. His father admonished him, "Now it is your job to take care of Mother. You see that nothing happens to her."[1] Katie and David moved into the Grant Hotel on the corner of 24th Street and Grant Avenue. David brought Katie her meals, accompanied her to doctor's appointments, and did whatever else her health and comfort required. He soon became a familiar sight in nearby restaurants where he ordered their meals. The task of taking his mother to the doctor's office was more difficult. Though the office was only a half block away, Katie's arthritis was so advanced and the pain so great that it often took a half hour to make that short trip.

George was able to visit them two or three times during the summer, and Katie's sisters were attentive. But most of the time David and his mother were alone. Despite her pain, Katie made every effort to keep him from being lonely, reading to him and talking about the ranch and family members and about his future. Katie also knew how difficult it was for David to be cooped up all day in a hotel room, so she let him spend time outside the hotel. He took the street car to the Hermitage resort in Ogden Canyon and the Bamberger railroad to Lagoon, a resort halfway between Salt Lake City and Ogden; he played jacks by himself if he could find no one else to play with; he discovered the soda fountain in the Hudson Building just up 24th Street and made friends with the soda jerks, who would sometimes treat him to a soda; he explored the Grant Hotel and learned in the process how to start the freight elevator by pulling on the rope; and he found the entrance to the roof of the building, from which he could see the entire city.

One voyage of discovery on which his mother sent him, on the first Sunday they were in the hotel, was to find a church he could attend. She was amused when she learned from his description of the service, which he said "was unusual," that he had mistaken the nearby Episcopal church for a Mormon chapel. David had promised his mother that he would go to church, and go to church he did. He was greeted cordially, and he stayed for the entire service, kneeling when the others knelt, standing when they stood, and making his contribution when the plate was passed.

George and Katie moved to Ogden that fall, and the family was reunited in a rented home at 330–23rd Street. They remained there four years, during which time David attended Madison Elementary School and then completed the seventh and eighth grades at Central Junior High School. The move from Randolph to Kaysville had disrupted his network of boyhood friends in Randolph, and the family's stay in Kaysville was too short for him to develop close friendships with schoolmates. But in Ogden he met Marlon Schade, who became a lifelong friend. The two boys explored Peter's Canyon north of Ogden, rode their bikes the ten miles up Ogden Canyon to Huntsville, where the best fishing was found, and slept and ate at each other's homes. They spent a summer together on the ranch in Randolph putting up hay, shooting ducks and sage hens,

David at ages ten and thirteen

swimming and fishing in the Bear River, and sleeping in the hay-loft. They liked to talk, as all young boys do, about what they were going to do in the future. One day as they rode their bikes around the playground at the Madison School, David told Marlon, "You know what I'm going to be when I grow up? I'm going to be a lawyer. My aunt said, 'David, you are such an arguer, you should be a lawyer.'" Marlon thought David's aunt knew him pretty well. As for himself, he told David, "I'm going to be a mechanic." Marlon was completely wrong about his own future, for he became a lawyer, while David was only partly wrong about his, for though he was to complete law school, his adult life would be spent in banking.

The years David spent in Ogden marked the beginning of his work outside the home. His brother Melvin had a job as an auto mechanic, and he arranged for David to earn pocket money by sweeping up the garage. When David was thirteen, he and Marlon were hired as bellhops in the Marion Hotel, where they worked from four in the afternoon until eleven each night for twenty-five dollars a month. The hotel did not have an elevator, so the boys carried bags up three flights of stairs, which seemed a long way for the nickel or dime tip they sometimes received. The great flu epidemic that swept the country in 1918 did not spare Ogden or the Marion Hotel. When some of the hotel residents fell sick, the boys brought them their meals and ran other errands. Although David and Marlon were in constant contact with victims of the flu, they both escaped the illness, protected by youthful vigor and the surgical masks they wore whenever they entered the rooms. The next year David was promoted from bellhop to desk clerk. He kept the books, and enjoyed having the owner, David Matteson, put his arm around him and tell him that he was the youngest hotel clerk in the United States.

Though the Kennedys left Randolph to seek better care for Katie and improved educational possibilities for their children, George's primary interest remained the ranch in Randolph. He spent part of each winter there, supervising L. G. and Karl, who were operating it. In addition, the family spent each summer in Randolph, returning to Ogden in the fall. Thus Randolph and Ogden were pulling the family in two different directions: Randolph meant a commitment to ranching that lured John Kennedy, Jr., out of the Almy coal mines; Ogden meant an education and a broadening of perspectives and opportunities. Katie sensed the tensions stemming from these divided loyalties, and she hoped that if George could find work in Ogden, he would be more satisfied to remain with the family the year around, thus reducing the tensions inherent in his absence. The winter of 1919 she persuaded him to take a job in the Golden Rule Store in Ogden, which was run by George's friend Guy Johnson. The experiment was unsuccessful, for George did not relish being a store clerk, and Johnson let him return to Randolph whenever he got bored with clerking. Katie finally persuaded George to turn the ranch completely over to L. G. and Karl and to begin a chicken farm. Consequently, the family bought seven acres of land in Riverdale, southwest of Ogden, that included a small but comfortable home surrounded by a lawn and fruit trees. George agreed to this plan, and shortly he had one of the largest chicken farms in the area.[2]

Despite all the doctor's efforts, Katie's arthritis continued to worsen. As a result, David not only worked alongside his father on the chicken farm but also did a major share of the heavy housework. He was no stranger to washing dishes, scrubbing floors, running the washing machine, and hanging the wash out to dry.

David Kennedy

25

All of the family were concerned about Katie's health, but David, perhaps because of the insights he gained during the summer they spent together in the Grant Hotel, was particularly sensitive to her needs. There was no question about George's devotion to Katie, for he was willing to leave the ranch and Randolph to seek medical help for her; but just as soon as he had moved the family into the house in Riverdale, which had no plumbing, he returned to Randolph. A year later when water mains were extended to Riverdale, the Kennedys' neighbor, Charles Mitchell, decided to put plumbing in his own home. George was in Randolph on one of his extended visits, so David suggested that if Mitchell would plumb the Kennedy home as well, he, David, would pay for the materials and help Mitchell with both installations. It was a fair bargain. David bought a set of tools, dug the trenches, and helped Mitchell plumb both houses.

Among the influences that shaped David's character as a youth was his membership in the Mormon church. He attended church as a youngster in Argyle and Randolph, where his parents were officers in the ward. This pattern of involvement in the programs of the Church continued in Kaysville, Ogden, and Riverdale. It was in the Riverdale Ward that the Church began to play a decisive role in his life. He took seriously the law of the tithe practiced by the Church, and when he was fourteen he found that he was behind in paying his tithing. Even at that age he believed in direct action, so he went to Commercial Security Bank and asked for a loan of fifty dollars to pay his tithing. The manager asked him how he was going to pay it back, thinking, perhaps, that David had not planned that far ahead. When David explained how much he was making at the Marion Hotel and how he had indeed foreseen the need to repay the loan, the manager drew up the documents and gave him the loan without even consulting his father, an unusual—and even illegal—procedure, given David's age.

David's growing ability to express himself clearly and forcefully provided him with numerous opportunities to speak in the Church's weekly worship service. At one of the meetings where he talked, Heber J. Grant, president of the Church, was in attendance and took time to congratulate him. Praise from President

Grant was a heady experience for an eighteen-year-old boy. More importantly, David began to understand with greater insight the wide-ranging discussion he had had with his father some years before as they were working together on the ranch. George surprised David by asking him what he thought was the purpose of life. David replied that he did not know. George said, "I'll tell you what the purpose of your life is. It's very simple. Your purpose in life is to serve God and your fellowmen, period. That's it. That's all you have to remember."

Katie's poor health posed a continuing challenge to David's emerging religious understanding. Her doctors seemed confident that her health would improve, but her arthritis continued to resist every treatment. David realized that the doctors could be mistaken in their assurances, but more difficult for him to accept in religious terms was her continued ill health despite fervent family prayers on her behalf. Sometimes he would feel after prayer that she was going to get better right away, and when she didn't, he was disturbed. Why weren't their prayers answered? he asked himself. Is it because the Lord doesn't hear prayer? Or is it because we

David Kennedy

27

don't have enough faith? He struggled with those questions without completely resolving them, but his mother's courage in the face of ill health and her continuing faith strengthened his commitment to the Church and his willingness to live by faith even when he could find no ultimate answers.

For David the years in Riverdale were the years in which his interests began to expand beyond those of boyhood. While he never lost his zest for visits to Randolph and the ranch, other pleasures now claimed his attention. He became aware of a growing power to express his thoughts in both writing and speech. As that power became recognized by others, he took every opportunity to develop it. He frequently spoke in the Riverdale Ward, and he represented the youth of the area by speaking at the celebrations on the 4th of July and at the 24th of July commemoration of the entry of the Mormon pioneers into the Salt Lake Valley in 1847. He took those assignments seriously. He would write a talk and then practiced it in the barn, hoping that if he had the attention of the cows, he would have the attention of the people. He not only inflicted his sermons on the cows but also on Marlon, who sometimes wondered what David found so exciting about giving another talk when he was asked to give so many.[3]

David's forensic ability brought him to the attention of Ernest L. Wilkinson, who coached debate at Weber Academy.[4] David began his high school years there in 1919. The academy, which was part of the Church's educational system, had begun as a combined preparatory and high school. The curriculum was later expanded to include courses leading to a teaching degree, and in 1916 the first two years of college work were added. The high school courses were later phased out, and by 1923 the college offered only college courses and the name was changed to Weber College in recognition of its status as a junior college.

At the academy David enjoyed the math classes of William Z. Terry, physics and chemistry classes taught by John G. Lind, and religion and history courses under John Q. Blaylock, but his principal academic interest was debate, which took him to tournaments throughout the state. He was also secretary-treasurer of the student body, on the boxing team, and sports editor of the school newspaper, the *Weber Herald*. The paper had been losing money, so David, in addition to reporting sports, started to sell ads. He was so successful that he was asked to be the business manager. As an added inducement, the editors offered to pay him a 20 percent commission on every ad he sold. With that incentive, he was able to sell enough ads to put the paper in the black and make more than enough money to meet his own expenses. Selling ads for the newspaper proved so lucrative that he accepted an offer to do the same thing for the yearbook, the *Acorn*, and he promptly sold eighteen hundred dollars worth of ads. The money he earned in these part-time jobs was enough that he did not have to depend on his father for spending money. That small measure of economic independence reinforced his growing sense of self-reliance and increased his determination to be free to follow his own inclinations without being beholden to others.

In his senior year in high school, David found himself in conflict with the academy's president, Aaron Tracy, over the way Tracy was administering the school's charter, particularly as it applied to student affairs. Some members of the faculty, including Wilkinson, agreed with the students and provided them with arguments they could use in support of a new constitution. Buttressed by that covert faculty support and driven by his own belief in the justice of his cause, David was successful in having the new constitution adopted. That success came to naught, however, for Tracy had the last word. He informed David that despite the adoption of the new constitution, the school would be governed by the old one, and if David wanted to continue his education at Weber, he would have to accept that decision. David protested that he was being told that he should be a good boy and go along without thinking, and "that's not what I've been taught at this school." The experience contributed to his decision to withdraw from the school in 1924. In his two quarters of college work at Weber, his grades were not any better than they had been in high school, when his involvement in extracurricular activities, a part-time job, and responsibilities at home had kept his grades at a C+ average. That first college year his highest grade was a B in English; a D in physics convinced him that his future was not in the sciences.

Simultaneous with David's expanding horizons at school and church came his first interest in girls. He knew that Bishop Adam Bingham, who lived across the street, had a pretty daughter, Lenora, whom he spoke to for the first time from the vantage point of his knees. She came to buy some eggs and found David scrubbing the kitchen floor for his mother. He did not know that he was already the subject of some discussion in the Bingham family—his method of hanging shirts out to dry by their arms amused the women in the Bingham home.

David and Lenora were not only neighbors but also worked together in the Sunday School of the Riverdale Ward, went to the same school, and had many mutual friends. But their romance did not flourish immediately. David and Marlon began to take girls from Riverdale and Ogden to school and church dances. They were caught up in the excitement of being with girls, but they were more interested in being sure that they were at the dances than

*David Kennedy and
Marlon Schade*

they were about dating the right girl. Many of the dates were arranged at the last minute and without thought to which of the girls each would choose as his date. Late one afternoon they called at the Bingham home to invite Lenora and her cousin, Marguerite Bingham, to a trout dinner at the Schade home. The boys drew straws, which resulted in Marguerite being paired with David and Lenora with Marlon.[5] Lenora thought the pairing was a mismatch. She liked Marlon and always welcomed the chance to dance with him at church dances, for he was the best dancer among the boys, but she would rather have spent that evening with David. Yet in the early days of their courtship, she did not reveal her true feelings, for she sensed that David would find her more interesting if he had to court her than if she were to show interest too soon. That assessment proved to be correct, for soon David began to pursue her with a singleness of purpose that excluded all other girls.

Soon after David and Lenora began to date regularly, Lenora's family moved to a new home in a cherry orchard about two miles west of Riverdale. David could no longer carry on his pursuit of her just by walking across the street; now he must make a two-mile trek either by foot or on horseback. If two miles did not deter him from his frequent visits with Lenora, neither did the seven miles that separated them after the Binghams later moved to Five Points, north of Ogden. Since by then he could drive the family car, their courtship continued. Much of their recreation centered around the Church, which sponsored a dance almost every weekend. There were also dancing dates at the Roman Gardens and Berthana Ballroom in Ogden, and on special occasions trips to the Odeon in Salt Lake City. Both David and Lenora enjoyed drama, and they acted in the Church's drama program in addition to plays at Weber Academy. Lenora's talent also found expression in dramatic readings of poetry. She was a popular attraction at church and school functions with her readings of Alfred Noyes's "The River of Stars" and "The Highwayman."

One summer David introduced Lenora to the Randolph he knew and loved. He invited her to join him in a fishing trip with his uncle Frank Kennedy and his brother and sister-in-law, L. G. and

31

Vilate. For three days they fished along Big Creek and ate their catch around the campfire at night. Frank caught most of the fish, while L. G. outdid his reputation as the best campfire cook in Rich County and filled the night air with his beautiful tenor voice.

David's attempts to acquaint Lenora with the beauty of Rich County and Bear Lake were not always that successful. On one trip, they set off from Ogden in his Model T Ford for a picnic on Bear Lake, accompanied by Marlon and his date, Ida Dalton. The disasters began when the brakes burned out as they descended the dugway leading from the summit of Logan Canyon into Garden City on the shores of the lake. To slow the car down when it got going too fast, David hit on the stratagem of bumping it into the mountainside. In Paris, Idaho, just over the Utah line, they found a mechanic who could put in new brake linings. Though the repairs took most of their money, they returned to the car in high spirits, and David, who took the successful repair as an omen that their bad luck was behind them, insisted that Lenora drive. She was reluctant at first, but with persistent urging she finally agreed. As they made their way back to Garden City, she began to feel more confident in her ability to guide the Model T along the dusty road. Suddenly her confidence was shattered by a high-pitched scream from the back seat. Turning around to see what had caused Ida to cry out, she lost control of the car, plunging it into a culvert.

This second disaster was even worse than the first, for a front wheel was so badly bent that the car could not be driven. They were rescued by a farmer, who took time off from haying to straighten the wheel in his blacksmith shop and charged them only $1.50. Their troubles were not over, however, for when they neared the top of the climb out of Bear Lake Valley, the car didn't have enough power to make the last steep grade. Everyone but the driver got out and pushed those last few yards. They finally arrived back at Lenora's home at four o'clock in the morning to find her mother waiting up for them. Lenora, who had been the innocent victim, got little sympathy from her mother, who awakened her at six with the observation, "You're not going to keep me up all night and expect to sleep all day."[6]

In the spring of 1924, David withdrew from school to work full time for the Ogden Gas Company, a subsidiary of Utah Power and Light Company. He did the bookkeeping and prepared the payroll. The job lasted only until the end of the summer, when he was displaced by a former employee who returned from school. Later David was given full-time employment with the parent company, Utah Power and Light, as complaint bookkeeper and collector of delinquent accounts. He was not a desk-bound bookkeeper, since he was expected to don electrician's spurs to disconnect the lines of people who had not paid their accounts. He also took advantage of a company offer of time off for employees to sell Utah Power and Light stock to the public. He found that meeting people and explaining company policy was more to his liking than office work. His work at the company so impressed company officers that when he resigned, they invited him to return at any time.

David still planned to be a lawyer when he dropped out of school, but he had more immediate concerns. He expected a mission call from the Church, but no mission call had come. In the meantime his courtship of Lenora had drawn them closer together and he had talked to her about marriage, but they both seemed too young for her to take the discussion seriously. However, in the summer of 1925, as his hope for a mission call dimmed, he began to think more seriously about marriage.

It took a lovers' spat to bring the couple to a decision. David angered Lenora by asking her to go home from a picnic with her parents while he and Marlon went off to Bear Lake and Cokeville, Wyoming. She was still resentful at that treatment when, soon after his return, he took her to a dance at the Hermitage in Ogden Canyon. At intermission they walked outside, where the light of a full moon filtered through the trees and etched their patterns on the surrounding garden. There David, properly repentant for his trip to Bear Lake, found Lenora ready to forgive, and in that moment of reconciliation he sensed that the time had come when a renewed proposal of marriage would not be refused. They sealed their engagement with a kiss. He was barely twenty and she had just turned nineteen.

While the Kennedys were newcomers to Riverdale, the Binghams were long-time residents. Lenora's grandfather, Sanford Bingham, had been baptized into The Church of Jesus Christ of Latter-day Saints in the very early days of the restoration, as a lad of twelve in Vermont. He joined the Saints when they moved from New York to Ohio, then Missouri and Nauvoo, Illinois. He married his first wife, Martha Ann Lewis, in the Nauvoo Temple in 1847, and sixteen years later, in 1863, married Lenora's grandmother, Agnes Fife, in the Salt Lake Endowment House. At the time of his second marriage, he was living in Riverdale. Sanford and Agnes's first son, Adam Aranthon Bingham, was born there November 14, 1865. Sanford served as bishop of the Riverdale Ward for twenty-five years, a record of service that was later matched by Adam. Adam married Annie Stratton, whose parents, Edward Stratton and Adele De Saules, were also early settlers in Riverdale. They had ten children—seven girls and three boys. Lenora was the seventh child and the fifth daughter.

Lenora came from a home that reflected her father's sunny, gregarious nature. Adam liked nothing better than to sit around the table after dinner and talk animatedly with his children about church activities, schoolwork, his thriving fruit farm, and events in the community. This was in sharp contrast to David's home, where work began as soon as the meal was over. When Bishop Bingham learned that Katie's painful arthritis restricted her movements, he made special efforts to visit her regularly. This kindness reflected his empathy for all who needed help and understanding. As bishop, he was reluctant to take church action against ward members who seemed to warrant such action. When David pressed him about the behavior of a certain member of the ward, Adam's first thought was for the effect such action would have on the member's family, and from that broader perspective he preferred to use persuasion and kindness as his spiritual tools.

While Adam presided over the Bingham home, its daily affairs were in his wife's capable hands. Annie Bingham's approach to managing the household was systematic and direct, with little room for nonsense. She worked hard and expected all the children to do the same. Her home reflected her own personal grooming; she

David on Old Alkali,
July 1924

appeared in the morning neatly dressed with each strand of hair in place, and made sure that the housework was done on time and to her satisfaction. With a large family and little ready cash, she became an expert seamstress with an eye for style. A taffeta dress of her own could be turned into an evening dress trimmed in silver lace for Lenora, who later would put the lessons learned from her mother to good use in restyling her own wardrobe. Annie's talents in cooking made mealtimes memorable. Her baked salmon, meat pies topped with hot biscuits, fruit salad, muffins with home-made jam or jelly, rice pudding, and sour cream cake were family favorites. Vegetables and fruits from their garden and butter and cheese made from the milk of the family cows assured that every meal was both nutritious and delicious. Annie's careful and thrifty management of the Bingham household was only part of her contribution to family life, however, for she was also an accomplished musician who introduced her children to the beauty of music and was wont to sing while she did her housework, often awakening her children with a song. Under her watchful eye, Lenora progressed in her piano studies until she could accompany her mother when Annie sang solos in church.

David was, of course, no stranger to the Bingham family that summer day when he approached Adam in the family's corn patch to ask if he could marry Lenora. He had been courting her for three years, and the families knew and respected each other. There was much to recommend the marriage: David was clearly a young man of considerable promise whose aspirations transcended those of most of his friends; Lenora had the household skills expected of a young bride; they were young but more mature than most couples their age; they both had carried family responsibilities beyond their years—David because of Katie's ill health, and Lenora in caring for the family one year when Annie was slow to recover from major surgery; and the two families shared a common religious heritage and both took their church membership seriously. Adam and Annie were not reluctant, therefore, to give the marriage their blessing; George and Katie joined in that approval, and the date was set for November.

David and Lenora completed preparations for the wedding and ordered, addressed, and mailed the invitations. One of the invitations went to Murray K. Jacobs, who had succeeded Adam as bishop of the ward. After receiving the invitation, he immediately asked David to come to his office for an interview. That interview was to change all the plans David and Lenora had been making, for David was asked to accept a call to serve a mission for the Church. Here was the call he had longed for but which had never come—and now it had come when he was about to take on the responsibilities of marriage and a family. David was at a loss to know what to do. A mission along with an education had long been his goals, and both he and Lenora were deeply committed to the Church. But when the mission call had not come as expected, they had plunged ahead with their wedding plans. When he reminded the bishop that his wedding invitations had already been mailed, Bishop Jacobs thought there was no problem. "You go right ahead and get married and then go on your mission," he advised. "I wouldn't ordinarily recommend this course of action, but I know Lenora and I know you, and there's only one girl for you and only one boy for Lenora, so I feel that's the thing to do."[7]

David's mother, who had hoped from his earliest youth that David would go on a mission, agreed with the bishop. She not only advised the couple to marry before David left, but she also invited Lenora to stay with the Kennedy family while he was gone. Lenora's father agreed; he thought it was bad luck to postpone a wedding and that they should go ahead with their plans. The support of their families made it easier for David and Lenora to reach their decision. He would accept the mission call, and they would proceed with their wedding as planned.

3

MISSION TO
GREAT BRITAIN

On November 4, 1925, David Matthew Kennedy and Lenora Bingham knelt across the altar in the Salt Lake Temple and took the vows that would join them as husband and wife throughout the eternities. It was a bittersweet day, for there loomed over their joy and happiness the anticipation of their impending separation. David's call to the British Mission of the Church had come, and he was scheduled to leave in January, just over two months away. In those two brief months there were difficult decisions to make. How to finance his mission was the first problem to be faced. He had saved one thousand dollars, probably short of the total needed. However, his father promised that he would supply whatever David needed beyond his own funds. There was also the question of what Lenora would do while he was gone. She appreciated Katie's offer of a home with the Kennedys, but in the end she decided to live with her parents and find a job in Ogden.

David's formal training was one week in the Mission Home in Salt Lake City. Systematic orientation for departing missionaries had just been introduced into the Church, and his group was one of the first to enter the home. The training consisted of a series of lectures on various theological topics by General Authorities of the Church. That part of the training he expected; what he didn't expect were lectures on table manners, proper dress, and how to meet

David M. and Lenora Bingham Kennedy

people. One instruction that amused him was the suggestion that the missionaries have pajamas or nightgowns to sleep in. After he saw the bright striped nightgowns some of the missionaries bought, he wondered if the ZCMI department store, where the missionaries were taken to shop, sold to unsophisticated farm boys what could not be sold elsewhere.

Until the advent of the modern airliner, the Union Pacific Railroad station in Salt Lake City was the departure point for thousands of Latter-day Saint missionaries. On January 15, 1926, David's turn came to stand on that platform, waiting for the conductor to call "all aboard." For Lenora this was the moment that had cast its shadow over the happiness they had shared since their marriage.

Determined that David's last glimpse of her would not be of tears, she sent him off with the smile that had won his heart some five years earlier. But when she could no longer see him waving from the train window, her tears came, and she wondered how long two years would really be.

David was scheduled to sail for England on the SS *Montnarin* from Montreal, but because of exceptionally cold weather the St. Lawrence River was frozen solid, so the ship sailed from St. Johns, New Brunswick. Though the steamer was comfortable, the crossing was anything but pleasant for the North Atlantic can be extremely rough in the winter, and the *Montnarin* immediately ran into a raging storm. David was one of the fortunate ones who, with the help of some inner gyroscope, were able to adjust to the pitch and roll of the ship and thus escape seasickness. When the steward asked him on one of the worst days if he was going to get up for breakfast, he responded, "I get up every day for breakfast." "If you can sail the seas today," the steward said, "you can sail the seven seas"—a prophecy that David remembered later when he found on numerous ocean voyages that he was not subject to seasickness. Though the voyage was rough, he did not learn just how precarious their situation was until he read newspaper accounts of how the storm swamped the SS *Antineau* and was too rough for the *Montnarin* to go to its rescue.

The British Mission occupies an important place in the growth of the Mormon church. Joseph Smith sent missionaries to England in the summer of 1837 to open the first mission outside the United States and Canada. They were joined in 1840 by several of the Quorum of the Twelve Apostles, notably Wilford Woodruff, whose successes as a missionary are legendary in the annals of Mormondom. By the end of his mission, Woodruff had brought more than eighteen hundred converts into the Church. Ever since, missionaries assigned to Great Britain have been measuring their efforts by that standard.

The British Mission that David entered in 1926 was not the vibrant, dynamic mission of a century earlier. Apathy rather than interest characterized religious life in England, partly an aftermath of World War I and to some extent attributed to the rise of an industrial society; but its deeper roots were in the rise of modern secularism, which challenged the relevance of religion in the modern world. However, the Church of England still retained at least the nominal allegiance of a majority of the English people, and there were active Catholic and Protestant congregations, while speakers at Hyde Park Corner continued to speak passionately on religious subjects. But these concerns for religion could not conceal the indifference toward religious issues that characterized a broad segment of English society.

The apathy toward religion had also taken its toll among the Latter-day Saints in England. The flood of converts of Wilford Woodruff's day, when 34,299 joined the Church in the decade 1840–50, slowly ebbed away until only 1,350 converts came from England in the first half of the 1920–30 decade. Moreover, the gathering of members that substantially strengthened the Church in Utah had weakened the Church's congregations in England. Branches that at one time had flourished there had fallen into decline as many members emigrated to the States. Not only did the emigration deprive the branches in England of leadership, but it assured that for the most part they would be composed of first-generation members with little experience in church government, a serious problem for a church that relies on a lay clergy to conduct its daily affairs.[1]

Missionary work in England in 1926 was also hampered by the fact that although polygamy had not been practiced by church members for more than thirty-five years, this reality had not yet penetrated the public consciousness in England. That ignorance was reinforced by the popular press, which still repeated lurid tales of Mormon missionaries who came to England to entice young English maidens to become their polygamous wives. In one of his first letters home, David instructed Lenora to address his letters to Mr. Kennedy rather than to Elder Kennedy. It was not long before he encountered this prejudice firsthand. In one of his first tracting experiences he met a woman who, upon learning that he was a Mormon missionary, accused him of coming to England to steal her daughters. "I told her I already had a wife," he reported to

Lenora, "and that I wouldn't trade my one wife for all the women in England, herself included."

The president of the British Mission when David arrived was James E. Talmage, a member of the Quorum of the Twelve Apostles. Talmage, who was born at Hungerford, Berkshire, England, was one of the most distinguished Latter-day Saints of his generation. By profession a geologist, he was also a leader among Utah educators. He had taught at Brigham Young Academy (the forerunner of Brigham Young University) and had served as president of the University of Utah from 1894 to 1897. After resigning the presidency, he remained at the university as professor of geology until 1907, when he became a consulting geologist. His call to the Quorum of the Twelve came on December 7, 1911. He was noted among his colleagues not only for his illuminating grasp of church doctrine and history but also for his exceptional command of the English language and his propensity to work long hours.

Headquarters of the mission were in Liverpool at Durham House, 295 Edge Lane, where President Talmage held his first meeting with David and the other newly arrived missionaries. During the meeting each of the missionaries introduced himself, and David told them that he had been married just before coming into the mission field. President Talmage commented, "I am glad you are so proud to be married, young man." This pleased David, who told Lenora that he was not ashamed to "tell people that I am married. . . . I am proud to be the husband of such a good girl." The mission president reminded the missionaries that they were strangers in a foreign land and should adapt themselves to English ways rather than expect others to adjust to theirs. If they wanted to be good missionaries, he said, they must be diligent and prayerful, avoid places of ill repute, and keep themselves morally clean. "I never will forget the spirit that existed at that meeting," David wrote to Lenora. "I told you that no one ever saw me shed a tear, but I guess I'll have to take that back now. The spirit manifest in that meeting was powerful and convincing." In that same letter, he touched on a theme that would be repeated over and over again: "Sister Lillywhite gave a reading about working for the ones we left behind. I thought of you, Lenora, and how I want to make good for your sake."

David's first assignment was to the mission's Liverpool District, headquartered at Blackburn, forty-five miles north of Liverpool. The district was in the heart of Lancashire, the birthplace of the industrial revolution; but while Lancashire includes some lovely areas, Blackburn and Accrington were grimy industrial cities made even more uninviting by the winter gray of February. David's companion, Grant Wilde, had already found them lodgings in Accrington, where board and room was $7.50 a week. At that rate, David estimated that his mission would cost him fifty dollars a month, which was more than he hoped to pay. He had always been careful with his money, but he was learning to stretch a dollar even further than in the past. "You know how I used to buy the best of things," he wrote to Lenora. "Now I buy the most for the least." After learning to live on fifty dollars a month, he thought his family might call him "old tight wad" when he got home.

When the first missionaries had arrived in England in 1837, they found potential converts by holding public meetings. But by the time David arrived there, missionary work was carried on by going from door to door and offering the people tracts, explaining religious principles, and inviting the contacts to meet with the missionaries in a "cottage meeting." David saw tracting as basically a way to extend invitations to cottage meetings, which he considered the most attractive environment for fruitful gospel discussions, a far more effective way of teaching the gospel than that time-honored institution of the British Mission, the street meeting. The most famous of the street-meeting sites in England was Speaker's Corner in London's Hyde Park, but every English city had an area where speakers representing every conceivable religious, political, and social position attempted to attract the interest of the passing crowd. In David's judgment, street meetings were more an arena for a contest of wits and strength of voice than a forum for preaching the gospel. Though he participated in such meetings in the Liverpool area, he believed that the missionaries made more progress if they could get the members to invite others and then "sit down and carefully talk about the gospel."

43

David brought to his missionary efforts the purposeful concentration to the task at hand that he had learned working with
his father on the ranch in Randolph and on the chicken farm in
Riverdale. Moreover, his brief two months with Lenora had made
him continually conscious of how much he had given up to accept
a mission call. He was determined to use his time in England to
preach the gospel to as many people as possible.

One distraction from missionary work that David did not anticipate was the time missionaries spent in visiting other Latter-day
Saints. These pleasant interludes from the rigors of tracting could
stretch into hours, and often they created expectations among the
Saints that visits from the missionaries would be made on a regular basis. Periodically David would resolve, as he wrote to Lenora,
to "cut down on visiting the Saints and get out among investiga-
tors and make new friends." He found that he had little patience
with, or gift for, "visiting just for visits' sake." In a despondent
moment he complained that it is "so seldom that we get to talk
about the gospel that it seems unnatural. I've had very few really
good, interesting talks, and believe me, it makes a fellow feel good

*David in kilt in Scotland
during mission to Great Britain*

44

to be able to explain the truth." He worried that his objections to visiting when there was work to be done led people to "think I'm backward and funny, but really, I can't help it. I guess they don't like me much for not wanting to mix, but I don't care, . . . I don't believe that is what we are here for, so I'm not going to do it."

Though David may have thought that the missionaries spent too much time visiting members, he also knew that some visits were necessary and that sometimes they provided opportunities to assist members through difficult times. It was those visits that pleased him the most. In a visit to one member family, he knew what to do when the visitors found the wife sick in bed and the family without supper. He reported to Lenora, "I cooked tea for the family. I toasted bread by the gas fireplace, fried eggs (I showed these Englishmen how to fry eggs), and made cocoa, we had eggs on toast and cocoa. I told them that you had taught me how to cook."

Despite David's impatience to forge ahead with the missionary work, he found time for relaxation as well. President Talmage encouraged the missionaries to absorb as much of English culture, history, and geography as possible. David made a survey of the historical sites that he might visit, went to the Liverpool Art Museum and the Anatomy Museum, attended an occasional movie, played tennis with his companion, participated in the baseball games organized by the elders, and attended operas and musical concerts, including a recital by the famed Austrian violinst Fritz Kreisler. In July 1926 David and his companion spent a week cycling through the Lake District of northwestern England. The following July he went to Scotland to visit his Kennedy relatives and found that his grandfather's cousin knew him at once for a Kennedy. "She brought the old family album out and showed me pictures of my ancestors," he wrote. "When she turned one page, lo and behold, there was a picture of Father and Mother—their wedding picture that I've looked at at home many times. I gave them one of my pictures, which will make a complete cycle."

At the end of April 1926, when David had been in the mission for just three months, Virgil Groo, the district president, asked him to become the district clerk. David was not enthusiastic about the prospect of working in the district office, but he was not unhappy about leaving Accrington for Blackburn; the Blackburn lodgings were cleaner, the food was better, and the price was the same as in Accrington. He spent about two hours a day in the district office preparing reports and answering correspondence, and he traveled more frequently, visiting the branches of the Church, but there was still time for tracting and cottage meetings.

In addition to their proselyting responsibilities, the missionaries were deeply involved in the administration of the branches of the Church. Not only did they conduct sacrament meeting on the Sabbath, but they were also responsible for the weekly Young Men's and Young Women's meetings of the Mutual Improvement Associations and, in some branches, the women's Relief Society. It was not unusual for David to be the only missionary in a meeting, and consequently he was "the presider, the prayer, the preacher, and the teacher—in other words the whole show."

One aspect of missionary work that he took to with a natural zest was speaking in church meetings. A compulsive keeper of records, he reported that after about two months in the mission field, he had given sixty sermons and talks, which meant he was speaking several times each week. When it became apparent that he would have to speak with increasing frequency, he began to outline a series of talks so that he could always be prepared. But the occasions that meant the most to the young missionary were those meetings at which his prepared remarks were discarded in favor of a message that came from his heart. He described one such meeting in a letter to Lenora:

"Yesterday evening, I went to Adlington to a cottage meeting; it was one of the most spiritual meetings I've attended in the field. I had a really good time, and my testimony was surely strengthened. . . . I usually speak last, but last night, I felt inclined to speak first. Sweetheart, I have never before felt the spirit as strong. I spoke about the gospel giving us something to live for and die for. It seemed like the words just came. I spoke for an hour and five minutes. It seemed like I could have gone on and on. . . . It's the first time that I've ever seen the people so full of the spirit that they cried when I was speaking. When we were going, they all said they would never forget that meeting."

David made the transition from student to missionary without much difficulty, but it took him somewhat longer to adjust to life in England. He was struck, as anyone would be coming from the browns and tans of the landscape in Utah, with the lush green of the English countryside. His eyes were also attracted to the lovely lanes fenced by rock walls or hedges of rhododendrons that the missionaries encountered as they tracted in the countryside. As spring came, he thought that the beautiful parks in Accrington and Blackburn seemed like jewels in contrast to the urban drabness that surrounded them. He was less enchanted with the rain that was the price that had to be paid for the beauty of the countryside, and he found it difficult to cope with the damp cold of English winters. Most of the homes were heated by fireplaces that did not "throw much heat around the room," he observed, so all had to sit almost "on the fire to keep warm. I've only seen two stoves since I landed in England, and they look like watch charms they are so small."

If David found it difficult to adjust to English weather, he was appalled with the poverty he found in Lancashire. His experience growing up in Utah had not prepared him for the slums of industrial England. There were, of course, poor people in Utah, but Utah in 1926 was still mostly rural, and rural poverty lacks the visibility poverty acquires when people are crammed together in heavily populated urban areas. Many English children he met left school at fourteen to enter the factories without hope for further advancement or promotion. As far as he could tell, the workers got only "enough wages to barely live on. The men have to work as long as they live—old men and old women going to work when they should be at home. They worship the lords and the dukes, and die in poverty." After a visit to the slums of Preston, he told Lenora, "It is pitiful to see how some of the people have to live— more like rabbits than human beings. Those poor little children haven't much chance in the world." The comparison of the fate of those children with the bright memories of his own childhood gave him a renewed appreciation of his Utah heritage. "I know

47

where Zion is now. I didn't used to know that, but I've found out now."

David's experience in caring for his invalid mother made him particularly sensitive to the way women were treated in England. Judged against the background of his own experience, it seemed to him that English women "are regular slaves to the men." He was scornful of men who could not even "spread a piece of bread," and who were waited on hand and foot by their wives. He was dismayed to find that in some homes the women were still cooking at the fireplace and that housework was done without any of the conveniences that American women enjoyed. His empathy included a healthy respect for the women, for they not only kept house and waited on their husbands, but they also worked in the textile mills of Lancashire for $2.50 a week.

Each of David's fellow missionaries had left family and friends to spend two years in the mission field, and each of them adjusted to that separation in his own way. There was a special poignancy in David's separation from Lenora, and he poured out his heart in letters to her. In one stretch of ten days in November 1926 he sent her six letters; and while he did not write that often throughout his entire mission, hardly a week went by that he did not write at least twice. He devised a unique method of keeping a count of at least some of the letters they exchanged. In an early letter he inserted a heart cut out of red paper and suggested that Lenora mark an "O" on it and send it back in her next letter. He would then mark an "X" on the same heart and return it with his next letter.

In his letters David shared his moments of triumph, his occasional despair, his hopes for the future, his disappointments in his failure to meet the high standards he set for himself, his enthusiasm in preaching the gospel, his appreciation for her support, and, transcending all, his love for her. "The old gag about the time going too fast is all bunk," he lamented when he had been away some nine months. That lament was triggered by hearing a fellow missionary play the violin with a power that touched David's heart. "You know how music makes you feel," he continued; "well, that's the way I felt also. 'Twas a message of love that I sent to you, 'twas a message of beauty, my sweetheart so true, 'twas that message I'd whisper each day in your ear, 'I love you, I love you.' Did you hear?"

David's letters were a means not only to let Lenora share in his mission but also to encourage her during their separation. He sensed that in many ways the separation was more difficult for her than for him. After all, he had the stimulation of new and challenging experiences to carry him through the days, while hers was a more mundane world. After he left, she went to work at Woolworths in Ogden for ten dollars a week and continued to live with her parents and to see the places and friends that constantly reminded her of David. Occasionally his younger brother, Ivan, would drive the family's Model T Ford to her parents' home in Five Points and take her to visit George and Katie in Riverdale. Though Lenora had been dry-eyed at David's departure, her tears after he left were never far from the surface. Her sister Georgia, a talented musician, gave up playing sad pieces on the piano, since they usually reduced Lenora to tears.

The familiar surroundings, then, both helped and hindered Lenora's adjustment to David's absence. A sensitive bishop in the Five Points Ward understood that church activity would help her cope with the separation, so he called her to be the president of the Young Women's Mutual Improvement Association (YWMIA). Thus, while David was growing emotionally and spiritually in the mission field, Lenora was keeping pace at home. The assignment to conduct YWMIA, as well as preparing for the monthly sacrament meeting for which the young men's and young women's associations were responsible, helped her overcome her timidity before groups. When she confided to David that there were some aspects of her calling that she didn't enjoy, he had some practical suggestions: "Why don't you appoint someone to take care of games, and so forth—an amusement committee or a master of ceremonies? You say this is the part you don't like, and by such an arrangement, it would take part of the responsibility off your

David on mission in England

shoulders." He assured her that she was doing good work and wrote that he would like to attend one of her YWMIA meetings, for "I can just imagine you up on the stand conducting." She served as YWMIA president the entire time David was away, and through their letters they shared each other's spiritual growth.

David's concern for English women who kept house under what seemed to him to be primitive conditions led him to assure Lenora that in their home he wanted her "to have every convenience possible." That promise underlined his conviction that he was responsible for the support of the family. Even though Lenora was working, he still felt responsible for her support. "You spoke of work, Lenora. Don't worry about that. Just let me know how your money is coming, and when you run out I will get you some more. . . . Get what you need; don't go without things, because I can get you some more money." His assurance that he could provide whatever she needed to live on reflected his assumption that she was working only to earn money for her own support while he was away. He was far less sympathetic about her working when he found from her letters that she enjoyed it and was even talking about continuing after he got home. That suggestion seemed to challenge his ability to provide for the family. "I should be able to provide amply," he wrote. "If I don't, it won't be because I won't try. I'll work hard, and with you to encourage me, sweetheart, I am sure to succeed." If he were the breadwinner, then Lenora had other work: "As I said before, so say it I again. Your work, Lenora, is in the home. For the sake of emphasis and clearness, maybe I'd better repeat and underline it. *Your work is in the home*."

Though in that letter David forcefully expressed his views on the roles the two of them should play in their marriage—a view that he would never change—he conceded that it would be all right for her to work for awhile after he got home. But, he couldn't help adding, "it depends on how long 'awhile' is." He softened his lecture on her duties as a wife by assuring Lenora, "What we will have to do . . . is to make it [a] matter of prayer; decide together, as we are a sort of two-in-one now, and always pull and work together. I know whatever is done in our lives, sweetheart, will be with best of intentions toward each other. We love each other, and are both concerned with the welfare of each other, so we will find happiness. Whatever you do Lenora, you will always be right in my eyes. You are my ideal, my helpmate, and my wife. I love you and will always. Together we'll find happiness and live eternally, as man and wife, as mother and father."

David not only tried to share his mission with Lenora through his frequent letters, he also made sure that his companions and the Saints he met knew about her. He never failed to tell them all that he was married, made sure that they saw her picture, sent returning missionaries and emigrating members to see her, and was pleased when one of the members reported back, "I have seen Elder Kennedy's wife, and she is the sweetest girl I've met over here." On one occasion David wrote Lenora, "I believe we will be better by having parted for these two years to fill 'our' mission. We have both found out that a life is not much without each other." The belief that they were sharing an experience that would enrich both of their lives, despite the distance separating them, was a theme he returned to time and time again, and which he tried to express in some lines of verse:

You Are My Happiness

Whither thou goest, I will go
All of my life's journey through,
Shoulder to shoulder, and palm pressed to palm;
Whether the pathway be stormy or calm,
I shall be happy with you.

When thou rejoicest, I will rejoice
All of life's journey through,
Sorrow I'll share when it touches thy heart,
Joy be my portion when joyful thou art,
I shall be happy with you.

David's experiences during his first year in the mission field did not result in a dramatic change in his life; rather they sharpened and intensified many of the qualities that gradually emerged in his boyhood and youth. His capacity to concentrate on the task at hand, his willingness to accept responsibility, his ability to express himself clearly, and his desire to be a good missionary were all present when he arrived in Liverpool. Over the course of that first year in the mission field, he found fulfillment in developing those qualities, but there were, of course, moments of discouragement. "Sometimes I get to wonder if it's worth the while," he wrote, "if I'm wasting our time, or if I'm doing any good. . . . Anything under the sun seems interesting to the people, including the Saints, except the gospel—religion."[2] But those moments were followed by a renewed intensity of effort to assure that the time spent away from home and Lenora was not wasted. "I have a little different outlook on life now," he confided to her.

"I hope I won't change so much that I'll get boresome to you. The old world looks so much different to me now. I can see so much I have to do and such a short life to do it in that I pause to know where first to commence. In the months to come I am going to serve the Lord to the best of my ability and work in the service of our fellowmen."

A call to serve as president of the Liverpool District came as a surprise to David, for President Talmage generally gave that assignment to older and more experienced missionaries. David was not yet twenty-two and had been in England less than a year, but his determination to succeed and his concentration on missionary work had caught the attention of the mission president who may well have seen in David something of himself. Though surprised at the timing of the call and aware of the amount of work it would entail, still David was willing to put in the extra time he knew would be necessary. The district, with headquarters in Blackburn, included branches in Liverpool, Nelson, Accrington, Wiggin, Burnley, Burkenhead, and Great Harwood. None of the branches owned a chapel; they all rented a house or a hall for their exclusive use. One or two of the meetingplaces had classroom space, but most were just a single room that held forty to fifty people. The hall in Blackburn was the largest, with sufficient room for the branch to hold socials. Fortunately, most of the branches were able to rent buildings in respectable neighborhoods.

When David became district president there were 635 members in the eight branches, but in the entire district there were only eight male members with sufficient experience and priesthood authority to administer church affairs. The limited number of local leaders meant that missionaries served as branch presidents and filled other vital positions in addition to their proselyting duties. In the absence of strong local leadership, there was a tendency for minor disputes to become disruptive conflicts. Soon after he arrived in England, David wrote, "I have never seen so much quarreling, backbiting and hatred among members as exists in some of these branches. It's more detrimental to us than the most severe outside criticism." It fell to his lot as district president to mediate these conflicts. In some cases, as when a dispute between the Sunday School superintendent and his assistant in the Burnley Branch erupted into an open argument during Sunday School, David patiently sought to negotiate a truce, if not peace, between the angry adversaries. But there was a limit to his patience. Conflicts continued to plague the Burnley Branch; and after one Sunday spent trying to resolve those conflicts, he wrote to Lenora, "I'm getting so it's easy to look a congregation straight in the eye and call them to repentance. . . . I'm starting to tell the people off. But this group would be starting on the road to apostasy if I permitted it to go."

District presidents in the British Mission were given substantial discretion in the administration of the district. The mission president made interdistrict transfers and appointed district presidents, but the assignment of missionaries to the branches within the district, the preparation of district conferences, the supervision of the proselyting effort, and the responsibility for the welfare of the missionaries all fell to district presidents. David soon learned that a responsibility of leadership was to listen to the woes of other missionaries. "I suppose that's what they think I'm here for. When the boys get homesick, I put a big, long smile on my face and cheer them up." When he discovered that cheering up the missionaries was part of his task, he thought that a little preventive medicine might make his job easier. He began to write letters of encouragement to each of the missionaries at least twice a month, praising them for their good work and telling them of his confidence in them. His own moments of discouragement did not disappear when he became district president, but, he told Lenora, "If I ever get a little down hearted myself," his therapy was to "get out your letters and reread them."

In addition to comforting homesick and discouraged elders, David sympathized with them through their health problems. Some suffered continually from the dampness of the climate, others battled boils, and three were stricken with appendicitis during the year he was district president. David had his own battle with poor health. When he developed two painful boils, he made light of them in a letter to Lenora. One of the boils, he said, "is right on my face; the left cheek; the other is on another kind of a cheek, so it makes things kind of bad. I don't look respectable, and have to sleep on one side. I can't sit down. That's a dickens of a fix to be in, isn't it."

David was less sanguine about an infection in his nose, which was not only painful but also continually drained from his sinuses. The doctor told him that he had a bad case of catarrh caused by a septal deformity and recommended that he have an operation, but President Talmage advised otherwise. He told David that in his opinion the problem was caused by the damp English climate and that the operation, which would leave part of the nasal bone exposed, would result in constant trouble and pain in the dry Utah climate. If the problem became so acute that an operation was necessary, he continued, he would rather release David and send him home immediately. David accepted the president's advice, but when there was a stretch of rainy weather, the swelling in his nose was so extensive that he could not see out of one eye and just barely out of the other. In letters to Lenora describing the difficulty, he constantly assured her that it was nothing to worry about, but there was an undertone of concern that his assurances could not conceal.

Early in his mission David became aware of the unfavorable image given the Church by the popular press. President Talmage had done a great deal to counteract the lurid stories about Mormons in the national press, and as district president, David took up that labor with the local Lancashire press. Following each branch or district conference, he wrote an article about the conference and took it to the local newspaper. He found that on the whole the newspapers were willing to give a more balanced view of the Church, though negative articles about the Mormons still appeared often. In any event, David felt that the change of attitude that resulted in more favorable publicity was a blessing. Any improvement in the way the Church was reported on in the press, he believed, could substantially advance the missionary effort. "It does more good than all the tracting a person could do in a mission period," he wrote.

David had accepted a mission call because he believed deeply in the message of the Church that through the ministry of Joseph Smith, the gospel of Jesus Christ had been restored to the earth. His conviction of the truth of that message was strengthened during the two years he spent in England. For him, that was the most

55

important result of his missionary experience, but he also recognized that his perception of the world had been changed dramatically during those two years. He left England with fewer illusions about life than he had entertained on his arrival. He tried to explain to Lenora how he had changed in his two-year absence: "Do you ever have any of those silly, but wonderful dreams we used to have? Yes, Lenora, we've had so many of those castles crumble to earth, that it seems hardly worth building them. I guess there is no such thing as making dreams a reality. One thing this mission has taught me, Lenora, is that reason is sometimes twisted by feelings, but reason is always more dependable. I am trying now to read between the lines of life, so to speak, and to forget those whimsical fantasies. I used to live in a pretty small world, but now things have changed, since I've seen a good bit of it. It is a glorious world, sweetheart, but we've got to be able to match our wits with it."

Paradoxically, David's newfound realism about the world was accompanied by an expanded vision of his own potential. In a letter to Lenora he confessed his desire to "get somewhere in life; to make good. I'm sure that with your help, I shall; I'll work, and I'll study at nights; anything to prepare myself for bigger things in life." That determination to "get somewhere in life" had its origin in his parents' hopes for him, but his success as a missionary and as district president strengthened his confidence in his ability to achieve his goals. His association with James E. Talmage introduced him to higher standards of excellence than he had known at home or at college. He became painfully aware of those standards during a district conference in September 1926, when he prepared a presentation for the conference on the theme of the apostasy. When President Talmage who had himself written a book on the apostasy, learned that David had prepared the presentation, he asked him if the presentation represented the best he could do.

"In the time I had, I did about the best I could do," David told him.

"Well now, wait a minute, is that the best job you could do?"

"No," David confessed.

"Then would you take it and do the best job you can d it?" President Talmage asked.

"Well, I'm not sure anybody ever does the best job they can do," David responded, but he agreed to try.

David spent the night working on the document—checking his references, looking up the exact meaning of words in the dictionary, and writing and rewriting sentences to improve their grammatical accuracy and rhetorical felicity. When he gave his revision to President Talmage the following morning, the question he had been asked the preceding evening was repeated again. David assured the mission president that he had done everything to improve the piece that he could think of. The President took the pages and began to read. David watched with some dismay as President Talmage swiftly applied his pen and began making editorial changes. When he finished, he handed the pages to David and asked, "Does this improve it or does it not? Will you accept these changes or won't you?" David agreed to accept the changes, but he was not sure all of them were improvements. Struck by his honesty, President Talmage told him to take the changes he liked and to ignore the rest. David tried to tell him what a great experience this had been. "Well," the president responded, "I like the way you work."

If James E. Talmage contributed to David's increased confidence in his ability, his successor, John A. Widtsoe, also a member of the Quorum of the Twelve Apostles, led the young man to consider educational possibilities beyond those offered in Utah. That change in leadership, barely a month before David was to leave for home, came at a propitious time. After two years of concentrated missionary work, David was faced with questions about his own future. President Widtsoe took the initiative to ask David what his plans were. When he learned that David was thinking of law as a career and was considering attending the University of Utah, the University of Chicago, or the University of Michigan, President Widtsoe suggested that he include George Washington University, in the nation's capital, among the list of possibilities. He pointed out that George Washington offered classes in late afternoon and evening and that David could work, attend school, and still be home at a reasonable hour. He offered to give David a letter of introduction to Senator Reed Smoot, another member of the Quorum of the Twelve, who could help him find a job in Washington. Those talks sharply increased the insight with which David approached the decisions he had to make about his future education. Whereas President Talmage gave David a greater vision of what he might do in life, President Widtsoe, ever of a practical turn of mind, showed him the way to realize that vision.

On February 1, 1928, David finished packing for the trip back to Utah. Before sailing on the SS *Olympic* one week later, he visited London and then made a whirlwind visit to Germany, Switzerland, and France before boarding the ship at Cherbourg. One of the "Castles in Spain" that David and Lenora had built during his absence was that she would meet him in Chicago or New York and travel home with him. That castle proved to be as illusive as their other dreams for she had to wait until he arrived in Ogden before the eagerly awaited reunion took place.

4

MOVING EAST: DESTINATION WASHINGTON, D.C.

The David Kennedy who returned home to Riverdale was more mature, more reflective, more sure of his ability, and more aware of his potential than the David Kennedy who left home two years earlier. His mission completed, he now had to decide what to do about school, make plans for earning a living, and choose where to live. Most importantly, David and Lenora must adjust once again to married life after David's long absence. Their most pressing need, a place to live, was resolved when George and Katie decided to return to Randolph and left their fully furnished home rent free to David and Lenora. The house had more room—a living room, dining room, kitchen, and two bedrooms—than they needed, and they were grateful for George and Katie's generosity.

The first few weeks after David's return were spent visiting family and friends. He teased Lenora that since she was working, he did not intend to look for a job until she was ready to quit. But after two or three weeks without work he was ready to accept a job offer from Utah Power and Light, where he worked full time until he entered Weber College that fall. Thus, within a month he made the transition from missionary to husband and bread-winner. Lenora continued working at Woolworths, but in April she became pregnant with their first child, Marilyn, who was born January 4, 1929.

As is the case with many former missionaries, David now took school more seriously. While he had a C average before his mission, he received four A's and three B's during the three quarters he was at Weber College during the 1928–29 academic year. His success in the classroom and as a member of the Weber debate team reinforced his hope to attend law school. But before he left for his mission, he had made two commitments he felt compelled to honor. The first was his grandfather Kennedy's expectation that he would take over the bank in Randolph in which his two grandfathers were major stockholders. Upon his return from England, he went to Randolph to see his grandfather, who was ill with pneumonia. They chatted briefly about David's entering the bank, but the details were left until his grandfather recovered. A second discussion did not take place, for his grandfather never recovered from his illness. What did take place was a discussion with his grandfather Johnson, whose only question was whether David wanted to enter the bank. When David said he had other career aspirations, his grandfather urged him to follow those plans and forget about the bank. But there was still one other commitment to be fulfilled before a final decision could be made about law school.

The second commitment involved a partnership with his brother Karl and his uncle Parley Lambert in a creamery in Roosevelt, a small town in the Uinta basin about 150 miles east of Salt Lake City. Before his mission he had borrowed thirty-six hundred dollars at the First Security Bank in Ogden on a ten-year note to finance his part of the venture. Despite David's mission call, the bank officials decided that Karl and Parley should go ahead with the creamery and that David was to retain a third ownership and participate in any profits. In return David promised to assume an active part in the creamery when he returned from his mission. During a visit David and Lenora made to Roosevelt in the summer of 1928, David told his partners that he wanted to return to school at Weber College; again it was agreed that he should continue as a partner sharing in the profits. Now that he hoped to go to Washington, D.C., and enter law school, he discussed those plans with Karl, who offered to buy his share for fifteen hundred dollars. The agreement was struck, and David and Lenora prepared for the trip east.

David's decision to go to law school was not hastily made, for he had talked about being a lawyer from his earliest youth. The choice of Washington, D.C., was due wholly to John A. Widtsoe's suggestion that in Washington he could work during the day while attending law school in the late afternoons and early evenings. Having reassured themselves that there was a branch of the Church in Washington, he and Lenora traded their Model T Ford for a Model A one-seat coupe, built a shelf in the window behind the seat for Marilyn's bed, loaded their meager belongings in the trunk, and set out for the nation's capital.

David and Lenora's departure from Utah for Washington came also in a period of transition for the extended Kennedy and Johnson families. David's maternal grandmother, Matilda Johnson, had died while he was on his mission, and her husband, Peter Johnson, Sr., died the summer of 1928, just three months after John Kennedy, Jr., David's paternal grandfather. David's parents had moved back to Randolph, and although Lenora's parents still lived in Ogden, David and Lenora had no plans to remain in the Ogden area. For David, the Riverdale years were only an extended interlude between his boyhood in Randolph and his adult years in the mission field and later in Washington and Chicago. He had moved to Riverdale because of his mother's health, and he left because there was no reason to stay. The transition from Riverdale to Washington was only the first in a long line of events that challenged his ability to cope with changes that pushed him in unexpected directions. Yet, what changed was the nature of the challenge, for he left Utah for the East with attitudes and values shaped in Randolph, Riverdale, and Liverpool that would remain constant over the rest of his life.

The constants in David's life began with a deep sense of identity with his roots in Randolph and in the extended Kennedy and Johnson families. For David, this intertwining of place and family was not just pride in a hometown and awareness of family ties, it was also an expression of his religious faith. This juxtaposition of place and family is not unique to Mormons, but it is a theme that runs to the heart of what it means to be a Mormon. Converts to the Church like the Kennedys and the Johnsons left their home-lands, as Neal Lambert has written, because they were called to establish "a series of sacred places and cities" in a promised land, "culminating with the establishment of a new city of Zion in the tops of the Rockies," where they came to have a "sense of place that far outweighed the power of old homelands or fatherlands." It was the Bear River Valley and Randolph that called to David across the years with its memories of family, ranch, and town, so wherever he lived, or wherever he traveled, or whatever position he held, or in whatever circumstance he found himself, home was always Randolph and family gatherings were nearly always com-mand performances.[1]

Another constant in David's life was the personal relation-ships created in his boyhood and youth that persisted through the years. Foremost, of course, was Lenora. She was the first and only girl in whom he showed more than a passing fancy. The stability of their relationship was matched by the ties of friendship that linked David to his youth. There was his cousin Orville Johnson, whose common sense and refusal to be awed by David's accom-plishments constantly reminded David of his roots in family and place. And there was his friend Marlon Schade, with whom David had climbed the mountains east of Ogden, fished the Weber and Ogden rivers, and spent a summer in Randolph. They slept and ate at each other's homes, double-dated together, shared their hopes for the future, would over the succeeding years spend vacations together with their families, and planned for retirement together in Huntsville, the scene of so much youthful happiness.

In addition to a sense of family and place and the persistence of ties of affection and friendship, David took with him to Wash-ington an unusual sense of responsibility and an ability for sus-tained effort in the achievement of a task. His father relied on that quality when he left David to care for Katie that summer in Ogden. James E. Talmage recognized it when he appointed him president of the Liverpool District ahead of more experienced and older elders. Throughout his life his concentration on tasks at hand would lead him to use the sharp tongue he inherited from his mother to urge family and coworkers to pay attention and to get on with the job.

Finally there was David's religious faith. In many ways David exemplified the outward manifestation of what it meant to be a Mormon. He was diligent, responsible, honest; he did not smoke or drink; he paid a tithe; he respected his parents and cherished his wife and children; he came from a pioneer family; and he served a mission and willingly accepted calls to serve in church organizations. Beneath those outward manifestations was a profound faith in the message of Mormonism that the gospel of Jesus Christ in its original purity was once again upon the earth. That faith defined for David the meaning of life, created a spiritual context that defined his priorities, and led him to understand that without love and compassion—the core of Christ's message—these outward manifestations were in danger of being empty rituals. David had not come to that faith without reflection; it was not just an inheritance from believing parents. As a boy he had struggled to understand why the prayers offered in his mother's behalf failed to restore her health. As a missionary he sometimes wondered if the work he was doing was worth the price of separation from Lenora. As each struggle, each doubt, was resolved in favor of faith, his commitment to the Church increased until it was impossible for him to think of himself apart from his identity as a Latter-day Saint.

If his family and his religious values and character were the constants in David's life, his professional life was a series of changes, most of them the result of opportunities that came to him unexpectedly. He left Utah fully planning to be a lawyer, and to that end he completed law school; instead his so-called temporary employment at the Federal Reserve Board resulted in banking becoming more attractive than law, and he became a banker. That decision ultimately opened the door to public service and to an appointment as Secretary of the Treasury and as ambassador-at-large for the United States. He planned to retire to Huntsville; instead he became the special representative of the First Presidency of The Church of Jesus Christ of Latter-day Saints. But as David and Lenora arrived in Washington and drove by the Capitol, the Supreme Court building, and the White House before even looking for a place to stay, all those changes were yet to come. The immediate task was to find an apartment and a job and to enter law school. Beyond those challenges they would entrust the future to the "tender light of faith."

When David and Lenora arrived in Washington in 1929, it was not unusual for young Mormons to leave Utah to complete their education and then return to follow their chosen careers. David and Lenora fully expected to do the same. There was, however, another pattern, not as well established, whose prototype was the career of J. Reuben Clark, Jr., who in 1903 left Utah to attend Columbia University Law School. Rather than return home, Clark remained in the East, first in New York and then in Washington, where he had a distinguished career in the Department of State before being named Ambassador to Mexico in 1929. As more and more Mormons left Utah and the valleys of the Intermountain West in search of professional opportunities, Mormon communities began to expand—first on the Pacific Coast, where stakes were created in Los Angeles in 1923 and San Francisco in 1927, and then in the East, where stakes were organized in New York City in 1934, in Chicago in 1936, and in Washington, D.C., in 1940. Thus, when David and Lenora arrived in Washington in the fall of 1929, the exodus of young Mormons from Utah was already underway; it would not reach its flood tide until after World War II, when along with new converts it resulted in the creation of stakes not only on both coasts but throughout the nation.

When David and Lenora arrived in Washington, they found a small contingent of Utahns that mirrored the social, religious, and economic structure of their home state. George Sutherland, who was born in Utah, was the most prominent non-Mormon in the group. He was appointed to the Supreme Court in 1922 by Warren G. Harding after serving two terms as United States Senator from Utah. He was joined after 1933 by George H. Dern, Secretary of War under Franklin D. Roosevelt. But the Utah community in Washington was predominantly Mormon, and it reflected the distinction well established in Utah between those Mormons for whom the Church was the focal point of their social as well as their religious life, and those who had Mormon roots but for whom the Church played only a peripheral role in their lives. Considering

David Kennedy in Rock Creek Park, Washington, D.C.

the importance of the Church in the lives of David and Lenora, it was inevitable they would become integrated into the former group.

The small, close-knit Mormon community that they encountered on arrival in Washington was composed mainly of fellow Utahns, but there were also members of the Church from Idaho and Arizona. That community was divided like Caesar's Gaul into three groups. There was the congressional delegation led by the senior senator from Utah, Reed Smoot, who was also a member of the Church's Quorum of the Twelve Apostles. A Republican, Smoot entered the Senate in 1903 after an attempt to exclude him because of charges that the Church had not really given up polygamy and that it controlled the political as well as the spiritual life of its members. He survived that challenge to become one of the most powerful members of the Senate. His patronage was sought by a succession of Utahns who came to Washington to seek work or attend school, since a word from his office to government agencies opened doors that otherwise remained closed. William H. King, the junior senator from Utah, a Democrat, was also an active member of the Mormon community, as was Congressman Don B. Colton.

The other Congressman from Utah, Elmer O. Leatherwood, who was a Methodist, died just two months after David and Lenora arrived in Washington and was replaced by Frederick C. Loofbourow, a Unitarian.

The second group was composed of people with Utah roots who had decided to make their home in Washington. Foremost among this group was Edgar Brossard, who in 1925 was appointed a member of the United States Tariff Commission.[2] He was president of the Church's Washington Branch and opened his home to students who enjoyed escaping from their meager quarters for a visit to the Brossard's tastefully appointed apartment. Also prominent was Gustave A. Iverson, who came to Washington in 1929 as a special assistant to the United States Attorney General. Younger members of this second group included Rosel Hyde, who eventually became one of the five commissioners of the Federal Communications Commission, and Samuel Carpenter, who became secretary of the Federal Reserve Board. Government service was not the only thing that attracted young Mormons to Washington as a permanent home. Merlo Pusey was just beginning his brilliant career at the *Washington Post*, and J. Willard Marriott was starting his first restaurant, which would result with his name on hotels throughout the world. The last group, composed of students, was drawn to Washington, as was Rosel Hyde a decade earlier, because "it was the only place in the country where . . . a man could combine work and a night-school program."

With the exception of the congressional delegation, the Mormons David and Lenora met on their arrival were not members of the governmental or private power structure. They came for the most part from middle-class or farming families, and if they were in government service, they were primarily in staff positions. Most of them were young, in their mid-twenties and early thirties, and none had much money. Hence, students living on a shoestring were easily and readily integrated into the social and religious life of the Mormon community. It was, in short, a homogeneous group brought together by their roots in the Intermountain West and a common religious faith.

The existence of a small, cohesive Mormon community made the transition from Utah to Washington easier for David and Lenora, but they faced a number of difficult challenges alone. They arrived in Washington with visions of a nicely furnished two- or three-bedroom apartment, but they soon learned that that was an unrealistic dream, for even unfurnished apartments that size were beyond their budget. They quickly revised downward the number of rooms they were willing to live in and revised upward the amount of rent they were willing to pay. Once they adjusted their expectations to fit their budget, they rented an unfurnished one-room apartment in the Marquette, a newly constructed complex at 2115 Pennsylvania Avenue Northwest. The rent was $47.50 per month. They furnished the apartment with a breakfast set, two chairs, a davenport, and a crib for Marilyn all bought at a secondhand store.

Apartments were not the only things that were more expensive in Washington. David ruefully wrote his father that he wished "you could sell your cattle for the price we have to pay for meat here. Every time we buy a piece of meat it is like buying a fourth interest in a steer." And still later he wrote his parents that he would send them a Washington newspaper occasionally. "You may be interested in the capital news. That is about the only thing that is cheap in this city, and it is possible to get a newspaper for two and three cents."

Finances were a constant concern for David and Lenora. They had some savings, but they expected to pay their living expenses, including school tuition and fees, out of David's salary. It was imperative, therefore, that he find a job as soon as possible. He had in his pocket the letter of introduction from John A. Widtsoe to his colleague in the Quorum of the Twelve, Reed Smoot. Dr. Widtsoe's letter informed Senator Smoot that David had "presided with success over one of the largest Districts in the Mission." He described David's skills in bookkeeping, stenography, and typewriting, and reported that he had business experience. "He is indeed a very competent man, trustworthy and reliable, and withal a man who has the gift of getting along with his fellow-men." In a final paragraph, Widtsoe assured the senator: "Brother Kennedy is the type of man who can be unreservedly recommended to you, and I know how much of your precious time and energy you have given to help young men achieve their life's ambition. In this instance I believe I am recommending a somewhat unusual man and have no hesitation in asking him to present this letter to you."

Armed with the letter, David went to the senator's office, showed it to Smoot's administrative assistant, Isaac Stewart, and asked for an appointment to see the senator. Stewart told David that the senator was busy, but if David would leave the letter he would give it to him. David shrewdly sensed that if he surrendered the letter his only chance of seeing the senator personally would be lost, so he declined Stewart's offer and said he would come back when the senator had time to see him. Stewart did give him a list of government departments where appointments were made outside the normal Civil Service procedures, but David found that he was at the bottom of a long list of applicants, so he turned to other sources of job opportunities. The student employment office at George Washington University gave him leads on some part-time jobs, one of which offered good pay as a male model for art classes, but when he found that on occasion he would have to pose in the nude, the pay suddenly seemed insufficient.

Disappointed in the Smoot connection—he tried to see the senator a second time but met the same rebuff from his staff—and by the suggestions of the student employment office, David began to look for a job on his own. He soon found that there were jobs for people with stenographic skills, and he reported to his parents on October 3, 1929, less than a month after arriving in Washington, that he had a job with the George Washington Stone Corporation in Alexandria, Virginia. "I started to work here yesterday," he wrote. His starting salary was $125 a month, and he could adjust his hours to meet his school schedule.

David had been at the company just six months when the onset of the depression forced the company to close and he faced unemployment. He had hardly started his search for another job when, in a chance conversation with Ken Iverson, Judge Iverson's son, he learned that a position was open at the Federal Reserve Board in the Division of Bank Operations, where Ken was working. David gleaned all the information about the job he could from

Ken and submitted his application to the board. He was invited back several times for interviews, but they only resulted in further interviews, not in a job offer.

As the time drew near for the stone company to go out of business, David grew increasingly impatient with the delay in the selection process at the Federal Reserve Board. He learned that the decision rested with Edward Smead, chief of the Division of Bank Operations, so he decided to ask Smead if he was actually being considered for the job or was he just a name on a list. Smead told him that the division had narrowed the selection to two candidates; David bluntly asked if he were one of the two; Smead said yes, and David replied, "Well, I'm still interested."

Knowing that he was one of only two applicants still being considered for the job did not make the waiting much easier. With some relief, then, he wrote his parents on April 10, 1930, that "yesterday the Federal Reserve Board called and said they had decided on me to fill a vacancy they have. So I will go to work for them tomorrow and at $150 to start with." He minimized the loss of his job with the stone company. "I did not write you before because I thought you might worry," he told them, "and I knew there was no need of it. Instead I got busy and looked around for work."

David recognized his good fortune in getting the job at the Federal Reserve Board, for as he wrote, "there were several fellows after the position and it was a nip and tuck proposition. . . . It seems that we have had the lucky breaks and now I have got to get to work and make good." There was, however, no premonition in his letter that the job with the Federal Reserve Board had any special implications for his future. Since he fully expected to return to Utah when he completed his schooling, any employment was only a means of financing his education. And the position with the Federal Reserve Board seemed attractive only because it offered an opportunity for advancement and an extra twenty-five dollars a month to ease his tight budget.

Even before getting settled in an apartment and finding a job, David applied for admission to the pre-law program offered by

Columbian College, an undergraduate division of George Washington University. He was accepted and was given credit for the classes he had taken at Weber College. He enrolled in Beginning French, Principles of Accounting, American Government, and Public Speaking. Soon finding that four classes coupled with full-time employment was more than he could reasonably carry, he dropped the French and American Government courses.

Although David came to Washington intending to study law, he became increasingly aware of how long that would take working full time and going to school at night. His salary was barely enough to live on, and the prospect of existing on the edge of poverty during the time it would take to complete law school was discouraging. He therefore began to explore the possibility of postponing law school to study accounting, with a view to becoming a certified public accountant. With that possibility in mind, he took four semesters of accounting and three of economics at Columbian College in Washington. By August 1930, he had decided to enter law school as soon as he could. However, he had not yet given up the idea of linking his interest in business with a law degree; he had merely shifted emphasis once again, as he told George and Katie in his letter announcing his firm intention to study law: "I have decided to study LAW. When I get my degree . . . I can go to Harvard for two years and study business administration. It will make me thirty-two . . . when I get out, but I will have some education. I can work and pay my way through. . . . Is it worth it for an education? I will get out of school broke, or practically so when I am thirty-two. . . . I will have some education though. If I haven't any money I will have a few letters behind my name. . . . How do you think the letters will look on my card—David M. Kennedy, A.B., L.L.B., C.P.A., M.A., and perhaps Ph.D."

The satisfaction and growth David and Lenora experienced that first year in Washington were marred by the tragic death on December 5, 1929, of David's brother Karl, who died from injuries sustained in a traffic accident. Although George offered to pay their way to Utah to attend the funeral, David and Lenora decided that because it would take five days to get to Utah if they drove, the

cost would be substantial if they went by rail, and David's schooling would be disrupted, they would stay in Washington. David
wired his father, "You understand conditions at both ends, wire if
best to come. Otherwise we shall mourn his loss here." In letters
to Karl's wife, Algie, he recalled how happy and vibrant Karl was
the last time they were together. "We shall cherish the remembrance of that visit," he wrote, "and always remember him as he
was, my strong, true and big-hearted brother." He expressed his
confidence that death was merely a "separation of body and spirit,"
and that through the miracle of the resurrection we all become
again living souls: "not as before exactly, no, more glorified, immortal! Family ties shall again then bind husband and wife, brother
and sister, father and child." When that day comes, he promised
Algie, "Karl will take up his place and be that same good son,
brother, husband and father that we all know him to be."

Karl's death increased the uncertainty that already clouded
David's ability to finance his education and support his family.
Under the agreement he made with Karl for the sale of his share of
the dairy, he was to receive $250 before he left for school and the
balance when he finished and was ready to begin his professional
career. Because of financial difficulties Karl had been unable to
make the initial payment, so at his death David had a claim for the
entire fifteen hundred dollars against the estate. As is the case in
many families, Karl had not kept his wife informed of his financial
affairs, so it was difficult for her to understand the basis of David's
claim on the estate. In a long letter to his father, David laid out the
history of his agreement with Karl with all the details needed to
make the matter understandable and clear to Algie. Although David
was convinced that he was entitled to the fifteen hundred dollars,
payment of his claim became impossible after the proceeds from
Karl's estate were invested in a business that failed during the depression.

The family ties that played such an important part in David's
life in Utah were not neglected when he and Lenora moved to
Washington. "Write to us often and let us know the news," he
urged his parents. "Ranch news is like ranch air, it is refreshing."
He not only liked to receive news from Utah but also sent home a

continuing stream of advice on a variety of matters. Melvin moved to Riverdale to help George on the chicken farm, and David advised him to explore the possibility of establishing a highway market or raising fryers for sale at retail. After Karl's death, L. G. considered buying Karl's share of the dairy, but when there was difficulty in coming to terms with his Uncle Parley, David was firm in his advice that L. G. should not buy under those terms. He took a special interest in Ivan, his younger brother, suggesting that Ivan come to Washington to study shorthand and typing as a prelude to finding a job. When it appeared that Ivan might seek his fortune in South America, David cautioned that, although there were opportunities in South America for ambitious young men, Ivan should make "connections with a good company before he goes. It is almost useless to go without having definite lines established beforehand."

But foremost in David's concern was his parents, who he thought were at an age when they should start thinking more of themselves and less about the boys. When he first learned of Karl's accident and read into George's letter the possibility that Karl might be crippled for life, David explored in his letters ways in which the family might rally to help Karl. He thought it might be possible for L. G. to move to Roosevelt to run the dairy, but then who would look after the ranch in Randolph? He proposed coming back to Utah and continuing his education at the University of Utah, and if not at the university, perhaps through correspondence courses. Even after Karl's death, David continued to explore the possibility of returning to Utah, particularly when he fell behind in his car payments and had to ask his parents for help.

Ill health continued to afflict Katie. In the months following Karl's death, she went to Logan for treatments for her arthritis, while George was in Randolph helping L. G. with the ranch or in Roosevelt trying to help Algie dispose of Karl's share of the dairy. Karl's death reinforced David and Lenora's desire to return to Utah during the summer months, but in the end David decided to attend summer school so that he could enter law school that much earlier. He suggested without success that George and Katie come to Washington that fall to visit them. In his usual methodical way he planned an itinerary for them, and "figuring the way it cost us to come here," he estimated that the cost would be about $150.

Despite David's urging, George and Katie did not make the trip, partly because they were trying to decide whether or not to sell the Riverdale property and return to Randolph for good. George had moved to Riverdale only to provide better educational opportunities for his sons and medical care for Katie. But the boys had left home and his hopes for improvement in Katie's health had not materialized, and he disliked farming and longed to return to the ranch and Randolph. When offered a chance to trade the Riverdale farm for property in Star Valley, Wyoming, he decided the time to leave Riverdale had come.

David's letters home that first year reflected the uncertainties that frequently follow on the heels of a decision to abandon familiar patterns for new and untried ways. Karl's death and the pressures of supporting a family added to those inevitable uncertainties and led David to vacillate between Washington and Utah as the best place to continue his education, and between accounting and law as the most promising career. By year's end those uncertainties were resolved. The job at the Federal Reserve Board promised enough income to support his family if they were frugal; his success in school had given him the confidence to settle on law as his educational goal; and the Mormon community provided them with friends who shared not only their religious values, but who could also understand and share their sometimes frantic attempts to juggle the demands of family, school, and work. They would stay in Washington for the next sixteen years while David completed his education and honed his understanding of economics and banking at the Federal Reserve Board. While there they would add three more daughters to their family and develop lifelong friendships that cut across religious, ethnic, and social lines—but it would never really be home. They would live in rented homes for those sixteen years, explore job opportunities in Utah where they expected to make their home, and in the end would move not to Salt Lake City or Ogden, but to Chicago, a city that they had at one time associated only with the crime of the prohibition era.

5

WASHINGTON, 1930–46:
FAMILY, CHURCH, SCHOOL

By September 1930 David and Lenora had decided after some vacillation to stay in Washington until David finished law school. That decision was made easier by his position at the Federal Reserve Board and the financial stability it promised. They had not given up their intention to return to Utah, but when and in what capacity could wait until he had his degree in hand. So having decided on a fixed course for the immediate future, they settled into the task of juggling the three components of their lives: family, work (including school), and church.

David completed his first year at George Washington University with all A's and election to the honor roll. His second-year grades slipped below that high standard but were still high enough to place him on the honor roll. By the fall of 1931 he had completed the prerequisites for admission to law school, although he still lacked enough hours for his bachelor's degree. Rather than complete his undergraduate studies, he applied for admission to the university's law school and was admitted on September 23, 1931. For the next four years, except for summer vacations, he worked full time at the Federal Reserve Board and attended classes each evening and on Saturdays.

David was not alone in juggling the demands of a full-time job with the need to attend class and to find study time, for almost all the students in the evening classes were also working full time. Since many of his friends from Utah were also studying law, they took turns meeting in each other's apartments to study together. But most of the daily preparation for each day's classes was done late in the evening, when David, with Lenora's help, would read the cases and try to make sure he understood the legal principles on which they rested. In those four years, Lenora read so many cases to David that she thought she learned enough law to merit a degree of her own.

During David's third year of law school, he decided to take the Washington, D.C., bar examination, since a law degree was not a prerequisite for taking it. In preparation for the exam, he enrolled in a law review course offered by August H. Moran, which had the best record of success. David learned that the cost of the course was $150 if he passed, $10 if he didn't. That proposal did not appeal to him. He had seen enough horse trading in Randolph to know not to take the first offer. He countered by offering to pay $75 regardless of how he did on the exam. At first Moran refused, but David's argument that he ought to try something new finally persuaded the man to take the offer. To pass the bar exam, in addition to reviewing familiar material, David had to study material covered in courses he had not yet taken. Considering what appeared to be David's over-optimism, Moran may well have thought that David's counteroffer was for Moran a smart gamble. Had he known of David's ability to apply himself so single-mindedly to the achievement of a task, however, he probably would have held to his original proposal. David passed.

David learned that the challenge of law school was not only to master the technicalities of the law but also to think clearly under the pressure of searching questioning. He learned that lesson well in the administrative law course taught by James Forrester Davison, who singled David and one other student out as targets for the most difficult questions. It seemed to David that Davison harassed him with probing questions that pushed him to the limits of his analytical abilities. After a semester of such treatment, he came to the conclusion that he was in danger of failing the class. Since he needed the class for graduation, he wondered if he should wait to send out graduation announcements until he knew for sure that he had passed. His efforts to determine his grade before grades were officially announced was initially rebuffed by the secretary in the registrar's office, but under his importuning she finally checked the record and told him to send out his announcements. As he was leaving the office the secretary stopped him with the remark that his was the highest grade she had ever seen in Davison's administrative law class.

David did well in those classes in law school that particularly interested him. In addition to administrative law, he had high grades in criminal law and civil procedure. But torts, the second year of real property, and municipal corporations pulled his average down, and at his graduation, in June 1935, he ranked 66 in a class of 117. Although he had graduated from law school, he did not abandon his determination to complete the work for his bachelor of arts degree. On June 9, 1937, after completing the second-year course of Spanish, he finally achieved that goal.

With the bar exam passed and a law degree in hand, David and Lenora began to explore the possibility of returning to Utah to practice law. The decision was finally made entirely on pragmatic grounds. During a vacation to Utah in the summer of 1935, David discussed returning to his home state with some friends who had graduated from George Washington. He learned that they were not earning enough to pay office rent and secretarial help, for when they did get a case, their clients could not pay them. Those reports made his job at the Federal Reserve Board that much more attractive. He also considered, then declined, an offer from Ernest L. Wilkinson to join his newly established law firm in Washington, D.C. David's friendship with Wilkinson had begun at Weber College and lasted until Ernest's death, but he was realistic enough to recognize that despite their friendship, he could not work for Wilkinson, who was already noted for his tendency to dominate his subordinates. Thus, the professional association never materialized, although the friendship endured.

David and Lenora's marriage before they reached Washington was beset with rapid change. Initially there was David's departure for the mission field, then the interlude in Ogden while they again adjusted to marriage, then parenthood, and finally the move to Washington that took them, particularly Lenora, away from the sheltering protection of family, friends, and familiar places. But even though it represented a dramatic change in their physical environment and circle of family and friends, it brought a stability into their lives that gave them a chance to create those patterns which undergird a successful marriage. They began, of course, with a shared set of religious and personal values that strengthened the strong ties of affection and love that led them to the marriage altar. All successful marriages must begin with shared values and love, but in addition they must also develop patterns of daily living that not only reflect similarities but also accommodate differences. It was in Washington that David and Lenora learned that differences as well as similarities can enrich a marriage.

David brought to marriage the same work ethic and task orientation that characterized his father and the dogged determination to overcome all obstacles that marked his mother's struggle against ill health. Likewise, Lenora personified her parents, particularly her father's sunny disposition and great capacity for warm, personal relationships. When church services ended, David wanted to leave for home; Lenora could not think of leaving until she told the speakers how much she enjoyed the talks, congratulated the singers, and chatted with a friend or two. Time for David was a commodity that must be husbanded and used carefully; for Lenora it was not to be counted against the pleasures of personal relationships. If Lenora had her father's disposition, she learned neatness at her mother's knee. David was not nearly so sensitive to those concerns as Lenora thought he should be. He on the other hand thought at times she made too much of them. There were occasions, such as departures for vacations, when Lenora's disregard for timetables and her desire to leave her home as neat as possible clashed with David's anxiety to depart on schedule. He would grumble as he followed her around the house while she put things aright, asking, "Well, aren't you going to scrub the ceilings too?"

David's strong sense of time, coupled with concentration on the task at hand, made him at times impatient with family, friends, and colleagues. That impatience in turn was expressed in sharper language than he normally used. Lenora came to recognize those moments of frustration and, without excusing them, made allowances for them. She also came to recognize that when David was sick, he retreated within himself, making it all the more difficult to care for him. David, for his part, came to appreciate Lenora's need for a network of personal relationships, her willingness to accommodate his demanding schedule, and her ability to manage a household on his salary. With the help of such adjustments and compromises, the two of them wove into the fabric of their lives the designs that would reflect not only the underlying harmony of their marriage but also the differences they learned first to tolerate and then to cherish.

Although David and Lenora decided to stay in Washington after David completed law school, they did not give up the intention of moving west sometime in the future. The continued tentative nature of their stay in Washington is best reflected in the fact that they lived in rented homes throughout the seventeen years they were there. When the apartment on Pennsylvania Avenue became too small, they moved to a larger apartment on Oates Street N.E., then to Owen Place, before moving to a house in Arlington, Virginia, in 1935. Their final move, in 1938, was to a three-bedroom home in Hyattsville, Maryland, where they lived until they left Washington for Chicago. At one time they bought a lot in the District of Columbia in a development where several of their friends owned lots. The shortage of materials during the war and difficulties with a contractor delayed a start on their home, and the project was abandoned when they left for Chicago.

Each move while they were in Washington was in part dictated by their growing family. In November 1930, as the birth of their second child approached, David decided for both family and financial reasons to send Lenora home to Utah for the birth. Barbara was born January 14, 1931, but David did not see her until he finished the school year in June and drove across the continent to bring his family back to Washington. When he arrived in Ogden he was greeted by his mother-in-law, who held two babies in her arms, for Lenora's sister, Ruth, had given birth to a son within a few days of Barbara's birth. "Which," she asked David, "is yours?"

David always asserted that it took only one look to know that Barbara was his daughter. "Well," he said taking her in his arms, "I'll take this one."

The family grew to five when a third daughter, Carol, joined the family on November 14, 1935. Her birth was both a time of joy and a time of trial for the family. Lenora did not receive the best medical care during the birth, and for the next eight years she struggled with poor health. Paradoxically, Lenora's health improved after the birth of their fourth daughter, Patricia, on November 13, 1943. Patricia's birth was preceded by a frantic race through the streets of Washington with David at the wheel and Lenora in the back seat being attended to by their friend and doctor, Ralph Stevenson, who alternated between telling David not to stop even

The Kennedy family, December 24, 1942: David and Lenora, back; Barbara, Carol, and Marilyn

for red lights and advising Lenora how she should breathe to delay what appeared to be imminent birth.

There are moments in every father's life when neither time nor intervening events can diminish their impact—they remain forever as if they happened yesterday. David experienced one of those moments when he took Carol, now eight years old, to the hospital while he visited Lenora. His first impulse was to obey the hospital rules and have Carol wait in the car while he visited a few minutes with Lenora. During the visit he remembered that a door and stairway near Lenora's room bypassed the nurses' station so he decided to bring Carol in that way. He went back to the car and asked Carol if she would like to see her mother. "In all my life," he recalled, "I had never seen an expression on anyone to beat it. Her eyes lighted up like a burst of fire." So father and daughter silently stole up the stairs and into Lenora's room for a cherished moment that both mother and daughter have fondly remembered through the years.

In those years in Washington, family traditions were created that have remained fresh in the minds of the Kennedy family over the years: the annual summer vacations in Utah, where the children came to know and love the scenes of their parents' youth; Randolph, where David taught them how to ride a horse, took them on camping trips, displayed his fishing skills, and introduced them to the numerous Kennedy and Johnson relatives; Riverdale and Ogden, where their parents attended school, where David courted Lenora, and where they were introduced to another set of relatives, the Binghams. A winter highlight was the Christmas season, with David gathering the family around him on Christmas Eve to read the account of Christ's birth from the scriptures or the story "The Other Wise Man." For the Kennedy children, these traditions and memories could not be separated from the religious faith that gave them a sense of family unity and tied generations together in a common bond. Regular attendance at church services each Sunday, participation in the youth programs sponsored by the Church, and church socials were not just family traditions, for ultimately each of the children transformed them into individual commitments to the faith those traditions represented.

By the time the Washington years came to an end, the older girls had already developed the characteristics that would mark their special place in the family. There was Marilyn, self-confident and independent, anxious to do her best in school and preparing to graduate from high school and enter Brigham Young University. She was at times conscientious to a fault, as when her father found that she had stayed up all night to complete an English assignment. Whereas Marilyn's approach to life was pragmatic and straightforward, Barbara's was dramatic and artistic. She was adept at persuading friends to take part in the plays she organized at home, and she was happy to spend time alone painting or reading. But her abiding passion as a child was animals; she was always pressing her parents to let her add another rabbit or two to her collection. Carol, only eleven when the family left Washington, was giving clear indications of being gregarious and having sensitive qualities that marked her as the daughter most like Lenora. Yet she was also introspective and analytical—her father's hallmarks. Patricia was only three when the family left for Chicago; for her, Washington would live only in the retelling of family memories by the others.

Every successful family gradually develops a division of labor, ways of resolving sibling rivalries, standards of behavior both in and out of the home, educational goals, and the values that provide a moral basis for family life. Lenora was, of course, closer to the problems that beset growing girls; they found it easy to bring their problems to her, for they knew she would give them a sympathetic and understanding hearing. Her own calm, sunny disposition and long-suffering patience made her the ideal confidant. She was less likely than David to let the petty annoyances of daily life upset her, and she was ever willing to play the role of the peacemaker. Furthermore, she was always readily available, since she had no competing responsibilities outside her home and children.

David's affection and concern for his family was apparent to all who knew him.[1] He took an active interest in the girls' schoolwork and in their intellectual and spiritual growth. Despite the growing demands on his time by his professional and church responsibilities, he was never the absent father. He extended to Lenora and the children the same measure of devotion that he gave to his parents. During the years of Lenora's poor health, he did as much as he could to share the burden of keeping house and helping with the children. Sometimes his helping hand was better intended than successful. The fried egg sandwiches he fixed for the girls' school lunches were accepted in the spirit they were given, but they were eaten out of a sense of duty, not because the girls shared their father's taste for egg sandwiches.

No father is ever fully aware of the impact he has on his children. David had the deepest respect and admiration for his own father, yet from an early age it was clear he was not a mirror image of his father, and consequently he became a different kind of parent. His independence of mind, his careful consideration of problems from every possible angle, his strength of character, his desire to excel, and his ability to express his ideas clearly and forcefully brought his children to endow him with qualities that he would not have claimed for himself. In later years, Carol reflecting back on her childhood, would use the word *infallible* to describe the way she remembered her father. While *infallible* is too strong a word to describe David as a father, he was certainly the patriarch of the family. That term too often conjures up unjustly an image of the domineering, autocratic, intolerant father. David was far from that. Believing that teaching by example was more important than teaching by precept, he sought to transmit his religious faith by demonstrating both his own commitment to church service and his tolerance for those whose lives took them along different paths. The sense of security and unity created by that devotion assured the girls that despite his impatience with their minor failings, in times of crisis they could count on their father's full support. Thus, he was for his children not only the dedicated teacher his father was to him, but also the loving adjudicator of family disputes, the symbol of family unity, and the guide to religious truth that his grandfather, John Kennedy, Jr., had been for the extended Kennedy family in a previous generation.

Lenora Kennedy, holding baby Patricia; Carol, Barbara, Marilyn

Since their teenage years David and Lenora had served in one way or another in church callings. In Washington they found ample opportunity for service in the small branch that met in the Washington Auditorium. The Washington Branch was not only the center of their religious life; it provided a focus for their social life as well. In addition, it was an informal network of information about job possibilities, low-cost apartments, school work, and news from the West. In many ways David and Lenora's move from Utah to Washington was a geographical move, for the existence of the branch there meant that no matter how great the distance from west to east, they remained within the boundaries of a familiar community.

The one thing missing in the life of the branch was a meeting place they could call their own. Without a chapel, they continued to have a sense of being strangers and pilgrims dependent on others for a place to pitch their tents. The branch members were therefore delighted with a decision by the First Presidency in 1930 to build a chapel on a corner of Columbia Road and 16th Street. The chapel was to front 16th Street on what was then known as Embassy Row. Branch members raised funds for the building with enthusiasm, but there were moments of doubt about the wisdom of proceeding with such a large project in the face of the deepening depression. Even after all the contracts were let, Senator Smoot wondered whether they should proceed until the economy improved. But the chapel was completed and dedicated in 1933 with the First Presidency and other General Authorities present.

By 1938 the branch had grown so large that the Eastern States Mission of the Church, which had jurisdiction over the area, decided to create a Washington district with three branches: Washington, Arlington, and Chevy Chase. David was called to serve as a counselor to Wallace Hales, who was installed as president of the Washington Branch. The Washington Branch became a ward when the Washington Stake was created in June 1940 with Ezra Taft Benson as the first stake president. Those two years between 1938 and 1940 were transitional years for the Mormon community in Washington. Until the creation of the district, the branch was the religious and social focal point for all Latter-day Saints in Washington and the surrounding area. The chapel was a handsome building of which they were all proud, its organ was excellent, and Edward Kimball, who had been one of the organists in the Salt Lake Tabernacle, provided public recitals on it several times a week. The recreation hall provided more than adequate space for socials as well as a basketball floor where the younger members worked off their excess energy.

During those transition years, the Kennedys remained members of what became the Washington Ward. Then, when the stake presidency decided to divide the ward in 1941, they became members of the newly created Capitol Ward, which took in all of Northeast Washington, with dependent branches in Annapolis and for a time in Baltimore. In addition to the organizational changes that inevitably follow the creation of a new ward, the Capitol Ward had to find a new place to meet. Leaving the building on 16th Street was for ward members almost like being expelled from the Garden of Eden. Their new meeting place was the Garden House of the

Washington D.C. Stake members at general conference of the Church in Salt Lake City: Left to right, Abe Cannon, J. Willard Marriott, C. Stevens Hatch, Ezra Taft Benson, Flora Benson, Milton Barlow, David M. Kennedy

Dodge Hotel, which was located about a block from the Capitol and not far from the Washington railroad station. The Garden House was the social area of the hotel, and it had one large room that could be used for sacrament meeting, but finding classroom space was a problem. The hotel permitted the ward to use some of the hotel rooms for classes, but at least one class had to meet in the lounge of a restroom.

When the Capitol Ward was created, it had about three hundred members. The ward membership was drawn from the less affluent part of the Washington Stake, including many young, recently married couples who moved to the area because of World War II. In May 1942, some nine months after the ward was organized, David was called to serve as a counselor to Ellis Overlade, the first bishop of the ward. He continued to serve as a counselor until October 1944, when he was called as bishop upon Overlade's release. David brought to his calling as a bishop the same singleness of purpose that had characterized his missionary work; at the same time he knew that if he were to meet his family and professional responsibilities and still assure that the ward functioned properly, he would have to rely heavily on his counselors and the heads of the auxiliary organizations. He therefore delegated as much responsibility as possible and concentrated his efforts on counseling with ward members and assuring the financial stability of the ward.

The spiritual welfare of the ward members was David's first concern, particularly the youth. He took a special interest in those young men who were ignoring the advice in the Word of Wisdom against the use of tobacco. When ward members spoke disparagingly of them, he was wont to ask of those who complained if they felt free enough from sin to cast the first stone. In addition, David thought the Church should give its members an opportunity to develop their talents. When the Sunday School superintendent expressed disappointment that David had not approved his proposal to call experienced teachers to teach in the Sunday School, David reminded him that the "purpose of the Church is to train people, and not just to have a well-oiled organization, running smoothly all the time."

The membership of the ward included the only two black members of the Church in the Washington area, Novella Sargent Gibson and her sister, Evalena Sargent Pendleton, both faithful attenders at church services but not fully accepted by some of the members, particularly those from other wards. David and Lenora had their own problems in adjusting to living in a city with a large black community, for their roots in rural Utah had ill prepared them for that experience.[2] But in the years they lived in Washington, they had made substantial progress in learning to live in a multiracial society. David made his own feelings clear when he learned that the two black sisters were not going to be invited to a stake Relief Society party. That proposal got his Kennedy dander up. "Why not? They're members of the Church. They attend Relief Society. They're entitled to come." When still more objections were raised, David became adamant. "Look, they're coming to that party. I'll bring them myself, and they'll be treated as equals." When David found that there were no membership records in the ward for the sisters, he repeatedly wrote the Church's membership office in Salt

Lake City until the original baptismal records were located and proper records were forwarded to the ward.

David also discovered as he went over the membership records that there was no record for Blanch Alberti, a faithful Primary teacher. When he asked her why the ward had no membership record for her, she said she was not a member of the Church. To David's query why she had not joined, yet had given such faithful service, she replied that no one had ever invited her to join. Simultaneously dismayed and amused at her answer, he promptly posed the long-awaited question and accepted her invitation to baptize her. Upon Blanch's baptism, David learned that her mother was upset because she too had not been invited to join the Church. David presided at her baptism also.

David's independence of mind, coupled with his willingness to see qualities in people that were not readily evident, provided two of his most satisfying experiences as bishop. Alan Young and his family lived not far from the Kennedys, and the two families became friends. Alan was a grandson of Brigham Young, and, although not indifferent to the Church, he was careless about church attendance, often excusing himself because his work frequently took him out of town. David wanted Alan to become more deeply involved in the ward, not only because he thought it would enrich Alan's life, but also because David needed him as the ward clerk. When David asked the stake presidency for permission to make that assignment, he was told to first bring Alan back into full activity and then call him to serve. But David knew his man. He convinced the stake president that if Alan said he would accept the position, he would do so with full fidelity to his responsibilities as a church member. David's confidence in Alan was fully justified, and their shared experience in church service forged an even firmer bond of friendship between them. In a letter to David after the Kennedys left Washington for Chicago, Alan wrote, after giving David and Lenora the latest news about the Capitol Ward, "The greatest among many things for which I shall be always grateful to you, Dave, is the influence you exerted on my life in bringing me back into activity in the Church. This has brought so much happiness and the finest of friendships to Ruth, to the children and to me. I owe you much that can never be repaid, except it be through service to the Lord and to my fellow men."

David had an even more difficult time persuading the stake president to approve his proposal that Alma Fife Heath should be called as his counselor in the bishopric. Alma had recently begun to attend church after a long period of being only a name on the ward records, but he divided his Sundays between attending the Capitol Ward and the Protestant church of which his wife was a member. David, therefore, not only had to persuade the stake presidency to approve the call, but also had to persuade Esther May Heath that if her husband accepted, he would need her full support. Faced with continuing opposition from the stake presidency, David finally suggested that he be released as bishop, since for him the proposal to call Alma as his counselor was an answer to persistent and fervent prayer. Impressed with David's sincerity and conviction, the stake president finally approved the call but reminded David that Alma's success as a counselor was his responsibility— a challenge that David was more than willing to accept. He had a much easier task obtaining Esther May's support for the call. "I'll never stand in the way of Dr. Heath's progress in the Church," she told him. She was as good as her word, and although it was almost twenty years before she joined the Church, she faithfully fulfilled her promise to David to give her husband the complete support he needed to carry his full share of the bishopric's responsibilities.

Along with the spiritual rewards that come with the calling as a bishop are the challenges of finding the resources, both human and financial, to sustain the many activities in which the ward is engaged. The ward needed money to pay rent on its meeting place, to fund the social activities sponsored by the ward, and to pay for the manuals and supplies needed for Sunday School, Primary, and MIA classes. Ward members were also anxious to have their own chapel, but that required creation of a building fund in addition to the monies needed to operate the ward. Hence, David spent much of his time raising money. Had the members of the Capitol Ward been more affluent, he could simply have assessed each family a portion of the annual cost of running the ward, including the building fund. But he was faced with a ward population that was relatively young and strugglinjg to make ends meet. Some were there for only short periods as a result of wartime assignments, and some were simply not interested in providing financial support. Given these realities, David and his counselors cast about to find ways of supplementing whatever donations there were.

The most successful fund-raising project was selling lunch at stake conferences, which were held quarterly in the Washington Ward chapel. The conference consisted of two sessions at 10:00 A.M. and 2:00 P.M. Since the chapel was far from a commercial district where church members could buy lunch, the stake presidency agreed that the ward could sell the box lunches. David called Victor Bartholomew, the Sunday School superintendent, to organize the project. The profit was enhanced because much of the food, especially the salads and cakes, was donated by ward members, including many who seldom participated in church activities. Members volunteered to bake hams in their homes, and those that were too big to be baked at home were baked in the ovens of the Marriotts' Hot Shoppes. Ice cream and sheet cakes to supplement those donated by members were also ordered from the Hot Shoppes, which frequently delivered the desserts with no bill attached.

Other fund-raising projects were not so successful. A project to raise tomatoes proved to be more difficult than expected. The summer was exceptionally hot and dry, water had to be hauled in buckets, and members were reluctant to use their gas rations to drive to the garden site to help with the watering and cultivation. The result was that although the vines produced an abundance of tomatoes, they were small, and not as many were bought as David expected. Lenora and Ruth Young canned batch after batch of unsold tomatoes, which were used to help the needy in the ward. Even though the project did not raise as much money as David hoped, he still believed it was a useful experience for the ward.

David enthusiastically continued one project that had started before he became bishop: fellowshipping servicemen who were temporarily on duty in Washington or who were in transit. The ward did more than welcome them to church services; ward members also provided Sunday meals for them. Because of food rationing, those Sunday meals were often built around baked beans and other nonrationed goods. It was impossible to know just how many to expect, so the ward learned to adjust to feeding from just a handful to as many as fifty.

Not having a chapel was another burden. The space in the Garden House was just barely adequate for Sunday meetings, and it was difficult to generate an atmosphere of reverent worship in its bare rooms. The difficulties of building a chapel seemed insurmountable. The war created a shortage of building materials, few appropriate sites within the ward's geographical boundaries were within the financial reach of the ward, and most members were struggling to raise growing families on very limited budgets.

But there was a solution. Alma Heath suggested that they consider a firehouse no longer used by the city. Since it was designed to match the colonial architecture of the surrounding area, he thought it could be converted into a chapel. David became convinced that, given the obstacles to building a chapel, the proposal offered a good alternative. After reviewing the issue with ward leaders, he reported to the stake presidency that it would cost an estimated thirty thousand dollars to buy the building and the adjacent land needed for parking and to remodel the interior. In June 1946 final approval for the purchase and remodeling was given by the First Presidency. David negotiated the acquisition of the building from the city and began organizing the ward for donations to start the remodeling. He did not, however, see the fruition of his efforts; on October 20, 1946, he was released as bishop in consequence of his decision to leave Washington for Chicago.

Though he would have many positions in the Church subsequent to the years in Washington, David always recalled those two years as bishop of Capitol Ward with singular affection. It was there that he learned more clearly than he had ever known that a bishop who was patient, sensitive, and open to spiritual insights could make a difference in the lives of basically strong, good people who were struggling to find an inner harmony in their lives. He would never forget that it is in the wards that the greatest work of the Church—changing the lives of people—takes place. Nor would he forget the members who shared those experiences with him, whose friendship he treasured across the years.

6

THE FEDERAL
RESERVE YEARS

When David Kennedy walked into the office of Edward Smead, chief of the Division of Bank Operations of the Federal Reserve Board, that April morning in 1930, he thought of his new position as merely a means of supporting his family until he could finish law school and return to Utah. But as the French are fond of repeating, there is nothing so permanent as the temporary. Kennedy's employment at the Federal Reserve Board came at the beginning of the Great Depression, which brought in its wake increasing unemployment with all of its attendant social and economic ills. Prior to that point the federal government played a limited role in most Americans' lives. Except for a brief period during World War I, the nation maintained a small military force and income taxes were low. The federal government managed federal land in the West and built dams for flood control, but it assumed no responsibility for the larger environment. It operated the postal service, but road and highway construction, schools, and most welfare services were left to the states. For most Americans, then, the federal government was only a shadowy presence concerned with foreign policy, tariffs, national defense, and a stable currency.

During the depression, the American people sharply and irrevocably shifted their expectations of the federal government. It became the employer of last resort, the protector of investors from "watered" stock, the regulator of industry, the insurer of bank accounts, the protector of collective bargaining, and the subsidizer of farm production. The federal government was expected to keep employment high, taxes low, interest rates stable, and the gross national product (GNP) growing steadily ever larger.

David Kennedy's years with the Federal Reserve would also see the emergence of the United States and the Soviet Union as the two great superpowers dominating the world. American foreign policy in the 1920s returned to its isolationist past following the unsuccessful efforts of Woodrow Wilson to lead the nation into the League of Nations. But by the end of the decade there were ominous clouds on the horizon: the fascists had come to power in Italy in 1922, and the unresolved issues of German reparations and Allied war debts still worried the statesmen of Europe and the United States. Any chance for a lasting peace was shattered by Adolf Hitler's rise to power in 1933 and by the increasing influence of the military in Japan. Hitler was determined to avenge the defeat Germany had suffered in World War I, and Japan's military leaders sought Japanese domination of Asia. The pursuit of those goals eventually brought both Germany and Japan into conflict with the other major powers, and a world war resulted. World War II ended with the defeat of Germany and Japan, but just as the restoration of economic health was not the only important result of the fight against the depression, the defeat of German and Japanese aspirations was not the only important result of World War II. Victory resulted in an international system marked by the emergence of two superpowers divided not only by national interests but also by sharply conflicting ideologies.

With the end of the war, American business began to expand abroad in ways unknown in the prewar years, and access to American markets became a necessity for those countries for whom exports were essential to economic stability. The United States became the economic, political, and military center of the free world with influence unmatched even by the British Empire at the height of its power. Those dramatic changes would all take place in the sixteen years David Kennedy was to spend at the Federal

Reserve. In addition, the New Deal would bring changes to the structure and function of the board that would, for better or worse, give it power to largely determine the monetary policies of the federal government.

The Federal Reserve system was created in December 1913 to provide a means of avoiding the money panics and credit crunches that periodically afflicted the economy. The system was based on twelve regional Federal Reserve banks, owned by the member banks in each region and governed by a board of directors representative of the major geographical and occupational interests in each region. The system was given the ability to manage the nation's money supply in three ways: first, and most important, by buying and selling government securities—what came to be known as its open-market activities; second, by regulating the reserves that member banks had to maintain with the Federal Reserve system; and third, by setting the interest rate on interbank loans. The act created a Federal Reserve Board composed of the Secretary of the Treasury, the Comptroller of the Currency, and five members appointed by the President for ten-year terms. The board was given supervisory powers over the entire system, but in the face of the substantial power given to the regional Federal Reserve banks, that authority was not effectively used.

Kennedy began his employment as a clerk in the Division of Bank Operations at a salary of eighteen hundred dollars a year, with a promise that after a year of satisfactory performance he would receive a substantial raise. The depression made that promise an empty one. Indeed, under the terms of the Second Economy Act of March 20, 1933, salaries of federal employees were cut 15 percent. Fortunately for Federal Reserve Board employees, that reduction lasted only until June 16, for the Glass-Steagall banking act gave the board complete control of staff salaries, which were not supported by tax revenues but from earnings of the Federal Reserve system. Even with that authority, it was not until August 1933 that Kennedy, after three years of waiting, finally received his promised raise to twenty-four hundred dollars a year.

When he accepted the job offered by Smead, Kennedy expected a clear description of his duties. To his surprise Smead suggested that Kennedy become familiar with the work of each section in the division, and then, from that review, identify for Smead tasks that needed doing but were being left undone. Kennedy expressed his reluctance to take on that assignment, since he was totally unfamiliar with the operations of the division. Smead overrode his objections and put him to work.

After familiarizing himself with each section, Kennedy discovered that the board was collecting data on bank failures, but nothing was known about the increasing number of bank mergers and their impact on the banking system. His proposal that he undertake a study of bank mergers—both past and proposed—was accepted, and he was assigned to work under Jack Horbett, one of the two assistant chiefs of the division. Horbett had a passion for accuracy and an eye for detail. When he discovered that Kennedy shared these traits, he made him his assistant, and his support helped Kennedy establish himself as a valuable addition to the division staff.

The usefulness of the information that Kennedy collected on bank mergers became fully apparent during the banking crisis of 1933. Although bank failures increased gradually in the 1920–30 decade, the depression precipitated a sharp increase in that trend. In 1929, 659 banks throughout the country suspended operations; that number increased to 1,350 in 1930 and to 2,293 in 1931, and although suspensions decreased to 1,453 in 1932, it was apparent that an increasing number of banks were barely solvent.

The rising tide of bank failures was the first crisis Franklin D. Roosevelt faced after his inauguration on March 4, 1933. His first action was to declare a four-day nationwide bank holiday during which all banks were forbidden to transact any business unless authorized by the Secretary of the Treasury. On March 9 Congress passed the Emergency Banking Act of 1933 after only eight hours of debate, which confirmed and approved the bank holiday based on Roosevelt's executive order and permitted the President to extend it if necessary. The act also empowered the Treasury to license member banks of the Federal Reserve System to reopen for business and gave similar licensing authority to the states for state-chartered banks. Kennedy was at the center of the whirlwind that the national bank holiday created. The bank histories he collected were a crucial part of the information the Department of Treasury needed to allow a bank to reopen. In an interview with Studs Terkel, author of *Hard Times*, Kennedy recalled that in the three days that those licensing decisions were made, he "never left the office. . . . I slept on the couch and had sandwiches brought in," he recalled.

The banking crisis of 1933 raised many questions about the effectiveness of the Federal Reserve system as a means of managing the nation's monetary policy. One of the most vigorous voices in that chorus of criticism was that of Marriner Eccles, who, like Kennedy, was a native of Utah. Eccles, unlike Kennedy, came from a family of substantial means. His father created a financial empire in the West with investments in lumber and sugar mills, railroads, mining, heavy construction, utilities, insurance, livestock, and, most importantly, in banking with the establishment of the First Security Banking Corporation. On his father's death in 1912, Eccles took over the management of most of his father's holdings and continued to build on that foundation. From then until the coming of the depression, his economic philosophy was governed by his father's career. But the depression forced him to rethink his views on economics, particularly the role that government could and should play in fostering economic growth as well as stability.

Eccles's outspoken views on the causes and cures of the depression brought him to the attention of Roosevelt, who decided that he was just the man to head the Federal Reserve system. But Eccles would not accept that challenge without some changes in the structure and function of the system. He became convinced that the system was too decentralized to function effectively, that the legal restrictions on the kinds of assets member banks could use as collateral for loans from the Federal Reserve banks were too restrictive, and that the open market function of the system must be restructured, as should the board itself. He argued that the board had to be given discretion to alter the reserve requirements as it saw fit and that national banks be permitted to make long-term real estate loans. After a stiff political struggle, the Banking Act of 1935 gave Eccles most of what he wanted.

The act centralized power in a new Federal Reserve Board that excluded the Secretary of the Treasury and the Comptroller of the Currency as *ex officio* members. The new board, now called the board of governors of the Federal Reserve system, was composed of seven members appointed by the president for fourteen-year terms. One of the board members designated by the President would serve as chairman of the board with a term of four years. Most importantly, however, was the greater control the board was given over the open-market operations of the system. Twenty years of experience had shown that open-market sales and purchases of government securities were the most powerful tool the Federal Reserve had in managing the money supply, for when the system bought government currencies, it put money into circulation, and when it sold them, money was taken out of the economy. The open-market mechanism worked because the system did not have to make a profit, so it could offer to buy or sell government securities at prices that always found a buyer or seller. Eccles was determined that responsibility for open-market operations should be vested in the board of governors. While he was not able to achieve that goal, the 1935 legislation created a Federal Open Market Committee composed of the Federal Reserve's board of governors and five representatives of the twelve Federal Reserve banks; thus the board had a majority on the committee. Moreover, the power to initiate open-market operations was clearly given to the new committee.

The Banking Act of 1935 also relaxed the restrictions on the kinds of assets member banks could use for collateral for loans from the Federal Reserve banks, thereby making it easier for banks to obtain the needed funds for seasonal or otherwise short-term fluctuation in their reserves. The system was given greater flexibility in determining the percentage of their deposits member banks held with the Federal Reserve, thus giving the system the power to increase or decrease the availability of credit. With some modifications, the Banking Act of 1935 has remained the basic framework within which the Federal Reserve system operates. And it was within that framework that David M. Kennedy worked for most of his career at the Federal Reserve. That experience would shape his understanding of the banking system, sharpen his understanding of the interaction between the private and public sectors, and contribute substantially to his success as a leader in the world banking community.

Following the banking crisis of 1933, Kennedy settled into the everyday routine of the Division of Bank Operations. Still in law school until 1935, he received periodic salary increases, and in January 1936 his salary was raised to thirty-two hundred dollars a year. The case histories he gathered on bank mergers and bank failures that were so helpful during the banking crisis of 1933 brought him favorable recognition from his supervisors. Indeed, the board decided that a thorough study of the history of bank failures after World War I should be thoroughly studied. An economist was hired to undertake the task at a salary substantially higher than Kennedy's but that proved to be unsatisfactory and Kennedy was given the responsibility for completing the study. He would ruefully remember that while he was given the responsibility, he was not given the salary, he did win the respect of his colleagues. In 1936 Horbett wrote to Smead: "So far as Mr. Kennedy is concerned, you know that I have on many occasions indicated that he is extremely valuable to me and to the Division as a whole, and I believe your view coincides largely with mine in this regard. I feel that he is qualified for almost any phase of the bank suspension study assigned to our Division, which in itself is quite complimentary considering the much higher-priced persons who are also working on the project. Frankly, if he should have an opportunity to better himself and should leave us, I would feel a great loss not only to myself but to the Division as a whole."

With his expanding experience at the Federal Reserve Board and the poor prospects for a legal career in Utah, Kennedy began to explore banking as an alternative career to law. As the first step in that direction, in the summer of 1936 he applied for admission to the Graduate School of Banking at Rutgers University in New Jersey. This two-year program was designed to provide junior bank officers with training in the more technical and complex issues in bank administration. Each student had to select a major and a minor, and Kennedy decided to major in banking and minor in trusts. The classes in banking would give him a better understanding, he assured his supervisors, of "the present-day problems concerning possible changes in the structure of the commercial banking system, and the use of statistics as a basis for formulating administrative policies." In a memo to Chester Morrill, secretary of the board, Smead said Kennedy's attendance at the school "should materially increase his value to the Division, particularly as he has demonstrated himself to be an apt student. Mr. Kennedy's value to the Division has, in fact, been constantly on the increase."

The Rutgers program included intensive two-week seminars for each of three summers, case studies to be prepared between summer sessions, and a thesis to be submitted before the end of the program. Kennedy was accepted for the session beginning June 1937. During the first year of the program, he paid the fees and other expenses out of his own pocket. A change in policy in 1938 made it possible for the board to pay his fees and travel expenses, but his meals and lodging were still his own responsibility. By April 1939 Kennedy completed his thesis on the "Structure of American Banking" in which he analyzed significant trends in American banking and their impact on the banking system. On June 30, 1939, after the last summer session, Lenora and the children watched him join the other successful candidates in commencement exercises on the Rutgers campus.

In the meantime, Kennedy's work at the Federal Reserve Board continued to bring steady advancement. In January 1937 his salary was raised to thirty-six hundred dollars, and at the end of the year his title was changed from clerk to technical assistant. His salary was raised to thirty-nine hundred dollars in January 1938 and to forty-one hundred dollars in May 1939. In his recommendation for this latest raise, Smead pointed out that Kennedy's responsibilities included a wide range of records and statistics "relating to branch, group and chain banking, and of the preparation of the weekly member bank condition statement and the weekly, monthly and annual bank debit statements." Moreover, Kennedy was now the general assistant to Horbett and assumed Horbett's duties as assistant chief of the division when Horbett was away. "His services in the Division," Smead wrote the board of governors, "have been and continue to be highly satisfactory." Satisfaction with Kennedy's performance resulted in two raises in 1940, to forty-three hundred dollars in May and to forty-seven hundred dollars in December.

Kennedy's work in the Division of Bank Operations attracted the attention of E. A. Goldenweiser, a distinguished economist who joined the staff of the Federal Reserve Board in 1919 and in 1936 was appointed the economist for the Open Market Committee in addition to his duties as director of the Division of Research and Statistics. Goldenweiser decided that he needed help in his duties with the Open Market Committee. He told Kennedy he was looking for someone who was already on the staff of the board, who had the confidence of the division chiefs, and on whom he could rely to keep confidential the decisions pending before the committee. When he asked Kennedy if he would be interested in the job, Kennedy replied that it would be a chance of a lifetime for him. The stumbling block to his appointment was Smead, who like any skillful administrator never gave up a good employee without a fight. But Goldenweiser knew the ins and outs of office politics as well as he did economics. He wrote the job description and asked Smead if anyone in his division could fill the post. When Smead assured him there was no one he would recommend, Goldenweiser had Kennedy apply for the position. He then told Smead that he had Kennedy's application and that Kennedy was his first choice. Smead tried unsuccessfully to dissuade Kennedy from taking the position, but Kennedy was ready for a change. The deciding factors were that the work of the Open Market Committee was at the heart of central banking and that working with Goldenweiser would be another step in his education in the banking system.

The result of those complicated maneuvers was Kennedy's transfer to the Division of Research and Statistics as an associate economist. From that vantage point, he was able to observe the operations of the Open Market Committee as it affected the supply of money and credit by its purchases and sales of government securities and the resulting effects on financial markets and their interactions with the entire economy. Specifically, he was responsible for keeping a detailed record, including statistical data on government credit agencies, the public debt, and on Treasury receipts and expenses. In addition, government securities became a special area of expertise for him, and when necessary he substituted for Goldenweiser at meetings with the board. In February 1942 Kennedy was promoted to assistant chief of the Government Securities Section, where he was making "important decisions involving the exercise of a high degree of independent judgment." He had, his supervisors reported, a "marked ability to organize, supervise, and coordinate research work and capacity for original research."

World War II thrust the Federal Reserve Board into the heart of the problem of financing the war. Kennedy's position in the Government Securities Section and his work with Goldenweiser in open-market operations involved him in crucial issues of war financing and made him exempt from military service. In November 1942 he became sensitive to his protected position at the board. He responded to a memo from Lawrence Clayton, Eccles's administrative assistant, which noted the "need of men to serve in the U.S. Army who are qualified in the fields of banking and finance and who will be expected to serve in occupied countries." Kennedy pointed out to Clayton that this was "the first opening in the armed services that has come to my attention where I have felt that my particular training and experience qualify me to do a job which might contribute as much or more to the war than my present position." Since LeRoy M. Piser, chief of the Government Securities Section, would still be on the job, Kennedy hoped "the Board will feel that I can be spared to go into the Army. . . . My principal interest is to use my energy and whatever abilities I may have where they will do the most for my country." Clayton took Kennedy's application to Eccles, who asked him to remain at the board. Perhaps Eccles expected that he would need Kennedy's services, because Clayton, who had come to Washington with Eccles from the First Security Bank in Ogden, left the board soon after. Early in 1943 Kennedy became Eccles's new administrative assistant.[1]

The coming of World War II brought with it important questions of how to finance the war. Both Marriner Eccles at the Federal Reserve Board and Henry Morgenthau at the Treasury were well aware that the war would have to be financed by deficit spending, but it would make a substantial difference how that deficit were financed. Winning the war was, of course, the first goal, and Morgenthau promised General George C. Marshall, Chief of Staff, that he could make his plans for achieving that goal without concern for financial issues. A secondary but nonetheless real danger was inflation, since the infusion of a substantial amount of money into the economy to pay for arms to fight the war along with a reduction in the production of civilian goods would mean that too much money would chase too few goods in an inflationary spiral.

Financing the war by relying totally on direct taxation would have eliminated the threat of inflation. But since that was thought impossible, it was necessary to rely on some combination of direct taxation, borrowing from the public and banks, and an increase in the money supply by the Federal Reserve system. Borrowing through the sale of government securities to the public did in fact produce substantial amounts of money to finance the war. But they were not nearly enough, so the government had to rely on the sale of bonds and other government securities to commercial banks and other investors. The key to the government's policy was the ability of the Federal Reserve Board through its open-market operations to assure an expanding money supply, thus creating the necessary reserves banks could use to finance their purchase of government securities. Borrowing from banks was inflationary not only because it depended on an expanding money supply created by the Federal Reserve Board, but also because it was in direct competition with the private commercial sector. Therefore, the government was reluctant to rely too heavily on the banking system for financing the war.

The challenge was to persuade the public to buy government savings bonds so that borrowing from the banking system could be kept as low as possible. Roosevelt and Morgenthau were convinced that if approached right, the American people would voluntarily invest enough in savings bonds to raise sufficient funds to meet expenses not covered by tax revenues. But in the end they had to face the harsh reality that sales of savings bonds to individuals would fall far short of the needs of the armed forces and that substantial government borrowing would have to come from sales to financial institutions—financed indirectly by the Federal Reserve.

The decision to finance as much of the war as possible through bond sales to the public resulted in vigorous and sometimes acrimonious struggles over the control of war-bond drives. That struggle for power brought into conflict Marriner Eccles as chairman of the board and Henry Morgenthau as Secretary of the Treasury. Although Morgenthau was an early supporter of Eccles, they soon split over the economic policies to be followed by the Roosevelt administration. Just before the war they differed sharply over the causes and solution to the depression of 1937–38, a battle that Eccles won— thereby deepening the rift between them. Now they disagreed over the organization of the war-bond drives. Kennedy's principal assignment as Eccles's administrative assistant was to work directly with Eccles on questions involving the financing of the war. Hence, he observed the battle from a front-row seat as he accompanied Eccles to a meeting on May 14, 1943, with Morgenthau and the presidents of the regional Federal Reserve banks, that brought the conflict to a head.

Prior to May 1943, two organizations were responsible for conducting the war-bond drives. The first was based in each state and managed by the Treasury; the second was based in the twelve Federal Reserve districts and managed by the chairman of the Federal Reserve bank in each district. For the December 1942 and April 1943 bond drives, these two organizations were merged into a single unit. It was generally agreed that this merging should be made permanent, and the May 14 meeting was called to confirm that idea. After praising the success of the April drive, Morgenthau presented a draft of a Treasury plan for a single organization. Following some discussion, the meeting was adjourned to allow Eccles and the bank presidents time to review the Treasury plan and to propose amendments. David Kennedy and Casimir Sienkiewicz, secretary to the conference of presidents of the regional Federal Reserve banks, were asked to draft an alternative to the Treasury proposal.

The Federal Reserve counterproposal was in most respects simply a clarification of the language in Treasury's draft. The Kennedy/Sienkiewicz draft, however, made the appointment and payment of the leaders of the proposed single organization the responsibility of the presidents of each Federal Reserve district, and the employees of the single organization were to be paid by the Federal Reserve banks on a reimbursable basis.

The counterproposal produced an outburst from Morgenthau. He accused the Federal Reserve of holding a gun to his head; warned the presidents that as long as he was Secretary of the Treasury, he was not going to turn the financing of the war over to the Federal Reserve system; and insinuated that the presidents were not supporting the war-bond drives out of patriotism but to curry favor with the banking community for their own benefit. Eccles and the bank presidents succeeded in mollifying Morgenthau to some extent, but the meeting closed without resolving the organizational issues. On reflection, the presidents resented deeply Morgenthau's implication that they lacked integrity and were guilty of a conflict of interest. In a letter to Morgenthau, Eccles suggested that the secretary call each of the presidents and express his confidence in them in order to correct a bad situation. He also requested that Morgenthau agree to have his remarks about the motives of the presidents expunged from the record. The matter was not resolved before it reached Roosevelt's desk. In a meeting with the President on May 24, Eccles gave him a memorandum outlining the conflict in the May 14 meeting,[2] which was taken almost verbatim from a report that Kennedy gave to Eccles, reviewing what had happened in the meeting. The resolution of the conflict was a compromise negotiated by the President. Morgenthau agreed to expunge from the record his remarks that so offended the presidents, but the Treasury was left clearly in charge of the overall direction of the war-loan drives, although the secretary authorized the Federal Reserve banks as fiscal agents of the Treasury to handle sales to commercial banks, mutual savings banks, insurance companies, and government bond dealers.

Kennedy's association with Eccles at the Federal Reserve was a stimulating yet frustrating experience. It was stimulating because

Eccles had a clear grasp of the complexities of monetary policy and the way the Federal Reserve Board should operate to have maximum influence over those policies. In addition, Kennedy became acquainted with all the presidents of the regional Federal Reserve banks as well as with leading Treasury officials. But the experience was also frustrating because Eccles had little taste for routine administration, had no sense of time, was given to long monologues, and on occasion required Kennedy to convey his displeasure to other members of the board. On balance, Kennedy would recall that working for Eccles was a "great experience" in which the advantages far outweighed the frustrations.

As interesting and challenging as David's work was, he and Lenora had not given up their hope of moving to the West. Late in April 1944, Kennedy wrote to Arch Anderson, president of the California Bank, that he hoped "to make a move sometime this summer or fall, if practicable." He described his current duties and asked that if Anderson knew "of any opportunity for a suitable connection in the meantime for which you think I might qualify, I would appreciate your letting me know about it." Later that year he also wrote to the Wells Fargo Bank in San Francisco and began a correspondence with H. G. Leedy, president of the Federal Reserve Bank of Kansas City, about opportunities in the Midwest. He began his search for a position in the West before the end of the war because as he explained to Anderson, members of the board thought it would be best for him to leave before the end of the war rather than to wait until "the readjustment period following the war when the System will be under heavy pressure." He also told Anderson that he wanted to move west because he thought Lenora's health would improve in a drier climate, and "I came from the West and like it much better than the East."

As Kennedy began exploring these and other career opportunities in banking, he kept in mind a discussion he had had early in the war with Francis M. "Hank" Knight, vice-president in charge of the bond department at the Continental Illinois National Bank and Trust Company of Chicago. Knight told Kennedy that if he ever wanted to get into banking, he should let him know. When he decided to leave the Federal Reserve Board, Kennedy told Knight that he was now serious about commercial banking as a career. Early in 1946, after more than a year of weighing job offers in California and New York against the possibility of accepting an offer from Knight to come to Chicago, Kennedy finally decided in favor of Continental. It was a difficult decision, since New York was the center of the government securities market and the salary offered in California was substantially above what Continental was offering. The deciding factor was Kennedy's assessment that in Chicago he "could supply some of the spark that would be needed" to help Continental reach its potential in an expanding market.

For six months Kennedy pressed Eccles to release him so he could accept Knight's offer. Eccles procrastinated; he suggested that Kennedy join the Eccles's own First Security Corporation. Kennedy did not completely reject Eccles's proposal, for in a personal letter to Eccles, he asked that "in case one of the propositions we have talked about in your organizations out West should develop, please keep me in mind as I am very much interested in returning eventually to the intermountain area." But in the end, Kennedy could not reconcile his strong sense of independence with employment in a family-dominated corporation. "My name was not Eccles," he recalled. Even though the offer was repeated by George Eccles, Marriner's brother who was running the bank, Kennedy withstood the temptation since, he told them, "I want to be completely on my own." Finally, in September 1946 Kennedy wrote Eccles that he had to make a firm decision about the offer from Continental, since "they feel that it would be an imposition to hold the position open much longer." He went on to state that he had decided to leave the Federal Reserve effective October 4, 1946. The letter, accompanied by his formal letter of resignation, expressed his appreciation. "I have benefited greatly from such close association and friendship with you, the most able, devoted and unselfish of public servants. . . . I shall always hold you in the highest esteem and treasure your friendship."

At Kennedy's farewell party, Eccles said that he had been accused of bringing in too many people from Utah to staff the board. Most of them, he pointed out, were hired before his appointment, so "somebody before me did a good job of taking care of the boys from Utah. I am proud of the good records they have made." He pointed out that Kennedy's steady advancement and promotions were indications that his work was of a uniformly high caliber. Eccles feigned amazement at the length of Kennedy's service at the Federal Reserve, since he did not look old enough to have been at the board sixteen years, let alone to have graduated from law school and reared four children in that time. Eccles was generous in his praise of Kennedy's work, and he expressed his appreciation for Kennedy's assistance in areas of Eccles's special interest: government bonds and the board's open-market decisions. He ended his remarks by presenting Kennedy with a watch as a departing gift from the board.

Kennedy's employment at the Federal Reserve ended with a classic American retirement ceremony: kind words of appreciation and the ubiquitous watch. Those were not, of course, the important legacies Kennedy inherited from his employment at the Federal Reserve. In those sixteen years the Great Depression and World War II permanently changed the role of government in American life. An important element in that change was the transformation of the Federal Reserve from a highly decentralized system with limited powers to affect the monetary policy of the nation into a centralized system dominated by the board with the substantial powers of a central bank. Kennedy watched that transformation firsthand and came to commercial banking with a clear understanding of how individual banks fit within the overall banking system and how that system was affected and influenced by policies adopted by the Federal Reserve Board. That experience alerted him to the possibilities for, and limitations on, individual banks as they sought to realize their potential in an economy where both market forces and government policies shaped the economic environment. There were others at Continental who knew much more about the day-to-day operation of a commercial bank than Kennedy did, for they came to the bank as junior officers and rose through the ranks. Theirs was an expertise essential to the efficient operation of the bank, but their perspective was shaped by that experience. Kennedy came to his banking career with the perspective of a central banker, and, therefore, he saw opportunities for Continental that were hidden from those who viewed the bank only in terms of stability and profitability. He was not sure when he left the Federal Reserve whether he would eventually gain enough influence to move Continental toward what he saw as its full potential, but it was a risk he was willing to take.

7

CONTINENTAL ILLINOIS: BANKING BECKONS

In retrospect, David Kennedy's decision to leave Washington and his position at the Federal Reserve Board to join Continental in Chicago seems farsighted. At the time, it had much more the appearance of an act of faith. In terms of salary, it was not even the best job offer he had; he could have gone to New York, which was the leading financial center of the nation, if not the world, and he was leaving the board just when it appeared that he would soon move into positions of increasing influence. His family was happy in Washington, where the children had a supportive circle of friends at church and school; Lenora's health was improving; and Kennedy was finding his calling as a bishop rewarding. Furthermore, he seemed to be giving up a position with the Federal Reserve Board, where he had an insider's view of the forces that shaped the monetary policy of the nation, for a position in the bond department of a stodgy conservative bank managed by men who were more interested in stability and liquidity than in being part of a dynamic and growing economy.

The management of Continental had sound reasons for its conservatism. During the boom years of the 1920s the bank pursued an aggressive lending policy that brought it heavy losses when the depression struck in 1929. It was saved from insolvency in 1932 when the Reconstruction Finance Corporation (RFC) bought fifty million dollars of preferred stock in Continental that permitted the bank to stay open. At the insistence of the RFC, Walter Cummings, then head of the newly created Federal Deposit Insurance Corporation (FDIC), was appointed chairman of the board and chief executive officer of Continental. Cummings made his fortune as the founder of a company that manufactured streetcars, and he was treasurer of the Democratic party during Roosevelt's campaign in 1932. He then entered government service with the coming of the New Deal.

Cummings came into the bank determined to retire the preferred stock held by the RFC as soon as possible and to assure the liquidity of the bank. He achieved both of those goals, first by collecting on some of the loans that were written off but became collectible as economic conditions slowly improved, and second by a restrictive lending policy in favor of investing in government securities. He had a simple philosophy, he told the bank's executives: "You people get the deposits in here. I will invest them in the bond account. And we aren't very anxious to make loans." Thus, between 1934 and late 1946, when Kennedy joined the bank, the conservative management policies followed by Cummings and Carl Birdsall, president of the bank, had firmly established the bank's financial stability.

Kennedy did not know Cummings when he joined the bank in the fall of 1946; all his negotiations were with Hank Knight, who headed the bank's bond department. Oddly enough, Kennedy came to the bank without a formal title and without a clearly defined position within the department. Knight advised against a title on the ground that it might arouse some animosity against him by people who had been there longer and still were not vice-presidents. It would be, Knight thought, to Kennedy's advantage to take a back seat for a while. Kennedy trusted Knight's judgment and did not insist on a title or on a clearly defined job description and thus entered the bank much as he had entered the staff of the Federal Reserve Board: with a challenge to carve out a meaningful position for himself.

Soon after joining the bank, Kennedy refused appointment as the bank's economist. His training and experience seemed to make him a natural candidate, but he had his heart set on a decision-making position. In any event, if being the bank's economist was to be his fate, he would have been better off at the Federal Reserve Board, where the crucial decisions were being made, rather than sitting in Chicago talking to customers about the future course of the economy and giving advice to members of the board of directors, and "then have them do what they darn pleased anyway."

Although Kennedy did not know Cummings, service in the bond department was the ideal place to become acquainted with him. Cummings and Knight met daily to discuss the bank's investments in government securities, and Kennedy was gradually drawn into those strategy sessions. He came to Cummings's attention also because of his challenge to the view held by many in and out of the bank that the danger of inflation was high in the post–World War II years because of a shortage of consumer goods until the conversion to peacetime production was complete. The danger in the long run, they believed, was recession (or even depression), partly because of the large national debt and partly because they doubted the industrial sector could absorb the returning veterans and simultaneously retain the thousands of workers who were employed in arms production during the war. Kennedy was of a different opinion. Because of his experience at the Federal Reserve Board, he could see clearly how the board's open market operations, coupled with federal taxing and spending policies, would first assure that the government debt was serviced and then provide the necessary increase in the money supply for the economy to expand. He also could see that federal policies provided the banking community with the opportunity to play a central role in facilitating economic growth.

At first, Kennedy's outspoken optimism about the postwar economy received a chilly reception from the senior officers at Continental, who told him that he was a "Washington maverick." He had been too long in Washington, they complained, and had too little practical experience to see the matter clearly. This criticism did not deter him from spreading his optimistic views about the future of the economy and the potential of the bank among the

*David M. Kennedy
in the 1950s*

bank's junior officers. He preached his gospel of growth and opportunity to these young officers during their daily coffee breaks, where there was a chance for wide-ranging informal discussion of the bank's policies. His message was that they should look beyond the present to Continental's future as the leading bank in Chicago and the Midwest.

Kennedy's principal benefit from assignment in the bond department was the opportunity to work with Knight. Knight was one of a small group of bankers in the nation who understood the full implications of the changes in the Federal Reserve system resulting from the Banking Act of 1935. Because of his experience in the government securities market, Treasury officials often consulted him on the response of the money markets to new government bond issues. Knight recruited Kennedy, promoted his career at the bank, and introduced him to the network of bank officers and bond dealers, who included the leaders in the government securities market. They were a perfect match: they respected each other's professional judgment, they closely agreed on major issues, and they shared a strong personal friendship.[1]

Ironically, it was a disagreement with Hank Knight that indirectly led to David Kennedy's appointment in 1953 as an assistant to the Secretary of the Treasury. The disagreement arose over the bank's investment in the first long-term bonds issued by the Treasury since World War II. Before the bonds were issued, the Treasury consulted with monetary experts throughout the United States, including Knight. Knight was enthusiastic about the bonds and proposed to commit the bank to $200 million in them. He was surprised to find Kennedy opposed the plan based on his assessment that the inflationary pressure resulting from the Korean War was still strong, the future of interest rates was unclear, and that the Federal Reserve Board was only supporting short-term government securities.

Knight decided that Kennedy's arguments made sense and agreed to support Kennedy's proposal that the bank purchase only $20 million of the $200 million he originally proposed. When the bonds fell below par soon after their issue, not only did Kennedy's sound assessment of the market save the bank a considerable sum of money but the incident also enhanced Kennedy's reputation with other executives at Continental and with outside banking experts. His assessment of the bond market brought him to the attention of George Humphrey, the Secretary of the Treasury, who wanted to know more about this young man in Chicago. He had to go no further than W. Randolph Burgess, his Under Secretary for Monetary Affairs, for the answer, since Burgess had known Kennedy well while he was on the staff of the Federal Reserve Board. The result was that Kennedy was invited to Washington to work with Burgess as a specialist in debt management.

There were many good reasons why Kennedy was reluctant to accept Humphrey's invitation. He was enjoying his work in the bank and his service in the Church, the family was settled happily in Evanston, and he would have to resign from the bank, forfeiting his pension rights. In addition, Cummings was opposed; after all, he argued, Humphrey could find someone else to fill the position at the Treasury. Knight had other advice for Kennedy. He pointed out that experience in the Treasury would enhance Kennedy's reputation in the financial community, and that the appointment would advance Kennedy's career at the bank. Kennedy's decision to accept Knight's advice was strengthened by the support of John K. Edmunds, president of the Chicago Stake, with whom Kennedy was serving as a counselor in the stake presidency, although some of the Church authorities in Salt Lake City thought it would be wise to release Kennedy if he went to Washington, Edmunds said he would rather have Kennedy as a part-time counselor than someone else full time. With this support, Kennedy agreed in October 1953 to go to Washington for one year.

Because the Washington assignment would be temporary, Kennedy and Lenora decided that she and the girls would stay in Chicago during the school year and join him in Washington for the summer. He took a small apartment—sitting room, bedroom, and kitchen—in the Jefferson Hotel at Sixteenth and M, where several other Treasury officials, including Burgess, were living. For the next fourteen months he became a familiar face on the Baltimore and Ohio Railroad's Capitol Limited as he commuted each weekend between Washington and Chicago and was often in Chicago midweek for meetings of the stake presidency. The overnight journeys made for an exhausting schedule that was justified only by the professional challenge Kennedy found waiting for him in Washington on the one hand, and the all-important family and church responsibilities that continued at home on the other.

When David Kennedy joined the Treasury Department in October 1953, Dwight D. Eisenhower's administration was still searching for ways to achieve its goals of balancing the budget and promoting economic growth and stability. Both of these goals proved elusive. The budget inherited by the new administration had a deficit of $9 billion. Inflation fueled by the Korean War was brought under control, but only at the cost of a recession in the latter half of 1953. In addition, it was not clear just how the then unprecedented national debt of $276 billion—largely the legacy of World War II and the Korean conflict—should be managed.

The cost of financing the national debt had risen after the Federal Reserve Board began letting market forces set the interest rate on all government securities. Secretary Humphrey and Burgess supported that policy because they believed low interest rates and government deficits were among the main causes of inflation and undermined their efforts to maintain a sound dollar. Kennedy agreed with them that free markets, including one in government securities, were the best means of achieving lasting economic prosperity. They knew that a free market in government securities would increase the cost of government borrowing. The answer, they argued, was not to peg interest rates at an artificially low level but to adopt monetary and fiscal policies that would assure a vigorous, growing economy. While the answers were clear to them, the task—how to make the transition from deficit spending to a balanced budget while maintaining economic growth, reducing taxes, and managing a large national debt—was difficult indeed.

A major goal of debt management, Kennedy believed, was to achieve a balance between long-term and short-term government securities. Maintaining that balance was difficult enough with a balanced budget, but it was exacerbated by an unbalanced budget because issuance of new government securities necessitated refinancing the existing debt and producing enough revenue to cover the budget deficit. When Eisenhower took office, the national debt was heavily weighted in favor of short-term securities. The Treasury was therefore constantly having to enter the market to refinance a portion of the existing debt as the short-term securities came due. This robbed the Treasury of considerable flexibility in choosing when to make a new offering of government securities. With more flexibility, the Treasury could take advantage of any fluctuations in the interest rate to lower the cost of government borrowing. Consequently a major goal of government policy was to increase the percentage of the debt held in long-term securities.

During the fourteen months Kennedy was at the Treasury, progress was made in lengthening the average maturity of the national debt. This was largely because of a $26 billion refinancing offering of long- and medium-term government securities that Kennedy persuaded Burgess to undertake. Kennedy not only thought the market would absorb this offering, but he also undertook a vigorous selling campaign with commercial banks across the country. The figures tell the tale. The marketable debt—that portion of the national debt that is represented by government securities largely owned by commercial banks and that can be traded in the market—which matured in under one year represented 33 percent of the debt at the end of June 1955 compared to 52 percent in June 1953. It might be asserting too much to say that Kennedy was solely responsible for the increase in the average maturity of the government debt. However, his vigorous advocacy of that policy and the crucial position he held in the Treasury as the expert on debt management suggest that much of the credit must be his.

During those fourteen months, Kennedy became involved in several issues that were only peripherally related to debt management. Among the most important of those issues was the St. Lawrence Seaway, a joint venture with the government of Canada that involved the construction of several canals and locks to open the Great Lakes to seagoing vessels. Eastern Seaboard states opposed the seaway because they believed that it would divert traffic from their ports, railroads were opposed for much the same reason, and others argued that the projected cost was too high and the anticipated benefits too low. Much of the controversy centered on the financing of the seaway. Those opposed on policy grounds argued that even if the seaway were approved, it should be funded by revenue bonds sold on the open market to the public. Since there was considerable doubt that tolls from the seaway would be sufficient to retire the bonds, opponents thought public funding would assure that it would never be built. Some proponents argued for revenue bonds sold to the public but guaranteed by the United States Treasury, and others wanted the government to pay for the cost of construction as it would for any other public works project. When Eisenhower took office, the desirability of the seaway was still being debated in Congress. After some initial hesitation, the

President came out strongly for the seaway, and that decision forced the Treasury to face the issue of how the project was to be funded.

David Kennedy became involved in the debate in early 1954 when, unexpectedly, Secretary Humphrey asked him to testify in favor of the seaway in hearings before the Public Works Committee of the House of Representatives. With only a brief examination of the files the Treasury had on the seaway, Kennedy appeared before the committee. He took with him William Heffelfinger, a senior civil servant at the Treasury who knew the background of the department's position on the project, to guide him through the maze of previous testimony Treasury representatives had given before the committee. In June 1953, Randolph Burgess had told the committee that the Treasury opposed the "issuance and sale of guaranteed obligations by Government corporations in the market." The Seaway Corporation, he argued, should borrow the funds to build the seaway directly from the Treasury at the same rates the Treasury paid to borrow money. Critics argued that this simply increased government spending by the $105 million that it was estimated the project would cost, at a time when the government was seeking to reduce government spending to balance the budget. Thus, the dilemma for proponents was either to agree to the revenue bonds sold to the public or to accept the stigma of favoring an increase in government spending. Kennedy thought he saw a way out of this dilemma. He proposed that the Seaway Corporation issue revenue bonds to be retired by the tolls generated by the seaway, but that those bonds be sold to the Treasury rather than to the public.

Kennedy began his testimony with what he would later recall as a "Fourth of July oration" on the importance of the seaway. Then, in answer to a challenge that the cost of the project would undermine the administration's policy of balancing the budget, he suggested that it be financed by a revenue bond. Before he could explain the rest of his proposal, Chairman George A. Dondero, an avid supporter of the seaway, adjourned the meeting, called Kennedy and Heffelfinger into his office, and complained bitterly that they had just killed the seaway by proposing to finance it by the sale of revenue bonds. The railroads were urging the same policy upon

Congress, he told them, because they knew such bonds could not be sold, thus effectively killing the seaway. Kennedy told Dondero that on the contrary, he had just "bought" the St. Lawrence Seaway, and that if Dondero would resume the hearings he would convince the committee it could be done. When the hearings resumed, Kennedy admitted that revenue bonds, given the current market, could not be sold on the open market, but that over the long run the St. Lawrence Seaway was an economically viable project and, therefore, the Treasury would buy the entire issue.

Dondero and Humphrey were skeptical of Kennedy's proposal, Dondero on policy grounds and Humphrey because he doubted the Treasury had the legal authority to buy the bonds. But both came to realize that revenue bonds purchased by the Treasury offered a way out of the debate over funding the project. After Dondero became convinced Kennedy's proposal was sound, the committee amended the St. Lawrence Seaway bill to substitute "revenue bonds" in lieu of "notes, debentures, bonds or other obligations" in the section of the statute that authorized the Secretary of the Treasury to provide up to $105 million for construction.[2]

At the time, Kennedy received great personal satisfaction and praise for his part in "buying" the seaway. Fifteen years later, when he returned to Washington as Secretary of the Treasury, he found that although revenues from the seaway had continued to rise each year, they were not sufficient—except in 1966—to pay the interest on the revenue bonds held by the government. In fact, by 1968 the seaway owed the government $19.2 million in deferred interest payments. It is little wonder then that Kennedy found the seaway was not the attractive investment he believed it to be when he delivered his "Fourth of July oration."

As a member of the staff of the Federal Reserve Board, Kennedy had come to understand how government economic policy was made. He witnessed firsthand the titanic battles between Henry Morgenthau and Marriner Eccles for control of the government's economic policies. At the Treasury he had an opportunity to observe the politics of policy making at a still higher level. Because the size of the budget was crucial to the management of the public debt,

Humphrey asked him to sit in on budget meetings at the White House. His only instruction was to take a strong stand on the budget so that no promises were made that the Treasury could not finance. Those meetings gave Kennedy a chance to assess Eisenhower's leadership abilities; he came away impressed. He thought the President was much stronger than he was represented to be in the media. He found that Eisenhower was not ideological in his approach to economic issues and he was, therefore, able to accept a budget deficit if that were necessary to assure economic growth and prosperity. Those budget hearings at the White House also gave Kennedy his first introduction to Richard M. Nixon, who sometimes sat in on the meetings and from time to time made comments and suggestions.

Kennedy's experience at the Treasury was really his first with partisan politics. In his youth he had considered himself a Republican. However, his experience in Washington during the depression led him to support Roosevelt during his first two terms; then he returned to the Republican convictions of his youth. He had avoided partisan political activity, and his appointment to the Treasury during the Eisenhower administration was not made because of his politics but on his merit as an expert in debt management. Still, his fourteen months at the Treasury gave his political views a somewhat more partisan cast than they had when he left Chicago. After all, it was Democrats such as Senator Paul Douglas of his home state of Illinois, and Representative Wright Patman of Texas, who were the most outspoken critics of the policies he helped to formulate and that he vigorously defended. Yet the most lasting impression he took from that experience was not resentment but a deeper understanding of the democratic process. "If we have a democracy and a system of government that you and I want," he told a group of bankers in Montana, "we must have at least two political parties—the majority party in power and a minority party—the loyal opposition—to keep the majority party on its toes." The existence of a minority party, he argued, was necessary to assure that decisions were the result of considered judgments. The concomitant of a minority party strong enough to "have its views felt and considered" was a majority party strong enough to have its policies adopted by the Congress. "I believe in a two-party system . . . and I have come to the conclusion that this give-and-take is one of the things that makes us strong," he said. The necessary consequence of his belief in the two-party system was the importance of politicians. He cautioned students at Brigham Young University not to think of a politician as "a bad man, an immoral, sinful man," but as one of the people who make democracy work. His own experience in defending the economic policies of the Eisenhower administration sensitized him to their importance and to the ways they can be misunderstood.

David Kennedy stayed on at the Treasury two months longer than he had expected, and he was anxious to return to private life. When he left Continental, he had every intention of returning, but his service at the Treasury opened other possibilities to him. Several banks in New York approached him with attractive offers. While he was considering what he should do, Carl Birdsall came to Washington and confided in him that although there was no question of Continental's solvency, it was losing ground. What the bank needed, Birdsall said, was someone who understood the current economic realities to represent the bank across the country—someone like Kennedy who could meet with Continental's correspondent banks, corporation officials, and other customers and discuss the issues he had been dealing with at the Treasury. Kennedy's reaction was that Birdsall was seeking someone to manage a public relations campaign, and he was not interested in that kind of position. Birdsall assured him that if he would take on the task, he would have a significant voice in developing bank policy. Kennedy was interested because he understood well enough the changes that needed to be made at the bank, but he had one last question: Was Birdsall speaking for himself or for Walter Cummings? Birdsall honestly confessed that he was speaking for himself, but he hastened to assure Kennedy that Cummings was more than eager to have him return to the bank. "You know your relationship with Cummings," Kennedy remembered Birdsall saying. "He thinks you're one of the boys and he wants you back."

Kennedy returned to Chicago and Continental with a promise that he would play a more significant policy-making role than he had enjoyed when he left. He was fully confident that he knew what needed to be done to make the bank an even more important factor on the Chicago and Midwest financial scene. That confidence was based in part on insights he gained from his experience in government and at the bank. At an even deeper level, his confidence was based on a belief in himself and in his own abilities. While some might have been surprised at his emerging influence in banking circles, he expected more of himself. He revealed some of the high expectations he had set for himself to his daughter Carol when she came to Washington to spend some time with him while he was at the Treasury. "Did you ever think you would be where you are now at this age?" she asked him one evening. "What do you mean where I am?" Carol remembered her father saying, "I thought I'd be a lot further." In view of that expectation, it is tempting to speculate that he returned to Chicago because he anticipated becoming president of the bank in the near future. There is, however, nothing in the record to justify the speculation. Kennedy returned for the same reasons he joined Continental in the first place: it was a bank that had great potential for growth in a market that itself offered unlimited possibilities of expansion. What had been an act of faith in 1947 was, in 1955, a decision that reflected his belief that his vision for Continental could be realized.

8

CONTINENTAL ILLINOIS: CHANGING OF THE GUARD

David Kennedy left the Treasury at the end of 1954 having realized some of the goals that took him there and with an enhanced reputation both in and out of the bank. Carl Birdsall occasionally asked him to undertake a special project, and loan officers turned to him for help in getting Walter Cummings to approve a loan.[1] Kennedy's intercession with Cummings was the turning point in the approval of a large loan to J. R. "Jack" Simplot, who was expanding his empire in the Intermountain West. The vice-president responsible for the business the bank did on the West Coast and in the Intermountain West came to Kennedy with a request for help after months of frustration when Cummings delayed approval of the loan. Kennedy presented the case for a loan to Cummings, who asked him only if it was a loan worth making. Kennedy said he knew Simplot, that he knew Idaho, and that this was the kind of business the bank should be developing. Cummings approved the loan, and Kennedy gave the approval to the pleased loan officer, but not without some surprise on his own part that Cummings had responded so quickly to his request.

Soon after his return to Continental, Kennedy assumed full responsibility for the bond department. Robert Drew, Hank Knight's principal assistant in the bond department and secretary of the board of directors, retired in April 1955, and Knight himself developed cancer and struggled with poor health until his death in 1958. Kennedy took Drew's position in the bond department and as secretary of the board, and with these increased responsibilities, he was made a vice-president.[2] His cousin and close friend Orville Johnson helped him keep his new title in perspective. Orville lived all his life in Randolph but was exceptionally well read and maintained a lively interest in current events. He told David that he had read of his promotion to vice-president in the bank and casually asked how many vice-presidents were in the bank. When David told him there were about eighty, Orville's shrug let David know that he was not impressed by a high-sounding title that was debased by the frequency with which it was bestowed.

Kennedy set about restructuring the bank's investments in government securities. Following the 1951 agreement between the Federal Reserve Board and the Treasury to let the market determine interest rates, the liquidity of the bank's large holdings in long-term bonds was undermined. Since other investment opportunities offered a higher rate of return, Kennedy's strategy was to sell Continental's long-term bonds at a loss, charge the loss against earnings, and then buy higher-yield bonds with the cash generated from the sale. The advantages of "tax swapping" were not readily apparent to other bankers since they tended to value the existing bonds at face value rather than in comparison to what the same money would earn if invested at a higher interest rate. But Kennedy brought all his vigor and powers of persuasion to the task and was able to generate a substantial amount of business for the bank.

Kennedy's increasing influence in the bank, his successful record at the Treasury, and his reputation as a specialist in government securities brought him to the attention of those outside the bank who were looking for executive talent. An attractive offer came from Newell Childs, president of C. F. Childs, a family firm and one of the large government bond dealers in the United States. Childs not only offered Kennedy an attractive salary but also offered to supplement it by placing a million dollars in a trust fund with the interest going to Kennedy. There were other inducements, such as stock options and retirement benefits. In the end Kennedy said no. Attractive as the offer was, he was not interested in working for a family firm whose business was limited to the buying and selling of government securities. What he sought was an opportunity to make a difference in an organization whose influence and impact on the community would transcend the pursuit of profits. He wanted to be a builder, not just a merchant.

A less lucrative opportunity, but one of far greater substance professionally, came from the Federal Reserve Bank of Chicago. The long-time president, Clifford S. "Hap" Young, had reached retirement age, and the board of directors, of which Walter Cummings was a member, was looking for a new president. Cummings called Kennedy in to talk to him about this offer and promised his support if Kennedy wanted the job. Kennedy replied that he did not want to leave Continental and that Cummings should carry that message to the board. The board was not persuaded that David was adamant about staying at Continental, so they enlisted the help of William McChesney Martin, chairman of the Federal Reserve Board. Martin told Kennedy that if he would accept the position, the salary would be raised from fifty thousand dollars to match the sixty thousand dollars then paid the president of the New York Federal Reserve Bank. In addition, he promised David a seat on the Federal Reserve's open-market committee and that he would participate in international monetary meetings on the same basis as the president of the Federal Reserve Bank of New York. These were persuasive arguments, but in the end Kennedy refused to accept the position. He knew the key decision-making authority in the Federal Reserve system resided in the board, not in the regional banks. If he were going to leave Continental for the Federal Reserve system, he wanted to be in Washington at the heart of things, not in Chicago on the periphery of power.

Despite Kennedy's expanding role at Continental and his increasing influence in the national banking community, he was not yet a senior vice-president when Carl Birdsall, who had been president since 1948, suddenly died on November 19, 1956. Unexpectedly, within a day of Birdsall's death, Cummings offered the position to Kennedy. The record is not clear why Cummings chose Kennedy, and there is no contemporary statement from him giving his reasons. On its face, the appointment seems incongruous in terms of the policies Cummings had followed since coming to the bank in 1933. Kennedy was known in the bank for his belief that those policies were out of date and had let Continental's chief competitor, First National Bank of Chicago, become the leading bank in the city, and hence in the entire Midwest. Lending money to the government was good business in the 1930s and 1940s, but by the mid-1950s, banking growth was "clearly in private lending—in mortgages, consumer financing, and imaginative loans to small, aggressive companies, which kept on turning into large, aggressive companies."

Although Cummings never publicly explained his reasons for choosing Kennedy, the circumstantial evidence suggests at least four factors were important in the selection. First, Kennedy had more access to Cummings than most officers in the bank. The bond department was for Cummings the heart of the bank, and he reviewed the investment policies of the bank every day with Kennedy. Second, Cummings was a member of the board of directors of the Federal Reserve Bank of Chicago and saw how enthusiastically members of that board pushed for Kennedy's appointment as president of the Federal Reserve Bank. That experience may have convinced Cummings that if Kennedy were not made president, he might well be tempted by future offers from other banks. Third, Kennedy's judgment when he came to the bank that the nation would not suffer a postwar depression proved correct. Fourth, his service at the Treasury gave him increased visibility and influence at the national level, and his role as a spokesman for the bank since his return from Washington made him the most viable presidential candidate, if not the most visible.

Yet, given all of these plausible reasons for Cummings's decision, Kennedy's selection was unusual because he lacked experience in managing a large organization. Neither his experience at the Federal Reserve Board nor at the Treasury gave him wide-ranging executive responsibility. At the bank he managed one of the smaller departments and one not directly related to the principal business of the bank—commercial banking. Election as president meant, therefore, a sudden and substantial increase in his administrative responsibilities, for he would be managing one of the largest banks in the country. In view of the rapidity with which Cummings moved to name Kennedy president of the bank, he obviously had few doubts about Kennedy's executive ability. Nor was he deterred from his choice because Kennedy had not risen step by step through the bank hierarchy to become a senior vice-president. After all, Cummings had become chairman of Continental without any experience as a banker. Thus, he probably saw nothing unusual in reaching down into the ranks to pick the person who in his estimation was the best candidate.

When Cummings offered Kennedy the position as president of the bank, Kennedy countered with several objections. First, he was deeply involved in his church work and he did not want to give up that involvement. Cummings brushed that objection aside with the comment that he too was heavily involved as a layman in the Catholic church. Kennedy pointed out that his religious convictions would place some restrictions on his representational functions as president since he did not drink. Cummings, Kennedy remembered, made short shrift of that objection: "You've got plenty of people around here that like to drink. Hire them." Kennedy reminded Cummings that there were officers in the bank who had been there longer than he, and who deserved to be considered as president, including some who thought they had been promised the position. When even that argument did not sway Cummings, Kennedy reminded him that they were in fundamental disagreement on the policies the bank should follow. Cummings disarmed Kennedy by promising him that as president he would have full operating authority, including the power to make policy changes. Kennedy had one last reservation that reached to the personal relationship between the two of them. He explained to Cummings that as president and as a director of the bank, he would have to make decisions about policy matters that would directly affect Cummings, including Cummings's retirement. He reminded Cummings that he was in favor of placing an age limit on the service of directors and officers of the bank, and that if he became president, he would pursue that policy. Cummings responded that he did not intend to "stay around forever" and that Kennedy would need him as chairman during his initial tenure as president. Kennedy asked for permission to discuss the offer with Lenora and the family and said he would give his answer the next day.

Yet even after he had accepted Cummings's offer following an expression of support from Lenora and the children, Kennedy faced a decision that could have forced him to withdraw that acceptance. That possibility arose with the receipt of a letter from David O. McKay, president of the Church, asking if Kennedy could meet with him in Chicago. Kennedy assumed that President McKay wanted to discuss the Church's involvement in the banking business, since they had had several discussions on that issue before. President McKay arrived with an offer to head the Church's bank in Utah with full authority to make all operational decisions. Kennedy asked President McKay if this was a church calling rather than a business proposition, for if it were, he would not hesitate to accept. When he was assured that it was a business proposition, he explained to President McKay that he had just accepted the offer to be president of Continental. Kennedy offered to come to Salt Lake City if that were in the best interests of the Church, but President McKay quickly said that he should stay in Chicago as head of Continental, although he extracted a promise that Kennedy would help the Church find someone who could manage the bank in Utah.

Kennedy's formal election as president of Continental Illinois National Bank and Trust Company came the following Monday. Cummings interrupted a lunch that Kennedy was enjoying with two old friends, John K. Edmunds and Harold B. Lee, a member of the Church's Quorum of the Twelve Apostles, to ask permission to take Kennedy to meet the board of directors, for he had just been elected president of the bank.

127

Kennedy was fifty-one when he became president of Continental. Except for the year at the Treasury, he had made his influence felt working behind the scenes at the Federal Reserve Board and at the bank. In both of those institutions he was part of the informal power structure composed of people who because of their ability have influence that extends beyond the position they hold in the formal organizational structure. But as president, he would have not only the influence that flowed from his ability but also the formal power that resided in the office. At last he was in a position in which he could achieve his ambition to make a difference by giving direction and purpose to an organization whose impact could be felt worldwide. During his years as a young missionary in England, he wrote Lenora of his desire to "get somewhere in life; to make good. . . . I shall; I'll work, and I'll study at nights; anything to prepare myself for bigger things in life." The fruits of that determination, of his ability to concentrate on the task at hand, of his honing of his intellectual and analytical ability, were now in hand.

When David Kennedy had been appointed a vice-president of the bank, his cousin Orville was not impressed. Soon after his appointment as president, David was in Randolph, and Orville, in his laconic way, asked how many *presidents* there were in the bank. When David assured him there was only one, Orville's response was "Congratulations, boy!" Orville knew the difference between one of eighty and being the only one.

Kennedy moved quickly to impose his own style on the office of president. He had an inner core of reserve, so he was far from being a glad-handler, but the influence he enjoyed both in the bank and in his church reflected his ability to make friends and his sensitivity to personal relationships. He also believed that top management should be more visible to the employees of the bank than were Cummings and Birdsall. Hence, his first act was to hold a reception in the president's office for all bank employees. It was the first time that most of them had seen the president's office. At Christmas time, just a month after he was elected president, he went throughout the twenty-four-story bank to wish every employee a Merry Christmas, a tour that became a Christmas tradition.

There was far more to the Kennedy style than the visible president. After his election as president, he carefully assessed the strengths and weaknesses of the bank. There was no doubt about its liquidity, for there were ample reserves against bad loans, and its relations with its large corporate customers were of long standing and were generally well managed. There were substantial opportunities for growth by expanding international activities and seeking more business from small- and medium-size firms, as well as by increasing the bank's share of the consumer credit market in Chicago. He knew that the senior officers were not only competent but also well respected in the banking community, though he wondered if Cummings's tight rein had robbed them of their initiative. He was, however, willing to give them a chance to show what they could do if given authority to make significant decisions on their own. He also realized that the board of directors would have to be changed, for most of them were of the same generation as Walter Cummings. Cummings, one of his critics bitingly said, had made Continental "an 'old man's bank.' "

Although David Kennedy's selection as president was generally well received among the bank's senior officers, some of them wanted to be sure he adopted their agenda for change. John Mannion came to him with an offer to take charge of the bank's commercial lending. While Kennedy recognized Mannion's ability as a commercial loan expert, he was not ready to turn those crucial decisions over to one man. He explained his own plans for a loan

Walter Cummings, chairman of Continental Illinois National Bank, and David M. Kennedy, president

committee with the chairmanship rotating among the top vice-presidents of the bank. Richard Aishton, whom Kennedy had strongly urged on Cummings as president of the bank in his place, told Kennedy that his major task was to force the immediate retirement of older members of the board of directors. Again Kennedy agreed with the goal but explained that the change had to be done with care so as to avoid ill will that in the long run might cost the bank important accounts. Fred M. Naber, who was in charge of the eastern part of the country for the bank, argued that Continental should leave the international field to the New York banks. Such advice was a challenge to Kennedy, who believed that the future of the bank must include vigorous development of the bank's international activities. In his view, the decision to expand internationally would determine whether Continental was to be a major American and international bank or a parochial bank confined to Chicago and the Midwest.

One by one Kennedy shared with the senior vice-presidents his views about what needed to be done for Continental to reach its full potential. A central part of that message was that no longer would all the important decisions be made in the front office. He was prepared to delegate to senior officers the authority and responsibility they needed to manage their departments. He was fully aware that he had no experience in the lending operations; he had never processed a loan, made a credit investigation, or administered a trust. What he brought to the office of president was wisdom and vigor, sound knowledge of the interrelationships of the public and private sectors of the economy, and substantial expertise in the securities market.

When it became clear that Kennedy really intended to delegate authority and responsibility to the bank's officers, he discovered how vigorous, innovative, and aggressive they could be if given the chance.[3] Indeed, he may have underestimated the extent to which the bank was ready for the kind of leadership he was offering. Those senior officers knew how most successful large banks operated and had chafed under the highly centralized operating style of Walter Cummings and Carl Birdsall. Then, too, as Cummings grew older, they anticipated that when he was gone there would be an opportunity to change many of those restrictive policies. Birdsall's death sped up that timetable, and Kennedy's own desire for change happily coincided with the general climate for innovation that existed in the bank.

Kennedy's appointment not only increased his administrative responsibilities but also included the representational responsibilities that inevitably fall to the president. That facet of his position raised the possibility of a conflict between the use of alcohol on social occasions and Kennedy's objection to that use, which was firmly grounded in his religious belief. There was no question about his personal use of alcohol; the issue was whether he would serve alcohol in his home or permit its use in the bank's dining rooms. At home he followed his religious inclination and kept an alcohol-free table. At the bank, he let stand the strict rule Cummings had established against serving liquor in the bank, including wine in the bank's dining rooms. An exception to that policy occurred in later years after Kennedy became chairman. Tilden Cummings,[4] who was then president of the bank, wanted to hold a reception for alumni of the bank who would be attending the American Bankers Association meetings in Chicago. As Cummings told the story, he knew Kennedy "was a good Mormon and wasn't very enthusiastic about drinking. So I went to Dave and said, We're going to have this alumni brunch on the second floor of the bank, and we want to serve bloody Marys and screwdrivers. He said, All right. So I rushed out of the office before he could change his mind, and I thought to myself, My God, I wonder if he knows they're alcoholic drinks."

While David Kennedy was attempting to change the direction of the bank, the presence of Walter Cummings as chairman of the board and chief executive officer was a constant reminder that those new beginnings could not be fully realized until there was a new board of directors, and, more specifically, until Cummings retired. The subject of Cummings's retirement involved conflicting emotions for Kennedy. He felt a deep sense of loyalty to Cummings; Cummings had promised him that as president he would have operational control of the bank, and for the most part he kept his word. Yet he believed that Cummings's retirement was in the best interests of the bank: Cummings was seventy-seven years old—substantially beyond the age when the chairmen of most large corporations retire—and he had been chairman of the board for almost twenty-four years. Furthermore, his presence symbolized the conservative policies of the past, whereas Kennedy wanted to push Continental into the future.

In early December 1957, Kennedy, accompanied by several members of the board of directors, approached Cummings informally about adopting a retirement policy for members of the board and setting a date for his own retirement. They suggested two options: Cummings would retire at the end of 1957 but continue as a member of the board for some time, or alternatively, he could stay on as chairman for another year "but have the by-laws of the bank amended to transfer the principal responsibility to the President of the bank."[5] They also proposed that directors who were officers of the bank should retire from the board when they retired from the bank, and other directors should retire from the board when they retired from their own businesses, but in any case not later than at seventy-two or seventy-five years of age. The meeting was incon-

David M. Kennedy on hunting trip, December 1957

clusive, but at least Kennedy and one other director came away with the impression Cummings would tell the board at its December 13 meeting that he would retire at January's annual meeting.

At the December 13 meeting, Kennedy read a prepared statement conceding that a discussion of Cummings's retirement was "a difficult matter for me to discuss either with him and particularly with the members of the Board, since however objective I might be, it appears that I am an interested party and might be asking for something for myself." He sought to place the issue in the broadest possible context, for he pointed out, he was "thrust into a position of leadership over night as it were. I hope this never happens at the Continental Bank again." What he wanted, therefore, was a carefully considered and planned transition of leadership. It was just as important in his view that the transition include a consideration of the top management team as it was to determine who would be chairman. "In these selections," he informed the board, "if I am to succeed Mr. Cummings in responsibility, I would like to have a free hand subject to the approval of the Board."

In the ensuing discussion, Cummings expressed his belief that January 1958 was too early, since Kennedy had been president for such a short time. Kennedy responded that he would not have accepted the presidency if he did not feel qualified to become chief executive officer. Twelve of the fifteen directors present spoke in favor of an early retirement date for Cummings and tried to commit him to a date not later than June 30, 1958. Cummings resisted fixing the date but promised that within the next six months he would notify the board as to the date of his retirement.

Cummings was as good as his word. At a meeting of the board on June 23, 1958, he expressed his desire to continue as chairman until January 1959, when he would have completed twenty-five years in that position. But he wanted to remain on the board and asked that the bylaws be amended so that he could "be elected by the new Board to a new position, Chairman of the Executive Committee, at the same salary I am now drawing." Relieved that Cummings had finally set a retirement date, the board adopted a resolution that made his statement a part of the official minutes of the

133

meeting. The resolution also provided that "the Board of Directors to be elected at the annual meeting of shareholders, to be held in 1959, take appropriate action to carry out the recommendations in such statement." On its face Cummings's statement and the resolution of the board seemed to put an end to the question of succession. That was not to be. His proposal that the bylaws be amended so he could be appointed chairman of an executive committee embroiled Kennedy in a conflict with Cummings that he thought involved issues even more critical than who should be chairman.

Kennedy asked Herbert A. Friedlich, a member of the law firm that represented the bank, to draft a resolution creating the proposed executive committee. The committee, he said, should be a committee of the board that would be given assignments by the board and report to the board on the completion of those assignments. Friedlich took the draft to Cummings, who insisted on changes that made clear his intention to retain a significant voice in the affairs of the bank. The revised draft made the executive committee an executive committee of the bank rather than of the board of directors, with the chairman of the committee an officer of the bank second only to the chairman. In addition, it made the chairman of the board a member of the committee, giving him only one vote on a committee that would have power to "consult with and advise the officers of the Association generally on matters of policy, administration and operations."

When Kennedy saw this draft, he realized that it compromised the position of the chairman and created in essence a two-headed administrative structure. He told Friedlich that the draft was unacceptable, and when Friedlich responded that the draft reflected Cummings's views and would have to stand, Kennedy fired Friedlich as the bank's attorney; it seemed to him that Friedlich was representing Cummings rather than the bank. He then took his own analysis of the draft proposal to John Edmunds, who thought that Kennedy understood the matter correctly. Between them they prepared an opinion, signed by Edmunds, laying out in detail the objections to the draft.

On the basis of Edmunds's signed opinion, Kennedy sent a long memorandum to Cummings containing the objections with a cover note in which he described Friedlich's proposal as impossible: "It is a hodgepodge of conflicting jurisdictions that could cause trouble." Kennedy's fundamental objection was that Cummings's proposed committee would have operational rather than consultative responsibilities. Acceptance of the proposal would create "a separate 'executive' branch that could prove to be a discordant, annoying anomaly, out of which many thorny problems might arise."

Kennedy gained approval of board members for his original proposal to create the committee under the existing authority of the board to create committees as it saw fit. The board also agreed to make it clear to Cummings that the committee would be merely advisory, that is, without operational authority. With this backing, Kennedy discussed the issues with Cummings and then sent him a blunt *aide mémoire* that noted that the board objected to

David M. Kennedy, Illinois Governor William G. Stratton, Walter Cummings, and Chicago Mayor Richard J. Daley on 100th anniversary of Continental Illinois, 1957

135

the use of the term executive committee and that no change in the bylaws was planned since the committee—whatever its name— was a temporary expedient to accommodate Cummings's wish to remain on the board. Cummings must "clearly understand," Kennedy wrote, "that this is retirement and that this agreement to permit you to head an advisory committee of the Board for a year is merely as a transition to full retirement." Faced with a unanimous board and with the prospect that if he resisted further he might even be denied his wish to stay on the board, Cummings agreed to fulfill his commitment to retire at the annual meeting and to nominate Kennedy as chairman. He wanted, however, to keep the symbols of power, even if he was to lose its substance. Hence, he wanted to keep the office he occupied while he was chairman. Kennedy remembered vividly his response to Cummings: "Mr. Cummings, that's been the symbol of power in this bank for twenty-five years, and I can't take another office." When Cummings urged him to take a larger office in the floor above, Kennedy reminded him, "Yes, it's above it, but it'll be below it."

For Kennedy, Cummings's retirement was a wrenching experience. He was convinced that the bank would be better off if Cummings retired, but at the same time, as he told the board, he was an interested party whose motives could be misinterpreted. He knew that he was not acting alone; the board of directors was in full agreement that the time had come for Cummings to retire. Even so, Kennedy was still disturbed by the tension between him and Cummings that was engendered by the conflict.[6] Faced with this problem, he turned to Edmunds, not in his capacity as a lawyer, but as his spiritual leader in the Church. How, Kennedy wanted to know, could he best heal the breach that threatened to divide him from Cummings? Edmunds told Kennedy: "If I were in your place and I was replacing a man who had been Chairman of the Board for years and had helped me along, had helped me come up through the ranks in the bank, I'd want to honor him as much as I possibly could. . . . You have to understand that after he's been there that long and had influence in that position, prestige, it isn't easy to give that up. Be kind to him and generous with him and praise him—wherever it's honest, praise him. You have to be your own man, but praise him where you can and hold him up among the Board members."

Edmunds reminded Kennedy of one of the most familiar and oft-quoted passages in Mormon scripture that lays out the principles of church leadership but applies to all administrative and personal relationships: "No power or influence can or ought to be maintained by virtue of the priesthood, only by persuasion, by long-suffering, by gentleness and meekness, and by love unfeigned; by kindness, and pure knowledge, which shall greatly enlarge the soul without hypocrisy, and without guile—reproving betimes with sharpness, when moved upon by the Holy Ghost; and then showing forth afterwards an increase of love toward him whom thou hast reproved, lest he esteem thee to be his enemy; that he may know that thy faithfulness is stronger than the cords of death."

Armed with this advice, Kennedy turned to the task of healing the wounds created over Cummings's retirement. Cummings remained a member of the board and chairman of the advisory committee—the board finally agreed to call it the executive committee—until the annual meeting of the board in 1961. He continued to have an office in the bank and lunched every day "at precisely the same time and at the same small table in the twenty-second floor dining room" until he became too feeble to visit the bank anymore. He died on August 19, 1967, just two months after his eighty-eighth birthday.

9

CONTINENTAL ILLINOIS: KENNEDY TAKES CHARGE

With his appointment as chairman of the board of Continental Illinois, David Kennedy moved with greater freedom to carry out the policies he had begun to put in place as president. His first priority was to increase commercial loans. He pressed an aggressive search for loan opportunities beyond the large corporations, such as U.S. Steel, Bethlehem, General Motors, Ford, and Swift, which comprised most of the bank's customers. Now the bank sought small and medium-size firms with substantial growth potential. The result was an increase in the percentage of the bank's assets invested in commercial loans from 37 percent to 63 percent from 1958 to 1966. As the bank increased its loan portfolio, it reduced its investments in government securities and changed their character. The percentage of the bank's assets represented by government securities declined from 29 percent in 1958 to 7 percent in 1966. Simultaneously Kennedy diversified those investments by reducing the bank's holdings in federal bonds and increasing those in state and municipal securities.

This policy shift was accompanied by a corresponding shift in operational policy. Prior to Kennedy's becoming chairman of the board, loan officers found it difficult to obtain approval for loans; even the top officials, other than the president and the chairman,

David M. Kennedy,
chairman of the board

could lend only $250,000. Loan officers chafed under these restrictions and pleaded with Kennedy for increased lending authority. In response, he established a graduated scale of lending authority, with senior vice-presidents authorized to loan up to the legal limit the bank could lend. This power led to caution as well as to aggressive and innovative loan management. Armed with that power, each of those senior officials "was smart enough to realize that if he had that big a loan he ought to sit down and talk with one of the other four or five," a bank officer recalled. In addition to delegating lending authority throughout the bank, Kennedy also had the loan committee conduct periodic reviews of each officer's decisions. This system had the advantage of giving customers a rapid

139

decision on their loan requests while giving loan officers feedback on their performance.

Kennedy also moved the bank into retail banking, an aspect that Continental had shunned. Many of the young officers of the bank, who had watched the First National Bank of Chicago aggressively pursue passbook savings and checking accounts from small depositors, had suggested on occasion that Continental do the same. Walter Cummings had always answered: "Never will we do that, we don't want that business." With Kennedy's ascension, Continental began to woo the small depositor, but there was more than an image change behind that decision. Small depositors in the 1930s and 1940s did not have much money; by the early 1950s the general prosperity meant that small depositors could be a significant source of deposits. In 1960 all the bank's retail-related activities— savings accounts, consumer loans including home mortgages, and low-cost checking accounts—were brought together as a Family Banking Center. Continental had once boasted of being "The Biggest Bank under One Roof." Now it wanted to be known as the "Big Bank with the Little Bank Inside."

Kennedy knew that to change the direction of the bank, he not only had to build a top management team but also to restructure the board of directors. He approached those two tasks with a mixture of careful planning, caution, and determination that moved him relentlessly toward his goal but saved him from impetuous mistakes. When he became chairman, he asked Richard Aishton, who had just eighteen months before he retired, to serve as president. Aishton, a competent, experienced banker, had been with Continental for twenty-five years. To those who came to Kennedy complaining that it was a mistake to name Aishton as president when he had so little time left with the bank, Kennedy argued that it was precisely because Aishton had so little time left that he was chosen.

Soon after Kennedy became chairman, he began to meet informally with members of the board to explain the need for changes and to ask for their agreement and cooperation. These discussions resulted in a consensus for a policy that required directors to retire at age seventy-two or two years after they retired from active management of their primary businesses, whichever date came first. Kennedy anticipated carrying out that policy in stages but hoped that one or two would voluntarily retire during 1959. Chauncey B. Borland, who had served as a member of the board since 1917, voluntarily resigned in September 1959. His graceful departure was the impetus for other elderly directors to resign, and by the end of 1961 eight of the older directors, including Walter Cummings, had retired.

As painful as that experience was for Kennedy (he said he would not repeat the experience for all the gold in Fort Knox) it permitted him to make his own appointments to the board. He was not interested in having lawyers, for Continental had its own law firm; neither was he interested in executives of consulting firms who might want to do studies of the bank or in investment bankers. He did not want to be tied to a single investment bank just because one of its executives was on the board of Continental. Ideally, he wanted directors who were active in the management of their own businesses and who as a group represented a broad spectrum of the business world. What he wanted from members of the board was their participation in matters where their action was required by law and their judgment on large policy issues.

Once Kennedy had put in place the process for retiring members of the board, he was ready to organize his top management team. Aishton retired as president on June 30, 1960, after having helped David make the transition from president to chairman. During that eighteen-month period they carefully considered Tilden Cummings and Donald Graham as candidates for appointment as vice-chairman of the board and as president. The two were a study in contrasts.

Tilden Cummings had been with the bank since 1932 and had become a senior vice-president in the commercial banking department. He readily seized the opportunity for a more aggressive loan policy that Kennedy's rise to power made possible, and he provided expertise in an area where Kennedy had no experience. He was considered by many to be the epitome of the hardheaded conservative banker, but that image was belied by his willingness to look beyond conventional criteria in making loans. He urged his loan officers to make a second or third effort to find "some legitimate way of helping the customer solve his financing problem." That's what he called "creative banking."

Donald Graham, trained as a lawyer, was brought into the bank in 1953 to organize the oil and utilities division. It was his superb management of that division as it grew in importance that attracted Kennedy's attention. In addition to his exceptional competence, Graham had a warm personality and a wide variety of outside interests, and, unlike most bankers, he was a Democrat with close ties to the party at the state and local levels. As an administrator he brought unusual vision and energy to his task. While he had little taste for administrative details, he always had time for people and found it difficult to turn down requests for appointments or pleas for help.

Kennedy made no secret of his intention to appoint Graham and Cummings as either vice-chairman or president, although he

Marlon Schade and David Kennedy catch swordfish in Mexico, January 1960

had not decided which. But he warned them that he was interested in whether they could work as a team; if they could not, neither would be appointed. In the end he was not disappointed; he appointed Graham as vice-chairman of the board and Cummings as president of the bank. A trio of top administrators was confusing to many of the bank's executives, who speculated among themselves about the exact pecking order. When the question was finally put to Kennedy, he said Graham was second in command, and he seemed surprised that the question had been raised. While a top management team of three people seemed odd to the bank's executives, it was a pattern natural to Kennedy. A council of three is the basis of administration in the Mormon church, and Kennedy's own administrative experience outside the bank was within that context.

Graham helped Kennedy in a variety of special assignments, with specific responsibility for energy, public and government relations, and personnel. Cummings continued his supervision of commercial lending and assumed responsibility for the trust department as well as for overall bank operations. Kennedy reserved the bond department and the international department for himself. This division of labor capitalized on the strengths of each member of the team, assured that each had the relevant information he needed, and made clear the lines of authority and responsibility. Kennedy also required that at least one of the three be in the bank during business hours and required separate air travel even when the other two were traveling to the same destination.

Large and complex organizations must constantly be concerned not only with top management but also with the way the organization is perceived by its employees. Kennedy moved rapidly to improve Continental's already good relations with employees by liberalizing medical and life insurances and other fringe benefits. His most striking innovation was the establishment of a profit-sharing plan in which the bank contributed 3 percent of its net operating earnings before taxes. Employees began to share in the plan after ten months of service at the bank, and their participation became fully vested gradually over a seven-year period. Earnings and contributions were credited to an individual account for each employee, and taxes on earnings on the bank's share as well as on voluntary contributions were deferred until the employee withdrew his share from the plan.

Kennedy's impact on the bank was also reflected by a complete renovation of the bank's headquarters. The task was assigned to Joseph Fitzer, chief of bank operations. "The psychological effect of this program on employees and customers alike was remarkable," Fitzer recalled. "It provided visible evidence that Continental Bank was moving again." Fitzer was struck by Kennedy's continuing interest and involvement in the project, commenting, "He showed a surprising sensitivity for aesthetic considerations, particularly where the main banking floor was concerned. This was—and still is—the largest, most impressive banking room in the world, and Mr. Kennedy was anxious that, in developing air conditioning, new lighting, new teller windows, and other improvements, we must not tamper with the architectural integrity of the room. He kept a close eye on the work to make certain we didn't."

The image that Continental was moving again was important. Continental was the largest bank in Chicago in the 1930s and 1940s, but it had lost that position to First National Bank of Chicago in the years following World War II. While Kennedy protested that he was not concerned that Continental was not the largest bank in Chicago—he just wanted it to be the best—he knew that size did count. Large corporations, which were Continental's principal customers, needed the services that only a bank with large assets could provide. Continental was close enough in size to First National—Continental had $2.4 billion in deposits, while First National had $2.6 billion—that it could compete equally for the business of the large corporations with which it traditionally dealt. If, however, First National should materially increase in size, Continental must inevitably be relegated to a secondary position in the Chicago market. Kennedy's determination to maintain Continental's position as one of the two leading banks in the city led to a merger of Continental with City National Bank, the most dramatic episode during his tenure at the bank.

The story began not in the offices of Continental but in the headquarters of City National Bank, whose offices were just across the street from Continental. The president of City National, Arthur Leonard, had reached retirement age, but the bank was not able to find a chief executive to replace him. Competent candidates were scared off by a conflict in the board of directors over the future of the bank. A group of New York investors, who owned 40 percent of the stock, thought that the bank had little or no future as a middle-sized bank in the Chicago market and wanted it to merge with another bank so they could liquidate their holdings at a favorable price. Against this background Leonard began in the spring of 1960 to discuss the future of City National with Chicago bankers, including Kennedy and Homer Livingston, chairman of First National. Kennedy offered to help Leonard find new management for the bank, but said that if Leonard finally decided that a merger were necessary, Continental would be interested. At a later meeting Kennedy again expressed interest in a merger with City National, but said the initiative for such action must come from Leonard. There the matter rested until early in December 1960, just after Kennedy returned from a trip to Europe. While he was away, rumors that City National would merge with First National began to circulate in Chicago banking circles. Graham heard the rumors and reported them to Kennedy. Kennedy decided that it was time for another chat with Leonard.

In a meeting with Leonard on December 6, Kennedy renewed his offer to help City National find a chief executive. When Leonard brushed aside these offers of help, Kennedy asked outright if City National was considering a merger with First National. Leonard hesitated but confessed that such was the case. Kennedy realized that the acquisition of City National would make First National clearly the largest bank in the Midwest. He was determined not to let that happen and quickly put Leonard on notice that if City National was contemplating a merger, Leonard was under obligation to his shareholders to consider an offer from Continental.

Thus began a week of feverish negotiations between Continental and City National. It began with Kennedy pressing Leonard to explain just how far the negotiations between First National and City National had gone. Leonard, without revealing its contents, admitted that Livingston had made a formal offer that he had not accepted. In fact, he had sent Livingston a memorandum saying that there would have to be some changes in the offer before it was acceptable. Livingston, reluctant to make any changes, asked Leonard to reconsider the original offer. Kennedy urged Leonard to send Livingston a written notice that First National's offer was unacceptable, lest Livingston should in the meantime decide to accept Leonard's suggested changes in the First National offer and thus create a binding contract between the two banks. Leonard was still concerned that even though there might be no legally binding contract, he had an ethical or moral obligation not to entertain an offer from Continental while he was still discussing the possibility of a merger with Livingston. Kennedy suggested that the two of them put the matter to Leonard Spacek, head of Arthur Anderson, a nationally known accounting firm with which both banks had done business. Leonard explained his concerns to Spacek, after which Kennedy said he wanted to make an offer to City National. Spacek's conclusion, which satisfied Leonard and delighted Kennedy, was that Leonard's true moral and ethical obligation was to present the Continental offer to City National's board of directors for their approval or rejection.

Kennedy now went to see Livingston to inform him that Continental intended to pursue a merger with City National. He went immediately to the heart of the matter: the impact that a merger of First National and City National would have on Continental. He explained that Continental "would not sit by and let the City National Bank go to the First National and thereby completely upset the balance between the two largest banks in Chicago." On the other hand, he argued, that the balance would not be upset by a merger of City National and Continental. Livingston was understandably upset that Continental should try to enter the picture at such a late date and tried to convince Kennedy that an agreement had already been reached. That argument was rejected by Kennedy, since he knew Leonard had sent a formal rejection of First National's offer to Livingston.

Kennedy then began to explore rapidly what terms Continental should offer to City National. As he recalled the events, he sequestered himself in a room at the Union League Club where over the next few days he and Leonard went over "the loans, the reserves of the bank, the earnings statements." They also discussed "in detail the staff, retirement program of the City, got a breakdown of the bank in various categories and list of the major customers." They enlisted the help of Lloyd Coveney of Arthur Anderson to prepare a presentation for the board of City National comparing the Continental offer with that of the First National. The substance of First National's offer would be known only to Coveney and Leonard until the comparison of the two offers was presented to the City National board. Kennedy had given his word to Livingston that Continental would make no effort to learn of the terms First National had offered to City National, either from Leonard or from Arthur Anderson. Continental would, he pledged to Livingston, "make a realistic appraisal of the bank and put a price on it which we thought was fair and reasonable."

The issue of what was a fair and reasonable price for City National was a question not only of what the bank was worth, but also of what price would assure that Continental's offer would be the best. Kennedy, of course, had no authority to commit Continental without authorization of the board, but until he was ready to make an offer, he did not inform the board of his negotiations. Finally, on December 9, he called a meeting of the board and asked in effect for a free hand to bring the negotiations to a close without revealing that they involved a merger with City National. He later explained to a director, who came to him privately to express concern over the "blank check" the board had given him, that the board would be given all the facts and could accept or reject the proposal. Before the meeting with the board, Kennedy discussed the issue with Lawrence Fisher, a director of General Motors and a former member of Continental's board. Fisher confirmed Kennedy's understanding that size was a factor in the decision of a large corporation like General Motors in choosing a bank, and he urged Kennedy to make a liberal offer to City National to assure that its bid would be better than that of First National. Following that discussion and before the board met, Kennedy discussed two possible offers with Graham and Cummings. The first was an exchange of one share of Continental stock for a share of City National stock.

The second would offer 1.10 shares of Continental stock for each share of City National stock. They both agreed that the higher price was acceptable; indeed they were willing to pay even more to assure that Continental could buy City National. Kennedy wavered between the two offers, believing that the one-for-one offer would carry the day, but fearing it might not be enough. Finally, he decided to split the difference at 1.05 shares of Continental stock for each share of City National stock.

The negotiations between the two banks were a tense drama. Kennedy moved so rapidly and restricted so closely the circle of those with whom he shared his plans that Livingston was unaware Continental was making an immediate offer for City National. He had not, therefore, changed his original offer, nor did he know that on December 13, just six days after Kennedy's visit to his office, the boards of directors of City National and Continental were meeting simultaneously in their separate boardrooms across the street from one another. The scenario Kennedy had carefully planned unfolded. Coveney was at City National with a chart that had blank spaces for both the First National and Continental offers. As the board meeting at City National began, Coveney filled in the figures of the First National offer from the information given him by Leonard. Meantime Leonard was in his office waiting for Continental's offer. The phone rang. It was Kennedy, offering $125 a share for City National's stock. He also said a formal written offer would be in Leonard's office within five minutes. Leonard said the offer was higher than he expected, but it was a fair price, and unless First National made another offer, Kennedy had just bought a bank. Kennedy had achieved his goal. Leonard went to the City National boardroom and gave the figures to Coveney, who filled in the missing blanks in his chart. Those figures made it clear that Continental's offer enhanced the value of City National's stock, so it was a pleased and surprised board of directors that accepted the offer, subject to ratification by Continental's board of directors. Leonard notified Kennedy of that decision and gave him the details of the two offers, and Kennedy presented them to his board, which voted unanimously and enthusiastically to approve the merger. As Kennedy remembered the sequence of events:

"I immediately at the end of the Board meeting released the announcement to the press. I then walked across the street to the City National and met with Arthur. I walked through the entire bank with him and shook hands with officials and employees and welcomed them to the Continental Bank family. Newspaper and TV people were asking questions and there was a reporter with a photographer taking some pictures. Then we were walking across LaSalle Street for Arthur to come over and shake hands with our people when the photographer stopped us in the middle of LaSalle and, with traffic stopped, we had a historic photograph taken with City National on one side of the street and Continental on the other, with the two chief executives shaking hands in the middle."

David Kennedy shakes hands with Arthur Leonard on LaSalle Street after purchase of City National Bank by Continental Illinois, December 13, 1960

149

The $125 a share Continental paid for City National's stock was $14 a share more than First National offered. Livingston admitted that First National was finessed by Continental, but he told the press that until the last minute he had not known that First National was in a bidding war. A reporter for the *Chicago Tribune* colorfully summed up Continental's successful merger with City National: "First National, currently the city's largest bank but about to be outranked in size . . . by the merged Continental-City, had been courting City National for months, unaware that a more ardent swain bearing a bigger bouquet was waitin' at the gate."

As a result of the merger, two members of City National's board were added to the Continental board and Leonard was made chairman of the executive committee. Kennedy, Graham, and Cummings remained the top management team of the merged bank, and it was expected that there would be no difficulty in combining the two staffs, since City National had only eight hundred employees and Continental had a personnel turnover of one hundred people a month. City National employees would have the advantage of Continental's more liberal pension, health, and group insurance plans, as well as participation in the recently adopted profit-sharing plan. City National customers also benefited from the merger because of the full range of banking services now available to them, and the merged bank's larger resources meant higher loan limits than City National previously offered.

The euphoria over outbidding First National was tempered by the requirement that federal approval for the merger would have to be obtained from the Comptroller of the Currency. Before granting approval the comptroller had to obtain the advice of the Federal Reserve Board, the Federal Deposit Insurance Corporation, and the Justice Department as to the impact of the merger on competition in banking in the Chicago area. Those agencies had thirty days in which to provide that advice, and when Continental submitted its application for approval on January 23, 1961, it expected the comptroller's approval soon after that thirty-day period expired. Those expectations proved wildly optimistic, for almost five years passed before the merger became a legal reality. The first sign that

Continental was in for a protracted struggle was a phone conversation Graham had early in March with Ray Gidney, Comptroller of the Currency, notifying the bank that both the Department of Justice and the Federal Reserve Board opposed the merger because it would reduce competition among commercial banks in Chicago. The bank's attorneys immediately wrote to the Justice Department, which had the most serious objections to the merger, asking that the department withdraw its objections and approve the merger. That petition was rejected, and in the ensuing months Continental was to learn that its hope for early approval was unrealistic.

Continental and City National entered merger negotiations on the assumption that the Bank Merger Act of 1960 vested in the Comptroller of the Currency the power to approve bank mergers similar to that of Continental and City National. Unbeknownst to Kennedy and Leonard, Robert F. Kennedy (then Attorney General), Douglas Dillon (Secretary of the Treasury), and Gidney had agreed that mergers to which the Justice Department objected would not be approved until after the Supreme Court ruled on bank mergers in Philadelphia and Lexington, Kentucky. The gravamen of the Justice Department's argument was that the Bank Merger Act of 1960 did not preclude the Justice Department from attacking bank mergers under previously existing antitrust legislation, namely the Sherman and Clayton Acts.[1]

Continental officers did not learn of this agreement, which David Kennedy promptly dubbed an "unholy alliance," until April 6, when Arkansas Senator J. William Fulbright, one of the sponsors of the 1960 legislation, released a letter to the press that he had written to Robert Kennedy and Dillon insisting that the statute "did not give the Justice Department veto power." Both Dillon and Robert Kennedy refused to back away from their previous agreement and thus left the Continental-City National merger in limbo.

Dillon and Gidney finally became convinced that the merger should be approved because further delay would create a hardship for City National and might result in irreparable damage to the bank. The chief of the antitrust division in the Department of Justice, Lee Leovinger, disagreed. Any hardship to City National was, in his opinion, because the merger was announced before approval

151

was received. Continental bombarded the Treasury with information on the declining position of City National, hoping that the Treasury would approve the merger. As hope faded for approval without some compromise, David Kennedy authorized the bank's attorneys to propose to the Justice Department that permission to consummate the merger be granted without prejudicing Justice's right to bring a suit for divestiture. After hard and sometimes bitter bargaining, the Justice Department agreed to permit the merger on that condition.

It was, Kennedy remembered, the only time he asked to be sued, but the alternative was to postpone the merger of the two banks until the Supreme Court decided the two pending cases or until Justice should relent, which it gave no signs of doing. Furthermore, Continental officials believed they had oral assurances that Justice was prepared to let the merger take place without further objection, since its right to sue for divestiture was protected. At the same time, Kennedy believed Dillon had convinced Robert Kennedy that the Continental merger should be considered an exception to the Dillon-Kennedy-Gidney agreement and that no suit would be filed. That assumption was reinforced by the letter Continental received from the Comptroller of the Currency on August 21, 1961, approving the merger. With that letter in hand, Continental and City National began to make plans to carry out the physical merger over the approaching Labor Day weekend. Because of the ban on branch banking in Illinois, City National had to be moved lock, stock, and barrel into Continental's building.

Even as preparations for the move were under way, Kennedy was told by a reporter that attorneys from the Justice Department were on their way to Chicago to seek a temporary restraining order to force delay of the merger. This prior notice gave Kennedy and the bank's attorneys a chance to explain to Federal District Judge Julius H. Miner that a temporary restraining order would kill the merger. The government assumed that because the judge was empowered to issue the temporary restraining order without holding a hearing, the injunction would be issued simply on the basis of the government's brief. Alerted to the consequences of that action by Continental's attorneys, Miner refused to issue the order without a hearing and ordered both parties to be in court the next morning.

In the heat of the battle, Kennedy and Leonard issued a press release alleging that the request for a temporary restraining order represented an act of bad faith by the attorney general. That allegation was headlined in the papers, and at the hearing Miner sharply criticized Kennedy for making the statement. So strong was Miner's reaction to the press release that Kennedy feared the case was lost. His fears were quieted by Graham, who told Kennedy that now that the judge had scolded them, he would rule in their favor. Despite the government's contention that the question should be "decided before there is a complicated, hopeless intermingling of assets that would make relief most difficult," the judge held in Continental's favor, citing three reasons: first, "This Court of equity cannot sanction irreparable injury upon any litigant, or prevent the proposed merger by a restraining order without a full hearing on the issues involved"; second, the comptroller had acted within his statutory authority in approving the merger; and third, the two banks properly relied on the agreed stipulation "in proceeding with the consummation of the merger."

With Miner's ruling in hand, the physical merger of the two banks was rapidly undertaken. Over the weekend of September 2–5, day and night, according to a Continental spokesman, the move of "600 desks, 1,000 chairs, 1,500 filing cabinets, 80 safes, $11.5 million in cash and more than $1 billion in securities" from the vacated quarters of City National to the Continental building went on. The process was guarded "by a small army of guards . . . 25 policemen from the Chicago Police Department, a total of 125 guards from both banks and more than 30 guards from Brink's, Inc." From the time the letter approving the merger was received from the comptroller until the move was completed, "staff members working on the merger were served 9,618 meals in the Continental cafeteria, consuming 1,260 pounds of pork, 560 pounds of beef, 600 pounds of chicken, and 410 gallons of coffee." The moving of the physical assets of City National was less complicated than the transfer of the accounting and bookkeeping chores connected with it. Yet, when the newly merged bank opened for business September 5, all the City National accounts were integrated into the Continental bookkeeping system and City National officers were in place to greet their customers.

Though the physical merger was complete, the government almost immediately filed a suit for divestiture. This began a long series of legal battles all pointing toward a trial when a court would decide if the merger was in fact forbidden by law. There was no great sense of urgency on either side, since the Supreme Court had not yet handed down its decision in the Lexington and Philadelphia merger cases. Then on June 17, 1963, in announcing its decision in the Philadelphia case, the court undermined Continental's hopes for an early resolution of the legality of its own case by holding that the Bank Merger Act of 1960 did not preclude the government from attacking bank mergers under the Clayton and Sherman Acts. The court also ruled that the merger violated Section 7 of the Clayton Act and Section 1 of the Sherman Act. The following April the Supreme Court struck down the proposed merger in Lexington, and later a federal district court in New York, relying on those decisions, rejected a proposed merger involving Manufacturers Hanover Trust Company.

David Kennedy was discouraged by these decisions, but he thought there was a good case that the Continental-City National merger should be treated differently. However, faced with the probability of a trial in which the trend of the law was against them, Continental's attorneys suggested that the bank consider two alternatives: a negotiated compromise that would limit the bank's right to merge with any other bank without the approval of the Justice Department but would avoid divestiture in the present case, or remedial legislation that would protect the existing merger.

In early April 1965, Kennedy met with Robert E. "Jeff" McNeill, Jr., chairman of Manufacturers Hanover, and officials from the Justice Department concerning the merger. Following those discussions, Kennedy and McNeill decided that some kind of remedial legislation exempting their banks from action by the Justice Department offered the best chance of relief. The task of getting such legislation promised to be difficult, but they could expect some support from the banking industry, from the Treasury Department, and particularly from some members of Congress who were angry at the Supreme Court's decision that, in effect, gave Justice a veto over bank mergers. Foremost among those concerned with Justice's enlarged role in bank mergers was Senator A. Willis Robertson of Virginia, chairman of the Banking and Currency Committee of the Senate. He agreed to introduce remedial legislation in the Senate and suggested that it would be easier to get the bill through the Senate if it had the support of Senator Paul H. Douglas of Illinois.

Because his relationship with Douglas was not the best, Kennedy asked Illinois Congressman Sidney R. Yates to intercede with Douglas on behalf of the bank, but Yates said this was something Kennedy would have to do for himself. Kennedy's discussion with Douglas never got to the substance of the bill, for Douglas only wanted to know why Kennedy was so opposed to the newly appointed Comptroller of the Currency, James Saxon. This sally astonished Kennedy since he strongly supported the appointment of Saxon. Once Douglas was satisfied that Continental was not opposed to Saxon, he expressed his willingness to back the bill. Kennedy was delighted for his support, even if for irrelevant reasons.

The Robertson bill reasserted the power of the Comptroller of the Currency over bank mergers, but it permitted the Justice Department to file suit under the Clayton or Sherman Acts within thirty days of approval of the merger, which would delay the merger until the suit was settled. The measure also exempted from the Sherman and Clayton Acts six bank mergers, including Continental's, that had relied on the Bank Merger Act of 1960 for authority to consummate their mergers. Senate action was just the beginning of the struggle, for the House of Representatives still had to act, and the chairman of the House Committee on Banking and Currency was Texas Representative Wright Patman, whose antipathy to large banks was well-known and of long standing. The Speaker of the House, Massachusetts Congressman John W. McCormack, told Kennedy there was little chance of getting the bill passed because committee chairmen could block legislation they did not like and Patman was a master at using parliamentary procedure to kill a bill in committee. Kennedy asked if it was impossible, and remembered that the speaker said that it was not impossible, "but I don't think it has ever been done and particularly where you have a committee chairman like Wright Patman."

McCormack's predictions came to pass. Patman, who was opposed to the bill, simply ignored its existence and proceeded with the committee's other business. But he was immediately challenged by twenty-six members of the thirty-three-member committee, who sent him a letter demanding that he hold prompt public hearings on the Robertson bill. The leader of the group was Representative Thomas L. Ashley, a Democrat from Ohio with, a *Wall Street Journal* reported, a liberal voting record, "but on the bank merger issue he was outraged by the chairman's foxy delaying maneuvers; their split finally became a bitter personal struggle for control of the committee itself."

The dispute was finally resolved after what the *Journal* called "The Bank Merger Bill's Zany Journey," which included a rump session of the committee in Patman's absence that sent the bill to the floor of the House. That rump session also proved that Ashley had the votes to replace Patman as chairman. McCormack was now dismayed by both sides: he was angry with Patman for his unreasonable delaying tactics and at Ashley for threatening to upset the time-honored congressional committee system. Kennedy, who had left the day-to-day management of the lobbying effort to Graham and John Perkins, was now brought directly into the negotiations by McCormack. The speaker asked Kennedy, now that the bill was before the House and likely to pass, if it was not time to call a truce between Patman and Ashley. At a meeting in McCormack's office, Kennedy, Ashley, Patman, and McCormack worked out a face-saving compromise. The action of the rump session of the committee would be "illegal," but the committee would adopt the Ashley bill unchanged and Patman would introduce it in the House. Patman, who was "clearly more interested in reasserting control over his committee than in murky legalisms," agreed to the compromise and the battle ended.

Kennedy's aggressive pursuit of the merger with City National, his willingness to outbid his rival, and his perseverance in seeing the battle through the courts and Congress were important factors in establishing his reputation as one of the most competent, resourceful, and farsighted senior bankers in the United States. It provided him with the same credibility outside the bank that the change in Continental's operations gave him inside the bank. The merger negotiations made explicit those character traits that had been maturing since his early youth. They reflected, as did perhaps no other incident in Kennedy's career, his willingness to plunge ahead on the basis of his own judgment and to take responsibility for his actions. There was also his ambition to make a difference wherever he could, undaunted by the formidable difficulty such tasks might present. Those negotiations showed his commitment to integrity, honesty, and morality, for it was only after he became convinced in his own mind that City National owed no moral or legal commitment to First National that he pressed his own case for a merger with Continental. The juxtaposition of Kennedy's personal integrity and his realistic approach to the task at hand was a legacy he had inherited from the past. There is far more of Randolph, Riverdale, and the British Mission in the merger negotiations than is revealed by the written record.

10

CONTINENTAL ILLINOIS: EXPANDING ABROAD

The Kennedy era at Continental coincided with a growing expansion of American business abroad. World trade disrupted by World War II had been reestablished, American manufacturers were increasing their sales abroad, and American investment in overseas companies was becoming increasingly attractive. The era of the multinational corporation was well under way, creating expanding possibilities for American banks to profit from their international operations. The increased involvement of the United States in world trade and international finance was changing the climate of the business world in Chicago and the Midwest. Completion of the St. Lawrence Seaway opened Chicago to the ports of the North Atlantic, and by 1963, 40 percent of American exports were generated in the heartland of the nation.

David Kennedy understood the implications of the United States's rising involvement in foreign trade, and from the beginning of his tenure as chairman he argued that Continental must rapidly expand its international operations if it were to stay at the cutting edge of American banking. He met some opposition in the bank from those who believed the possibilities for growth in the domestic market were so substantial—and, of course, the domestic market remained the source of Continental's strength—that only limited funds should be devoted to the expansion of the bank's international activities. He recognized the force of these arguments and also believed that expansion of Continental's international business was an integral part of the service the bank must offer to both new and old customers. As Midwest businesses expanded their sales beyond their traditional domestic markets, he believed, they would want to deal with a bank that could furnish them with a full range of services. If Continental could service only their domestic business, they would gravitate to a bank that could meet all their needs. He also believed that such expansion, rather than reducing the bank's ability to compete in the domestic market, would be a source of funds to expand the bank's lending capability to American firms.

Kennedy had other reasons for establishing Continental as a worldwide bank that were more humanitarian, psychological, and emotional than practical. He saw Continental in a larger context than its immediate midwest markets, and banking as more than the accumulation of profits. Consequently, he saw Continental's expansion abroad as contributing to the interdependence of nations, and that interdependence in the long run would benefit all nations, rich and poor. Seen in that light, a long-time associate wrote: "Kennedy's mission was more important than the simple ambition of a capitalist to expand the business empire he managed. Anyone who knew him and his motivations would surely agree that he viewed the issue to a rather major degree in humanitarian terms— the imperative of world peace, the frightful problems of Third World countries, and the need to defuse the culture shock resulting from faster transportation and communications that made next-door neighbors of people living in different hemispheres."

There was, in addition, his abiding desire to build rather than just manage, and international banking was an area in which he could make a singular and significant contribution. He was, after all, not the traditional commercial banker; he understood commercial lending, but he was not the expert in that field that Tilden Cummings was. And while he admired Donald Graham's success in building Continental's stake in the energy industries, he was not familiar with the details of the operation. His expertise was in the securities market, but the bond department was no longer the center of the bank's activities. What Kennedy could provide was the vision of how all the bank's functions fit into an overall operational strategy, coupled with the skill and contacts to integrate Continental's international business into that strategy.

As early as his service on the staff of the Federal Reserve Board, Kennedy had established contacts with bankers and other businessmen from throughout the world. His appointment as an assistant secretary of the Treasury broadened that circle of acquaintances. He intended to use those contacts in expanding Continental's international activities, but first he had to create a base of operations at home. He decided at the outset that the international division would report directly to him, and appointed Roger Anderson, who came into the bank as a trainee in 1945 after service in the navy during World War II, to head a revitalized international division. He was also fortunate to have the services of Alfred Miossi,

David M. Kennedy

who joined the bank in 1953 after being with the Bank of America in Japan.

For Anderson, working with Kennedy was an education in geography, politics, and economics. On their first trip abroad together in 1959, Anderson learned that his task was to make recommendations of what commitments might or could be made in the countries they visited. His recommendations, Kennedy told Anderson, should be based on the political and economic situation of each country and take into consideration Continental's current business activity in that country. That was not the end of Anderson's education, for he met Kennedy for breakfast, outlined the agenda for the day, and briefed him on all the people they would meet—all this without assuming that Kennedy was familiar with the country or the people they were to see. At the end of the day, Anderson sent cables to Chicago summarizing what had been accomplished during the day. He was also startled to learn on that trip of the extent of Kennedy's plans for Continental's expansion, for Kennedy told him that within the next few years Continental should have five branches abroad—a bold vision at a time when the bank had none.

Kennedy and Anderson explored three ways to begin operations abroad. The easiest was to establish offices that would represent Continental in its dealings with major banks and businesses in the host country but would not receive deposits or make loans. A second way was to acquire a minority interest in an already existing bank, with Continental officers being put on the board of directors. Affiliated banks would give Continental greater influence in the countries where such relations were established, but the success of the bank still rested on the skill and effectiveness of local management. The third—and preferred—way was to create a branch of Continental that could take deposits and make loans on the same basis as banks of the host country.

Just as there was a preferred way for the bank to operate abroad, there was, Kennedy believed, a preferred country in which to begin: England. Europe was the principal market for the products offered by Continental's customers, London was at the center of the world financial network, English regulatory legislation was more easily understood by Continental representatives, and there was the advantage of a common language.

Kennedy's first choice of a site was in the area known as the City, where London's major financial institutions were located, for he wanted Continental's branch to be in the mainstream of London banking. He and Anderson finally found a five-story building at 58-60 Moregate, just a few minutes' walk from the Bank of England. After extensive remodeling, Continental's London branch was opened March 1, 1962. To celebrate the occasion, the bank invited the Chicago press to an English lunch at its Chicago headquarters. The lunch was a prelude to a transatlantic press conference with Kennedy, who placed the call from the new branch. His pride in the London branch was evident as he stressed the importance of this event not only for Continental but also for Chicago and the Midwest. It was not only Continental's first overseas branch, he told the press, but Continental was the only American bank other than those on the east and west coasts with a branch in London.

The most perplexing problem David Kennedy faced in pushing into the international arena was finding competent people to manage Continental's affairs abroad. Continental could not rely on its small international staff in Chicago; experienced personnel like Alfred Miossi were needed at the home office. Furthermore, Kennedy realized that he could not send an inexperienced young banker to represent Continental in one of the most sophisticated financial centers of the world. For leadership, then, he turned to a retired vice-president of the bank, Carl Johnson, to manage the London branch. Since Johnson had not lived abroad and knew nothing of British banking practices, Kennedy and Anderson hired a British banker, Norman Laughland, who had retired to London after a banking career in India, to guide Johnson through the shoals of English banking.

Kennedy's search for capable people to staff Continental's expansion abroad continued throughout his tenure. Gradually, as the international division in Continental's Chicago headquarters increased in size, experienced personnel were recruited from that pool, but the problem was never really solved because the need continually exceeded the resources.

The choice of London for Continental's first branch abroad rested primarily on economic grounds, but the existence of a common language was an added incentive. A common language helped communication—as long as the words meant the same thing on both sides of the ocean. Miossi recalled a confrontation between the American and English members of the staff over the assignment of offices. It was resolved only after it was discovered that the term "first floor" meant the ground floor to Americans, but to the English members of the staff it meant the first floor *above* the ground floor. That minor strife foreshadowed the more serious conflicts Kennedy and Anderson had to resolve as Continental moved into countries where the culture was sharply different from that which they knew as Americans. In no other country was that truth brought home to them more forcefully than in Japan, which became the next goal in Continental's move onto the international scene.

The prospect of a move to Japan came unexpectedly after Anderson learned that a Dutch bank, Nationale Handelsbank, whose assets were taken over by the Rotterdam Bank, and had five branches in the Far East—Singapore, Hong Kong, Bangkok, Osaka, and Tokyo—that the parent bank now wanted to sell. Anderson reported this conversation to Kennedy, who sent him off to Rotterdam to discuss the possibility of Continental buying those branches. Anderson first considered buying all five branches, but after the difficulty he had experienced in finding competent personnel to man the London branch, he was chary about taking on five branches in countries where Continental had no experience. He decided, therefore, to buy only the branches in Osaka and Tokyo.

Kennedy found that it was easier to buy the branches from the Dutch bank than it was to obtain approval from the Japanese government to operate them as branches of Continental. He expected Japanese officials to let Continental change the name of the branches and continue to do business as before, but the officials in the Ministry of Finance, which regulated the admission of foreign banks into Japan, saw things differently. They insisted that there was no connection between the Handelsbank and Continental; the fact that the parent banks were in different countries precluded such a simple transfer of ownership. What Kennedy envisaged as a routine change of ownership turned into a long series of negotiations lasting well over a year.

When Kennedy entered the negotiations in June 1963, he turned for advice to Shigeo Horie of the Bank of Tokyo and to Makoto Usami, president of the Mitsubishi Bank, both of whom did considerable business with Continental. Continental did business with several Japanese banks, and Kennedy feared that if it were known that Continental intended to open branches in Japan, those banks would oppose approval. He was confident, however, that Horie and Usami would understand the argument that Continental's branches in Japan would increase rather than curtail the business that Japanese banks placed through Continental. Those discussions with Horie and Usami guided Kennedy in mapping out his strategy as he began his negotiations with the Ministry of Finance.

The problem confronting Kennedy was how to enter into discussions with ministry officials without making a formal proposal that, if turned down, would lock the ministry into a rejection from which there would be no appeal. The Kennedy strategy turned on the lessons he learned from his Japanese mentors, what he later termed a "kabuki" strategy. Therefore, Anderson was sent to tell officials at the Ministry of Finance that Kennedy was in Tokyo, and that before he made a formal call on the minister, he would like to meet with them informally to explain what Continental hoped to achieve in Japan. In the meeting that took place a few days later, Kennedy repeatedly stressed that their discussions were informal and that he would talk with them officially and formally only after he had an interview with the minister, Kakuei Tanaka. In those informal talks, Kennedy was told that it would be impossible to approve the transfer of the Handelsbank branches to Continental, but since the discussions were informal, each side understood that that advice did not constitute a refusal. Furthermore, the talks let Tanaka's aides know in advance what Kennedy would discuss with the minister, thus saving them from being surprised when the minister raised the issue after Kennedy's formal visit.

Now that the first step in the "kabuki" strategy had been taken, Kennedy was ready for the second: the formal meeting with Tanaka. At that meeting Tanaka called in his aides as Kennedy had anticipated. After a general discussion of Continental's plans, Kennedy suggested that he and Anderson should continue to discuss details of the proposal with Tanaka's aides. To this Tanaka readily agreed. Thus, Kennedy recalled, "I took it off the Minister's back, put it there and then took it off, without asking permission. I didn't embarrass him. He had no face to lose. He put it back where it belonged."

The first fruits of the "kabuki" strategy came in October 1963 when Kennedy and Tanaka both attended the meetings of the International Monetary Fund (IMF) in Washington, D.C. But those fruits matured only after tough negotiations in which Tanaka said it was difficult to give branches in Japan to Continental when the Bank of Tokyo could not have a branch in Chicago. Kennedy asked Phillip Cordes, a Continental officer, to see if there was a way the Bank of Tokyo could enter the Chicago market. Cordes reported back that, while a state-chartered bank could not be a branch of the Bank of Tokyo, it could be managed by the Bank of Tokyo. The result was the creation of the Chicago Bank of Tokyo with capital raised by Japanese trading companies. The only aid Continental provided in that venture was Cordes's time, but Kennedy has remained convinced that the creation of the Chicago Bank of Tokyo was a major factor in obtaining approval for Continental's branches in Japan.[1]

At the IMF meetings in Washington in October, Tanaka, in obviously good humor, was a bearer of good news. He told Kennedy that he was making an exception for Continental: approval for the transfer of the Nationale Handelsbank's branches to Continental was forthcoming but would be limited to only one branch, Tokyo. Kennedy then put to use the lesson on "face" he had learned from Horie. He wrote Tanaka that Continental must have both branches or none. He recalled telling Anderson, "He has to make a decision now whether he will go this extra mile. . . . And I think he's now in a position that he can't turn me down, because I'll lose face, and I don't think he'll want to put me in a position of losing face."

Kennedy profited from Horie's instruction; in a few weeks, approval came for both branches, which began taking deposits and making loans in 1964. Continental was in business in Japan at a cost of over a million dollars, including the purchase price as well the administrative cost of opening the branch offices.

While Kennedy and Anderson were carrying on the tortuous negotiations with the Japanese, the pace of Continental's overseas expansion was quickening. The bank began its involvement with affiliated banks with the purchase of a minority interest in banks in Argentina and Colombia in 1963. Simultaneous with the opening of the branches in Tokyo and Osaka in 1964, a second London branch was opened in Berkeley Square. That year also found the bank creating a representative office in Switzerland and purchasing minority interest in an affiliated bank in Holland. Additional investments in affiliated banks in Belgium, Italy (including Sicily), and Spain were made the following year. Representative offices were opened in Belgium, Italy, and Mexico in 1966, followed in 1967 by offices in Spain and the Philippines. Further investment in affiliated banks was made in 1967 when Continental acquired a minority interest in banks in Ecuador, Morocco, Switzerland, and the Bahamas. During 1968, Kennedy's final year at the bank, branches were opened in France and Germany, a representative office was opened in Venezuela, and an investment was made in an affiliated bank in Lebanon. In addition, plans were made for additional representative offices in Argentina and Brazil, as well as a branch in Holland, all of which were opened in 1969.

When Kennedy became chairman in 1959, Continental was not operating outside the United States and there were only six officers in the international division at bank headquarters. When he left at the end of 1968, there was a network of branches, affiliated banks, and representative offices traversing the world, with nineteen officers assigned to supervise an expanding corps of personnel in the overseas offices. The Kennedy era saw the establishment of Continental's wholly owned subsidiaries, Continental International Finance Corporation in Chicago and Continental International Banking Corporation in New York. The impact of Continental's rapid expansion into the international arena not only resulted in additional business for the bank but also stimulated other Chicago banks to expand their own operations.

Traveling abroad as the chairman of one of the largest American banks meant not ony meetings where discussions turned on millions of dollars but also a whirl of world-class hotels, limousines, lunches, receptions, and formal dinners. As chairman of Continental, Kennedy came to know people of power and influence: Georges Pompidou and Valery Giscard d'Estaing in France; Lord Cobbold, Governor of the Bank of England; Antonio Ortiz Mena, Minister of Finance in Mexico; Hermann Abs, the most influential banker in West Germany; and leading bankers and ministers of finance in each country where Continental had substantial interests. In Korea and the Philippines, where Continental made large loans to advance industrialization, Kennedy became a particularly welcome visitor who was courted with zeal.

Even in those countries where Continental was not directly involved, his name was known. That was brought home to him in May 1967 when he was in Casablanca to complete negotiations to purchase a part interest in a Moroccan bank. While he was there he was invited by Field Marshal Abdel Hakim Amer, a close friend of President Gamal Abdel Nasser, to visit Egypt with a select group of American businessmen, who were guests of the Egyptian government.

During the visit, Kennedy's hopes to see an Arabian horse show were interrupted by a request that he come to Nasser's office. Nasser wanted to talk about Egypt's relations with the United States, which had been disrupted by the Suez crisis of 1956 and the subsequent withdrawal of American financial support for the construction of the Aswan Dam. He also wanted to know why Continental was not making loans to Egypt as it was doing to Japan. To Kennedy's response that Japan could be depended on to repay the loan, Nasser with good humor, pointed out, as Kennedy recalled, "Well, you know, there are two ways to pay a loan. One is with money and the other is with another note, just renewing the note."

During the three-hour meeting, the discussion turned to Israel. Israel will need more land to accommodate its increasing population, Nasser predicted, and it will try to expand at Egypt's

Lenora Bingham Kennedy

expense. The problem created by Israel's presence in the Middle East, Nasser told Kennedy, had its origins in the ancient past, in biblical times, not with the coming to power of Nasser, and "trouble with Israel will last after Nasser is dead and gone." Kennedy considered this meeting important enough to report to Secretary of State Dean Rusk. Kennedy told Rusk that in his opinion, war in the region was not imminent. When war between Egypt and Israel broke out just one month later, Kennedy learned that foreseeing the course of international events involves even more imponderables and a greater risk than forecasting the stock market.

The 1967 trip to Morocco with the Egyptian interlude was memorable not only because of the long talk with Nasser but also because the Feast of the Sacrifice took place while David and Lenora were in Rabat. This feast takes place each year sixty days after the end of Ramadan, the Moslem holy month of prayer and fasting. The ceremony began with King Hassan II of Morocco killing a ram as a symbol of the ram that the Lord provided to Abraham in place of his son Isaac. Following the ceremony, David and Lenora were taken to the palace, where they were unexpectedly separated. Lenora was taken into another part of the palace, while David was ushered into the presence of the king and his cabinet. There, in an impressive ceremony, the king and each of his cabinet members drank goat's milk dipped from a wooden cask by a copper dipper from which each took a sip, then ate dates coated with sugar. The goat's milk and the dates were not idly chosen, for the prophet Mohammed always broke his fast with a simple repast of goat's milk and dates. Kennedy, honored by an invitation to participate in the ceremony, was impressed with the similarity of that ceremony with his own church's monthly fast, which is broken by partaking of bread and water in remembrance of the Last Supper.

That evening the Kennedys were guests at a lavish dinner hosted by the chief of the cabinet. For the Kennedys, the experience of eating roasted lamb with only their hands for eating utensils was a novel experience. But even more novel was to find that the second course was lamb eaten with unleavened bread, followed by a third course of lamb cooked in a melange of fruit. The three courses of lamb were followed by chicken, and the chicken by couscous sweetened with fruit, which the diners rolled into a ball with their fingers. Lenora came away from the dinner not only with a surfeit of lamb but with the gift of a beautiful kaftan.

One of David Kennedy's strong points was his willingness to innovate; but the cost of innovation is the risk of failure. Two of the investments he engineered for Continental in the Middle East started with promises that eventually proved to be hollow. The first, an investment in a bank in Lebanon, was made only after difficult negotiations with Lebanese regulatory agencies. The negotiations were not the end of difficulties, however, Continental soon found that banking practices in Lebanon were unique and that loans were made without adequate study or collateral. Eventually Continental brought in its own people to save the bank from failure. Both the investment in Lebanon and one in Iran had to be written off after Kennedy left the bank because of the political chaos in Lebanon and the revolution that engulfed Iran.

These failures reduced the profits of the bank, but Continental's investment in the Banco Privata Finanziaria in Milan, Italy, although returning a profit for Continental, ultimately imposed a heavy personal cost on Kennedy. Continental preferred to open a branch in Italy, but the Italian government refused the bank's application. Kennedy then turned to the possibility of buying an interest in an existing bank. A search of such possibilities turned up the Banco Privata Finanziaria and its owner, Michele Sindona. Both of them came highly recommended to Continental from the head of the Italian Central Bank and from the representative of the Vatican on the board of Banco Privata Finanziaria. Convinced by those recommendations, Continental bought 20 percent of the bank in 1965 and placed a representative, Peter Shaddick, on the board of directors of the Italian bank. Shaddick was later replaced by Miossi. Business relations between Continental and Finanziaria were no different from those with Continental and its affiliates in other countries, and the relationship proved to be profitable. When Continental finally received approval—partly with Sindona's help—to open a branch office in Italy, it offered its stock in Finanziaria to Sindona at a profit. The sale was made with the provision that Continental would retain a small participation in the bank so that it would not appear that Continental was selling out because of dissatisfaction with Finanziaria.

In retrospect, there was far more to Sindona than appeared on the surface. He seemed to be the Italian version of Horatio Alger— the poor boy who made good. He had left his native Sicily for Milan and had become a lawyer specializing in tax law.[2] He expanded his business operations into manufacturing and banking, and at the age of thirty-two, his name was already known in other financial centers in Europe. Through his friendship with Pope Paul IV, he became the Vatican's principal financial advisor. He entered the American market by purchasing substantial interests in American Oxford Electric and Libby, McNeill & Libby, the American canning giant. There was, however, a darker side to Sindona that he kept carefully concealed from his friends in the Vatican and from his influential business associates in the United States and other countries. When his Italian empire came tumbling down, it was clear that he had used the Vatican's unwitting support to finance many private deals that were dangerously unsound from the beginning.

One of Sindona's business associates from whom he was careful to conceal the dark side of his business empire was David Kennedy. Sindona was aware that Kennedy's name and friendship could be useful to him in opening doors both in Europe and the United States, and he did not want to surrender that advantage by sharing with Kennedy the full extent and nature of his Italian business dealings. Rather, he did everything possible to ingratiate himself with Kennedy. He was a man of considerable charm, and, knowing Kennedy's affection for his own family, he was careful that Kennedy saw him as a devoted husband and father.

In January 1973 Sindona told Kennedy, who was then serving as ambassador to the North Atlantic Treaty Organization (NATO), that he was increasing his involvement in the American financial market. To do so he had organized Fasco International Holding, S.A., a company incorporated in Luxembourg and wholly owned by him. Then in July 1972, acting through Fasco, Sindona had purchased 21.6 percent of the common stock of Franklin New York Corporation, the holding company that owned Franklin National Bank, Long Island, New York. When Sindona visited with Kennedy in 1973, he asked Kennedy to become a director of Fasco International with power to vote Sindona's shares in case anything happened to Sindona. Kennedy pointed out that he was still in the government and could not join any company as long as he held that position. Moreover, Kennedy thought the purchase unwise because the bank was overextended in real estate investments and also had a substantial position in long-term municipal and school-district bonds at low interest rates.

When Kennedy resigned as ambassador, Sindona renewed the invitation and Kennedy accepted. In addition, Kennedy and Sindona explored the possibility of several joint ventures. They held tentative negotiations with Hill Samuel, a British banking firm, but those negotiations proved fruitless. Sindona, through Fasco International, loaned Kennedy $200,000 to finance an investment opportunity in Arizona, a loan that Kennedy repaid. Although their search for a joint venture was unsuccessful, Sindona tried to entangle Kennedy in the affairs of Franklin National Bank. He asked Kennedy to become chairman of the bank, but Kennedy was not interested in a second career in banking. He did, however, serve as a consultant, advising Sindona on economic trends, foreign trade, currency movements, and financial developments in the United States, Asia, and Europe. Kennedy also discussed Franklin's financial and personnel problems with Sindona and introduced him to James Smith, Comptroller of the Currency, and other private and public banking officials in the United States and abroad.[3]

Because of Kennedy's association with Sindona, some commentators have sought to link Kennedy to Franklin's later difficulties. But that assertion ignores the fact that Franklin was in trouble even before Sindona appeared on the scene. As Joan Spero has pointed out in her carefully researched book *The Failure of the Franklin National Bank: Challenge to the International Banking System*,[4] the roots of the bank's decline and fall go far deeper than Sindona's purchase of 21.6 percent of the bank. The same point is made by Sanford Rose. In a *Fortune* article, Rose argues that the bank "had been run amateurishly for decades." Franklin had a protected market on Long Island because New York law excluded the large New York City banks from operating in that market. When the law was changed in the early 1960s, Franklin responded to this increased competition by moving into the highly competitive New York City market. It had neither the resources nor the experienced personnel to compete in that market. All of these problems existed when Sindona bought into the bank, but he compounded them rather than solving them.

A case in point was Sindona's pressure on Harold Gleason,[5] Franklin's chairman, to hire Peter Shaddick, who had once worked as a foreign-exchange trader at Continental. Apparently, Sindona expected that Shaddick would produce enough profit to offset the bank's losses in its other operations. Kennedy advised Sindona not to hire Shaddick except as a foreign-exchange trader. There were limits, he believed, to Shaddick's abilities, and if he were given broad administrative and policy responsibilities at Franklin, the bank would suffer. Disregarding Kennedy's advice, Sindona gave Shaddick complete control over the bank's international department that operated as a "bank within a bank," answering neither to Gleason nor to the president, Paul Luftig, but to Sindona.[6]

The stage was set for disaster: Franklin's normal banking operations were fundamentally unsound, Shaddick was undertaking high-risk speculations in foreign-exchange markets, inflation and interest rates in the United States were rising sharply, and there was pending chaos in the international exchange markets triggered by the oil embargo of 1973. In November 1973, because of Franklin's weak financial position, bankers in Europe and the United States refused to deal with Franklin or sharply reduced their relationship. By the spring of 1974, the bank's affairs were in shambles: Shaddick's foreign-exchange operations piled up loss after loss, and he turned to deceptive practices to conceal the real extent of the losses. In turn, the bank attempted to stave off disaster by increasing its loan portfolio, but it was paying more for money in the market than it was earning on its loans.

In the face of increasing losses, Luftig became convinced that a merger with another bank was the only way for Franklin to remain solvent. Manufacturers Hanover Trust Company was interested, but before the merger could be agreed upon, Franklin was forced to announce additional losses in its foreign-exchange operations, to suspend payment of dividends, and to request a suspension in trading of Franklin shares. Manufacturers Hanover backed down. A Sindona plan to rescue Franklin with a $50 million offering to shareholders was put aside in favor of a loan to Franklin from the Federal Reserve Bank of New York to assure that the bank would remain solvent.

Although Kennedy was aware of the deteriorating condition of Franklin and had discussed the problems of the bank with Sindona, he was not monitoring the activities of the bank on a day-to-day basis. However, he intervened along with senior officials at Franklin to prevent Shaddick from carrying out a plan to sell to Edilcentro International Limited, a merchant bank in Nassau that was a subsidiary of an Italian firm controlled by Sindona, almost $100 million in Italian government bonds that Franklin had underwritten but was unable to sell. When Kennedy learned of the proposal, he insisted that it be cancelled because it was not an arm's-length sale. He learned later that Shaddick and Sindona ordered Franklin's

London branch to transfer enough funds to Edilcentro to buy the bonds.

Kennedy was not entirely surprised by Franklin's financial difficulties, for he warned Sindona about the bank's investment portfolio before the Italian financier invested in the bank. Furthermore, he knew that the bank's losses in the foreign-exchange markets had made the bank's financial difficulties even worse than he expected. As those losses mounted and the stability of the bank was threatened, he arranged for Sindona to meet with Comptroller Smith to explore ways of assuring the bank's viability. Still, he was not prepared for the crisis that broke over the second weekend in May 1974.

The first notice Kennedy had that Franklin might fail was calls from both Smith and Sindona on May 10 while he was in Los Angeles on his way to the Far East as the head of a trade mission. They reported that merger talks had failed because Franklin had suffered substantial losses in its foreign-exchange dealings and could not pay a quarterly dividend, the first American bank to suspend dividend payments since the Great Depression. Given Kennedy's experience at the Federal Reserve Board during the banking crisis of 1932–33, he was fully aware of what this meant. His response was to warn Sindona and Smith that the loss would probably be substantially greater than estimated.

Kennedy, though well aware of the seriousness of the Franklin situation, could not let the trade mission go on without him. He continued on to Seoul, where he was besieged by a series of transoceanic phone calls from both Smith and Sindona. They both thought they could restore confidence in Franklin by placing Sindona's stock in an irrevocable voting trust for one year,[7] with Kennedy as the trustee. Kennedy agreed to this request but rejected their insistent demands that he return immediately. He did not arrive in the United States until May 31. As soon as he returned to Washington, he and Sindona met with Smith. The upshot of those talks was that Smith asked Kennedy to try to sell the bank and to find new management for Franklin. Kennedy spent the next two weeks trying to find a buyer for the bank. Since he had full control of Sindona's stock, he could assure buyers that Sindona would not be a problem, not only because Kennedy could vote his stock, but also because by that time Sindona had given up his drive to retain his stock and was willing to sell. At one point Kennedy thought that the Bank of America would buy Franklin, but that proposal was shot down by the Federal Reserve Board, which was determined to keep the California-based giant out of New York. Kennedy's other efforts to sell Franklin to other New York banks were equally unsuccessful. Franklin was, after all, in bad financial difficulties, and none of the larger banks wanted to take on the risk. There was considerable "group think" in the decision of the New York banks not to buy Franklin. It was the collective judgment of the market that it would be unprofitable to merge with Franklin, and that collective judgment kept some banks from doing what was in their own self-interest and certainly in the interest of the American banking community.

Although Kennedy was unsuccessful in finding a buyer for the Franklin, he was successful in persuading Joseph Barr, who had been Secretary of the Treasury for a brief period during Lyndon Johnson's administration, to become the chief executive officer at the bank. From June until October Franklin limped along, supported by continuing loans from the Federal Reserve Bank of New York, as Barr, officials of the FDIC, and officers of the New York Federal Reserve Bank sought to put together a package that would be attractive to buyers. Finally, in October Franklin was declared insolvent and its assets sold to a consortium of European banks, which reopened the bank under the name European American. Sindona lost his entire investment, but by this time the Italian authorities had also discovered irregularities in his financial operations in Italy, and the extensive financial network he had so carefully woven began to unravel as incident after incident of fraud and deception was exposed. Finally, on June 13, 1980, Sindona was convicted of bank fraud in the United States Federal District Court of Manhattan and sentenced to twenty-five years in a U.S. prison. He appealed his conviction, but it was upheld by the Second Circuit Court of Appeals and he remained in prison until September 1984, when he was extradited to Italy to face charges arising from the crash of his Italian financial empire.[8]

The collapse of Franklin was not the end of the Sindona episode in Kennedy's life. He was a government witness at the subsequent fraud trials of Harold Gleason and Peter Shaddick, and the government took his deposition in the preparation of the case against Sindona. The Italian government, convinced that an element of fraud was attached to all of Sindona's business dealings, brought suit against Kennedy and a group of Utah businessmen who bought Talcott, a successful factoring firm, from Sindona. The basis of the suit was the charge that Sindona purchased Talcott in 1972 as part of a pyramid scheme; hence, he used money that was not his to make the purchase. The case was dismissed because the statute of limitations had run. At the time of his conviction, Sindona made one last request of Kennedy. He asked Kennedy to deliver a letter to the White House in which Sindona appealed to President Ronald Reagan for a pardon. Without any suggestion of advocacy on his part, Kennedy agreed to this last request.

In retrospect, it is easy to criticize Kennedy and the government regulatory agencies that tried to work with Sindona to assure the solvency of Franklin. Yet in 1972, when Sindona purchased 21.6 percent of Franklin, he was a force in international finance. His widespread financial interests involved him deeply in the financial affairs of the Vatican. He controlled several banks in Italy and a one-third interest in Societa Generale Immobiliare, a giant Italian real estate development firm that developed the Watergate complex in Washington, D.C. In August 1973, *Fortune* estimated his worth at $450 million and reported that though he was feared by some of his Italian competitors, "one after another attests to his brilliance, judgment, courage, imagination and decisiveness." His almost unbroken series of successes suggested that he would be successful in keeping Franklin solvent. It was only after the Franklin crisis that the darker side of his financial manipulations became known and an assessment of his achievements and failures was made with some precision.

"Banking," Sindona claimed, "is a matter of connections." It is difficult, therefore, not to see a high degree of self-interest in his relationship with David Kennedy. It was only after the Franklin failure, when Sindona's hidden agenda came to light, that Kennedy realized how Sindona had used his name and influence to advance interests of which Kennedy had no knowledge. If Sindona had a hidden agenda in his relationship with Kennedy, the same was not true of Kennedy, whose concept of friendship rested on candor, trust, and loyalty. Those old-fashioned qualities made it possible for a so-called friend to exploit them for selfish ends, but they also meant that after Kennedy's disappointment and disillusionment passed, his integrity remained.

11

CONTINENTAL ILLINOIS: THE KENNEDY DECADE

Statistical measures cannot tell the whole story of David M. Kennedy's decade of leadership at Continental, but they are both prologue and epilogue to that tale. From the time he became chairman of the board at the beginning of 1959 until he left in January 1969, the bank's resources increased from $2.9 billion to $7.4 billion, and deposits increased from $2.6 billion to $6.3 billion. The most striking change was the dramatic rise in loans from $1.1 billion to almost $4.2 billion, a growth of 272 percent. Growth of that magnitude required an increase in employees, and the size of Continental's staff rose over that ten-year period from 3,800 to 6,918. Shareholders could look back on the Kennedy decade with some satisfaction. In a decade of low interest rates (the prime interest rate rose from 2.5 percent in 1958 to a fraction under 6 percent in 1968) and when stock dividends averaged 3 percent, Continental's stock kept abreast of the market. One hundred shares of Continental stock held on December 31, 1958, had a market value of $11,600. By December 31, 1968, stock dividends and a 1963 four-for-one stock split had increased this investment to 484 shares with a market value of $21,901; meanwhile, cash dividend income amounted to $4,866.20, or an average of 4.2 percent over the ten-year period.

All divisions of the bank shared in that growth. In an era of rising prosperity, the trust department served an increasing number of individuals who made the bank the trustee of their estates. The sophisticated investment division department, as reported in a review of Kennedy's decade as chairman, Kennedy, "broadened greatly the scope of investment opportunities available to personal trust customers, pension funds, and profit-sharing funds." When the government made it possible for self-employed individuals to set up their own pension plans, Continental expanded its pension-fund management to accommodate individual accounts. In addition, the trust department had a long record of serving as the trustee for bond sales and agent for stock transfers, but still it was not prepared for the challenge it faced as a result of Kennedy's appointment in 1963 as one of the incorporators of the Communications Satellite Corporation (Comsat).

It all began with a telephone call while Kennedy was on bank business in Idaho. The call was from the White House; President John F. Kennedy was calling Chairman David M. Kennedy to ask that he serve as an incorporator of the Comsat. David Kennedy, with tongue in cheek, suggested to the President that there were enough Kennedys in Washington without adding one more. The President entered into the banter by recalling that Robert F. Kennedy was suing Continental over the merger with City National. Kennedy remembered, continuing the conversation, "That's right. He's the Attorney General of the United States and your brother, and you have no appeal from your brother. That's the part I don't like." "Oh," the President responded, "you're a Kennedy. You can take care of that all right." The upshot was that David Kennedy accepted the appointment as one of the incorporators of Comsat, and what started out as his personal involvement in the corporation ended in Continental participating in the underwriting of Comsat and the trust department undertaking what was at that time the largest stock transfer in the history of American business.

Congress established Comsat as a privately owned corporation created to provide telecommunications services by satellites circling the earth. The legislation provided that there would be two classes of stock: Class A stock, for sale to the public, and Class B stock, for sale to communications companies. Class A stock would have voting rights; stock ownership by any one individual was limited to 10 percent of all the stock, or 10 percent of the stock outstanding. The act also provided that half of the stock issued by the corporation would be Class A stock, which sale was expected to raise $100 million. The statute fixed a maximum price of $100 a share on Class A stock; the actual selling price would be determined by the incorporators based on their best judgment of market conditions.

The project no sooner got started than two problems emerged. The first was the erratic behavior of Philip Graham, publisher of the *Washington Post*, who was interim chairman of the incorporators. When it became apparent that Graham had serious emotional problems, most of the other incorporators agreed that he would have to be replaced. They were relieved of the need to force the issue with President John F. Kennedy when Graham was hospitalized because of a nervous breakdown. David Kennedy was then appointed along with two other incorporators to find a new chairman. Upon their recommendation, Leo Welch, who had just retired as chairman of Standard Oil of New Jersey, was asked to take on the responsibility, which he eventually accepted.

The second problem was how to find enough working capital for the corporation to do business until the stock was issued and sold. The incorporators decided that the corporation would need a loan of five million dollars, but there was no one to sign the note; Comsat did not yet exist and no stock had been sold. Kennedy, always decisive, committed Continental to $500,000 and asked the ten largest banks in the United States to match its commitment. There was no collateral except Kennedy's assurance that the loan would be repaid out of the proceeds of the stock sale. That was not enough for Fritz Larkin, chairman of Security Pacific, who protested, Kennedy recalled, that "this is the wildest loan I've ever heard anybody propose. It's a cloud nine loan. You've got no one to sign the note." Despite the tenuous nature of the collateral, Kennedy convinced ten banks—not including Security Pacific— that the loan was viable; he sweetened the pot just a little by promising the banks that Comsat would carry an account with each bank when the corporation became operational. His efforts were remembered in Comsat folklore as the "Kennedy Cloud Nine Loan."

As a result of his role during the period of Comsat's incorporation, Kennedy was elected a director of Comsat, and Continental became the transfer agent for issuing the stock. Planning for the task of printing the certificates, registering the stock in the shareholder's name, and completing delivery of the stock was based on a price of $20 a share and 500,000 individual transactions. That decision was just the beginning, for entirely new techniques of stock transfer based on the pioneering use of computers had to be developed. Computer consultants were brought in from IBM, other departments were combed for competent supervisory personnel, training classes were created, and high school graduates and college students were brought in on a temporary basis. In the end, the "paper tiger" was tamed, and the bank successfully issued all $200 million of Class A and Class B stock at $20 a share. The effort was not without cost, primarily because the work of other departments had been disrupted by the transfer of personnel to the Comsat project. The rewards were, however, substantial. The bank obtained a valuable account; stock transfer procedures based on the use of computers, which had been under development at the bank even before Comsat, were refined and perfected to the point where they could be applied to all the bank's transfer business; and, finally, it was another success that enhanced the image of Continental as a bank on the cutting edge of modern bank operations.

Kennedy's penchant for innovation was also reflected in the Continental/Sears connection. Charles Kellstadt, chairman of Sears, Roebuck & Company and a member of Continental's board of directors, raised with Kennedy problems Sears was having because of sharply increasing sales on credit, which it was financing out of its own funds. The problems arose because Sears's tax books were kept on an accrual basis; that is, each sale was recorded as completed even though full payment had not been received. Under the law Sears had to pay taxes on the sale as soon as it was made. Sears could have postponed the tax if it changed its accounting system to reflect the cash received rather than the sale. The Internal Revenue Service made that a costly decision by requiring companies making the change to begin paying full taxes on each dollar collected—even though some of these dollars would have been taxed already, when they were accrued. The solution that seemed so simple on its face would have cost Sears twenty-five million dollars in additional taxes in the year the change in the accounting system was made. There was a way out of this dilemma, Kennedy explained to Kellstadt, a way that had been used by some smaller companies. The solution was to sell Sears's accounts receivable just before the change in the accounting system, which would result in no double taxation, for Sears would have no accounts receivable.

Kellstadt was not ready to move on such a large refinancing— Sears had $1.6 billion in installment sales whose terms ran from one to two years—without seeing what other bankers thought of the proposal. Those discussions left him pessimistic because he was told that the sale of Sear's accounts receivable was too big for the market to absorb without creating unhealthy competition among other borrowers. Kennedy told Kellstadt that he was not frightened by size, for when he entered a 1 in his accounts at home it only stood for one dollar, at the bank the same 1 stood for a million dollars, and when he was at the Treasury the same 1 stood for a billion dollars. Besides, the key to his solution was not to give Sears cash for its accounts receivable but to pay for them with a special certificate of deposit, with maturities tailored to fit Sears's seasonal needs for money. Hence, no money would actually leave the bank until the certificates matured, and then on a staggered basis. Kennedy had expected that New York banks would participate, but they backed away from a transaction where a Chicago bank was the lead bank. Finally, Kennedy decided that the sale could be made if Continental's correspondent banks would buy with the certificates of deposit the accounts receivable generated by Sears in their local trading area. That proposal broke the log jam, and John Hoffmann, who spearheaded the transaction for Continental, could happily report that the sale was completed and that a check for $960,242,000 was ready for Kennedy to present to Kellstadt.

Because of Continental's location in the heart of the Loop, Chicago's principal business district, Kennedy was concerned that the area not become spoiled by urban blight. That concern alerted him to an opportunity that arose out of a casual conversation with Arthur Rubloff, a land developer with nationwide interests, who complained that the city would not approve his proposal to develop what became the Carl Sandburg Center on Clark Street just north of the Chicago River. Not only was Rubloff having trouble with the city, but First National of Chicago, where he usually did business, would not finance the project. Kennedy invited him to bring his plans to the bank and, if the project was all Rubloff claimed it to be, Continental would undertake the financing. He also promised Rubloff that if the project was in the best interests of Chicago, he would talk to Mayor Richard J. Daley about the difficulty Rubloff was having in getting approval from the city planners. Rubloff had not exaggerated; Continental found the project to be all he said it was and more. Approval from the city was

Groundbreaking for the Carl Sandburg Center in Chicago, 1961: Second from left is David M. Kennedy, then Mayor Richard J. Daley, then Arthur Rubloff, chief promoter of the project (others unidentified)

183

promptly forthcoming, and Continental not only provided Rubloff with a construction loan but also arranged long-term financing for the project. And the risk Continental took in financing this massive project was repaid not only in monetary profits but also in Rubloff's frequently expressed assertion that he had never seen a bank move a project ahead as effectively as Continental had done.

A major reorganization of Continental's corporate structure was undertaken in 1968 just before Kennedy left the bank. In 1956 Congress passed the Bank Holding Company Act, which permitted the organization of a bank holding company, under which the holding company could be the parent company of one bank in addition to other companies. Although Continental was a leader in the discussions that led to the passage of the act, it was not among the first to create a holding company. Finally, in 1968, after more than a year of study, Continental decided to establish a holding company to be called the Conill Corporation. The name, a contraction of Continental Illinois, was the subject of much discussion among senior Continental officials, and both praise and blame for its selection was laid at Kennedy's door.

The growth that Continental experienced in the years between 1959 and 1968 was reflected not only in statistics but also in the internal reorganization that took place in those years. One of Kennedy's first concerns when he became chairman was the retirement of the older members of the board of directors. By the end of 1968, only two members of the board who had been there to vote for Kennedy's election as chairman were still serving. The composition of the board reflected Kennedy's views that board members should be involved actively in the management of their parent companies and that they should reflect the breadth of Continental's activities. There were no lawyers on the board, no representatives of consulting firms, and no educational or religious leaders. It was a board of business leaders. David Kennedy, Donald Graham, and Tilden Cummings, along with John Perkins and Roger Anderson, who had just been named executive vice-presidents, represented Continental on the board. The other directors were officers of corporations with interests in oil, transportation (airlines and railroads), insurance, merchandising, manufacturing (steel and electronics), meat packing, finance, and communications. An explicit retirement policy was in place so that there would be a continual renewing of the board. Kennedy did not want to leave his successor with the unenviable task he had faced of asking for the resignation of older board members.[1]

A revolution in bank operations came to Continental during the years Kennedy was chairman. He had had no experience in bank operations when he joined Continental, but his penchant for delegation made him a ready listener to the officers in charge of operations who listed the advantages of computerization. They told him that they could not promise it would cut costs or mean a reduction in personnel, but "it was an absolutely mandatory step if the bank was to prevent an explosion in costs as the volume of transactions swelled inexorably in the years ahead." If Continental was to keep abreast of the technological changes wrought by the computer in the way customers did business and with the services offered by other banks, it had to move decisively and rapidly. One colleague reported: "Kennedy got the message. By the end of 1963 a large amount of accounting, including all demand deposit accounting, had been automated. Two or three years later Continental was not only handling demand deposit work for correspondent banks but was also letting them store their savings accounts in its computers and giving them access to update the accounts via remote 'on-line' terminals."

Kennedy's years at Continental had their share of frustration and difficulties along with the satisfaction and pride that comes with achievement. He ruefully recalled that at the bank he was the officer in charge of bad news. Bad news always seems to come at unexpected moments, as in the telephone call from Tilden Cummings while Kennedy was on vacation at Acapulco, Mexico. Cummings's particular bad news was that the bank faced the possibility of a substantial loss because collateral that had been given to the bank against loans might prove to be worthless. The culprit was Anthony "Tony" De Angelis, who operated a vegetable-oil refining and export business in New Jersey. De Angelis would buy raw materials, refine them for the oil, and then export the oil to overseas customers. Between refining and export he stored the vegetable oil in tanks owned by American Express Warehousing, a subsidiary of American Express. To finance his business, De Angelis borrowed money, giving warehouse receipts as collateral. Those lenders would then use the receipts to borrow money from banks and other lenders.

Up to this point, De Angelis was running a risky but normal business. He soon added a wrinkle, however, that made his business not only more risky but also illegal. He began to obtain fraudulent warehouse receipts for vegetable oil that never existed. The scheme was based on his success in inducing American Express Warehousing to surrender to him responsibility for taking the periodic inventory of the storage tanks that was supposed to assure holders of the warehouse receipts that the oil represented by the receipt actually existed. Once De Angelis got control of the inventory procedure, he was able to fool even independent inspectors hired by some lenders, including Continental, to inventory his stocks. In some cases oil was pumped from tank to tank just ahead of the inspectors, who thus measured the same oil over and over again. In others, tanks were partially filled with water on which floated a thin layer of oil. De Angelis plunged ever deeper into the murky world of fraud and deception when he entered the futures market in vegetable oil, using phony warehouse receipts to finance his operations. He began to buy enormous quantities of vegetable oil in advance, betting that the price would rise. At one point he was committed to buy 1.2 billion pounds of vegetable oil, almost as much as the United States exported in a year. When the price of vegetable oil broke in late 1963, his paper empire came tumbling down and the American banking community found itself faced with substantial losses. Whatever else could be said about De Angelis, he was not a petty thief, and when all claims were totaled in the bankruptcy proceedings, they added up to $318 million.

Continental got caught in De Angelis's web of fraud and deception not because it had dealt directly with him, but because the bank had accepted warehouse receipts issued by American Express Warehousing as collateral from its customers who were dealing with De Angelis. Nevertheless, the bank, which had loaned almost

$35 million based on the fake warehouse receipts, stood to lose a considerable sum. Rumors began to circulate in the Chicago banking community that Continental would lose $35 million, and Kennedy was confronted with that figure by Marshall Field, publisher of the *Chicago Daily News*. He fended Field off, saying that he supposed the bank would lose that much because, like Will Rogers, all he knew was what he read in the newspapers.

Kennedy refused to be forthright with Field, not because of any reticence to discuss the bank's loss, but because he really did not know just how great the loss would be. Some of Continental's customers who dealt with De Angelis would be hurt—but not destroyed—by their losses and could repay the bank, and some of the loss was covered by insurance. Kennedy was also confident that American Express, the parent company of American Express Warehousing, would make some compensation, if only to protect its reputation. Kennedy took the lead in negotiating a settlement with American Express. Although both sides initially refused to accept his formula, his solution was finally accepted because it was fair, and, as important, if it were rejected, American Express would face a long court battle with Continental.

Kennedy, therefore, could tell the stockholders at the 1964 annual meeting that the bank did not expect to lose more than $5 million from the De Angelis scheme and that the loss might well be less when all insurance payments and recovery from customers were made. Each year some stockholder would want to know how much the bank had lost. Each year until the 1969 meeting, when he was leaving to be Secretary of the Treasury, Kennedy would repeat the $5 million figure. But that year he said he would turn the question over to the incoming chairman, Donald Graham. Graham took some pleasure in reporting that the loss would be under $1 million.

The bad news about De Angelis and his vegetable-oil scam came out of the blue and with only a minimum of fault on the part of the bank; the bad news associated with the entry of Continental in the credit-card business came gradually and resulted almost completely from the way the bank introduced its Town and Country credit card. Before 1966 there were no bank-sponsored credit cards in the Chicago area, but in that year several banks began examining the possibility of combining forces for a joint credit-card operation. Continental was part of that planning group, but the bank also made its own cost-benefit studies on the basis of which it decided to issue the Town and Country card.

The ostensible reasons for Continental to begin a credit-card operation were to increase profits, enlarge the number of the bank's consumer customers, strengthen Continental's ties with its correspondent banks, and prepare for a checkless, cashless society. The real reason was the threat that some other lending institution, either a bank or a major firm like Sears, might issue credit cards before Continental was prepared to compete, and would thus preempt the market. In a brilliant memorandum, Selden Swope, head of Continental's retail banking department, put the matter bluntly. Although he estimated that it might take fifteen years to recoup the investment losses from being the first to offer credit cards in Chicago, Continental must act rapidly to prevent a competitor from controlling the consumer market. Kennedy clearly understood that this was the issue before he approved the decision to go ahead in September 1966. Though the decision was not one that the board had to approve, the arguments for going ahead were rehearsed for the board by Graham, and the board unanimously resolved to approve the decision.

The success of the credit card hinged on reaching a high volume of business as soon as possible. Therefore, when the decision was reached in September, the bank set November as the target date for distributing its credit cards. The public argument for that early date was to have the cards in the hands of consumers before the Christmas holidays; the private argument was that Continental was ahead of its competitors in its preparation, and, therefore, an early introduction date would give it a competitive edge. But the arguments for quick distribution of the cards were the source of the major problems that the bank encountered.

The operational question Continental faced in achieving rapidly a high volume of credit-card business was how to put the cards in the hands of potential users. The safest way was to advertise the card and invite the public to apply for one, but it would have meant a piecemeal introduction of the card, and, hence, it would not satisfy the need to develop quickly a high volume of business. In place of that piecemeal strategy, Continental decided to distribute cards to selected consumers in the area served by the bank and its correspondent banks without requiring an application. The first list was generated from Continental's own customers who had checking or savings accounts. Each correspondent bank provided lists of people to whom the cards should be sent. Going beyond that, the bank bought lists of names from various sources and sent cards to those people. This high-volume strategy did indeed assure a wide distribution, but it also opened the door to substantial fraud and theft.

Those twin evils stemmed in part from the nature of the lists of people to whom the card was sent. Continental's expectation was that the lists would be checked to eliminate bad credit risks; that expectation turned out to be utopian. Frequently the cards, with a credit limit of three hundred dollars, went to low-income groups with no experience in the use of credit and whose ability to repay was limited. Some of that loss was taken into account in assessing the start-up costs of the operation, but what was not reckoned with was the large amount of fraud associated with the use of the card on the part of both consumers and retailers. Continental did have a verification center, but the personnel were new and the technology was not yet sophisticated enough to identify the multiple ways in which the card could be abused: customers going from store to store charging all that they could, and retailers falsely reporting the sale of a large number of a single item to one person.

If the fraudulent use of the card had been limited to a portion of the card recipients with petty larceny in their hearts, the problem might have been manageable. But many of the cards never reached the person to whom they were sent; they were stolen from mailboxes, and whole trays of envelopes containing credit cards never left the Chicago post office. Continental finally took to mailing the cards through post offices outside Chicago in hopes that at least the cards would reach the designated holders. But the thefts meant that a substantial portion of the cards were falling into the hands of criminals, who found theft by stolen credit card much easier than breaking and entering.

Although theft and fraud made the start-up costs—which totaled some ten million dollars—greater than Continental expected, the introduction of the Town and Country card achieved the bank's goal of forestalling a competitor from dominating the consumer credit market. In the process, however, Kennedy came under fire. One customer expressed his concern at "the manner in which these charge cards are promoted and to the inflationary pressures which they cause as a result of encouraging people to extend their indebtedness. Also, if you make a charge on merchants offering your service, this would inflate prices if enough people do go along with your system."

In a speech to stockholders in January 1967, barely two months after introduction of the credit card, Kennedy defended the bank against these charges. He could readily answer the charge that credit cards were inflationary, since the discount the merchants paid on each purchase was really an accounting charge they would have to bear if they operated their own credit plan. The charge that the bank was luring people into lax and irresponsible use of credit touched a raw nerve, for Kennedy grew up hearing warnings from the leaders of his Mormon faith against buying on credit, and J. Reuben Clark, Jr., a member of the First Presidency of the Church, had, on occasion, bantered with Kennedy over the role of bankers as purveyors of credit. The tension that the credit-card concept created in his own mind is reflected in his talk to the stockholders. He recognized, he told them, that not asking for applications before issuing the cards to prospective users was a "new— and to some surprising—approach to the concept of credit." Moreover, he pointed out, "many of us . . . were brought up under the more conservative financial and banking circumstances and feel a natural reluctance to accept some of the seemingly radical innovations that are upon us." That "natural reluctance," which Kennedy obviously shared, "must give way in the face of increasingly strong competition for the consumer credit market," he argued. He sought to assure the stockholders that the bank screened the credit-card recipients for credit worthiness, although he admitted that errors were made.

In retrospect, as Kennedy himself recognized, the errors in assessing credit worthiness were more numerous than he thought they would be, but fraud and theft were more important in the initial losses than the existence of poor credit risks. In any event, the first year was the worst because the first issue of cards had a one-year expiration date, and after that date was reached, bank employees reviewed the list of card holders and eliminated all the poor credit risks they could identify. Furthermore, the bank's verification center soon developed the capability to provide merchants rapid response to authorization requests, which materially reduced losses from stolen cards as well as from fraud.[2]

David Kennedy's decision to plunge ahead with the introduction of credit cards reflects his understanding that Continental's expansion entailed a continuing willingness to take risks. Those risks were not reckless gambles but were taken to assure the bank's ability to compete across the full range of financial markets. He never forgot that the core of Continental's business was with large corporations. While he was chairman, the bank improved the quality of its service to those primary customers, and it vigorously expanded its loans to middle-size and small firms. Kennedy risked expanding the bank's foreign operations because he foresaw the rising involvement of the bank's principal customers in overseas operations. Wherever his customers went, he wanted Continental to be, in order to provide the widest possible service. He risked taking the bank into the retail credit market—which Walter Cummings had deliberately shunned—because he believed that Continental could not abandon that market if it was to justify its claim to being the leading Chicago bank. There were, of course, sound economic reasons for taking risks; they were all taken with the hope that they would in the long run increase the profitability of the bank. Likewise, some risks were forced on the bank by competitive pressures, but a more cautious chairman might not have

Ralph Walters photo, © with permission of the Chicago Sun-Times, Inc., 1987

David Matthew Kennedy on balcony overlooking the lobby of the Continental Illinois bank

transformed those pressures into opportunities to expand the bank's activities beyond the traditional role of commercial banks. Kennedy's image of himself was that of a builder, someone who wanted to do more than just manage a smoothly functioning organization. His record of achievement in the decade he directed the affairs of Continental reflects how well his performance matched that image.

12

CHICAGO, 1947–69:
CHURCH AND FAMILY

When David and Lenora Kennedy arrived in Washington in 1929, they had only one child, Marilyn, who was born just before they left Utah. When they left Washington for Chicago in October 1946, the family included three more daughters. Marilyn had graduated from high school and was attending Brigham Young University in Provo, Utah, and the youngest girls, Carol, twelve, and Patricia, four, found the move exciting. But for Barbara, who was just beginning her junior year in high school, the move was a wrenching experience. The first year, when the family lived in a small apartment in Rogers Park, was the most difficult for her. She was relieved when the family decided to move to Skokie, a suburb of Chicago, and she enrolled in Niles High School, a much smaller school than the one she attended in Chicago. She quickly made friends at Niles and became a member of the debate team. Her happiness at Niles threatened to be short-lived, however, because David and Lenora decided to move to Evanston. When Barbara was determined to stay at Niles despite having to pay tuition as a nonresident, David rehearsed with her, in discussions that sometimes became heated, all the reasons why it would be better to attend high school in Evanston rather than stay at Niles. Finally he realized how difficult the move to Chicago was for her and agreed she could complete her senior year at Niles.

While Barbara was finding it difficult to adjust to Chicago during that first unsettled year, Marilyn was swept up in the excitement of being at college and away from home. In letters to her parents following her first Christmas away from home, she began to mention dates with Verl Taylor, a senior at BYU. Nothing in those letters, however, prepared them for the phone call they received from her on May 14, 1947, announcing that she and Verl had just eloped to Elko, Nevada. David and Lenora were stunned that their oldest daughter, who was just eighteen, had eloped with a man they did not know. Transcending all of their immediate concerns was one that went to the heart of their religion. Mormon parents who are as committed to their faith as David and Lenora want their children to be married in a temple, for only there can the marriage ceremony assure the eternal unity of the family, a central belief in Mormon theology. Marilyn's call took David and Lenora on a hasty journey to Utah to meet their new son-in-law. Fortunately, they found him a thoughtful young man who proposed elopement only because he feared losing Marilyn; he had clear career plans and was as anxious as they were to have the marriage solemnized in the temple.

The Kennedy family was no sooner settled in the apartment in Rogers Park than David found himself deeply involved again in church assignments. The first stake had been organized in Chicago in November 1936, and by 1947 there was a sizeable Mormon community in the Chicago area. When David Kennedy arrived, the stake president was John K. Edmunds, who in February 1947 called him as a member of the stake high council. In September 1947 David became second counselor in the stake presidency, and in September 1952 he became first counselor. Since the stake covered a large geographical area from Gary, Indiana, in the south to Milwaukee, Wisconsin, in the north, the stake presidency traveled almost every weekend visiting the wards and branches. There were also weekly meetings of the presidency that sometimes ran late into the night, for Edmunds was a methodical planner who liked to review stake problems and progress in detail. What began for David Kennedy and John Edmunds as a formal relationship in church service soon became a rich friendship. They served together for sixteen years, but in 1947 neither of them could foresee that their association would last as long as it did and that they would come to rely so heavily on each other.

By the end of 1947 it appeared to David and Lenora that most of the trauma of moving to Chicago was behind them. They had no way of knowing that 1948 would bring a serious crisis that threatened to undo all their carefully laid plans. In early summer David developed a high fever, resulting in a diagnosis of viral pneumonia. He was in the hospital for a number of weeks and then recuperated several months at home with no noticeable improvement. In those trying months, Hank Knight, head of Continental's bond department, was a tower of strength. He visited David almost every day in the hospital and continued his visits after David went home.[1] When his health failed to improve, David decided that in all fairness to the bank it would be best for him to resign. The response to his letter of resignation was both surprising and gratifying, for in a personal letter, Walter Cummings refused to accept the resignation, telling him that he had been hired for life.

David was sustained in his battle with poor health by Lenora's faith in his eventual recovery and by her unselfish concern for his every need. He would always marvel that she was able to devote so much time and attention to him without endangering her own health. Both David and Lenora were buoyed up in those long months by their deep religious faith and by the support they received from their friends in the Church. Edmunds and the first counselor in the stake presidency, Ariel L. Williams, were determined that David should continue to feel a part of the presidency, so whenever it was possible they held their meetings at his bedside. Despite these constant gestures of support, David felt guilty that others were burdened with his share of the work. On December 31, 1948, he wrote Edmunds and asked to be released, explaining, "John, at times I feel that I am not making the progress that I should. It is now quite clear that after seven months of letting others carry my load I still am not able to do my share. I had hoped and expected that by this time I would be able to assume the responsibilities of my office and calling in the Church. This is not the case. . . . I have given this matter a good deal of thought over the months, but put off taking it up with hoping [*sic*] that it would be unnecessary. Now the course of action is clear—I must step aside." The letter was rejected with the same vote of confidence he had received when he had attempted to resign from the bank. In both cases his reasons for writing the letters was a reluctance to be a burden on his associates; battling poor health, his inability to carry his share of the work at the bank and in the Church weighed heavily on his mind and increased his frustration as the day of his recovery was delayed.

As Kennedy's health failed to improve, he was advised by his doctors to leave Chicago for a drier climate and to seek a less demanding occupation. Not knowing what else to do, he and Lenora, before making any final decision to leave Chicago, decided in January 1949 to go to Utah to see if the change in climate would indeed help him recover his health. Barbara and Carol stayed in Chicago with Marilyn and Verl, while Patricia went with her parents. Lenora put David in a Pullman berth, and the three of them set out for Ogden.

As David fought his battle with viral pneumonia during the fall and winter of 1948–49, he had two deeply moving experiences that buttressed his conviction that there is a power in faith and prayer that transcends the limits of human knowledge. The first of those experiences came one cold winter evening in Chicago before the family left for Utah. David suddenly developed difficulty in breathing, and Lenora rushed downstairs to call the doctor—just as the doorbell rang. She opened the door to find Edmunds and another member of the Church, E. A. Christensen, standing on the door step. Each of them decided independently to visit David and arrived simultaneously at the door. Lenora pulled them quickly into the house, breathlessly explained that he was having trouble breathing, and asked if they would administer a blessing to him. Following the blessing pronounced by Edmunds, David began to breath with greater ease and made it through the night without difficulty.

The second experience occurred after David and Lenora arrived in Ogden and were staying with her parents. David was in bed, still too weak to leave the house, when again there came a knock at the door. Lenora's mother went to the door, and there stood a man whom she recognized as Matthew Cowley, a member of the Quorum of the Twelve Apostles. He asked if David Kennedy was there. "Yes," was her response, "he is in bed upstairs." Cowley said he had come to give David a blessing. Although David had known Cowley in Washington, his appearance at David's bedside was a surprise. David had not asked him to come, nor, as far as he knew, had anyone else in the family, yet there Cowley was, unbidden but gratefully welcomed. Cowley blessed David that he would recover his health and strength and would be able to resume his normal activity. It was not long after the events of that startling afternoon that he was able to get out of bed, then out of the house to walk a half a block, and finally he triumphantly walked completely around the block without difficulty in breathing.

When it became clear that David was gradually regaining his strength, the family returned to Chicago. He did not return to work immediately, but as his strength increased he began to spend a few hours a day at the bank. Finally he recovered his full strength and was able to resume work at the bank and service in the Church. When Hank Knight learned that David was still active in his church assignment, he tried to persuade him that he could not do both and that his first priority should be his professional career. But for David Kennedy there was no alternative—he had to do both. He assured Knight that he was confident of his ability to do justice to both assignments. Knight on only one other occasion had tried to counsel David about his church life and the demands of his professional career. Soon after David joined the bank, Knight gently suggested that if he wanted to succeed in the bank, he would have to bend his rigid rules about drinking to join fully in the social life of the bank's officers. David did not accept that advice, and he was now determined to continue his service in the Church with renewed vigor in order to make up for the time he had lost.

David's experience with poor health made him even more conscious of the price his mother paid for almost a lifetime of ill health. David and Lenora maintained close contact with Katie and George, writing often, spending part of each vacation with them in Randolph, and occasionally helping them financially. In 1936 Katie and George spent a month in Washington visiting historical sites and getting better acquainted with their grandchildren. But the arthritis that made Katie an invalid finally won out over her will to live; she died on November 19, 1950, at the age of seventy-one.

David spoke at his mother's funeral, which was fitting because there was much of Katie in David. They shared a determination to make the most of their abilities, an independence of mind, a profound commitment to shared religious values, and a determination to overcome the obstacles placed in their way. They also shared little tolerance for those unwilling to pay the price in hard work that success demands, and impatience with the minor errors of family and friends, while at the same time being thoughtful, considerate, and understanding in the face of major crises.

George, who devoted much of his life to caring for Katie, particularly after the children left home and she became confined to a wheelchair, was uncertain what to do after her death. He did not want to live with his children, so he rejected David's invitation to come to Chicago. But David did persuade his father to come for a visit; George stayed through the winter, and thereafter he spent

David and Lenora Kennedy, Christmas 1967

winters in Chicago with David and Lenora, but summers took him back to the familiar haunts of Randolph.

Each of the Kennedy children had sharply different memories of Chicago. Marilyn was already away at college when the family moved there, but she and Verl joined the family later while he studied at Northwestern University. After Barbara finished high school in Chicago, she then followed in her older sister's footsteps by attending BYU, only to return to the family home in Chicago with her new husband, Carl Law. For the two younger girls, Carol and Patricia, Chicago was truly home.

As they grew older, they began to take part in school activities and to enjoy their friends both in and out of the Church. Some church members would not let their children take part in school activities because they thought it would subject them to harmful influences. David and Lenora felt differently. They believed that if their children were firmly grounded in religious and family values, they could represent those standards and win the respect and acceptance of their non-Mormon friends. That decision opened the way for Barbara to take part in drama and debate at Niles, and the pattern was set for Carol and Patricia when they faced the same decisions.

The decision to let their children participate actively in school activities and to date young men who were not Mormon did not mean that David was reticent to take direct action when necessary. A case in point: During her high school years, Carol's charm and emerging beauty attracted a bevy of boys, one of whom was Robert McKiever, a football star at Northwestern. McKiever invited Carol to a New Year's Eve party where David suspected there would be some drinking. David recalled extracting a promise from McKiever, much to Carol's embarrassment. "What I want you to do," he told McKiever, "if you take one drink, you give me a call and I'll pick her up and bring her home. . . . Now I don't mean two drinks. I mean one. . . . Don't worry what time it is," David insisted. "But one of the things I don't want her to do is to be riding in a car with somebody that has been drinking, because we love her and we don't want an accident to happen, if we can prevent it." On those terms Carol left on the date, and McKiever was as good as his word; he brought Carol home without having taken a drink.

Carol followed Marilyn and Barbara to BYU, where, after her freshman year, she married Jack Whittle on December 16, 1954, a month after her nineteenth birthday. David was known to grumble that he sent his daughters to BYU to get an education, not to get married, at least not so soon. With three daughters married, only Patricia remained at home with her parents, and of all the girls, her memories of growing up in Chicago were the longest and the most diverse. She was fourteen when her father became president of Continental, sixteen when he became chairman. She fondly remembered the home in Evanston, and she was seventeen when the family moved to their fashionable new home in Northfield. She was the only one who knew the luxury and embarrassment of being driven to high school in a limousine—she would always have the driver let her out a block away from school—and the excitement of trips to Europe with her parents, staying in the best hotels and having dinner at the best restaurants. David liked Lenora to travel with him as much as possible, and Patricia was often a traveling companion to her mother. The two of them would sightsee and shop while David was in business meetings. He would join them as often as his schedule would permit, but trips through art galleries and historical sites under the pressure of his tight schedule were often exercises in rapid appreciation.

When Patricia finished high school, she too went west to BYU, but not before David threatened to send her to a nunnery to assure that she would finish her education before marriage. She responded to that parental concern by completing her degree even though she too was married after her freshman year. When David and Lenora learned that their youngest daughter intended to marry Lewis Campbell, a young man they had never met, they immediately flew to Provo to meet him—and take his measure. While David was well-prepared for the interview, Patricia neglected to tell Lewis just who David was, other than that he was her father and a banker. The interview began with David showering Lewis with pointed questions about his intentions, his plans for supporting Patricia, and his plans for a career. The Campbells, no less than the Kennedys, have some Scotch blood in them, and Lewis got enough of his "Scotch" up to ask David what he did for a living. He was poorly prepared for David's answer that he was chairman and chief executive officer of the Continental Illinois Bank and Trust Company of Chicago. Despite that unexpected and some-what intimidating response, Lewis stayed the course and won the day with the proviso that Patricia spend the summer with her parents in Chicago to see if indeed absence made the heart grow fonder. It did. Patricia and Lewis were married with her parents' blessing on August 24, 1963.

The Chicago years not only brought changes to David and Lenora's immediate family but also in their extended family. Lenora's father died in 1948; and in 1962, her mother, who was approaching her ninetieth birthday, died in Ogden. The Chicago years also saw the deaths of David's remaining brothers. L. G. died in 1959, Ivan in 1961, and Melvin in December 1968, just before David left Chicago to become Secretary of the Treasury. David's father passed away in late May 1964, at almost ninety years of age. David spoke at his funeral. Different from his father in his chosen profession, David was like him in his capacity for hard work, in his love for his family, and in his devotion to the gospel of Jesus Christ.

David and Lenora had learned when they moved to Washington that a change in geographical location did not mean an exit from the Mormon community. That experience was repeated in Chicago, for in many ways the Chicago Stake was similar to the Washington Stake: a large percentage of stake members came to Chicago to complete their education, intending to return to the West, but many stayed on to make their homes in the Midwest. John Edmunds originally intended to return west but remained to make his career in Chicago. Dallin Oaks, of another generation, took the same path. Others came because of the business opportunities Chicago offered. Whatever the reason they had for coming to Chicago, those who stayed developed a sense of identity and loyalty to Chicago that has drawn them together across the years.

As a religious leader David Kennedy was not only interested in the spiritual welfare of stake members but also became deeply involved in their temporal problems as well. Since Edmunds was a lawyer and Kennedy a banker, members of the stake came to them individually with legal and financial problems. Often, all they needed was advice, but sometimes they needed more substantial help. Kennedy's knowledge of financial affairs and banking practices enabled him to assist a member of the stake in buying a home. The problem centered on the member's intermittent income as a salesman, which precluded his qualifying for a home loan. Kennedy got ten stake members to sign a note on which the bank could lend the money for a house, but E. A. Christensen, a member of the stake, offered to lend the money from his savings. The house was bought, the loan was repaid according to the agreement, and a major problem was solved that bound stake members even more tightly together. At other times Kennedy helped stake members, particularly students, out of his own resources. That help sometimes came back to him manyfold, as was the case of John Vandegraaf, whom he helped through dental school. Vandegraaf repaid that help with dental care for the Kennedys. Whenever Kennedy tried to pay for Vandegraaf's services, Vandegraaf's response was that he considered David a partner, and he didn't take money from a partner.

The Mormon church relies on a lay clergy to administer all the affairs of each stake. The stake presidency was therefore not only involved in counseling members with spiritual and temporal problems but also in directing church dealings in real-estate transactions and construction projects. As the stake grew, there was an increasing need for a stake center that could house one or more wards and be large enough for stake conferences and other activities. Edmunds proposed to solve the problem by building a new stake center in Wilmette, where the Church owned property conveniently located for public transportation and easily accessible by automobile. Since many of the beautiful buildings in Wilmette and Evanston, including those on the campus of Northwestern University, were faced with lannon stone, the stake presidency wanted to use the same stone in the construction of the stake center. Edmunds and his counselors knew that the stone would increase the cost of the building, but they were willing to bear the extra cost. That argument was not persuasive with the First Presidency, particularly President J. Reuben Clark, Jr., who told them they could have any kind of chapel they desired as long as it was constructed with red brick. The Church, he told them, was not in the business of building monuments.

The impasse was settled improbably by a downturn in construction in the Chicago area. Hard times in the construction business made stonemasons anxious for contracts. In that environment, the stake presidency contacted Caesar Fiocchi, whose firm had won national prizes for its work on the Wilmette library building. Fiocchi was in a quandary, for if in this slow period he let his master masons go, he might not be able to hire them again. On the other hand, if he kept them without work, his outlays for wages could break him financially. He was, therefore, anxious to accept a contract even at a loss. In their discussions with Fiocchi, the stake presidency told him that he had to compete with brick contractors, for the bids had to be submitted to Salt Lake City. The bids amazed the General Authorities in Utah and pleased the stake presidency, for thus forewarned, Fiocchi submitted the lowest bid. Faced with this favorable cost estimate and the perseverance of the stake presidency, approval was given to build the Wilmette chapel of lannon stone.

The dedication of the stake center took place May 6, 1962. President David O. McKay, then in his eighty-ninth year, gave the dedicatory prayer. When President McKay saw the beautiful new chapel, he confessed to Edmunds that he was glad the stake presidency had held out for stone. Kennedy had known President McKay since his student days at Weber College and was thus prepared for the deep spirituality of the dedicatory prayer and the courage with which the President faced his physical infirmities. But he also found that President McKay had not lost his sense of humor. The stake presidency was especially solicitous of him because of his advanced age and difficulty in walking. As Edmunds and Kennedy each took an arm to help him up the incline to the Edmunds home, where they were to have lunch, President McKay stopped, as Kennedy recalled the incident, and said, "You know, I can pull one of you up here, but I can't pull both of you up this hill."

Lenora Kennedy, John K. Edmunds, David O. McKay, and David M. Kennedy at the Chicago Stake Center dedication, May 6, 1962

Mormons have been highly praised for their welfare program, which provides assistance to members who are out of work or in need for various reasons. An aspect of the welfare plan emphasized by church leaders is storage by each family of enough food supplies to last for one year. As a member of the stake presidency, Kennedy began to feel a sense of guilt that his own supply was woefully inadequate. He decided that at least he should have a year's supply of wheat. The result was a phone call to Lenora's cousin, Delbert Wright, who was a vice-president of General Mills, asking if he could supply the Kennedys with some good clean wheat for storage. Wright said he had just what they needed. It turned out that he had more than they needed. "The railroad's on the phone. Did you order some wheat?" David's secretary asked one day as he was about to leave the office. David admitted that he had and said he would pick it up on his way home. To his surprise he found that Wright had sent two *tons* rather than the two bags he expected to pick up. After Kennedy donated a year's supply of wheat to Edmunds and Paul W. Jespersen, the other counselor in the stake presidency, he still had something approaching a decade's supply.

The next step was to buy a grinder, but then David found that he was grinding wheat for the whole ward. Skilled in the art of negotiation, he offered Barbara the grinder and the wheat if she would provide him and Lenora with a weekly supply of home-made bread. The deal was struck; Barbara not only supplied her father with homemade bread, but she sweetened the bargain with two cats to rout the mice who threatened to make David's wheat their own.

In 1963, when John Edmunds was released as stake president and the Chicago Stake was divided into three stakes, David Kennedy's sixteen years of service in the stake presidency came to an end. The association with Edmunds was one of the most reward-ing experiences in Kennedy's life. Theirs was a reciprocal loyalty; Edmunds kept Kennedy as a counselor through his extended ill-ness and during the year when he worked in Washington, com-muting between the capital and Chicago each Wednesday for stake presidency meeting. Later, when Kennedy became president and chairman of Continental and was deeply involved in the affairs of the bank and the community, Edmunds still preferred to have him as a counselor than someone else who might be able to give more time to the Church. For Kennedy's part he made every effort to carry his share of the burden that fell on the stake presidency. As long as Edmunds felt he was needed, he was willing to juggle his busy schedule to give pride of place to church service.

Kennedy's position at Continental, his service in the Treasury Department in 1953 and 1954, and his rising influence in the bank had attracted the attention of authorities of the Mormon church even before he became chairman. Continental was one of the larg-est banks in the country; many Utah banks were part of its corre-spondent bank network, and Kennedy had many friends among Utah bankers. As his reputation grew, it was inevitable that church leaders would seek his advice on a variety of issues related to the banks the Church then owned.

When Kennedy was consulted about the management of Zions First National Bank, owned by the Church, he urged President McKay to delegate more authority to the bank's officers. As part of that delegation process, he convinced President McKay that he should become the chairman of the board and relinquish the title of president to Orval Adams, who was performing that function but with the title of executive vice-president. Kennedy was instrumental in persuading Church leaders to have William F. Edwards undertake a study of the bank's lending and investment policies, which resulted in changes that improved the bank's profitability.

One Church leader who sought out Kennedy—not for specific advice on church-related banking and financial problems but for general information on economic and financial matters—was Harold B. Lee, a member of the Quorum of the Twelve Apostles who later became President of the Church. The two men met for lunch frequently when Lee was in Chicago, and discussed current economic trends both on the national and international scene. Lee was not merely content to discuss these issues with Kennedy; he also asked for additional reading material that would broaden his understanding of the world in which the Church had to operate.

A church project in which Kennedy became deeply involved was the restoration of Nauvoo, a community in southern Illinois that had been headquarters for the Latter-day Saints in the 1840s until their exodus west. The project began with the enthusiasm and energy of J. LeRoy Kimball, who purchased the Heber C. Kimball home, refurnished it with carefully selected furnishings from the period, and restored the exterior. With that beginning, Kimball was able to persuade Church authorities that something ought to be done about the rest of Nauvoo. The result was the creation in 1962 of Nauvoo Restoration, Inc., and Kennedy was asked to be a member of the board of trustees. When he accepted the assignment, he had little idea what the organization intended to accomplish at Nauvoo, and he soon found that no clear consensus existed among members of the board.

The absence of a clearly defined plan created confusion, not only about the funding of the project but also about its nature and purpose. One suggestion was to portray Nauvoo as part of the overall migration of the American people westward; the emphasis would be on Nauvoo in its historical setting. The story of the Church would be an important—but not overriding—element in that concept. A competing concept was to emphasize the place Nauvoo played in the Mormon drama, as more than just another frontier city. The purpose of the project, it was argued, should be to tell the story of Joseph Smith, the city he founded, and the faith that led the Mormons to Nauvoo and beyond. The matter was resolved in 1971 when the Nauvoo restoration project was brought under the overall direction, including budgeting and planning, of the Church Information and Historic Arts Committee of which Mark E. Petersen, a member of the Quorum of the Twelve Apostles, was the chairman. This reorganization made it clear that the role of the Church would be the dominant theme of the project. Once the conceptual was solved, the restoration of Nauvoo and the message it conveyed was integrated into the expanding network of the Church's missionary system.

While these discussions were under way, Kennedy found himself in a semi-comic correspondence with nationally known author Samuel Taylor after Hugh B. Brown, a counselor in the First Presidency, suggested that the board invite Taylor to write a drama about Nauvoo. Taylor came to a meeting of the board and outlined his suggestions for the play. It seemed to Kennedy that Taylor wanted to concentrate on the events leading up to the martyrdom of Joseph Smith, and in Taylor's version of Nauvoo's history, many of the Saints' difficulties were of their own making. Kennedy thought it a story of conflict and death. In contrast, he told Taylor, for him the story of Nauvoo was one of "preparation, gathering, the building of the priesthood, the building of a temple . . . moving westward, the development of the whole Western United States." He then asked Taylor what he had written and said he would like to see some of his writing.

Taylor responded to Kennedy's query with a long letter detailing his professional career as a writer, with more information, he wrote, than what was provided in "the happy little puff-sheet typed up by my wife." But Taylor's letter was not just a casual response to Kennedy's request for information. He was piqued that Kennedy did not know who he was, and he could not resist a rhetorical thrust. Perhaps the information he was sending along would "be enough to establish that there *is* a Sam Taylor. Next question: Is there a David Kennedy? Nobody has given me a puff-sheet on *you*."

Kennedy's response acknowledged his ignorance of Taylor's work: "Apparently Sam Taylor does exist. And your letter proves that he has written widely for many publications and on many subjects. It is no wonder that you were shocked that I was not acquainted with your work." But he was not overawed with the recital of Taylor's credits, declaring: "You question whether there is a David Kennedy since no one has given you a puff-sheet on me. I have been required on many occasions to give an account of my background and experience together with references to or copies of (the limited) material that I have written. I had to do this again just recently in connection with Continental Bank's application to establish a branch in Paris. It could not be expected that you would know of me—a boy from a ranch in Randolph, Utah, and in any event this is not important. But it is important that I know you

Original board of Nauvoo Restoration: A. Hamer Reiser (left), J. Willard Marriott, Alice Marriott, Lenora Kennedy, David M. Kennedy, Ed Kendrew, Mrs. Kendrew, Harold Fabian, LeRoy Kimball

and your work if I am to approve as a Trustee of Nauvoo Restoration of your writing the script for the Nauvoo story."

In the end Taylor did not receive the commission to write the story of Nauvoo; the trustees had a script written that Kennedy did not much like, but at least the tone was right. Taylor went on to write his own account of Nauvoo in his novel *Nightfall at Nauvoo*.

Whether in the capacity of a formal calling within church organizations or as an informal advisor, Kennedy took his church membership seriously. It was, after all, an integral part of his youth in Randolph and Riverdale, and he had left a young bride almost on their wedding day to undertake a mission for the Church to England. David and Lenora's involvement in church programs immeasurably eased the transition from rural Utah to cosmopolitan Washington, and he learned during his service as bishop and in the stake presidency how the Church could change and enrich the lives of its members. That was merely prelude to his conviction, which Mormons describe as a testimony, that the doctrines of the Church represent truth in its ultimate and transcendent sense. His commitment to his religious faith does not explain all there is to know about David Kennedy, but without taking that key element of his character into consideration, the inner core of the man will be missed. That commitment gave a broader meaning to his professional life, for it formed the basis of his father's explanation that the purpose of life is to serve God and one's fellowmen. It buttressed and reinforced his strong natural affection for his family, for it taught him that family ties stretch across the eternities. And it gave him strength to resist the temptation to see success solely in terms of professional achievement.

13

PUBLIC SERVICE:
MAKING A DIFFERENCE

In tracing David Kennedy's career in the bank along with his church work, it must be kept in mind that until he was released from the stake presidency in 1963, he was fitting both of those tasks into an ever more demanding schedule. Yet in addition to the claim on his time by the bank and the Church, he took on still other demanding commitments. His position at Continental involved not only managing internal affairs but also representing the bank on the local and national scene. Walter Cummings had focused his energies on the bank, while the time he gave to activities outside the bank was reserved for his support of the Catholic church. The story is told that when someone suggested that the bank might contribute to some of the great educational institutions in the Chicago area, he ignored the University of Chicago and Northwestern University to suggest that the bank give five thousand dollars each to Loyola, DePaul, and Mundelein.

David Kennedy became chairman with a much different administrative style and with an already sharply developed sense of public service, which was reflected in his church work and his appointment to the Treasury in 1953. His interest in public service heightened the sense of civic responsibility of other bank officers. Continental employees had always participated in the Crusade of Mercy, a citywide effort to raise funds for charitable purposes.

When Kennedy became president of Continental, he encouraged bank employees to increase their contributions to the crusade. More importantly, he freed up the time of top bank executives to chair the crusade, a year-long assignment. In addition, Continental created the Continental Bank Foundation in 1962 to formalize the institution's support of health, welfare, cultural, educational, and other community causes. Kennedy's recognition of Continental's civic responsibility made it easier for bank officers to be involved in their own community interests.

Kennedy himself set the example by his personal commitment to a variety of civic programs. The most notable of these was his appointment as chairman of the Mayor's Committee for Economic and Cultural Development. That appointment made him an ally of one of the most fascinating political figures of mid-twentieth century America: Mayor Richard J. Daley. During Kennedy's years at Continental, Daley was the undisputed political boss of Chicago, one of a new breed of big-city bosses who while maintaining their traditional power base—in Daley's case it was the Cook County Democratic party—won the support of influential business and civic leaders. These modern political bosses, Edward Banfield has pointed out, were able to mobilize this support by a fourfold strategy to provide "good government." As Banfield notes: " 'Good government' is some kind of mixture—the proportions vary greatly

David M. Kennedy, right, accepts the President's "E" Certificate of Service on behalf of Continental Illinois from Secretary of Commerce Luther Hodges

from context to context—of the following principal ingredients: (a) 'reform' of the old-fashioned kind, i.e., the suppression of vice, crime, and political corruption; (b) 'efficiency' in the sense of doing what public administration "experts" recommend with respect to organization structure and 'housekeeping' functions like budgeting and personnel management; (c) following 'progressive' policies in the fields of housing, planning, race relations, and welfare; and (d) executing big projects—airports and exhibition halls . . . to boost the size, business, and repute of the city."

Daley was a master of this strategy, which gained for him the reputation as mayor of "The City That Works." The alliance of Daley (born and raised in Chicago, a Catholic, and a passionate Democrat) and Kennedy (a product of rural Utah, a Mormon, and a Republican) was on its face an unlikely one. They shared, however, an interest in the improvement and development of Chicago, and that interest bound them together in a fruitful alliance. It was a classic case of a diverse set of interests converging on a common policy. While in both cases there was an altruistic element in that common policy, there was at the same time a hard core of self-interest. Daley enhanced his political power in Chicago by providing "good government." That policy forestalled the emergence of a "good government" party centered in the business community with a base sufficiently broad to topple him from office. Kennedy's interest centered on the need to assure a viable central business district in downtown Chicago, where Continental had its headquarters. Also, he was aware that his visibility as a civic leader was helping him to make Continental "the bank of Chicago."

Kennedy's chairmanship of the mayor's committee led to a request from Daley in 1965 that he head a committee to study ways to improve public services in Chicago. Recognizing that such improvements would significantly enhance the overall attractiveness and viability of the downtown area, Kennedy accepted. With the help of his staff at Continental and individuals from other firms, he proposed a bond issue of between $200 and $300 million dollars to improve city lighting, public transportation, the sewer system, and fire services. Daley liked the thrust of the report, but since Chicagoans had defeated a bond proposal in 1962, he thought the committee was too optimistic about getting such a large bond issue approved now. He decided, therefore, to propose a $195 million bond issue to finance only the most pressing of the projects proposed by the committee. Kennedy, believing that one of the reasons for the 1962 defeat was that the issue was part of a general election, suggested presenting the new bond issue at a special election. Although Daley had some misgivings about the cost of a special election, he agreed to schedule one for June 1966.

Kennedy now became the head of the Citizens Bond Committee for a Greater Chicago, which included representatives of the major civic, religious, and business organizations. He viewed Daley's influence and control of the Democratic party as crucial to the success of the election. The mayor would have to sell this election precinct by precinct, he told Daley, and he expressed confidence in Daley's ability to do so. The combined efforts of the Citizens Bond Committee and Daley's political influence assured a two-to-one margin of victory for the bond issue. While some would charge that Kennedy's interest in the election was based primarily on the profits that would accrue to Continental from its underwriting of the bonds, the benefits to Chicago, which were enormous, belied the charge that Kennedy's involvement was motivated purely by self-interest.

Economic development, Kennedy found, was easy to sell to the public particularly to the business community. Cultural development was another story. While he was on vacation in Idaho, a phone call from Mayor Daley telling him that the Chicago Symphony needed $300,000 to settle a dispute between the Chicago Symphony Foundation and the musicians gave Kennedy his most telling lesson in raising money for the arts. When he heard the amount to be raised, he protested that it would be difficult. When he hesitated, the mayor admitted that he had already agreed to the settlement. At that point Kennedy gave in. "All right," he said "we'll make you honest." After trying a variety of schemes, all of which on closer examination promised to lose money, Kennedy turned to "arm twisting." At a meeting of the executive committee of the mayor's committee, he promised that Continental would match the contributions from other members of the group. When the last arm had been twisted, he had the $300,000, but the mood of the group was sullen, and they gave their money only after extracting a promise from Kennedy that he would not use that particular strategy again.

Kennedy supported civic projects because they promised indirect as well as direct ways to benefit the bank. Other appointments he accepted because of their intrinsic interest. Perhaps foremost among these was his appointment in 1957 to serve on the board of trustees of the University of Chicago. He was a member of the investment committee of the board and headed several successful fund-raising drives. He was in charge of the Chicago area for a $300 million fund-raising effort that was one of the largest an American university had undertaken up to that time. His major interest as a trustee was the business school headed by George P. Shultz, who later was Kennedy's colleague in Richard M. Nixon's cabinet as Secretary of Labor. Together, Kennedy and Shultz promoted an exchange program giving students at the University of Chicago the opportunity to study at universities in Belgium and England and to serve internships with firms in the host countries as part of their degree program. Likewise, Belgian and British students took part of their training at Chicago in internships with Chicago-based firms.

In 1966, Kennedy's experience at the University of Chicago brought him a request from N. Eldon Tanner, a member of the First Presidency of the Mormon church, to head a major fund-raising drive for Brigham Young University. Kennedy had learned from his experience at the University of Chicago that the primary source of support for a university is its alumni. In the case of BYU, most of the alumni were members of the Mormon church, and President David O. McKay was reluctant to approve fund-raising drives that would place additional financial demands on people who were already under commandment to tithe and were expected to contribute to missionary work, building projects, and welfare needs. However, after mulling the matter over, he finally gave his approval for the university to target its alumni as potential donors.

When Kennedy accepted President Tanner's request, he knew he would be working closely with Ernest L. Wilkinson, president of the university. In their discussions, Kennedy found Wilkinson unrealistic about the difficulties involved in raising money from foundations, warning him that raising money from foundations for a church-related school would be far more difficult than doing so for a secular institution like the University of Chicago. BYU, Kennedy predicted, would raise money from foundations only if the foundation was interested in a specific area and if it was convinced that the university was doing some of the best work in the world in that field. After knocking on several foundation doors to no avail, Wilkinson found that Kennedy was right. Kennedy regretfully acknowledged that, although Wilkinson was a longtime friend, he was a hindrance rather than a help in raising money from foundations, because he was known for strong political opinions that were critical of many of the programs supported by those he was asking for contributions. His age also worked against him, for he was well beyond the age when most university presidents retire, and foundation executives told Kennedy they couldn't understand why the Church had kept him in office for so long.

BYU alumni proved to be the major source of funds, and before Kennedy resigned to become Secretary of the Treasury, the fundraising team he put together raised twenty-seven million dollars in an era when BYU had losing football teams. Non-alumni Church members who were supporters of the university also proved to be generous contributors. Many of these gifts, however, were property or businesses that had to be managed to be profitable. Kennedy knew that the University of Chicago had turned down gifts of this kind because the administration felt it lacked the expertise to manage the properties. When BYU began to accept these gifts, it became apparent to Kennedy that some other organization was needed to provide the management skills the university lacked. Out of that concern, as well as other problems, grew the Deseret Trust Company, which now manages gifts of property and businesses that come to the school or the Church.

A Washington-based organization on whose board of trustees Kennedy accepted an appointment was the Brookings Institution, the original "think tank." The appointment was made in 1961, and Kennedy resigned from the post only when he became Secretary of the Treasury in January 1969. His involvement in Brookings went beyond attending board meetings. He was actively involved in speaking and in leading discussion groups, and he brought members of the Brookings staff to the bank for discussions on economic issues. Whether or not he agreed with their conclusions, he admired the work done at Brookings. However, when he became Secretary of the Treasury, he found reason to complain about some of its activities.

Brookings was created as a nonprofit, nonpartisan research organization concerned with a large variety of public policy issues. Over the years, many of its staff members became closely associated with the Democratic party. Kennedy found during the struggle over tax reform in 1969 that Brookings staff members were not only testifying against the administration's bill, which Kennedy thought well within their rights, but were also serving as advisors to the Democratic policy committees of the Senate and the House. Without mentioning Brookings by name, Kennedy suggested that tax-exempt organizations ought to be careful about their partisan activities, or they might well be found in violation of internal revenue laws and regulations. Kermit Gordon, head of Brookings, correctly assumed that there was more to Kennedy's comment than a general warning. Acting on that assumption, he asked Kennedy why, after his long association with Brookings, there was this veiled threat. After all, members of the Brookings staff frequently testified before House and Senate committees. Kennedy put the matter bluntly. As he recalled the conversation, he told Gordon, "I have no objection to men testifying. We testify. They can testify for or against, whatever their position. But when they step aside and act on the side as advisors, then it's not open testimony. You've got a Democratic organization over there. You haven't any Republican in your organization."

Gordon admitted that Kennedy was right, but when he asked for the names of some reputable Republican economists Brookings might hire, Kennedy conceded that the new administration had brought the best of them into the government. The meeting ended with an agreement that Brookings staff members would cease to serve as advisors to congressional policy committees.

David Kennedy learned that no matter what area of community service he entered, he always ended up raising funds, but it also enriched his life. Service on the boards of two hospitals in Chicago gave him a circle of acquaintances and friends from other churches. He was a trustee of Presbyterian–St. Luke hospital in Chicago, one of the finest in the area, and also served as treasurer for fund-raising drives on behalf of Mercy Hospital, a Catholic institution. The latter association not only brought him the satisfaction of helping a great hospital but also the friendship of the administrator, Sister Mary Huberta. Each Christmas Eve Sister Huberta and members of her staff visited the Kennedy home and brought homemade whole-wheat bread to the Mormon banker.

In addition to his civic activities, Kennedy continued to be active in the American Bankers Association. He was elected a member of the government borrowing committee in 1955 on his return to Continental from the Treasury. In 1960 he became chairman of the committee, serving in that capacity until 1965. The borrowing committee was for the most part a self-perpetuating body with the same people serving year after year. While he was chairman, Kennedy, with the cooperation of his friend and competitor Homer Livingston, president of Chicago First National, broke up the self-perpetuating clique in favor of rotation in office. Service on the

David and Lenora Kennedy at American Bankers Association meetings, White Sulphur Springs, West Virginia, in April 1968

committee was an important assignment, since the committee was consulted by the Treasury on problems of managing the national debt and financing budget deficits.

During the years he was chairman at Continental, Kennedy was a member of the boards of directors for numerous large corporations, including Abbot Laboratories, Adela Investment Company, Commonwealth Edison, International Harvester, Robert Morris Associates, Swift & Company, Pullman Company, and U.S. Gypsum Company. These appointments took time, for he had to absorb enough of the welter of reports and other information to make a worthwhile contribution. Had it not been for the ability of Donald Graham and Tilden Cummings, on whom Kennedy could rely with complete confidence to manage the day-to-day affairs of the bank, he could not have carried such a heavy representational load.

Kennedy's public service brought him the honors that traditionally come to those who willingly give their time and resources to worthy causes. He was awarded honorary doctor of law degrees by Brigham Young University in 1960, Roosevelt University of Chicago in 1964, George Washington University in 1965, Northwestern University in 1969, and Illinois College (Jacksonville) in 1972. In addition, Lake Forest College of Chicago presented him with an honorary doctoral degree in humane letters in 1967, and Weber State College awarded its former student with an honorary degree of doctor of humanities in 1969.

Among the other recognitions that came to him were the Business Statesmanship Award from the Harvard Business School Association of Chicago in 1965, the Founders Day Award from Loyola University in 1966, and the Meritorious Achievement in the Field of Business Award from the College of Business at the University of Utah in 1967. The Chicago chapter of the Public Relations Society of America recognized his commitment to Chicago with its Public Relations Award for Community Service, and the American Marketing Association named him the Marketing Man of the Year in 1965; that was followed by the American Statistical Association honoring him with its Decision Maker of the Year Award in 1968. Typically, the citations accompanying the awards stressed his

218

Among guests at dinner of the Public Relations Society of America, Chicago chapter, honoring David M. Kennedy: John K. Edmunds, left; Kennedy; Chicago Mayor Richard J. Daley; Governor George Romney of Michigan; J. Darold Johnson of LDS Chicago Stake presidency

achievements as a banker, public servant, and civic leader and recognized the personal qualities of integrity, vision, and judgment that characterized his career. These awards and honors were, as an economist might say, nonpecuniary rewards for the time and energy he spent in public and civic service.

David Kennedy's knowledge, experience, and prestige were in demand at the national level as well as in Chicago. He served on a variety of national advisory groups, including the Federal Advisory Council of the Federal Reserve System, the council of the Radio Free Europe Fund, and the Council for Latin America. In 1965 he was invited to participate in the White House Conference on International Cooperation, held in conjunction with the designation by the United Nations of 1965 as the "Year of International Cooperation." He was chairman of the committee on International Cooperation in Monetary and Development Finance Matters. The recommendation of the committee that aroused the most interest was a proposal that the international monetary system "be further reinforced as a result of concerted action to devise supplementary assets to be held in official reserves." Although the committee report did not mention reducing the role of gold in the international monetary system, the suggestion of "supplementary assets to be held in official reserves" sparked a sharp debate over the "tyranny" of gold in the international monetary system.

Kennedy's most significant public service resulted from a request by Lyndon B. Johnson that he chair a presidential commission to study how to improve the organization and presentation of the federal budget. The commission's recommendations fundamentally changed the way the federal budget is reported, and decades later, Kennedy's successful leadership of the commission remains one of his most lasting contributions to public service.

Johnson appointed the commission because considerable confusion had long existed over the meaning of the word *budget*. At least three different meanings had been given that word. Traditionally, the budget simply meant the amount of money the federal government takes in and pays out each year. In the 1960s this was called the administrative budget, and it was this budget that got the headlines. A second meaning of the word developed after the 1930s when the government began financing programs, principally Social Security, highways, unemployment, and railroad and civil service retirement, from earmarked tax revenues deposited in a trust fund. Receipts and payments from these funds were not included in the administrative budget so another set of figures that included them was designated the consolidated cash budget. A third set of figures, which included the trust funds but excluded government loans and some other transactions, was called the national income accounts budget.

Each of these budgets had its uses, and each of them had its strong advocates. The problem, however, was that each gave a different picture of government spending. In fiscal year 1968 the administrative budget estimated government receipts at $126.9 billion and expenditures at $135 billion, resulting in a deficit of $8.1 billion. The consolidated cash budget estimated revenues at $168.1 billion and spending at $172.4 billion—indicating a deficit of $4.3 billion. The national income accounts budget gave still another set of figures: receipts of $167.1 billion, expenditures of $169.2 billion, and an apparently more palatable deficit of $2.1 billion. These different budgets, which both confused the public and were used by Congress or the administration to attack or defend a political position, brought complaints from economists, congressional leaders, and the press, and led Johnson to appoint the study commission—and Kennedy.

Kennedy was at first reluctant to accept the President's invitation. At a meeting with Charles Schultze, who was then director of the Bureau of the Budget, Kennedy said he believed that presidential commissions do a lot of work but nothing ever comes of them. He repeated that concern in a meeting with the President: "This is a political thing. You'll want to use it politically, and our report will not be implemented." Kennedy was surprised when Johnson promised that if the commission made a report, it would be implemented. Relying on that presidential promise, Kennedy agreed to accept the chairmanship of the commission, which included Secretary of the Treasury Henry H. Fowler; Carl Hayden and Milton Young, chairman and ranking member, respectively, of the Senate Appropriations Committee; George Mahon and Frank Bow, chairman and ranking member, respectively, of the House Appropriations Committee; Elmer Staats, Comptroller General; Schultze; and prominent economists and leaders from the financial community.

Johnson's letter of March 17, 1967, appointing Kennedy chairman of the commission, welcomed any suggestions the commission might have for improving the presentation of the budget. "The principal areas for the Commission to examine, however," he wrote, "is the set of concepts that underlie the major budgetary totals and their summary presentation." He expressed the hope that the commission would be able to complete its work by September so that "at least some of the recommendations of the Commission can be incorporated in next year's budget."

With that charge, Kennedy set to work with a small staff that never exceeded six people and was headed by his colleague at Continental, Robert Mayo. Furthermore, given the September deadline set by the President, he decided that the commission would meet only two days each month but all members of the commission would have to be present—they could not send substitutes. This would alleviate the confusion and delay of having to clear agreements reached with absent commission members. Kennedy made his point about substitutes when he would not accept a substitute for Fowler, even if it was the under secretary, Joseph Barr.

Kennedy's strategy was not to push for an early agreement but to give members a chance to have a wide-ranging discussion of the issues. As areas on which there was consensus and conflict became apparent, Mayo and his staff began work on a draft of the report, which Mayo reviewed with Kennedy before it was presented to the commission. Each successive draft was discussed in detail in commission meetings and then given to members of the commission or the staff for preparation of a final draft. The writing and rewriting of these drafts, although tedious, finally produced a report that commission members could unanimously support, a goal Kennedy pushed with single-minded determination.

The commission met the deadline imposed by the President, and on October 10 the commission submitted its report. A central thrust of the final report was that "a unified summary budget statement be used to replace the present three or more competing concepts that are both confusing to the public and the Congress and deficient in certain essential characteristics." The "unified summary budget statement" should reflect the full scope of the government's activities, including the trust funds administered by the federal government. All told, the commission made thirteen major recommendations for improving the process of presenting the budget to Congress. All of them were designed to make as understandable as possible a document whose length and complexity made that task difficult at best. It was no easy task, and agreement was sometimes difficult, as inferred in the report's statement that "not every member of the Commission subscribes to each and every observation, premise, conclusion, or recommendation in the Report." There was one minor dissent by Fowler, Schultze, and Robert Turner on a technical point, but Kennedy met his goal of unity within the commission, for members reached "complete unanimity regarding the main objective of a unified budget system."

On December 12 Schultze thanked the commission for its service. The President has directed, Schultze wrote, "that we make as many of the necessary changes as feasible in the budget documents that are now in preparation." At a news conference two days later, Schultze announced that "the fiscal 1969 budget will offer a unified budget statement to replace the three concepts presently in use—the administrative budget, the consolidated cash budget, and the national income accounts budget."

It was a remarkable achievement that would have a lasting effect on the American budget process. Kennedy's patient but firm leadership made that success possible. Because of his close association with staff director Mayo, as chairman he was never caught between the staff and commission members. While he gave members the widest possible latitude, considering the deadline against which they were working, he moved them with all deliberate speed toward his goal of a report they could all support.

Ironically, Kennedy might well have been sitting in Henry Fowler's place as a member of the commission had he been in greater agreement with Johnson's economic policies. Early in 1965, C. Douglas Dillon, then Secretary of the Treasury, notified President Johnson that he would be leaving in the spring. Speculation immediately began on who his successor would be. Finally, two names emerged: Donald C. Cook, president of American Electric Power Company, and David M. Kennedy, chairman of Continental Illinois Bank. When Cook refused the appointment, the press made Kennedy the front-runner. A United Press International (UPI) release on March 18 reported that "Kennedy's impending appointment was announced during a closed meeting of the House Ways and Means Committee by its chairman, Wilbur D. Mills, D-Ark." Unbeknownst to the press, the President *had* decided to offer the position to Kennedy, but he changed his mind after Kennedy expressed his belief that the cost of Johnson's "Great Society" was too heavy a burden on the economy. Consequently, he recalls telling the President, "I'd either be Secretary for a short duration or else I'd have to compromise on my own views." Johnson did not comment on

Kennedy's views, but they evidently dissuaded him. UPI had to follow up its prediction that Kennedy would be Secretary of the Treasury with a news bulletin some forty-three minutes later announcing that Henry Fowler was the nominee.

John Glenn, astronaut (and later U.S. senator from Ohio) with David M. Kennedy

14

SECRETARY OF THE TREASURY: NOMINATION AND CONFIRMATION

Richard M. Nixon emerged victorious in the 1968 presidential election in one of the most remarkable comebacks in American politics. Barely two years before, when he was defeated in the California gubernatorial election, his concession speech ended with a sardonic comment that the press wouldn't have Richard Nixon to kick around anymore. Yet on November 6, 1968, he was President-elect of the United States. It was a turbulent period of American history. The war in Vietnam divided the country, and student protests against the war spread across the nation and culminated in the tragedy at Kent State. The protests had moved beyond the college campus into the streets and reached an intensity that drove Lyndon Baines Johnson to the conclusion that he could not govern the country. The civil rights movement was still dismayed over the assassination of Martin Luther King, and hovering over the campaign was the death of Robert Kennedy. Nixon's rival was Hubert Humphrey, a long-time leader in the Democratic party, vice-president under Johnson, and an orator of some power. The election was complicated by the presence of George Wallace, who attacked both of the parties for their stand on civil rights. In the end Nixon won the election because Wallace won five states that normally voted

225

Democratic and Humphrey refused to repudiate Johnson's policies in Vietnam, thus failing to draw a sharp distinction between his and Nixon's positions on that conflict.

Nixon was one of the most controversial politicians in American history. Beginning with his successful campaign for the Senate against Helen Gahagan Douglas, he aroused either enthusiastic support or implacable enmity. His role in exposing Alger Hiss, his famous "Checkers" televised speech explaining the political slush fund raised for his use, his forceful political attacks on all Democrats, and his kitchen debates with Khrushchev were all equally praised and damned by supporters and detractors. He came within an eyelash of being elected president in 1960; then in a statesman-like act, he refused to challenge the outcome of the election to avoid disrupting the country for an extended period of time. Even in his 1968 victory he could not claim vindication, for he was elected with only a plurality of the vote. If he were to disarm his critics, it would not be with an overwhelming mandate from the voters but by a performance as president that would give the lie to their predictions of disaster.

Nixon's first term in office must be seen on its own terms, untainted by Watergate and his resignation. He faced formidable problems: the war in Vietnam was still unresolved, the tension between the United States and the Soviet Union continued unabated, and he inherited a troubled economy weakened by Johnson's determination not to let the war interfere with the construction of the Great Society. Nixon could not do much immediately about the ills of the nation, but he could set the tone of his administration by selecting cabinet members whose reputation, ability, and integrity would silence his critics. Past presidents had dominated the headlines in the weeks following their election by announcing one by one the members of their cabinets. Nixon decided to make a television spectacular of that process by announcing his appointments simultaneously on a nationwide television broadcast.

There was, of course, speculation by the press immediately after the election about the composition of Nixon's cabinet. Press interest has always centered on the three most important positions: State, Defense, and Treasury. As early as November 28,

Rowland Evans and Robert Novak reported that David Kennedy was a front-runner for the Treasury. That public speculation had an interesting background: a rumor was abroad that Maurice Stans would be named Secretary of the Treasury as a reward for his successful fund-raising efforts during the campaign. That possibility dismayed Charls Walker, executive secretary of the American Bankers Association. To forestall the Stans appointment, Walker decided that an alternative candidate must be put forward. Walker's candidate was David M. Kennedy, and he immediately began to enlist support among his friends in the banking community, including Robert B. Anderson, a former Secretary of the Treasury under Eisenhower, and Howard Laeri, chairman of National City Bank and a close friend of John Mitchell, who became Attorney General in the first Nixon administration.

The first that Kennedy realized this underground effort was nearing success was when a telephone call came November 26 from a close friend, Senator Charles Percy from Illinois, who asked if he would accept an appointment to Treasury if it were offered. Kennedy's response was to list all the reasons why he should stay at the bank. But when he was pushed to the wall, he admitted that he would give the matter careful consideration.

The day after Thanksgiving, this informal approach from Percy was replaced with a formal offer to become Secretary of the Treasury. The offer was transmitted by Laeri, who said that he was making the offer at the request of John Mitchell. Laeri explained that they had used this indirect route so that if Kennedy refused, they could deny that the president-elect had been turned down. Kennedy told Laeri that William McChesney Martin, then chairman of the Federal Reserve Board, was the best qualified man in the country to be Secretary of the Treasury and that Nixon ought to look to him. Laeri's response was that Nixon would not consider Martin under any conditions and would probably not reappoint him as chairman of the Federal Reserve Board. Finally, Kennedy authorized Laeri to tell Mitchell: "I sincerely prefer and hope that President-Elect Nixon will not ask me. There are other qualified men and I will be glad to give additional names. If he does pursue this further I will, of course, give the matter very careful, soul-searching consideration. I have a health problem and would have to consult my doctor." His protests were swept aside, and his conversation with Laeri was followed by a telephone call from Mitchell on December 1 asking if Kennedy could meet with Nixon in New York on December 4. Kennedy agreed, and the meeting was held in Herbert Brownell's apartment so he would not be seen at the Hotel Pierre, where Nixon had his headquarters.

Kennedy began the conversation by telling the President-elect how flattered he was by the offer that had come to him through Laeri. Nixon explained that the procedure had been chosen to avoid any unnecessary publicity, and Kennedy said that he understood and suggested that their discussion be treated as preliminary with neither of them to reach a decision that night. What Kennedy was suggesting was a replay of the "kabuki" strategy he had learned in his negotiations with the Japanese. If, he told Nixon, what was under discussion was the possibility of Kennedy becoming Secretary of the Treasury and Kennedy decided not to pursue the matter further, then in "no case could it be said he asked me and I turned him down." Kennedy also did not want the pressure of having to make a decision in Nixon's presence; he wanted a chance to talk to Donald Graham and Tilden Cummings at the bank, and most of all with Lenora and the children.

In their wide-ranging discussion, Kennedy expressed concern about his health. He wondered if he could keep pace with the younger, more vigorous men in the administration. He had been examined by his doctor, Robert Moore Jones, before meeting with Nixon, and the verdict was ambiguous. He had a history of bleeding ulcers, and lately he found that after working long hours under intense pressure, he required a day or two of rest. Nixon was sympathetic but not deterred by Kennedy's health problems. Most men who work under pressure get ulcers, he reminded Kennedy, and with the choice of good subordinates, Kennedy could delegate many of the tasks that former secretaries had made their own.

Kennedy then turned to his concerns about the relationship between the President and his Secretary of the Treasury. He wanted some assurance that he would not have to deal with the President through the White House staff. He told Nixon that he had no objections to working with the staff, but he worried about the way messages got garbled as they moved through the staff structure. Kennedy's recollection of the President-elect's response was that four departments—Treasury, State, Defense, and the Attorney General—would report directly to him and have access to him whenever they desired. He assured Kennedy that he, Kennedy, would have full control of appointments within the Treasury, and that Treasury would have the dominant voice in making fiscal and monetary policy.

Kennedy also raised the issue of the appointment of the chairman of the Council of Economic Advisors (CEA) and the director of the Bureau of the Budget, since he would be working closely with them. He expressed his approval that Paul McCracken had been appointed chairman of the CEA and was pleased to learn that Robert Mayo, his colleague at Continental, was under consideration as director of the Bureau of the Budget. As they discussed personnel, Kennedy repeated his belief that there were others more qualified to be Secretary of the Treasury. Specifically, he mentioned David Rockefeller. Nixon said that Rockefeller had taken himself out of consideration because he had just become chairman of Chase Manhattan Bank and felt that he could not leave for another two or three years. Kennedy also suggested that he could best serve on an ad hoc basis as he had done as chairman of the Commission on Budget Concepts, or as a consultant to the President or the Secretary of the Treasury, roles he had played effectively in the past and in which he felt comfortable. Throughout the interview Kennedy was eager to discuss policy matters, but Nixon demurred, protesting that he was not an expert and relied heavily on his advisors on those issues. As Kennedy left, he recalled, he told Nixon that the presidency was the hardest job on earth: and "I don't know why you wanted the job, but you asked for it and now you have it, so may God bless you."

At the end of the meeting that evening, Kennedy agreed to give the President-elect his decision by Friday, December 6. His discussions with his family, colleagues, and friends did not make his decision any easier. Graham and Cummings hoped he would remain at the bank; the family worried whether his health would hold up under such weighty responsibilities. On the other hand, his friends urged him to enter the administration. John Edmunds was strongly in favor, and N. Eldon Tanner urged him to accept, as did Harold B. Lee, with whom he had breakfast the morning he met with Nixon. The matter was still much in the air December 6 when, at about 5:00 P.M., Kennedy received a call reminding him that the President-elect was waiting to hear from him and would be available until 7:00 P.M. Los Angeles time.

Given that deadline, Kennedy sat down and outlined what he intended to say. He reviewed with Lenora the major points in the outline: his health was not the best (Lenora was particularly concerned about that aspect of the call, but she would do whatever David decided); there were qualified people to take the position and he would help recruit the best possible man; and he would accept ad hoc consulting assignments of various lengths where he could serve well—all of which added up to an expression of a preference that Nixon choose someone else. After going over that outline with Lenora, David was realistic enough to realize that if Nixon brushed aside these objections—as he had in their discussion the previous Wednesday—he was in effect accepting the position as Secretary of the Treasury. Faced with that reality, they both agreed he should accept the appointment if Nixon still wanted him.

Kennedy called Nixon a few minutes before the seven o'clock deadline. He expressed his appreciation for the chance to talk with Nixon on Wednesday and signaled his support by saying that he had voted for him twice for President. In good humor, Nixon responded to that opening sally by asking if Kennedy's votes were counted.[1] Amused, Kennedy assured him that they had been and then launched into making the points he and Lenora had agreed upon. Nixon did not let him get all the way through before he countered with the reasons why he, as well as the country, needed the skills and experience Kennedy could bring to the Treasury. Kennedy's resistance was broken; he agreed to enter the Nixon administration as Secretary of the Treasury, with the caveat that he could not commit to a full term of office and might have to

Melvin Laird, Richard Nixon, William Rogers, and David M. Kennedy on the occasion of the announcement of Nixon's cabinet, December 11, 1968

submit his resignation within a year or two. Nixon then asked to speak to Lenora, who in their conversation expressed her own fears that David's health might not be strong enough to bear the strains of office. Nixon told Lenora that between the two of them they would take good care of her husband, and that he would see them the next Wednesday, when he would announce his cabinet to the nation.

On December 11, 1968, the Nixon cabinet was announced as planned on a nationwide television presentation. The twelve men who comprised the cabinet were for the most part middle-of-the-road Republicans. An editorial in the *New York Times* described them as a group very much "like their chief, intelligent, moderately conservative, competent and rather colorless." There were no women or blacks among them, nor did the cabinet include a Democrat—contrary to speculation that had appeared in the press immediately following Nixon's election. Yet Nixon clearly sought to include men from the full spectrum of the Republican party. Some—like Robert F. Finch, who became Secretary of Health, Education, and Welfare; William P. Rogers, Secretary of State; Melvin

R. Laird, Secretary of Defense, and John N. Mitchell, Attorney General—had long been associated with the President-elect and could be described as old friends. Most of them had been active in Republican party politics for many years. George Romney, tabbed to lead the Department of Housing and Urban Development, had been governor of Michigan; John A. Volpe, slated for the Department of Transportation, was governor of Massachusetts; and Walter J. Hickel, who would become Secretary of the Interior, was governor of Alaska. Maurice Stans, appointed as Secretary of Commerce, had impeccable Republican party credentials, as did the new Postmaster General, Winton M. Blount, who led volunteers for Nixon-Lodge in eight southeastern states in the 1960 presidential campaign. George P. Shultz, who would take over the Department of Labor, and Clifford M. Hardin, in Agriculture, were not known for their political partisanship nor were they longtime friends of the President-elect, but they enjoyed substantial reputations in their fields of expertise.

Kennedy was neither a close friend of Nixon's—they first met in Washington in 1954 and on ceremonial occasions in Chicago when Nixon was vice-president—nor was he active in Republican party affairs. His close association with Mayor Richard Daley was well known, and he described himself to Nixon as a Daley Democrat in Chicago and a Nixon Republican in national politics. His appointment rested on his ability and on the respect with which he was regarded in financial circles. The strong support for him from Rockefeller, Walker, and Anderson was based on their belief in his competence. They and other supporters recognized that his career at the Federal Reserve and as chairman of Continental gave him the necessary experience to deal with the public policy issues that would face the Secretary of the Treasury.

Kennedy's professional and personal qualifications to be Secretary of the Treasury were widely recognized by the press. Hobart Rowen, writing in the *Washington Post*, reported: "In the opinion of many economic and political experts in Washington, Kennedy will bring excellent equipment to the prestigious job of Secretary of the Treasury. He has the respect of his peers here and abroad, first of all as an eminently successful banker." The *Times* of London noted that Kennedy's appointment was "widely expected and will be greeted with enthusiasm both on Wall Street and in Washington." The *New York Times* described Kennedy as "a soft-spoken Mormon banker of moderately conservative views." What struck the writer was that while Kennedy was "orthodox in his financial outlook," he was "progressive in his views on the urban crisis, as both his words and actions show."

The laudatory press comments were echoed by letters and telegrams that poured in from friends and colleagues from across the nation. A telegram from David O. McKay, president of the Mormon church, was followed by a letter from Archbishop John Cody of Chicago, warning Kennedy about the lumps in the Treasury Secretary's chair in the cabinet room: "About a year and a half ago, during a meeting which President Johnson held in the Cabinet Room, I had the honor of being seated alongside of him in the Treasurer's chair. I remarked to the President after our two-hour meeting, that there were a few bumpy spots in that chair, and smilingly he said, 'You ought to be sitting in this one.' By the time you take over your new position, I am sure that all of the bumps will have been smoothed out."

Robert McNamara, president of the World Bank, sent a handwritten note telling Kennedy, "I don't know when an appointment has pleased me more." The same message came from Rockefeller: "Your appointment as Secretary of the Treasury is the best thing that could have happened from the point of view of the economy of the United States and indeed of the world." Reassuring was a note from Douglas Dillon, himself a former Secretary of the Treasury: "I can't tell you how delighted I am at the news that you will be taking over the Treasury. With you at the helm, we can all feel confident that we can successfully steer our way through the difficult times that lie ahead." There was also a letter of congratulations from Kennedy's old boss at the Federal Reserve, Marriner Eccles. But Eccles's letter, true to his style, was not only a letter of congratulations but also a lecture on the economic ills of the country being caused by the war in Vietnam. "There is little that the fiscal and monetary teams can do," Eccles wrote, "until the economic and social effects stemming from the Vietnam War are eliminated."

The six weeks between the announcement of Kennedy's appointment and his taking office were hectic. There were constant interviews in the media, a smooth transition of leadership at the bank had to be arranged, decisions about housing in Washington had to be made, briefings by outgoing Treasury officials had to be worked into the schedule, and plans for meeting conflict-of-interest statutes had to be developed. In that interim Kennedy also met briefly with the former president, Dwight Eisenhower, who advised him to work closely with the Democratic leadership in Congress on the major issues and suggested that Robert Anderson, who had been Secretary of the Treasury in the second Eisenhower administration, could be relied on for sound advice. That visit was followed by a trip to Texas to spend a day with Lyndon B. Johnson on his ranch. Johnson showed Kennedy around his ranch, followed by a pleasant lunch with him and his wife, Lady Bird. Later Johnson and Kennedy discussed the war in Vietnam, how to get along with Congress, and the budget. Kennedy was careful not to reveal any changes the incoming administration would make in the budget, but he told Johnson that he was carrying on extended talks with Joseph Barr, the new Secretary of the Treasury (he replaced Henry Fowler on December 21, 1968), on the budget figures. Whatever inner feelings Johnson may have had about leaving the presidency, they were not evident the day Kennedy spent with him, although he did seem to be preoccupied with the future of Vietnam.

Before the hard work of being Treasury Secretary began, there came the excitement, glitter, and glamour of the inauguration. David and Lenora invited their four daughters and their husbands, along with David's cousin Boyd Christensen and his wife Jean to be their guests for the inaugural activities. The family found it a once-in-a-lifetime experience. They were housed in gracious suites in the Mayflower Hotel, limousines were at their disposal, a military aide was assigned to accompany them, and guides were provided to make sure they found their way from place to place. It was a time to be enjoyed, relished, and remembered. The climax of the inaugural activities would be, of course, the inaugural ceremony, when

David and Lenora Kennedy with their four daughters at the inauguration

Nixon would take the oath of office as the thirty-seventh President of the United States. But the activities leading up to that climax began two days earlier, highlighted by an All-American Gala at which inaugural guests were entertained by internationally famous stars. Sunday, the day before the inaugural, the Mormon Tabernacle Choir and the Washington National Symphony Orchestra gave an inaugural concert in Constitution Hall.

Inauguration Day, January 20, 1969, dawned bitter cold, but the weather did not dampen the spirits of the Kennedy family. The day began for them with an event that was not in the schedule but that enriched the meaning of the day for them. N. Eldon Tanner of the First Presidency was the Church's official representative at the inauguration. Early in the morning he came by David and Lenora's room to wish them well and to give both a blessing in anticipation of the heavy burdens they would bear in the coming months. In that blessing he promised David that his health would not hinder him in the carrying out of his duties, a promise that meant much to both David and Lenora in view of the concern they had expressed to President Nixon. Those moments of spiritual renewal with President Tanner were the prelude to the first event of the day, a prayer breakfast at the Department of State with Nixon, his wife, Pat, and the other cabinet members.

After the prayer breakfast, the day swept on to the swearing in of the President. When the ceremony was completed, the President and members of the cabinet and other guests had lunch at the Capitol and then left for the inaugural parade. David and Lenora watched from the heated presidential reviewing stand, while their family viewed the parade from the Treasury building. The day's activities were climaxed by gala balls at six hotels that evening, with cabinet members presiding at each. The Kennedys shared a box with Interior Secretary Hickel and his wife, Ermalee, at the Mayflower Hotel; they stayed throughout the evening, savoring this last moment of celebration before facing the harsh realities of the problems that the morrow would bring.

The day after the inauguration, before he was sworn in as Secretary of the Treasury, Kennedy stood in the large, impressive Secretary's office in the Treasury building with Henry Fowler and Joseph Barr. The three of them chatted about the office and the tasks Kennedy faced. Then on an impulse Kennedy asked if they would consider it inappropriate for the three of them to pray together. It was a touching moment that Kennedy would later recall: "So in the Secretary's office Joe Barr, Henry Fowler, and I knelt in

David M. Kennedy, center, flanked by President Nixon and Lenora Kennedy, is sworn in as Secretary of the Treasury by Earl Warren, Chief Justice of the Supreme Court

prayer, and Henry Fowler was asked to offer the prayer. He offered a beautiful prayer asking for the blessings of our Father in Heaven to attend us, calling upon Him to guide and direct us and putting ourselves in His hands." Kennedy then went to the White House, where, before his family, other cabinet members, and a few close friends, Chief Justice of the Supreme Court, Earl Warren administered the oath of office. David Matthew Kennedy, at sixty-three years of age, was the Secretary of the Treasury of the United States of America.

Even before that impressive ceremony, Kennedy knew that the appointment involved a close examination of his personal and professional life and a heavy economic burden. During his years at the bank, principally in the decade when he had been president and then chairman of the board, he had amassed an estate of approximately $3 million. The largest share was represented by an option to buy 30,855 shares of Continental stock under the bank's stock option plan. The remainder of his estate consisted of a portfolio of stocks and bonds whose worth in 1969 was approximately $469,000, but stocks worth $222,000 were pledged as collateral against outstanding loans. In addition, Kennedy had $645,000 invested in the bank's profit sharing plan, the family home in Northfield, and some undeveloped property in Arizona. But appointment meant that he would give up his salary of $200,000 a year and accept a cut in his pension payments of some $30,000 a year because of his early retirement from the bank. Still, he expected to protect the major corpus of his estate. His loss of income and reduction in pension payments was softened by $200,000 in severance pay voted by Continental's board of directors to be paid in five annual installments after he left government service. The bank also paid the premiums on a life insurance policy. To satisfy the conflict-of-interest statutes, Kennedy proposed to put all of his holdings in blind trust to be administered by Continental's trust department.

At his confirmation hearings before the Senate Finance Committee, Kennedy explained his intention to create the blind trust and to exercise his stock option by borrowing money from a bank other than Continental and pledging the shares as collateral for the loan. He told the committee he would hold the shares until August 15, when they would be placed in the blind trust. By holding the shares for six months, he could treat the proceeds of any sale of the stock as long-term capital gains and thereby pay income tax on the profit, if any, at a much lower rate. Thus, he would be in the same economic position as he would have been had he completed his term as chairman of the bank and retired as a private citizen. Accompanying this statement was a letter from Kennedy's lawyers stating that they had reviewed these financial arrangements and they believed the arrangements conformed with the conflict-of-interest statutes.

Kennedy found to his dismay that these arrangements, particularly his proposal to have the blind trust administered by Continental's trust department, did not satisfy Senator Albert Gore of Tennessee. In a letter to Senator Russell B. Long of Louisiana, the chairman of the committee, Gore said the proposal was a superficial bookkeeping arrangement. He acknowledged that under the terms of the trust Kennedy would have no control over it: he would not receive dividends nor could he withdraw any bank stock from the trust. However, Gore insisted, "If Continental is to be trustee with full power to sell and manage the nominee's assets, of which Continental stock is a major component, then it seems to me that the nominee will still have a significant association with Continental." If these arrangements were not changed, Gore threatened to vote against confirming Kennedy as Secretary of the Treasury.

At first Kennedy was adamant about the propriety of having Continental as the trustee. To suggest that the bank's trust department would violate the terms of the trust or that he would seek to induce the bank's officers to do so was unthinkable to him. What he considered a matter of principle, his supporters on the committee saw as points on which it would be wise to compromise. Senators Wallace Bennett of Utah and John J. Williams of Delaware finally convinced him to transfer the trust to another bank or individual and promised that if he did so, Gore would make the vote for confirmation unanimous. Kennedy finally agreed to make three changes in his original proposal to the committee: the Old

Colony Trust Company of Boston was substituted for Continental as the trustee of the blind trust; the trustee would be directed to diversify the holdings of the trust so that Continental bank stock "would not constitute, in terms of value, a majority of the corpus of the trust"; and Kennedy would either exercise or relinquish his stock option prior to taking the oath of office. If he exercised that option, the stock would be placed in the blind trust within six months and would be subject to the diversification terms of the trust. Agreement on those changes brought a unanimous vote in the committee and in the full Senate for Kennedy's confirmation as Secretary of the Treasury.[2]

The concessions Kennedy made were a heavy economic price to pay for the honor of serving as Secretary of the Treasury. They should have been enough to put the matter to rest. There was, however, an old adversary waiting in the wings to charge that the Kennedy-Gore agreement did not go near far enough and that the Secretary of the Treasury continued to violate the conflict-of-interest statutes. On January 27 Wright Patman, that ancient foe of bankers and high interest rates, rose on the floor of the House of Representatives to fire the first salvo at the new Secretary of the Treasury. "Not since the days of President Hoover and his infamous Secretary of the Treasury, Andrew Mellon," Patman intoned, "has Washington been flooded with so many bankers in official policy-making positions." The chief culprit was the Secretary of the Treasury, "a man who has been a leading executive in the banking industry for decades."

Patman renewed the attack when Kennedy appeared before the joint Senate-House economic committee of which Patman was chairman. He accused Kennedy of retaining a vested interest in the banking industry by placing his Continental stock in a blind trust. Just placing the stock in a trust was not enough for Patman; he wanted Kennedy to sell all his stock. If he did not, Patman suggested, he might face the same fate as Mellon, against whom Patman had led an impeachment attempt in the Hoover administration. Even though the Senate had confirmed him, Patman told Kennedy, that did not prevent the House from taking action. That implied threat stirred Kennedy to a rare display of public anger: "Mr. Chairman, if you're going to impeach me, I suggest you do it right away." Patman denied that he had made a threat, but he repeated his assertion that Senate confirmation did not preclude House action to impeach.

Over the next two months Patman repeated his charges that Kennedy was in violation of the conflict-of-interest statutes. Kennedy refused to answer the charges in the press. He was encouraged by President Nixon, who called to say that Kennedy was following the right course and who jested that every headline Patman got won the administration fifty votes in the House of Representatives. At the same time, Kennedy was quietly carrying out the agreement he had reached with the Senate committee. As promised, he notified the bank on January 22, before he took the oath of office, that he intended to exercise his option rights to acquire the 30,855 shares of stock at the stipulated price of $39.26 a share—a value of over $1.2 million. He borrowed the money from a bank, and, as he told the committee he would do, he pledged the shares as collateral for the loan. All other Continental Bank stock was in the trust and subject to the diversification terms of the trust. He took two other actions that he did not make public for reasons that are not entirely clear. On April 7 he exercised his stock option and bought the shares of Continental stock, which he was entitled to do, and two days later, April 9, he sold all the stock for $43.00 a share, which netted him a profit of just under $117,000 on which he paid income tax at a rate of 70 percent. Further, under the profit-sharing plan in which all employees of the bank were eligible to participate, Kennedy was entitled to take part of his shares in stock rather than in cash. He opted to relinquish that option and to take all his return in cash from that profit-sharing plan.

On April 29 Paul W. Eggers, general counsel of the Treasury Department, released to the press a detailed statement refuting allegations that Kennedy was guilty of the charges of conflict of interest that Patman repeatedly made. Eggers reviewed the action Kennedy had taken to comply with the terms of his agreement with the Senate Finance Committee and found that he had in every way fulfilled his commitment. That should have ended the matter.

But Patman's repeated accusations and the media's continued willingness to write about and publish the Congressman's remarks kept the story alive long after Eggers's report should have laid it to rest.

Spurred on by the publicity his charges were getting in the press, Patman broadened his attack by alleging that the Secretary had misled the public on the sale of his stock. He charged that the severance pay the Secretary was to receive after he left government service, the pension payments he was receiving under the bank's pension fund, the payments from the profit-sharing plan, and the Continental stock in the blind trust all constituted a conflict of interest. Patman's alleged justification for these continued attacks was to assure that Kennedy as Secretary of the Treasury would not be induced to make decisions favoring banks because of his personal stake in the profitability of the banking industry. On the face of it, that justification is specious, since the Secretary is under the unending scrutiny of the responsible press, and it is unlikely that such favoritism could escape notice. There was, of course, Patman's long-standing feud with the banking industry and his suspicions about all bankers. He hated the idea of a commercial banker as Secretary of the Treasury, and his behavior suggests that his intent was perhaps not to force Kennedy from office but to limit his influence and to induce him to follow policies closer to his, Patman's, own.

There is, of course, another probable motive for Patman's unending enmity toward Kennedy: the struggle over the legislation that permitted Continental to merge with National City Bank. As we have already seen, Patman fought that legislation with all the powers he could command as chairman of the House Committee on Banking and Currency. It was a battle he not only lost, but one in which his capricious behavior almost cost him the chairmanship of the committee. Faced with that prospect, he had dropped his opposition to the legislation and agreed to sponsor its passage in the House, but, with his prejudice against bankers, he was not one to forget that particular losing battle, and now that he thought Kennedy vulnerable, he was prepared to push his advantage.

241

Unfortunately, an increase in the prime rate from 7.5 percent to 8.5 percent on June 1, 1969, gave Patman an additional opportunity to continue his vendetta against Kennedy. This was not only the highest the prime rate had been in recent history, but a jump of one full percentage point in a single movement of the prime was also unprecedented. When Kennedy was called to testify before the Committee on Banking and Currency, Patman began the hearing by putting him under oath, an unusual and demeaning procedure to impose on a cabinet member. Patman badgered Kennedy for not taking action to restrain the banks from raising the prime rate. The Secretary tried patiently to explain the economic forces that were driving up the interest rate regardless of any action the Treasury might take, but Patman continued to imply that because of his financial ties to Continental, Kennedy had done nothing to reduce the prime rate. The Secretary, he said, ought to take action to prove to the country that he did not serve two masters. Kennedy's rebuttal was sharp and personal: "I have proved that to the country but not to you."

Kennedy was not without his supporters on the committee. Representative William E. Brock was particularly incensed that the Secretary had been required to take an oath before giving his testimony. Brock told him that the administration of an oath to a person in his capacity was not only an affront to him but also "an affront to the dignity of this body, and I apologize for it." Representatives Garry Brown and Lawrence G. Williams both joined with Brock in apologizing for the behavior of the chairman. From the other side of the aisle, Representative Tom S. Gettys also put distance between himself and Patman declaring: "Mr. Secretary, I have no knowledge of the merits of charges of any conflict of interest that may exist in connection with your duties as Secretary of the Treasury, but in the absence of proof to the contrary, I assume there is no such conflict, and as a Democratic member of this committee, I extend to you my apology for any personal harassment or embarrassment that may have come to you because of discourses on subjects unrelated to your appearance here for the sole purpose of helping this committee attempt to understand recent increases in prime interest rates."

Ultimately, Patman's attacks on the Secretary faded away, undermined first by Kennedy's prompt compliance with his agreement with the Senate Finance Committee, and second, by the flimsy evidence Patman was able to muster to support his claim. The concessions he demanded would have impoverished Kennedy and his family—essentially punishing him for accepting high office in the service of the country. He would have given up his pension; surrendered his severance pay, a stipend normally granted to chairmen of large corporations on their retirement; and forgone his share of the bank's profit-sharing plan, much of which was simply a return of the money he invested in that plan along with the interest the investment earned over the years. While Patman failed in those objectives, Kennedy had to focus a substantial amount of his time and physical energy in coping with Patman's drumbeat of charges. That was time and energy that the Secretary sorely needed in the first months of his tenure to assemble his team, get a firm grasp on the policy issues, establish a working relationship with the White House, and create his reputation with the public and the press. Patman's obsessions with bankers and banks, which he focused on Kennedy, made all these tasks more difficult.

15

SECRETARY OF THE TREASURY: MANAGING THE DEPARTMENT

David Kennedy's appointment as Secretary of the Treasury thrust him into the high politics of domestic and international economic policy. In Chicago he spoke authoritatively for the bank; in Washington he spoke for the nation. In Chicago he had been the chairman of the board and his success was reflected in the performance of the bank, which could be measured by balance sheets, deposits, and satisfied customers. In Washington he headed only one department, albeit an important one, in a large and complex bureaucracy. There, success was measured not in the hard figures in the annual statement but on the scorecard kept by the constituencies he had to satisfy. In Chicago the final decision was his; in Washington the final decision on things that mattered most was made in the White House, often not by the President but by the White House staff, whose agenda were governed by power and politics.

In Chicago David and Lenora had a private life, though it often had to be sacrificed to the demands of Kennedy's professional life. In Washington the circle of their private life was drawn ever tighter as the demands of the office became more and more incursive. Both in Washington and on their trips overseas, David and Lenora followed the pattern of entertaining that they had established in

David and Lenora Kennedy ride horses in celebration at Randolph, Utah, July 6, 1970

Chicago. They did little entertaining at home, since their apartment was not suited for large parties. But as Secretary of the Treasury, he could use the Secretary's dining room in the Treasury or schedule the dining room at the Blair House for hosting visiting dignitaries. On special occasions the President made his yacht, the *Sequoia*, available to Cabinet members; and, if he were not in residence at Camp David, Cabinet members could take foreign guests there for a weekend. Invitations to Camp David were ardently sought, and high-ranking foreign guests were disappointed if their stay in the capital did not include a day or weekend at Camp David. Lenora proved invaluable in helping David to fulfill his representational responsibilities. She was a gracious hostess whose sunny disposition and genuine liking for people made it easy for her to put others at ease and to feel comfortable in the company of a wide range of people. On one occasion, when she was seated next to Golda Meir, the prime minister of Israel, they fell easily into a conversation about the trials and joys of being grandparents.

Despite the many demands on his time, Kennedy tried to keep some semblance of a private life. Though he did not hold an official church position while he was Secretary of the Treasury, he and Lenora attended church faithfully when they were in Washington. He also spent as many evenings as possible at home with her. He refused to be caught up in the pattern of many government executives of spending long hours in the office after the working day ended. His usual practice was to leave the office at 5:30 or 6:00 P.M.—a practice that seemed strange to the press, who equated effectiveness with presence in the office. For Kennedy, who all his life retired early and arose early, the morning hours, as the Germans say, were golden hours. Alone in his study, he could think about the major problems facing the Treasury and formulate plans for dealing with them. That criticism may have bothered him, since it reflected a lack of understanding, but it did not deter him from a pattern of life he enjoyed and found comfortable and that served him well professionally. There was another reason that he maintained office hours that seemed to the press and others out of harmony with the Washington norm; that was the need to conserve his health. In their first interview, Nixon had suggested that he protect his health by reserving his strength for the major issues. That policy had been more difficult to follow than either the President or Kennedy expected, however, and his health was a continuing concern that dictated a judicious husbanding of his strength.

When Kennedy assumed office as Secretary of the Treasury, he knew that five powerful constituencies would seek to influence his every decision. First was the President and the White House staff. Each department wants the President to see issues as it sees them, and the President in turn wants each department to see issues from his perspective. The President has to balance the views advanced by the various departments and then integrate them into an overall policy. The President's need to persuade departments to see issues from his point of view has far-reaching organizational consequences. Presidents must choose between two organizational strategies: either they will have a strong cabinet with a White House staff whose task is to manage the policy process, or a strong staff that not only manages the policy process but makes policy as well. The first model predominated during the first half of the twentieth century, but in recent years White House staffs have acquired increasing control over policy. Nixon was undoubtedly sincere when he assured Kennedy that as Secretary of the Treasury he would not have to deal with the President through his staff, but not even he could foresee that under Henry Kissinger, H. R. Haldeman, and John Ehrlichman, the White House staff would become the most powerful in presidential history.

The second constituency Kennedy had to reckon with was the Treasury staff. It is an old saying that where one stands depends on where one sits. The view from Treasury is different from that of Agriculture, or of State. The Secretary is expected to see the problems as his staff sees them, to defend those views in conflicts with other departments, to articulate those views in hearings before congressional committees and in press conferences, and to persuade the President that the Treasury position should be his, the President's position.

A third constituency the Secretary must satisfy is Congress. The White House and the Secretary's colleagues at the Treasury expect him to fend off congressional attacks by explaining administration policy so clearly and persuasively that critics are disarmed, if not converted. That task is not only difficult, it is often impossible. Political differences over the content of public policy often reflect philosophical differences that simply cannot be bridged by skillful explanations. And beyond those philosophical differences are the objections Congressmen raise because they believe such confrontations will enhance their chances for reelection. Congressional hearings ostensibly called to examine public policy sometimes, then, become occasions for committee members to pursue their political ambitions.

The need of the Secretary to balance these first three constituencies flows from the structure of the federal government. The fourth constituency, while not a part of the federal government, has its roots in the essence of a democratic society: the press. No aspect of the secretary's performance is outside the concern of the media: the content of his policy recommendations, the choice of his staff, his administrative style, his relations with the White House, or his personal life. What normally attracts media interest is not cooperation but conflict, not successes but failures, not substance but style. A story once printed acquires a life of its own, and retractions are rare; accounts from sources often anonymous are considered more reliable than official sources contradicting them. Statements to the press sometimes come out differently than they are intended, either because the reporter chooses to emphasize some secondary aspect of a statement or because the issues are not understood. But once a story is printed about the Secretary, it is a permanent part of his profile that is added to, line by line, by the press until a public image is created that may or may not be an accurate reflection of reality.

Finally, the Secretary of the Treasury is not responsible to but is held accountable by the financial community, which has a vital interest in the government's monetary and fiscal policies. Management of government debt, tax policies, and international monetary agreements materially affect the financial community, which watches with a critical eye the Secretary's policy decisions. On the other hand, the Secretary watches with equal interest the financial community's reactions to Treasury decisions, for therein may lie the difference between success and failure.

Kennedy's first step in dealing with these constituencies was to fill two key positions: the Under Secretary of the Treasury and the Under Secretary for Monetary Affairs. As under secretary he chose Charls Walker, who was then executive secretary of the American Bankers Association. Walker had a doctoral degree in finance from the University of Pennsylvania's Wharton School of Finance and taught at the University of Texas before leaving teaching for a career in banking. He served as a special assistant to Treasury Secretary Robert Anderson before joining the American Bankers Association. His forceful personality, his experience in dealing with Congress, and his knowledge of the domestic issues facing the new administration persuaded Kennedy that he was the right man for the position.

The Under Secretary for Monetary Affairs, Paul Volcker, also had previous experience at the Treasury, first as director of the Office of Financial Analysis in 1962–63, and then as Deputy Under Secretary for Monetary Affairs, 1963–65. He left the Treasury to become vice-president for forward planning at Chase Manhattan

Bank in New York City, where he served until Kennedy called him back to the Treasury. Volcker's knowledge of international finance was unsurpassed, and he was superb in hearings before congressional committees, since he had an uncanny ability to escape from the traps set for him by committee members. Although some White House staff members were concerned that Volcker was a Democrat, Kennedy was able to have his way.

There were other strong members of the staff. Murray L. Weidenbaum, a distinguished economist, left his position as chairman of the economics department at Washington University in St. Louis to become Assistant Secretary for Economic Policy; Edwin S. Cohen was a member of the faculty at the University of Virginia Law School when asked to serve as Assistant Secretary for Tax Policy; and Paul W. Eggers left his private law practice to become general counsel. Some of Kennedy's top aides were already in the Treasury Department including Eugene T. Rossides, Assistant Secretary for Enforcement Operations; Artemus E. Weatherbee, Assistant Secretary for Administration; John K. Carlock, Fiscal Assistant Secretary; and John R. Petty, the Assistant Secretary for International Affairs. In addition to these department heads, James E. Smith was Kennedy's assistant for Congressional Relations; Anthony J. Jurich, National Security Affairs, and Dixon Donnelley, Public Affairs. The executive secretariat in the secretary's office was directed by Paul R. Beach, while Donald A. Webster served as assistant to the Secretary.

Kennedy procrastinated on only two appointments: the Treasurer of the United States and the Director of the Mint, for two strong candidates—Dorothy Elston from Delaware and Mary Brooks from Idaho—both wanted to be the Treasurer. They each had a strong claim for recognition because of their effective and vigorous support of Nixon in the 1968 campaign. Three months after the inauguration, Kennedy was still undecided, and his indecision brought a call from the President complaining mildly about the delay, since both candidates had raised the issue repeatedly with him and his staff. Kennedy assured Nixon that the matter would be handled without further presidential involvement.

In view of the tension over the appointment, Kennedy called each of the candidates in and extracted from them a promise that they would take whichever position was offered. Once he had that promise, he pointed out the importance of the mint and the possibility to make a substantial contribution in a challenging administrative position. When that ploy failed to induce either of them to volunteer to become Director of the Mint, Kennedy named Elston as Treasurer.[1] If Brooks was disappointed in being named Director of the Mint, Kennedy never knew about it, for she brought to the position substantial administrative skills and won Kennedy's well-deserved recognition for her distinguished service.

Kennedy was fortunate to have Mary Harris as his personal secretary. She had served in that position with Kennedy's predecessors, Henry Fowler and Joseph Barr. Although she wanted to leave government, she was willing to stay on until Kennedy found a replacement. Kennedy explained to Harris how he wanted the office organized: "I want three secretaries. I want one before I get up in the morning and one after I leave at night, and that's six or seven days a week. But with three of them they can take time off. They can keep their government hours, and when I press the button, I won't care whether it's you or one of the others. . . . When

President Richard Nixon meets with Henry Kissinger (foreground), David M. Kennedy, Peter Peterson

I travel I want one of you with me, so you wouldn't have to travel all the time. Any one of you could go."

Harris shook her head at such an unorthodox idea and assured the Secretary that it would not work, but she was willing to help him organize the office on that basis until she left. Sometime later Kennedy called Harris in to tell her that he was ready to look for her replacement. He noted with pleasure that she asked if she could stay on; she confessed that somehow the system was working. Not only did the system work, but she stayed with Kennedy during his two-year tenure at Treasury and then went with him when he became ambassador-at-large. "It was," she would remember, "one of the best things I did in my life."

Kennedy was interested not only in recruiting a staff within the Treasury Department in whom he had confidence, but also in having a comfortable relationship with the other principal economic advisors in the administration: the director of the Bureau of the Budget and the chairman of the Council of Economic Advisors (CEA). Fortunately both of these positions were filled by men he knew and trusted, Paul McCracken at the CEA and Robert Mayo as budget director. The three quickly established a good working relationship. They constituted what came to be known in previous administrations as the "troika" and met once a week for breakfast at the Cosmos Club. In those early morning meetings they reached agreements on the direction economic policy would take and prepared for their periodic meetings with the President. Once a month they were joined by William McChesney Martin, Jr., chairman of the Federal Reserve Board, and then they were dubbed the "quadriad" by the press. They chose the Cosmos Club rather than the White House mess for these meetings since they wanted full privacy. The meetings were resented by the White House staff, particularly John Ehrlichman. Mayo recalled, "I don't think Ehrlichman ever forgave us for . . . being so secretive."

Although Kennedy spent most of his time on high policy issues, they did not occupy his entire schedule. The scope of the Treasury Department reaches from taxes to the White House police force, from negotiations with the International Monetary Fund to enforcement of the customs laws. Therefore, during a typical day a wide variety of issues crossed his desk. The day might commence with a briefing to prepare him for an appearance before a congressional committee, followed by a staff meeting to plan Treasury's strategy for winning congressional approval to raise the interest rates on savings bonds. His attention was then claimed by a White House memorandum asking Treasury's opinion on the advisability of going ahead with the financing of the supersonic transport. The White House also asked for his recommendation on where the office of the Special Trade Representative should be housed. As mid-day approached, Henry Kearns and officials from the Department of Commerce came to discuss trade policy and the financing of nuclear power projects through the Export-Import Bank.

A working lunch followed, perhaps with the officers of the American Banking Association. Early afternoon brought a final meeting on the establishment of a Consolidated Federal Law Enforcement Training Center managed by the Treasury Department. Then the Secretary returned to his office to approve and sign a letter to Secretary of State William Rogers opposing exempting employees of international organizations from American income tax. Another letter for his signature requested that the Social Security Administration furnish the Internal Revenue Service with information on payments of more than six hundred dollars to doctors receiving Social Security payments for medical services under Medicare and Medicaid programs. Kennedy then reviewed the speech he was to give at the opening of the new facilities for the Mint in Philadelphia.

The letters signed and the speech reviewed, he was reminded by Mary Harris that he had a staff meeting to consider cuts that the Bureau of the Budget wanted to make in funds for the Customs service. The Secretary's day was drawing to a close, but there was still a letter to dictate to Kendall Garff, a friend from the mission field who was now a leading businessman in Salt Lake City, and who had written protesting high interest rates. Mayor Richard Daley had also written from Chicago to tell Kennedy that $78 million of the $195 million bond issue Kennedy helped to get adopted was still unsold. At day's end there was a letter to be signed as chairman of the Library of Congress Trust Fund, authorizing the

Librarian of Congress to accept a gift made to the library. It was followed by letters of appreciation to members of Congress for their support of crucial legislation. At the bottom of the pile was a letter from a student who wanted the secretary's opinion on how important the study of English was for his future career. "Words are our tools of thought and communication," Kennedy wrote the student, Gerald Ferch from Kenosha, Wisconsin. "By mastering them, you will increase your ability to think out your ideas, and to communicate them to others clearly, accurately, and effectively."

Ever present among the issues that demand the Secretary's time is the need to coordinate Treasury's activities with those of other government agencies where there is overlapping jurisdiction. Ordinarily, conflicts in the coordination process are handled by the Treasury units directly responsible, but the tension between the Bureau of Customs and the Bureau of Narcotics and Dangerous Drugs (BNDD) in the Justice Department became so intense that Kennedy and Attorney General John Mitchell were drawn into the debate.

The issue was the jurisdictional boundaries between Customs and the BNDD. A proposal by BNDD would have limited the power of Customs officials to contact foreign enforcement officials in fulfilling their responsibilities to enforce the antismuggling laws. Had the dispute been settled on the grounds the BNDD proposed, Customs officials would have had to obtain permission from the BNDD whenever Customs wanted to admit the smuggled goods and then trace them to their final destination so that both the smuggler and the recipient could be arrested in possession of the evidence.

When negotiations with the Justice Department proved fruitless, Kennedy appealed to the White House. What he offered was a compromise: the statute defining smuggling should be amended to define "smuggling, any attempt to smuggle, or any conspiracy to smuggle" as including, specifically, "acts preparatory and subsequent to the actual or attempted entry or introduction of any merchandise into the United States." In exchange, the statute should make an exception for "controlled dangerous substances" and limit the definition of smuggling in those cases to the "passage of undeclared merchandise through the custom lines." This proposal was never taken to Congress, for the threat to do so was enough to bring about a renewal of negotiations, which resulted in an inter-agency agreement that followed closely the statutory amendment Treasury proposed.

Kennedy had to protect Treasury interests not only in the arena of interdepartmental politics but also in its relations with the White House. Before the Nixon administration took office, Henry Fowler advised Kennedy to insist on being included in the meetings of the National Security Council (NSC). Fowler tried to persuade Congress to make the Secretary of the Treasury a statutory member of the Council but failed. Kennedy recognized the importance of Fowler's suggestion not only because of the contribution Treasury could make to NSC deliberations, but also because Nixon intended to make the NSC, under the direction of Kissinger, his principal for-eign policy forum. Kennedy went to the President and asked that he be invited to NSC meetings; the President agreed. "He called Henry and told him to see that I was invited to all the meetings," Kennedy recalled. "Well, I was and I was not. They'd forget to invite me. I put Tony Jurich on our staff to watch the National Security Council and follow every move they made, so he knew when the meetings would be held and he'd tell me. Then some-times if I didn't get a call from Henry's office to go, I'd just show up, because I was invited. He couldn't turn me down. We never corrected that."

The daily ebb and flow of matters that crossed the Secretary's desk was interrupted at times by crises that appeared randomly and without warning. Kennedy's most challenging crisis began May 9, 1970, in Hot Springs, Virginia, where he was attending a meeting of the Business Council. At lunch he looked up to see Stuart Saunders, chairman of the Penn Central Railroad, walking by. They exchanged greetings and Kennedy asked Saunders, "How's business?" That question, Kennedy would recall, "was the biggest mistake of my life." Saunders told him that it was not good and asked if he could come see him. Kennedy extended an invitation and a week later Saunders called for an appointment and brought with him David Bevan, financial vice-president of Penn Central. The duo complained to Kennedy that the government's economic policies were making it impossible for them to market a $100 million bond offering. Kennedy was surprised, since other companies were not having trouble selling their paper if they were willing to pay the market interest rate. He asked to see Penn Central's financial statement, and while in that short meeting he could not determine the full extent of Penn Central's difficulties, he learned enough to know that the company had a liquidity problem. He advised Saunders to consult his investment banker, for in view of the company's financial condition, the sale of bonds might be illegal. After Saunders and Bevan left, Kennedy called in Paul Volcker and his assistant, Bruce McLaury, and asked them to gather all the information they could on Penn Central.

From Kennedy's discussion with Saunders and from McLaury's investigation, it became apparent that Penn Central had to have $50 million immediately, since that amount in payroll costs and bond redemptions was due in the next few weeks and the company had only $7 million in cash. By June 9 Treasury's investigation and Kennedy's consultations with other government officials and leading bankers, including Walter Wriston of First National City Bank in New York and Gaylord Freeman of First National Bank of Chicago, led Kennedy to believe that Penn Central might be saved. A plan was developed that called for a consortium of banks to loan the company $200 million on a short-term basis; the Department of Defense would guarantee the loan, under the authority of the Defense Production Act of 1950, which authorized the Department of Defense to make such loans if the national defense required it. In the meantime, Transportation Secretary John Volpe would seek congressional approval for a fund of $750 million to help ailing railroads. The short-term loan from the banks would then be turned into a long-term loan. The linchpin in the proposal was the guarantee of the short-term loan by the Defense Department, for without the guarantee, the bank consortium would not extend the short-term loan. Since the Treasury Department was the President's principal advisor on the financial aspects of the plan, it fell to Kennedy to see if this package of public and private financial aid could be put together in time to save Penn Central from bankruptcy.

To prevent failure of Penn Central, Kennedy had to move on two fronts. First, he must convince the Defense Department, particularly David Packard, Under Secretary of Defense, that the department should guarantee the short-term loan. Second, he had to put together a consortium of banks to provide the $200 million. He began negotiations with Packard and sent Volcker to New York to talk to the banks. Meanwhile, Volpe and the Under Secretary of Transportation James Beggs undertook the task of obtaining congressional support for the long-term government loan. They talked to the two key figures, Wright Patman in the House and Warren Magnuson in the Senate, both of whom gave their support, and expressed the same intention to Kennedy.

The scenario called for Kennedy to produce a letter from the Defense Department guaranteeing the short-term loan; the bankers would then sign off on the $200 million loan, and legislation authorizing the $750 million in long-term assistance would be introduced and quickly approved. On June 2, 1970, the Secretary of Defense, Melvin Laird, wrote White House aide Peter Flanigan that the Department of Defense was "not in a position to act as a guarantor of a V-loan. DoD's requirements for the services of Penn-Central are not that significant." Laird also cited budgetary constraints that made it "impossible to expect Defense either to justify a role as guarantor or to make good as a guarantor should a loan of the magnitude contemplated be defaulted." Under strong pressure—essentially a demand—from Kennedy, the Department of Defense reluctantly reversed that position and gave Kennedy the letter of guarantee.

With that step taken, it appeared that the rescue of Penn Central was in hand. Patman, however, began to suspect that what on the surface was a plan to save a railroad was really a way to bail out the banks that were the railroad's creditors. Then Magnuson began to back away from his support, and in place of a ready approval of the legislative package that had appeared likely a few days earlier, there now loomed a drawn-out, bitter legislative battle. Furthermore, when officials in the Department of Defense saw the erosion of legislative support, they became even more reluctant than they had been to provide the key guarantee. Finally, Volcker, who was coordinating the negotiations with the bankers, began to have second thoughts about the rescue effort. On June 19 after a meeting with representatives of the other departments involved in the rescue effort—notably Flanigan and Packard—Volcker told Kennedy that the group doubted the success of the plan.

Kennedy left Volcker and went immediately to the oval office, where Nixon was waiting for him. That climactic meeting began with the Secretary reminding Nixon that the Justice Department believed the guarantee was legal and that it would stand up in the courts. Despite that opinion, Kennedy told the President that his major concern was the uncertainty about the ultimate cost. The Penn Central was not just a railroad but a complex conglomerate whose success or failure depended on so many different factors that there was no reliable estimate on what the final cost would be to the taxpayers. Kennedy's own assessment was that the cost to the government might be at least two billion dollars, or, as he told the President, it might be four billion dollars. "When you get into a situation like this, my experience has been that it's far more than you ever can see in the figures." In fairness to Volpe, who was not present, Kennedy rehearsed the arguments in favor of Volpe's rescue plan and suggested that the President might want to talk to someone who could see more clearly the political ramifications of saving Penn Central. At that point, the President looked out into the Rose Garden "for I don't know how long," Kennedy said. "At the time I thought it was an hour, but it was probably only two or three minutes or a minute. Then he turned to me and he said, 'You make the decision.' "

Kennedy didn't hesitate; if the President would give him his full backing, he would advise the Defense Department not to guarantee the loan, and Penn Central would consequently fail. Nixon assured him of that support, and thus ended the government's efforts to save Penn Central from bankruptcy. Volcker told the bankers to go home; there would be no government guarantee of the $200 million loan. Packard was pleased that the Defense Department was not required to guarantee the loan; Volpe was dismayed that he was not at the final meeting in the White House and wanted Kennedy to help him persuade the President to change his mind;

and Arthur Burns, chairman of the Federal Reserve Board, called to tell Kennedy that he had just made the biggest mistake of his life. Kennedy, relieved that the deed was done, moved to limit the damage by telling the regional Federal Reserve banks that the Treasury would support the commercial paper market to forestall any possible panic stemming from the failure of Penn Central.

The routine management of department bureaucratic politics and periodic crises was overshadowed by the ever-present high policy issues. Domestically, the economic issues that faced Kennedy can be summed up in one word: inflation. After minimal inflation in the first half of the decade, the rate of inflation gradually increased until it reached 5 percent in the last quarter of 1968 and promised to be even higher in 1969. At the same time the unemployment rate was just 3.3 percent, the lowest since 1953. The juxtaposition of rising inflation and low unemployment presented the Nixon administration with a dilemma: Prevailing economic theory held that the way to fight inflation was to limit government spending and reduce the money supply, but at the cost of increased unemployment. In economic terms a higher rate of unemployment was justified, because in the long run inflation was the greater threat to the stability of the economy. But the policy entailed substantial political danger, for great economic crises in American history were associated with recessions and depressions rather than inflation. Hence, an increase in unemployment would raise the specter of a depression with unacceptable political consequences.

If the economic problems facing the nation on the domestic front can be summed up in one word, the economic challenge the United States confronted internationally in 1969—and in later years as well—can be summed up in one phrase: balance of payments. During World War II the governments of the United States and Great Britain led an effort to create an international monetary system to replace the gold standard that historically had been the basis of international exchange rates. Their goal was to create a stable international exchange system that would enhance international trade but leave governments considerable freedom to manage their domestic economies. The result was the Bretton Woods conference of 1944 at which the participants agreed to a system of fixed exchange rates. Participating nations also created an organization, the International Monetary Fund (IMF), to manage this system of stable exchange rates. The IMF supervised a fund created by contributions from member states that was used to make loans to nations with temporary balance of payment problems. The system never worked exactly as it was planned because the economic disruption in the aftermath of the war was more extensive than the Bretton Woods planners had foreseen and because of the predominant position of the United States in the decade or so following the war. In that period of American dominance, the dollar gradually assumed the role of a reserve currency, that is, the currency that nations hold in their own reserves and that becomes the preferred medium of exchange in international trade. The dollar provided the stability and liquidity needed to finance expanding world trade because during those years the United States purposely ran a deficit in its balance of payments by extending large amounts of aid to Europe and Japan to recover from the ravages of the war.

The dollar-led international monetary system was successful as long as other countries needed dollars and viewed the American economy with confidence. But in the early 1960s those twin pillars of support began to weaken. First, two of the leading industrialized nations, West Germany and Japan, were holding more dollars than they needed for adequate reserves. Second, the war in Vietnam was raising doubts about the future of the American economy, particularly as inflationary pressures began to build after 1965. As inflation increased in the United States, the value of the dollar began to decline internally. But because exchange rates were fixed, the dollar retained its value on foreign exchange markets, which made it overvalued in relation to other currencies. This disparity between the dollar and other currencies resulted in increased American investment abroad, a higher level of imports, and more and more dollars held outside the United States.

There was an economic answer to this problem, and some countries that held their reserves in gold urged it on the United States: devaluation of the dollar. The United States steadfastly refused to consider this alternative for two reasons. First, since most countries held dollars as part of their monetary reserves, it would have unilaterally reduced the value of those reserves. Second, few nations wanted to surrender the trading advantage they had *vis-à-vis* the dollar, and they would have had to devalue their currencies to maintain their position relative to the United States. Some pressure on the dollar was relieved by an agreement in 1968 to create a two-tiered gold system, under which the United States continued to sell gold to other countries at thirty-five dollars an ounce, but sales to individuals by the United States or Western European countries were discontinued.

Although, as we shall see, the fight against inflation took a considerable portion of the Secretary's time during his first year in office, events on the international scene demanded a major commitment. Kennedy approached the balance of payments problem with a strong bias toward free trade. His experience at Continental reinforced that bias, and his statements during his stewardship as Secretary continued to reflect those views. He was not, however, writing on a blank tablet; past policies and current economic realities had to be carefully taken into consideration.

Although the Nixon administration hoped to rely primarily on fiscal and monetary policies to attack the nation's balance of payments deficit, there were measures to be taken on the international scene as well. As the dollar came under increasing pressure after 1965, the IMF began to play a more important role in international financial affairs. While the IMF had been useful in helping member states cope with balance of payments problems, there was a growing demand for some medium of exchange for financing international trade that was not tied to the dollar. In 1967 an amendment to the IMF charter was adopted that was intended to create just such an international currency. The amendment provided for "Special Drawing Rights" (SDRs) that member states agreed to treat as if they were convertible currencies. Hence, they could be used by IMF members to settle international accounts during temporary balance of payments difficulties. A fund of $9.8 billion over a three-year period was authorized.

The amendment was agreed to by the governors of the IMF but had not been ratified when Kennedy came to the Treasury. He pushed ratification because SDRs were seen as an alternative to devaluation of the dollar or floating exchange rates. Originally Kennedy had been more flexible on the issue of devaluation than had other members of the administration, but he took the occasion of the appointment of Volcker to put his office squarely against devaluation. "It will be our purpose," he told the assembled press, "to maintain a strong dollar both at home and abroad. We will not seek an answer to our problems by a change in the monetary price of gold. We see no need or reason for such action."

On the other hand, the possibility of some flexibility in foreign exchange rates attracted more and more attention from Kennedy and his colleagues at the Treasury. Pressure on the American balance of payments eased during the spring and summer months of 1969, yet the long-range prospects for the balance of payments looked increasingly negative, primarily because the large trade surplus the United States traditionally ran was disappearing. These pessimistic long-term analyses intensified American hope for greater flexibility in the IMF-monitored exchange rates. Most IMF members were opposed to increased flexibility in exchange rates, but the United States was able to get an agreement at the September 1969 meeting that a study of the problem would be undertaken.

Even as IMF members agreed to discuss flexibility in exchange rates, foreign exchange markets came under increasing pressure in September 1969. The immediate crisis had its origin in a threat that England would have to devalue the pound to protect its deteriorating balance of payments. A devaluation of the pound would make American efforts to solve its own balance of payments problem almost impossible within the existing international agreements. As a result, the United States would have to choose between two unpalatable choices: cut the link between the dollar and gold by making them unconvertible, or change the price of gold. An alternative to the devaluation of the pound was a revaluation of the German mark, for West Germany and the United States were England's largest creditors. Kennedy and Volcker much preferred this solution. But it was not at all certain at the beginning of the crisis that the Germans would revalue.

As the crisis developed, Kennedy, in a farsighted memorandum, told the President that it was in the United States's interest to solve the balance of payment problem within the framework of existing international agreements. The threat, Kennedy warned, was the possibility that time would run out before that goal could be reached, and the United States would be faced with the necessity of taking unilateral action. In that case, the administration would have to choose between three alternatives: refuse to convert dollars into gold, thereby forcing the world onto a "dollar standard"; raise the price of gold; or adopt a system of completely free exchange rates. On balance, Kennedy believed that the first of these alternatives was the least disruptive, particularly if it were possible to negotiate a series of agreements with some key countries that would agree, as Germany had already promised, not to convert dollars into gold.

The Nixon administration was saved, at least for the present, from making this difficult decision by the revaluation of the German mark by 9.3 percent following Willy Brandt's electoral victory in October. That decision, which was made under some pressure from the United States, brought calm to the international exchange market and permitted the Nixon administration to pursue its goals of bringing greater flexibility into the operations of the IMF, achieving a limited adjustment in current exchange rates, inducing other members of the IMF to agree to at least some marginal flexibility in exchange rates, and in the long run relieving the United States of the obligation to convert dollars into gold. It was also the prelude to the activation in January 1970 of SDRs, as Kennedy's persistent efforts to obtain ratification finally came to fruition.

David Kennedy's concern with international financial issues extended well beyond the United States's balance of payment problems and the stability of the international monetary system. His experience at Continental made him aware that many underdeveloped countries could not provide even a minimum standard of living for their people. He was convinced that the bank should help those countries create viable economies. Now as Secretary of the Treasury, he was in a position to assure that American aid policies would contribute to reaching that goal. Kennedy's genuine interest in Third World countries, as Paul Volcker recalled, was unusual for a Secretary of the Treasury. That interest was reflected in his efforts to increase the effectiveness of the International Bank of Reconstruction and Development, better known as the World Bank. Member countries can borrow funds from the bank for development projects at conventional financing rates. The World Bank has a subsidiary, the International Development Association (IDA), which extends credit to the poorest countries in the world that would not normally qualify for a loan from the World Bank. Recipient countries do not pay interest, but they do pay a small yearly service charge to defray administrative costs.

When Kennedy came to the Treasury, the United States had already agreed to contribute $480 million to increase the IDA's funding capacity. Appropriation of these funds was approved by the House of Representatives, but some senators wanted to limit American contributions to the IDA to that contributed by the World Bank from its earnings. Kennedy opposed that limitation, since it would reopen negotiations over increasing IDA funds that were painstakingly conducted with member states in 1967. He was also convinced that IDA funding materially advanced American policy in the recipient countries. Further, funds contributed by the United States could be used only to buy American goods and services, a concession the IDA made in view of the disparity in the American balance of payments. There were also complaints from the Senate that too high a percentage of IDA funds was going to India and Pakistan. Kennedy recognized the legitimacy of those complaints and supported a promise given by the previous administration that those countries would receive less in the future.

Another step in Kennedy's strategy to win Senate support was to persuade the World Bank that it should increase its contribution to the IDA. Robert McNamara, president of the World Bank, realized the problem Kennedy faced and agreed to increase the bank's contribution in 1968 to seventy-five million dollars from ten million dollars in 1967. With that solid evidence of the bank's willingness to increase its contribution to the IDA and McNamara's promise that the World Bank's contributions would increase as its earnings increased, Senator John Sherman Cooper of Kentucky agreed to lead the fight in the Senate against the amendment to the IDA bill. He was successful, and the President signed the authorization on May 23, 1969.

Two other multilateral international assistance organizations in which Kennedy took substantial interest were the Asian Development Bank (ADB) and the Inter-American Development Bank (IDB). As Secretary of the Treasury, he was a member of the board of governors of both banks and attended their annual meetings whenever possible. Kennedy was willing to back his interest in Asia and Latin America with a vigorous effort to gain congressional approval for increased funds for both organizations. He asked Congress to appropriate $100 million to the ADB for a special operations fund. In addition, he sought two billion dollars to increase the capital stock of the IDB, plus one billion dollars for the bank's special operations fund, with the least-developed countries of Latin America to have first call on the special development fund. It was a battle he lost in the closing days of his tenure as Secretary of the Treasury. Senator Albert Gore was able to halt passage of the omnibus international financial institutions bill until the funds for the ADB were cut from the bill and the one billion dollar appropriation for the IDB was cut to $100 million. Kennedy was dismayed at the outcome, since the House had already voted the funds and there was every hope that the Senate would follow the House in voting approval for the appropriation. In a telegram to the president of the ADB, Kennedy expressed his disappointment and promised to introduce the bill again in 1971 when the "special factors which caused deletion will no longer be present."

Even though Kennedy was sensitive to the economic problems of other nations, he was ever mindful of American economic interests and pushed for protection of those interests when others thought to do so would be politically unwise. He faced that objection when he insisted that the return of Okinawa to Japan not be approved unless the United States received some compensation for the roads, schools, power stations, and housing built by the U.S. during the occupation. Kennedy raised that issue with Nixon and got his approval of compensation in principle, only to be warned by Secretary of State Rogers that such a demand would seriously upset the already delicate negotiations then under way with the Japanese. But with the President's backing, Kennedy raised the issue with Japanese finance minister Takeo Fukuda in the spring of 1969. In their discussions, Kennedy and Fukuda agreed that the United States should receive some compensation as part of the agreement returning Okinawa to Japan, but Fukuda did not want to be put in the position of appearing to buy Okinawa back from the Americans. Therefore, Kennedy agreed to help Fukuda save face by accepting Fukuda's oral assent to the final terms.

On November 12, 1969, Anthony Jurich, who conducted the negotiations for the Treasury, initialed a pact providing the United States $520 million in compensation for its investment in Okinawa. Written approval by the Japanese came several weeks later in a meeting between Nixon and Eisaku Sato, the Japanese prime minister, when the Okinawa reversion treaty was signed. Kennedy's willingness to accommodate Japanese sensitivities by keeping the compensation issue in the background served the interests of both the United States and Japan: the United States received just compensation for its investment in Okinawa, and the Japanese were able to pay that compensation without appearing to be paying for territory that was rightfully theirs. Good deeds done behind the scenes are often unnoticed, but that is not so in this case. Sato not only sent an emissary to thank Kennedy for his part in the Okinawa negotiations, but he also followed that up with a personal word of appreciation.

Not all the pressing international economic issues that crossed Kennedy's desk while he was Secretary of the Treasury were resolved in the sense that they ceased to be troublesome. But they were all managed with insight and skill. An international monetary crisis was averted. SDRs are still an essential part of the international monetary system, and the United States still participates in providing aid to underdeveloped countries through multilateral agencies. On the other hand, the larger issues of the United States's balance of payments problems and the stability of the international monetary system are still with us. Although those issues were not resolved while Kennedy was Secretary of the Treasury, it was not his policy recommendations that were at fault, but the dominance of politics over economics. It is that same dominance of politics over economics that has transformed the United States from a creditor nation into a debtor nation and made the budget process a permanent crisis.

16

SECRETARY OF THE TREASURY: FIGHTING INFLATION

As we have seen, David Kennedy and his colleagues in the troika chose to attack simultaneously the twin problems of inflation and an unsatisfactory balance of payments. Their approach, which came to be known as gradualism, sought to fight inflation by adopting the proper mix of fiscal and monetary policies. Kennedy described the goals of that policy to the editors of *U.S. News & World Report*: "Our aim is to take some of the steam out of the boiler without causing such serious problems of a business slump that you would have to start building a fire in the boiler again. We want an orderly cooling down—and then to hold with it over a period of time."

Gradualism was the strategy. Fiscal policy—notably changes in tax policy, reduction in government expenditures, tightening the money supply by the Federal Reserve Board, and debt management policy were the tactics. Gradualism did not include an incomes policy—fixing guidelines for prices and wages, or jawboning—attempts by the President and other administration officials to persuade businessmen to hold the line on prices and labor leaders to reduce their wage demands. Richard Nixon opposed an incomes policy because it was contrary to free-market principles and was self-defeating in the long run. He rejected jawboning because he was a realist and thought it utopian to expect business and union

leaders to place the national interest above that of the organizations they represented.

Kennedy came to the Treasury convinced that the monetary
and fiscal policies of the past administration had been the root
cause of inflation. The large budget deficit in fiscal 1968 and the
expansion of the money supply by the Federal Reserve in 1967–68
built into the economy an inflationary impetus that would be difficult to curb. Although the Federal Reserve Board moved to a tight
money policy in the first half of 1969, Kennedy thought that monetary policy—control of the supply of money and credit by the
Federal Reserve Board—could not carry the entire burden of fighting inflation. It had to be buttressed by a sound fiscal policy, which
in the face of inflation required a balanced budget. After a budget
deficit in fiscal 1968, the Johnson administration left office with a
projected budget surplus in fiscal 1969 based on the reduction of
American troops in Vietnam. Kennedy entered office determined
to maintain that surplus by continuing a surcharge of 10 percent
on personal and corporate income tax rates that was scheduled to
end July 30, 1969. He was faced with a political as well as an economic problem. Nixon promised that if he were elected, he would
not renew the surcharge. Now Kennedy and the other members of
the troika had to convince him that he must back away from that
promise. Finally convinced, Nixon asked Congress in April 1969 to
extend the 10 percent surcharge until January 1, 1970, with a
reduction to 5 percent until June 30, 1970, when the surcharge
would be phased out.

While the extension of the surcharge made good economic
sense, it was a political lightning rod. The Democratic leadership
in the Senate was unwilling to deal with the surcharge until a
comprehensive tax-reform bill was passed, some Democrats wanted
it eliminated, and labor leaders were for the most part opposed to
it. Faced with this formidable array of opposition, Kennedy sent
Nixon a long memorandum on May 21 repeating the arguments
for continuing the surcharge and outlining the steps Treasury was
taking to mobilize public support for its extension. The memorandum stressed the need of support from three key organizations:

President Nixon and Secretary of the Treasury Kennedy

the U.S. Chamber of Commerce, the National Association of Manufacturers, and the American Farm Bureau Federation. In addition, Kennedy suggested that Vice President Spiro Agnew lobby for the support of state and local government leaders. These measures were necessary to bring pressure on Congress, for as Kennedy told the President, "the major trouble in the Congress seems to center around those Democratic liberals who insist that meaningful tax reform precede enactment of the surcharge. This desire simply cannot be met in the time available, but steps will have to be taken to convince them that a meaningful tax reform bill will be reported out of the Ways and Means Committee this year. This is a task that primarily confronts Chairman [Wilbur] Mills, but the Administration can help by reaffirming its support of significant reform."

The administration tried to anticipate the demand of Democratic leaders in the Senate that tax reform precede extension of the surcharge, and it proposed a far-reaching tax reform measure in mid-April. As the House Ways and Means Committee began hearings on those proposals, the Treasury published a formal statement in which every living former Secretary of the Treasury joined to express their conviction that "the financial health of the nation demands prompt action by the Congress to extend the income tax surcharge for one year." That same belief was echoed by sixteen leading economists, including Walter F. Heller, Arthur M. Okum, Paul A. Samuelson, and Charles L. Schultze, who argued that the surcharge was "a key element in the anti-inflation strategy. If it is not extended, the federal budget will again be stimulating the economy with a deficit which is totally inappropriate to present conditions."

Kennedy captured the headlines by warning that although he opposed wage and price controls, they would have to be considered if inflation continued to rise. The statement was an effort to increase pressure on Congress to move rapidly on the surcharge. The House needed little persuading: on June 30 it passed a bill extending the surcharge until January 1, 1970. But in the Senate proponents of linking tax reform with the extension of the surcharge were able to prolong the debate. Meantime, both the House and the Senate passed temporary extensions of the surcharge until the Senate could decide on the matter. Finally, all action on the tax measure, except the extension of the surcharge, was delayed until Congress could act on a tax-reform bill being considered by the House Ways and Means Committee. The surcharge was extended until January 1, 1970, by tacking it on as an amendment to a bill dealing with unemployment insurance.

The battle over the extension of the surcharge brought considerable speculation in the press about David Kennedy's role in the new administration. The press made much of a statement by presidential press secretary Ron Ziegler that Nixon was not considering wage and price controls if the surcharge were not extended. The United Press story on Ziegler's statement reported it as a contradiction of the Secretary of the Treasury. A story in the *Washington Post* was headlined "Wage Price Control Talk Drops Stock." The damage was done, even though later in the day Ziegler insisted that earlier he had meant to say "the same thing as Treasury Secretary David Kennedy, who declared on Tuesday that the question of controls had to be left open if Congress failed to extend the surtax." There were reports in the press that Kennedy's comments on the possibility of wage and price controls angered Nixon and that he was politically naive. For example, David Broder of the

Washington Post wrote that "Secretary of the Treasury David Kennedy, who has managed to convince both parties that he is a man of impeccable political naiveté, talked and acted as if any measure endorsed by two Presidents of opposing parties was certain to become law."

These contemporary press reports are contradicted by the record. Kennedy's memorandum to the President dated May 21—more than six weeks before the Broder article—reflects how clearly he saw the political difficulties ahead. In a June 28 letter to his friend Glenn Nielson, he wrote: "You have been reading in the paper, I am sure, about the difficulty we have had with our tax bill. We were able to get it back on track this week . . . President Nixon has given full support, for which I am thankful. Otherwise we could not have succeeded. Even after action in the House, we will have difficulty in the Senate. It has become a political issue with the Democrats and is being used by the liberal group to try to gain control over the Democratic party. The hope we have is that we can get solid Republican support and sufficient Democratic conservative support that will carry us through."

This letter and the memo to the President reflect Kennedy's awareness of the political forces he faced in Congress. He, as well as Charls Walker and other Treasury officials, may well have underestimated how adamantly some Senate Democrats would hold out for linkage between tax reform and extension of the surcharge. But then so did Representative Hale Boggs, who, because of Mills's illness, shepherded the surcharge through the House Ways and Means Committee. Boggs released a statement to the press just a day before Broder accused Kennedy of underestimating the drive for tax reform. In that release, Boggs charged the Democratic leadership in the Senate with playing "a game of brinkmanship" with this crucial fiscal measure. Since Kennedy's appreciation of the situation was similar to that of Boggs, who was far from being a political tyro, the charges that Kennedy was politically naive are in retrospect not persuasive.

The press report that somehow Kennedy, in his political innocence, surprised and angered Nixon with his comment on the possibility of wage and price controls if the surcharge were not extended seems to have had its origin in the White House, but not with the President. Kennedy's statement, after all, was made at the press conference he held with the President's other leading economic advisors. He mentioned wage and price controls as only one alternative, one that he opposed. The report that the President was angry at Kennedy's statement was published in a Rowland Evans and Robert Novak column in the *Washington Post*. When Lyndon K. "Mort" Allen, who reviewed the press for the President, brought the Evans and Novak story to Nixon's attention, Nixon told Allen that it was absolutely false.

Not only was there press criticism to deal with, but Kennedy was also under fire because of the increase in the bank prime interest rate, which rose in June from 7.5 percent to 8.5 percent. Wright Patman summoned Kennedy before the House Committee on Banking and Currency to explain the reasons for that sharp increase in the prime rate. Kennedy argued that there were three causes: a continuing strong demand for credit; inflation, which caused lenders to hedge against continuing inflation by adjusting their interest rates upward; and excessive reliance on monetary policy to fight inflation. Those rational explanations carried no weight with Patman, who was convinced that the increase in the prime rate was purely and simply a conspiracy by the big banks to increase their profits. In his view, the best friend of those big bankers was the Secretary of the Treasury, who sat supinely by while his friends raped the country. "Did you do anything preceding the increase of the prime interest rate to 8.5 to prevent it or discourage it?" Patman demanded. When Kennedy explained that he had no legal authority to roll back the prime rate, Patman wanted to know if he had discussed a rollback with the banks.

"No, I did not."

"Did you discuss it with anybody?"

"No."

"Why didn't you?"

"Why should I?"

"You mean you were helpless? You couldn't do anything?"

"I could have done no more than you did. You shouted from the housetops and nothing happened."

This exchange between Patman and Kennedy reflects a fundamental difference in economic philosophy. Patman believed that the government ought, by either moral suasion or by direct controls, to keep interest rates low, so that neither the cost of government borrowing nor the cost of consumer purchases would rise. For Kennedy, the issues were more profound than Patman was willing to concede. The increase in the prime rate was only a surface symptom of much deeper economic dislocations. Those dislocations, which Kennedy believed were caused by the three conditions he outlined for the committee, would be made even worse by the policies Patman was urging the government to adopt.

Simultaneously with the fight over the extension of the surcharge and the flood of international problems that came in the fall of 1969, Kennedy had to worry about the way Congress was mauling the administration's tax-reform proposal. The reform included not only the extension of the surcharge but also the repeal of the 7 percent tax credit for new investment, elimination of income taxes for those in the lowest income brackets, a minimum income tax for all wealthy individuals, and several other changes designed to make the tax structure more equitable. Early in May the Treasury completed work on a tax reform bill and sent it to the House Ways and Means Committee. As soon as it was received, Mills scheduled immediate hearings on it. Kennedy tried to persuade Mills to postpone the hearings until he returned from the meetings of the Asian Development Bank (ADB) in Australia. Mills rejected the request and forced Kennedy to choose between being present at the hearings or missing the ADB meetings. Caught on the horns of the dilemma, Kennedy—unwisely, as he later recognized—chose to attend the bank meetings and left Charls Walker to carry the burden of testifying before the committee in its initial hearings on the bill.

A principal goal of the Nixon tax-reform package was to remove about six million people from the tax roles by reducing tax rates at the lowest income levels by some 56 percent. In addition, the Treasury recommended that Congress close some of the loopholes the wealthy used to escape paying taxes. Kennedy was impatient with those who complained that this change would eliminate the incentives for investment then in the law. He explained to a friend in Chicago, Foster McGaw, that when it became known in early April 1969 that 150 individuals with incomes of more than $200,000 paid no federal income tax, the Treasury received more "gripe mail than it did in all 1968." "Now, Foster, you know as well as I do that every incentive in the tax laws was put there for a specific purpose and was hailed as a reform at the time it was enacted. However, these laws were never intended to make it possible for individuals—some with incomes in excess of $1 million—to combine these various incentives to avoid all Federal taxes."

For Kennedy, tax reform was secondary to the extension of the surcharge, but when he saw what the House of Representatives did with the Treasury proposals, he realized that what for him was a chance to achieve tax reform was for the Democratic-controlled Congress an opportunity for tax reduction. When the costs of the changes made in the House were added up, there was a revenue loss of $2.4 billion, twice what the Treasury had anticipated. The worst was yet to come. The Senate Finance Committee reported out a bill that was little different from the one that passed the House. But on the floor of the Senate, Albert Gore proposed an increase in the personal exemption from $600 to $800, which was reduced in the conference committee to $750. This loss of revenue, coupled with a 15 percent increase in Social Security benefits—5 percent higher than the administration recommended—increased the projected annual revenue loss to $5 billion.

Kennedy was double-minded about the tax-reform cum tax-reduction bill as it came to the President for signature. With Paul McCracken and Robert Mayo, he sent drafts of two statements to the President: one for him to make if he vetoed the bill; one if he signed the bill. In the end, they recommended that the President sign the bill, offering three reasons for doing so: the act did provide for a more equitable tax structure than existing law, there was a loss of revenue involved in either signing the bill or vetoing it, and a veto would create additional tension between Congress and the President. The prudent course seemed, therefore, to sign the bill and then ask for taxes to balance the budget in the next session of Congress.

The President did not like the act, but he signed it. However, he signed it in private and left his Secretary of the Treasury to face the press. David Kennedy tried to put the best face on the President's approval and praised the bill as a milestone in tax reform. When a reporter wanted to know why, if the bill was such a success, "didn't the President propose Congressional representation and sign it in public," Ron Ziegler brushed the question aside with the lame explanation that Congress had adjourned.

Income tax reform and extension of the surcharge had united support in the executive branch. In contrast, the principal battles over other domestic economic issues while Kennedy was Secretary of the Treasury involved interfraternal conflicts within the Nixon administration. Kennedy, Paul McCracken, and Robert Mayo insisted that the battle against inflation should be the administration's first priority, but other members of the Cabinet and some of the White House staff urged the President to undertake a far-reaching and expensive welfare reform that would make the fight to control inflation even more difficult. The proposal, backed by Daniel Moynihan, who chaired the Urban Affairs Council, and Secretary Robert Finch of Health, Education, and Welfare, was known in the early stages of its formulation as the Family Security System (FSS). The crux of the proposal was to provide a minimum income for every family with dependent children headed by a father as well as by a mother. It would therefore replace the existing program of Aid to Families with Dependent Children (AFDC). Critics of AFDC argued that it was discriminatory because it provided no aid for families with a father at home, even if he were unemployed.

The battle lines over the Moynihan-Finch proposal were drawn within the administration by the opposition of Arthur Burns, the President's counselor for domestic affairs, because it looked too much like a guaranteed annual wage and was too expensive. Secretary of Labor George Shultz and the White House staff, which saw substantial political advantage in the Moynihan-Finch proposal, backed the FSS. Kennedy sided with Burns on the issues, for he feared that if *any* costly welfare reform program was presented to

275

Congress before the surcharge was extended, the credibility of the administration's determination to fight inflation would be undermined.

Kennedy pressed the matter hard with the President. In a memorandum dated July 12, 1969, in addition to his concern that its introduction would imperil the extension of the surcharge, Kennedy questioned the estimates of how much the program would cost and pointed out that no matter how the plan is presented, "it will be interpreted as a guaranteed annual income." That memorandum was followed by one on July 22 to Kenneth R. Cole, Jr., special assistant to the President, who had asked for Treasury's comments on the FSS. Kennedy again urged the President to postpone action on welfare reform until the surcharge was enacted. In lieu of a new welfare program, he backed a proposal, first advanced by Burns, that would assure "the transition into the labor force of potential employable people now on welfare," provide "training . . . to increase the productive earnings of workers with low incomes, to give them incentive to stay off welfare," and provide "improvement of the assistance for those who cannot make the transition from welfare." Acceptance of these proposals, Kennedy argued, "should make it clear that the deferral of a public announcement of a major welfare reform because of the current domestic economic restraint effort is just that—a temporary but unavoidable deferral."

Kennedy's final attempt to forestall the introduction of the FSS to Congress was a memorandum that he sent to the President on July 31. "In this recommendation," Kennedy wrote, "I am joined by Messrs. Mayo, McCracken, and Burns. The Vice President also has asked to be associated with our position. In addition, . . . the point of view we express is consistent with positions taken by Messrs. Romney, Stans, and Harlow." Kennedy told the President that there were better and cheaper paths to welfare reform than the FSS. His objections rested on both fiscal responsibility and political credibility. The projected cost of the program would undermine the hope of the administration for a balanced 1971 budget without the surcharge. "Moreover," Kennedy reminded the President, "the credibility of sending now to the Congress a proposal . . .

which flies in the face of your emphatic statements within the past two weeks that you are determined to achieve and maintain fiscal responsibility becomes questionable."

It was a losing battle. John Ehrlichman rather than Arthur Burns now had the President's ear on domestic issues. It was Ehrlichman who flew to Bucharest on August 1 to present the FSS—and the Kennedy-Burns objections—to the President, who was on his way home from a round-the-world tour. Kennedy was reluctant to let Ehrlichman take his memorandum, for he was doubtful that Ehrlichman would present his views to the President with any precision. Ehrlichman insisted that he take the Kennedy memorandum so Nixon could consider it on his way home.

Soon after Nixon arrived home, he called Kennedy to thank him for the memorandum, but said he was sending the FSS to Congress and that the final version of the plan would be presented to the Cabinet at Camp David on August 6. Then, playing on Kennedy's strong sense of loyalty, Nixon said, as Kennedy recalled, "I hope you will not oppose me at the meeting, that you will not comment adversely on it." This hope, which Kennedy took more as an instruction than a request, put him in an embarrassing situation when one after another Burns, Mayo, and the Vice President asked him to take a strong stand against the program in the Cabinet meeting. Without telling them why, he told each of them that though he was strongly opposed, he would remain silent. "They couldn't understand me," he ruefully recalled.

At a luncheon following the meeting, Nixon made it clear to the Cabinet just how strongly he felt about the program. The President spoke of the need for unity in the Cabinet and expressed the hope that none would oppose the program in testimony before Congress. There was in his remarks a subtle implication that if they could not give him their full support in this matter, he was ready to accept their resignations. Nixon won the support of the Cabinet, but it was all for naught. Opposition in the Senate killed the measure, which had been renamed the Family Assistance Plan (FAP) to make it sound less "New Dealish," and Nixon's hope for welfare reform was swept aside.

The dispute over welfare reform was probably the turning point in establishing Ehrlichman's power over domestic policy. Presidents must devote the major portion of their time and energy to the most pressing problems, which in Nixon's eyes were clearly foreign policy issues. Furthermore, there is ample evidence that Nixon had little interest in economic issues. In Kennedy's first interview with Nixon, the President-elect refused to discuss economics, saying that he left such matters to the experts. McCracken thought Nixon approached economic issues "somewhat like . . . a little boy doing required lessons." Nixon always gave politics precedence over economics, for as he told Charls Walker, "You can't explain economics to the American people." In the development of economic policy, he wanted a consensus position that he could validate without having to spend his time and energy mediating disputes. The dispute over welfare reform presented Nixon with just the opposite situation. In that case he had to intervene personally in an interadministration conflict that deeply divided the Cabinet and the White House staff. He therefore gave increasing power to his two principal aides, H. R. Haldeman and Ehrlichman, to settle those issues without his intervention. Certainly, the rise to power of Ehrlichman made it more difficult for Kennedy to influence policy, since two of his closest allies in the White House, Arthur Burns and Robert Mayo, were by the middle of 1970 out of the administration. Burns became chairman of the Federal Reserve Board, and Mayo became president of the Federal Reserve Bank of Chicago after he lost his position as budget director in a reorganization of that office.

One aspect of the Nixon advocacy of welfare reform that survived and prospered was revenue sharing. The proposal that the federal government share part of its revenue with the states had been raised in the Johnson administration, but no action was taken then. Republican governors of major industrial states, such as George Romney of Michigan and Nelson Rockefeller of New York, picked up the idea and made it part of their political platforms. For most Republicans, the attractiveness of the idea was that it promised a way to strengthen the role of the state and local governments. When the Nixon administration came into office, Arthur Burns wanted to go slow on revenue sharing, but as part of his opposition to the Moynihan-Finch welfare reform plan, he shifted to active support for revenue sharing. He called Charls Walker and asked him to take charge of developing a revenue-sharing program. Walker protested that he had too much to do as it was. But when Burns would not take no for an answer, Murray Weidenbaum, who was a well-known advocate of revenue sharing, was recruited as Assistant Secretary for Economic Policy and assigned the revenue-sharing task. Weidenbaum and Robert Nathan of the White House staff became the principal architects of the proposal.

Kennedy's initial reaction to revenue sharing was cautious, because his first priority was the battle to stem inflation, and revenue sharing would make achieving a balanced budget more difficult. But when Congress refused to pass the FAP, the administration rescued the revenue-sharing proposal and decided to give it top priority in its domestic program. Kennedy loyally supported that decision, no doubt urged on by Weidenbaum. In November 1969 he praised revenue sharing as the heart of Nixon's "New Federalism," and in April 1970 he welcomed a statement by officials of the National League of Cities, the U.S. Conference of Mayors, the National Association of Counties, the National Governors Conference, and the National Legislative Conference supporting revenue sharing. In a letter to the editor of the *New York Times* on December 4, 1970, the secretary complained that a recent editorial in the paper urging prompt action on revenue sharing had not laid the blame for inaction squarely where it belonged: on Congress. He declared: "I was astonished that your editorial made no mention whatsoever of this unfortunate lack of progress by the Legislative Branch. Certainly revenue sharing deserves a prompt and thorough hearing. Recurring accounts of serious fiscal distress in our local governments only serve to underscore the high priority which revenue sharing has assumed. This is one instance where Presidential leadership needs to be joined by Congressional responsibility."

Kennedy's last word on revenue sharing before he left the Treasury was a draft of a statement for inclusion in the President's

President Nixon with leaders of Mormon church on steps of Church Office Building, July 24, 1970. In front row are Harold B. Lee, Joseph Fielding Smith, Nixon, and N. Eldon Tanner; back row are Pat Nixon and daughter Tricia, David M. Kennedy, George Romney

annual budget message. That draft committed the President to revenue sharing as a means "to transfer decision-making responsibility, as well as funds, back to the American people." Although the President's 1971 budget message did include a recommendation that Congress enact revenue-sharing legislation, he had to wait until October 1972 before the revenue-sharing act was sent from Congress for his signature.

Kennedy's most persistent theme throughout his tenure as Secretary of the Treasury was the danger of inflation. On the basis of that assumption he supported the extension of the surcharge, justified his opposition to the early introduction of welfare-reform legislation, including revenue sharing, and opposed the introduction of new programs before the budget was in balance. The government, he repeatedly argued, must reduce government spending and restrain the availability of credit if inflation was to be stemmed. Yet candor compelled him to admit that if these measures were not successful, the administration might have to consider the possibility of wage and price controls. For his part, Kennedy hoped the need to consider seriously that alternative would never arise, yet as 1970 began, wage and price controls became the subject of debate not only in Congress but also within the administration.

The early hopes of Kennedy and the other members of the troika that gradualism would reduce inflation with only a minimum increase in the unemployment rate were never realized. By mid-1970, inflation was close to 6 percent, up from 4.7 percent at the beginning of 1969, while unemployment had risen from 3.3 percent to 4.7 percent during the same period. This persistence of inflation in the presence of rising unemployment ran counter to the basic assumption of gradualism, which held that even in the short term, inflation and unemployment should move in opposite directions. Some economists, including Arthur Burns, Murray Weidenbaum, and Paul Volcker, concluded that the cause of the inflation was not only an excess of demand over supply but also the anticipation of businessmen and labor leaders that inflation would continue. Hence, those leaders were protecting their interests by raising prices and demanding higher wages. After all, the government's monetary and fiscal policies were no secret, and business, industrial, financial, and labor leaders could see that the strong growth of the money supply during the 1960s, particularly the sharp rise in 1967–68, foretold the coming of inflation. Therefore, businessmen raised prices anticipating inflation, bankers raised interest rates on the same basis, and labor leaders based their wage demands on anticipation that prices and interest rates would increase. These expectations led to what was called "cost-push" inflation, which could not be controlled without some dramatic government action to make the government's war on inflation credible.

As a result of these conclusions, consideration began to be given in both the White House and the Treasury to the possibility of an incomes policy to supplement gradualism. This internal debate became public after Burns, now chairman of the Federal Reserve Board, suggested in a speech on May 18, 1970, that "there may be a useful—albeit a modest—role for an incomes policy to play." What he had in mind was not a long-term incomes policy, but short-term restrictions that would break the psychological impulse of cost-push inflation and make gradualism truly effective.

In the ensuing public discussion of the possibility of adopting an incomes policy, clearly the term meant different things to different people. To some it meant an appeal to responsible behavior; to some, a set of general guidelines for prices and wages; to others, a temporary freeze on prices and wages; and to still others statutory limitations on wages and prices. Throughout this debate Kennedy continued to oppose statutory controls on wages and prices. But as early as January 1970, in a memorandum to the President, he suggested that the time had come for some "jawboning": "I believe that you and other senior members of the Administration should use appropriate opportunities, both in public and in private, to urge consumers, businessmen, workers, and Government officials as well, to responsibly restrain their demands so as to achieve the reduction in inflation which is to their mutual self interest. Such action could be useful in holding public confidence in our policies."

Although in a subsequent speech the President rejected "jawboning" as a basic part of an incomes policy, the administration was moving toward some kind of action beyond gradualism. Burns's May 18 speech was preceded by a report in March by the Joint Economic Committee that recommended that the Council of Economic Advisors (CEA) adopt "specific voluntary standards for price and incomes behavior." In testimony before the Joint Economic Committee on June 2, Weidenbaum acknowledged, under close questioning from Senator William Proxmire of Wisconsin, that "the time has come to seriously consider incomes policy." Weidenbaum would not discuss the details of what an incomes policy might include, since that involved confidential advice he was giving the Secretary of the Treasury. He hinted, however, that his concept of an incomes policy lay somewhere between mandatory controls and "jawboning." Burns and Weidenbaum's support for an incomes policy was opposed by Shultz—who left Labor to become the director of the Office of Management and Budget—on the ground that it would induce business to increase prices quickly to get ahead of the imposition of that policy. The result was a presidential address on June 17, 1970, denying that the administration was considering an incomes policy. President Nixon also said he had instructed the Council of Economic Advisors to issue periodic "inflation alerts" to highlight the danger inflation created for the nation.

David Kennedy, asked to comment on a draft of the speech, thought that it understated the difficulties that lay ahead in controlling inflation. He objected specifically to a passage that promised that full employment and price stability would be accomplished with "as little pain along the way as possible," saying, "Obviously, we want as little pain as possible, but the general tone still sounds as though we think we can accomplish our objective in a manner that won't hurt much. I doubt if that is a very credible or useful line at this point. Certainly we should defend and stick to our general monetary and fiscal policies. But, to pick up the metaphor of the speech, instead of talking about 'easing a boat into the dock,' I think we would be better off admitting that we are still in pretty choppy waters—and that it will take a steady hand, strong men, and some pain to ride it out, as we will and must."

The President took out the "little pain along the way as possible" passage, but he kept the line about easing the boat into the dock, although in retrospect Kennedy's "pretty choppy waters" metaphor was more appropriate. Indeed, in retrospect, his metaphor turned out to be very accurate—and has continued to characterize the American economy since.

During the late summer and early fall of 1970, Kennedy believed that the policies encompassed in gradualism had broken the back of inflation and that if they were continued, it would be possible to move to a slow but steady growth of the economy. On October 6, Kennedy told the National Press Club that no conditions in the foreseeable future would justify the imposition of wage and price controls. His troika colleague, Paul McCracken, held the same view. In a speech to the Economic Club of Detroit on October 19, he said the economy has "stronger gains in output, larger increases in productivity, a slower rise in the price level and in other costs per unit of output, and further gains against inflation, . . . a phase where we more nearly have the best of both worlds." These optimistic views of the economy were shattered by a recession that fall. Unemployment rose to 6 percent, partly because of a strike against General Motors that began in September and closed down that industrial giant for three months. The strike and a serious downturn in the construction industry increased total unemployment without bringing about a corresponding decrease in inflation. This experience reinforced the growing conviction in the administration that cost-push inflation was not responding to reductions in aggregate demand. This perception was sharpened during October and November when it became apparent that the settlement of the General Motors strike was likely to be inflationary, as were other wage negotiations in progress.

In the early fall, before this became clear, Nixon told Kennedy that political considerations made it necessary to reinflate the economy. As much as it may seem so, however, this primacy of politics over economics was not the result of the recession in the fall of 1970. It was implicit from the beginning of Nixon's administration. The President decided in the summer of 1969 to move ahead with welfare reform even though it would have resulted in a larger budget deficit and thus made the fight against inflation more difficult. His decision to reinflate the economy by sending to Congress in January 1971 a budget that had a deficit of $23 billion simply showed how deeply political factors influenced White House decisions. Kennedy thought that the President was moving too fast, but his objections were brushed aside with the assertion that a recession or depression would hurt Nixon's political future more than would continuing inflation. That argument troubled Kennedy, and he told the President so: "If you are going to inflate to be elected, then inflation is a way of life, and those people who said we would not stay with our course are right and we are wrong." Kennedy was not persuaded by the President's response that if he were to achieve his goals he had to win elections. "Well, if that is the argument," Kennedy responded, "then it's a question of who will out do the other one for election." This conversation convinced Kennedy that the President was "pushing more for reelection to a second term than for any other one thing." Despite Kennedy's insistence on the priority of economics over politics, the election defeat that the Republicans suffered in November seemingly justified Nixon's belief that politics must come first.

It was against this background that Kennedy sent a proposal to the White House for the creation of a wage-price panel with the power to review for its impact on inflation any wage or price decision on a case-by-case basis. The panel, Kennedy argued, would provide a " 'shield' for a more expansionary thrust from our conventional economic policies, without fomenting new inflationary expectations." Kennedy recognized that his proposal was not "an easy, painless escape" from the paradox unforeseen in prevailing economic theory of simultaneous increases in unemployment and inflation. The plan, he acknowledged, included "the danger that one can be propelled down the road toward direct controls." Yet, he thought, "even if we should fail to satisfactorily reconcile our price and unemployment objectives, it seems to me incomparably better to have been willing to make this new effort. If the effort is successful, we will have achieved a great deal."

This memorandum was Kennedy's last effort as Secretary of the Treasury to influence the Nixon administration's economic policy. Three weeks later John Connally was the new Secretary of the Treasury, and nine months later, when Kennedy was ambassador-at-large and the costs of reinflating the economy finally had to be paid, the President went way beyond Kennedy's wage-price panel to announce a wage-price freeze. In retrospect, in the context of 1969–70, it is clear that Kennedy and his associates were right in their conviction that inflation was the greatest danger. But the Nixon administration abandoned gradualism because its advocates underestimated the hold that the fear of recession and depression still had on the American people. Any increase in unemployment was unacceptable—as Kennedy learned when scorn was heaped on him for admitting that a 4 percent unemployment rate was an acceptable cost to pay in the effort to reduce inflation. The Great Depression brooded over the nation in the Nixon administration the way the fear of double-digit inflation has dominated contemporary economic and political debates. It was then probably inevitable that both Congress and the President lacked the will to accept the political consequences of gradualism. In the absence of that will, the Nixon administration was launched on a search for new policies that required new faces.

285

17

AMBASSADOR-AT-LARGE

For David Kennedy, the fall of 1970 was a time for decision. He was at the end of the two years he had promised to remain as Secretary of the Treasury; his health was not the best, and he was having trouble with a blood clot in his eye; and he turned sixty-five that July and was the oldest member of the cabinet. Yet he believed he still had a contribution to make as Secretary of the Treasury. However, his future was not decided on either of those grounds but by presidential politics. While Kennedy never lost faith in gradualism, increased unemployment coupled with rising inflation imposed greater costs than the political system could bear. Consequently, in the November election the Republicans lost nine seats in the House of Representatives, and, although they gained two seats in the Senate, they remained the minority in both houses by a substantial margin.

Kennedy recognized that the failure of the Republican party to make headway toward reversing its role as the minority party was partly due to the economic policies of which he was a leading advocate. Therefore, he offered himself to President Nixon as the scapegoat for the party's election defeat. That offer was at first refused, but there were forces at play in the White House that ultimately would induce the President to accept the resignation Kennedy offered.

First was the rise to power of H. R. Haldeman and John Ehrlichman, who were more interested in political victories than economic stability. The results of the 1970 election foreshadowed a difficult presidential race in 1972, and they wanted to strengthen the administration's ability to fight that coming political battle. Second, Nixon was impressed with John Connally and wanted to bring him into his administration. Connally was the leader of the conservative wing of the Democratic party and, like Nixon, was far more a pragmatist than an ideologue. He was, however, a man of great ambition—he would later become a Republican and seek the presidential nomination under that label. He was willing to serve in the Nixon cabinet but only in one of the top three positions: Defense, State, or Treasury. Nixon took the course of least resistance. He already had Kennedy's offer to resign, while he would have had to force Melvin Laird out to make Connally Secretary of Defense, and there was no point in making Connally Secretary of State as long as Henry Kissinger was in the White House. If Connally was to come into the administration, it had to be as Secretary of the Treasury.

Nixon and Kennedy had several discussions about Kennedy's situation. News of these meetings leaked to the press, and there was speculation about Kennedy's future that ranged from his being forced out to his being promised that he could finish Nixon's first term as Secretary of the Treasury. In those discussions, Nixon asked Kennedy whom he might appoint in his stead. Kennedy thought Charls Walker would do a good job, but Nixon revealed that he was after bigger game. He then asked Kennedy what he thought of Connally. Kennedy responded that Connally was a Democrat who would never change his stripes, but he also told the President that he would support whatever decision he made.

Even though Nixon was prepared to accept Kennedy's resignation as Secretary of the Treasury, he was not prepared to let him leave government service. He asked Kennedy if he would stay on as a member of the cabinet, serving as an ambassador-at-large specializing on international economic issues. Despite his preference for leaving government, Kennedy decided to accept the appointment. He would be free from the administrative burden of managing a large department, he would escape the ever-watchful eye of the press, and he would be involved in issues where he could make a substantial contribution. Thus, John Connally was brought into the administration as Secretary of the Treasury, and David Kennedy was appointed ambassador-at-large.

Kennedy's first assignment as ambassador-at-large was a fact-finding mission to Vietnam, Indonesia, Thailand, and Micronesia. It was merely the prelude to the President's request that he undertake sensitive negotiations with Japan, Korea, the Republic of China (Taiwan), and the Crown Colony of Hong Kong to restrict their textile exports to the United States. This assignment presented him with his most challenging task in his new position; it also brought into play his substantial experience in the Far East and permitted him to make the most of his negotiating skills and his personal qualities of integrity, patience, and persistance. Donald Webster remembered it as no easy task: "Kennedy took a plane over there and he literally camped on the doorsteps of those countries. . . . They didn't want to really deal with him. They knew what he wanted and they didn't have to give it to him. . . . It was really tough. I used to refer to it as our economic Vietnam. It was just brutal."

Long before Kennedy appeared on the scene, the American textile industry had sought reductions in Asian textile exports to the United States. In 1955 the Japanese imposed voluntary restrictions on the shipment of cotton textiles to the United States. That agreement led to a multinational pact on trade in cotton textiles in 1962 known as the Long Term Agreement. After 1962, the problem was no longer cotton textiles but man-made fibers and wool. The American textile industry wanted similar restrictions placed on imports of these textiles. On the other hand, the textile industries in Japan, Hong Kong, Taiwan, and Korea were adamant in rejecting such restrictions since they depended so heavily on the American market.

The plight of the American textile industry became an issue in the 1968 presidential campaign, and Nixon, as part of his southern strategy, promised that if he were elected, he would come to the aid of the textile industry. Although Nixon was basically in favor of free trade, he remembered the 1960 campaign when John F. Kennedy's promise to impose restrictions on cotton imports helped him hold the South against Nixon's challenge. Nixon's campaign tactics eight years later, therefore, called for a similar promise: to restrict man-made fibers and wool.

The assignment to negotiate a textile agreement with the countries of the Far East came to Kennedy only after others, including Secretary of Commerce Maurice Stans, had failed. Even Henry Kissinger had tried his hand at settling the issue, but by the spring of 1971 it was clear that his efforts as well as all others had failed also. When White House efforts came to naught, Wilbur Mills, chairman of the House Ways and Means Committee, entered the picture as an unofficial—and for the White House an unwanted—negotiator. Under his urging, Japanese textile industries agreed to limit their exports to the United States and set forth a detailed plan for doing so.

The Mills initiative was opposed by the American textile industry and by Nixon, who said it "fell short of the terms essential to the United States." The Japanese reaction to the President's rejection was on the surface bitter, but privately they speculated that his sharp rejection was for domestic consumption. They hoped that faithful compliance with the terms of the Mills agreement would quiet the demand in the United States for further restriction. That hope was falsely based, for Nixon was determined to keep his pledge to American manufacturers. Enter ambassador-at-large David M. Kennedy.

Kennedy brought to this assignment qualifications that none of the other negotiators possessed. He was well and favorably known in Japan[1] and understood the way Japanese did business, particularly the way they negotiated agreements. As Secretary of the Treasury he maintained good relations with Japanese leaders, who admired Kennedy, the man. They respected his advancing age, and they were impressed by his dignity, decency, stately appearance,

289

and, above all, patience and tenacity. They were, therefore, comfortable dealing with him, even when he advocated a policy they opposed.

Kennedy was faced with four interrelated but separate problems. First, he had to convince the Japanese that the United States would settle for nothing short of a government-to-government agreement. Eisaku Sato, the Japanese prime minister, was caught in a political vise. He had repeatedly told Nixon that he was willing to settle the textile problem, but he was unable, or unwilling, to translate that commitment into government policy. Furthermore, once the Japanese industry agreed to consider voluntary controls, Sato apparently hoped that such action would provide the American government with sufficient reason for not insisting on further action by the Japanese government.

Second, Kennedy found political tensions at home equal to those in Japan. The President was under continuing pressure from the American industry to keep his campaign pledge to restrict textile imports. At the same time there were those in his administration, particularly in the State Department, who thought that textiles were unimportant within the larger context of the alliance. They argued that the United States should avoid making textile restrictions appear to be a trade-off for the agreement to return Okinawa to Japanese control. They were also concerned that pushing the Japanese too hard on textiles would erode Japanese support for American policy in Vietnam and make it more difficult to negotiate the continued existence of American bases in Japan.

The third problem facing Kennedy was how to coordinate the agreements among the four Asian countries exporting synthetic and woolen textiles to the United States. On the one hand, the Japanese thought that restricting their cotton textile exports to the United States had not helped the American industry, since exports from Hong Kong, Korea, and Taiwan had filled the gap left by those restrictions. On the other hand, those three exporters thought they merited American support for their domestic industries as they struggled to raise their standard of living. Furthermore, they doubted that the Americans were serious about imposing restrictions. White House statements of determination were countered by private conversations among diplomats describing those statements as intended for domestic consumption, and if restrictions were imposed at all, they would be ones the exporting countries could accept.[2]

The fourth problem Kennedy had to tackle was how to find a negotiating strategy that would avoid the mistakes of the past. He decided his only chance for success was to adopt the Kissinger strategy—even though Kissinger had failed to get an agreement—of negotiating over the heads of both the American and the Japanese bureaucracy. As part of this "back channel" diplomacy, he arranged to use Central Intelligence Agency communication facilities linked directly to the White House, thus bypassing the State Department and other agencies. So, during the entire negotiations, Kennedy dealt directly with Peter Peterson, a senior White House aide to whom Nixon assigned the textile problem.

Kennedy's negotiating strategy was so unorthodox that it raised considerable concern among some American diplomats, who feared he would disrupt other American policy in the Far East. He was later told by a friend that during the textile negotiations "back channel" diplomacy was the principal topic of conversation at a regional conference of American ambassadors to Asian countries. This involved him in a continuing conflict with the Department of State, which sought at every stage of the negotiations to bring them back within normal diplomatic channels. His assignment, however, was to negotiate an agreement that would fulfill the President's pledge to the textile industry—and to achieve that goal, he must be the President's man, unhampered by State Department review of either his policy choices or his negotiating strategy and tactics.

If Kennedy's unorthodox methods were to be successful, he also needed a personal staff he could fully trust. His principal aide was Anthony Jurich, who was joined by Rex Beach. Two other key aides were Seth Bodner from the Department of Commerce and Harry Phelan from the State Department. Webster was assigned as an assistant to Peter Peterson in the White House. Thus, Kennedy not only had the full backing of the President and control of the communications channels, he also had a staff, both in the field and in Washington, in whom he had full confidence.

Kennedy began his task by visiting each of the exporting countries. The White House announced that he would undertake a worldwide trade mission involving consultations with the United States's trading partners but would not have any specific proposals at this point. In these early talks, Kennedy refused to discuss details of the textile problem. His concern was to establish a basis of trust—and to repeat over and over again three points: "how serious the President was about the issue, how important it was to remove this major irritant to U.S.-Japanese relations, and how impractical it was for the Japanese (and the Koreans, Taiwanese, and Hong Kong Chinese) to expect they could really expand textile exports to the United States very much more."

Kennedy also suggested that each country appoint someone at a high level with whom he could deal. He explained his intent to keep the negotiations out of the press as much as possible, and, for his part, to never make a statement to the press that would embarrass them. In Taiwan, Chiang Kai-shek expressed appreciation for that sensitivity and appointed Y. S. Sun, the economic minister, to work with Kennedy. Korean President Park Chunghee wanted to keep a close watch on the negotiations, so he insisted Kennedy deal only with him. Park repeatedly reminded Kennedy of Korea's special relationship with the United States and how American failure to provide Korea with enough aid to support its development plans was forcing that country to be increasingly dependent on Japan.

Upon his return to the United States, Kennedy told Nixon that he thought an agreement could be reached and reemphasized the necessity of keeping the negotiations confined to a small group outside normal diplomatic channels. Additionally, he asked for and got a presidential directive giving him full authority to conduct the negotiations without interference from other government agencies. Nixon suggested that Kennedy prepare a draft of such a directive for his signature. When the President signed the draft, he told Kennedy it was the strongest directive he had issued. Kennedy responded that he knew it was strong and he would use it only when necessary.

Kennedy's first stop when he returned to the Far East was Taiwan, where he reached an "agreement in principle." Negotiations with the Koreans were far more difficult. His visit to Seoul in June was greeted by a rally of over three thousand textile workers protesting any cuts in exports to the United States. Moreover, Korean officials still believed that the President's strong stand on textiles was intended only for domestic consumption. Kennedy finally had to show ambassador William J. Porter the presidential directive before his American colleagues believed that the President was really serious about reducing Korean textile exports to the United States. Hong Kong was not any easier than Korea, for the British government was opposed to any agreement, and when Kennedy arrived in the Crown Colony, he was described in the press as the most unwelcome visitor to Hong Kong.

While an agreement with Japan was key to negotiations with the other three countries, the strong objections to any agreement in Hong Kong, Taiwan, and Korea convinced Kennedy that more than an agreement with Japan was needed for leverage with those three states. Therefore, on his return visits he came prepared with options that were dubbed "carrots and sticks" by his negotiating team. There was little that could be offered Hong Kong, but both Taiwan and Korea had large and expensive U.S.-equipped military establishments and might be influenced by increased economic and military assistance. Therefore, in the ensuing discussions with Taiwanese and Korean officials, Kennedy could offer increased aid as a carrot. The stick was implied more than stated, since failure to agree would wipe out the promised benefits. The most threatening stick was the continued threat of unilateral restrictions imposed by the United States.

In the meantime, the Japanese were engaged in an internal debate over whether the agreement Wilbur Mills had wrung from the Japanese industry should be put into effect. Finally, after the Japanese government promised to compensate those firms hardest hit by the restrictions under the Mills agreement, the leaders of the textile industry decided to impose the restrictions July 1, 1971.

Anthony Jurich, David M. Kennedy, and Japanese Prime Minister Eisaku Sato

Kennedy's task was to persuade Prime Minister Sato and his colleagues that the voluntary restrictions did not change the situation and that eventually they would have to accept the necessity of reaching a government-to-government agreement. He began to hope for success after Sato made changes in his cabinet, assigning Takeo Fukuda as foreign minister and Kakuei Tanaka to head the Ministry for International Trade and Industry. Both men, Sato told Kennedy, were flexible on the textile issue.

Fukuda soon gave evidence that Sato was right, for at his first press conference he spoke in favor of reaching a final solution to the textile dispute, which he publicly conceded was not resolved by the industry plan. Tanaka had to be more cautious, but he too was in favor of greater flexibility, although in public he supported the Mills agreement. Kennedy's expectations that with the appointment of Fukuda and Tanaka a government-to-government agreement could be reached were upset, however, by the announcement on July 15, 1971, that Nixon would go to Peking to discuss American-Chinese relations with Chou En-lai. That announcement, which caught the Japanese government by surprise, brought Sato under vigorous attack for failing to anticipate and prepare for the shift in American policy. He now became cautious about reaching any agreement on textiles, and it became impossible for Kennedy to get serious Japanese consideration for a set of proposals that he, Jurich, and Beach had drafted.

Nixon's decision to visit Peking had repercussions not only in Tokyo but also in Taipei, where the aging Chiang had to be told of the President's decision before it became public. Kennedy was not eager to be the bearer of bad news, but the task fell to him nonetheless. After he finished telling Chiang of Nixon's forthcoming trip to the Mainland, Chiang looked out of the window for some time, then turned to say that, despite his great respect for Nixon, he thought the President was making a grave mistake. He warned Kennedy about communist duplicity but reassured him that his government would continue its policy of friendship toward the United States. He also expressed his appreciation for receiving advance notice of the President's trip.

As Kennedy left the Far East for Washington in early August, he knew that matters were at a stalemate. A general belief had emerged that the United States would not take the firm measures necessary to reach a solution. In Hong Kong, Korea, and Taiwan, there were doubts that the United States could negotiate a government-to-government agreement with Japan and, therefore, they would not have to take action; Japanese officials believed that agreements with the other three countries were beyond American power, hence no restrictions beyond the voluntary ones already accepted by the Japanese industry would be imposed.

Kennedy recognized all of these difficulties, but he was still hopeful that patient and quiet diplomacy would produce a solution. However, the American textile industry was increasingly impatient with the delay. He was the object of that impatience at a tension-filled meeting in Taipei with the overseas staffs of the American textile firms, who accused him of selling out to foreign textile interests. Kennedy reminded them, "You are not going to run these negotiations. I am, and I alone. . . . You can help me or you can oppose me, you can upset the apple cart—I couldn't care less.

This is the way it is going to be done." To make his point even stronger, he walked out of the meeting. Subsequently, Frederick Dent, an industry representative, came to Kennedy's hotel to smooth ruffled feathers and told Kennedy that the textile representatives knew his efforts were their best chance to obtain meaningful restrictions on East Asian textile exports to the United States and that he had their support.

Kennedy returned to Washington to find that the President's political advisors had decided that the economic problems besetting the Nixon administration—increased unemployment, rising inflation, and an unsatisfactory balance of payments—must be dealt with dramatically before the 1972 elections. On August 15 Nixon declared a national emergency and a temporary freeze on wages and prices, suspension of the converting of dollars into gold, and the imposition of a 10 percent surcharge on all imports. These measures were just as great an economic shock to Japan and the other textile producers in East Asia as the President's China trip was a political shock.

These shocks notwithstanding, the Nixon administration was not content to let the textile issue become entangled in international negotiations or to rely on the controls imposed by the Japanese industry. While Kennedy was being told by Sato that the time was not ripe for an agreement, Nixon's economic advisors in the White House were searching for a legal basis for imposing quotas on the offending textile imports. Paradoxically, the legislation that offered the best basis for presidential action was the Trading with the Enemy Act, adopted during World War I but amended just after Pearl Harbor, which provided that "during the time of war or during any other period of national emergency declared by the President, the President may . . . regulate . . . any importation or exportation of . . . any property in which any foreign country or a national thereof has any interest." Nixon had set the stage for using the act by inserting a declaration of a national emergency in his August 15 speech. Kennedy assisted in drafting the speech, but, he recalled, he "chose to regard it not as a final decision to go ahead, but rather adding another arrow in his quiver, increasing his leverage on the Japanese."

Kennedy increased the pressure for a government-to-government agreement on textiles with the Japanese at the eighth cabinet-level ministerial conference of the two governments, which began September 9 at Williamsburg, Virginia. At a secret meeting September 8, he gave Fukuda and Tanaka a memorandum stating that "President Nixon does not consider the textile issue to be resolved, in whole or in part, by either the Japanese unilateral restraint program or the measures he proposed and implemented on August 15." The memorandum ended with a threat wrapped in a hope that they could "in a final effort, reach accord before the United States is compelled to resolve the issue unilaterally to its satisfaction."

In his report of these meetings to the President, Kennedy expressed his belief that only Sato could finally convince Japanese textile leaders that some solution to the issue would have to be found before serious steps would "be taken toward resolving other economic issues between the two countries." Consequently, Kennedy urged the President in his meetings with both Fukuda and Tanaka, but especially with Fukuda, to "reaffirm . . . the great importance you attach to resolution of the textile issue. I firmly believe . . . that such a personal effort on your part is essential," he wrote, "if we are to seriously keep alive the prospects of resolving the textile issue by means of a voluntary accord rather than through unilateral action."

Kennedy's meetings with Fukuda and Tanaka at Williamsburg set the stage for the final solution. Out of those meetings came an agreement between Kennedy and Tanaka—with Fukuda really calling the tune—not on the details of an intergovernmental agreement on textiles but on a strategy to reach an agreement. In order for Tanaka to resist the domestic political pressures against an agreement, it must have the appearance of a forced settlement. The key steps involved Tanaka's continuing to take a firm stand against American pressure for an agreement during the ministerial conference, followed by an American ultimatum that a solution had to be found by October 15 or the United States would take unilateral action. For Tanaka, the ultimatum would be the equivalent of "Commodore Perry's 'black ship,' the ostensibly unwanted but overpowering external force that produces internal policy change." Kennedy and Tanaka agreed to negotiate a final settlement after Tanaka pounded the table "kabuki-style" and gained some final U.S. concessions.

Kennedy was confident after his visit with Fukuda and Tanaka that he could bring the textile negotiations to a successful conclusion if he could keep control of the negotiations in Washington and in Tokyo. He knew that Anthony Jurich could be trusted to carry out his instructions with skill and tact, but keeping the various agencies in Washington in line was another matter. There were still those in Washington who thought that the United States was making too much of the textile issue and that much of the President's public posture on the issue was purely for domestic consumption. Kennedy knew that a settlement depended on his ability to convince everyone at home and abroad that the United States intended to negotiate an acceptable agreement or to impose unilateral restrictions.

The final act of the drama began when Jurich returned to East Asia in late September to notify Japan and the other three exporting countries that the United States would unilaterally impose quotas on textiles on October 15 if an agreement satisfactory to the United States were not reached by October 1. The media in both Japan and the United States were critical of the decision to send Jurich back to Japan. But most critical of all were leaders of the Japanese textile industry, who described Jurich as a "ninja," a phantom character clothed in black who steals about in the night doing mischievous deeds.

Yet, even as Jurich arrived in Japan with the ultimatum, Kennedy was startled to read in the newspapers on September 24 an assertion by a State Department press officer, Charles W. Bray, that the American position on textiles was negotiable. Kennedy was furious. How could the threat contained in the ultimatum Jurich had just presented to Tanaka be credible if the State Department was saying publicly that the American position was negotiable? Not only the success of his mission but also the President's personal credibility, he argued, depended on the American government maintaining a united front on this issue. When Kissinger insisted that Kennedy was right on the credibility issue, he knew that his argument had at last been persuasive. His anger and frustration in learning of the Bray statement were apparent in the memorandum he sent to the President. He stated:

> The question of credibility is extremely serious and may well frustrate our objectives unless strong measures are taken immediately. I know, for example, that Hong Kong, Japan, and Korea have been probing the State Department for give in our position. This is particularly disturbing in view of several conversations I have had with Alex Johnson, who obviously is opposed to our terms and our deadlines. In addition, the State Department responded to a question in last Friday's press briefing that our proposals were negotiable. This comment touched off a flood of speculation and a barrage of questions from the Japanese and Koreans.
>
> John Connally, Paul McCracken, Pete Peterson and I have spent the weekend trying to patch up the damage caused by that statement. I don't know how successful we have been. I do know that any further comment of that sort—issued either publicly or privately—can well torpedo the whole effort.

Kissinger backed Kennedy strongly on the importance of American credibility, with the result that the President again notified agencies with an interest in the textile negotiations that Kennedy had full responsibility for the negotiations. Kennedy also insisted that reporters should be told that "Ambassador-at-Large David M. Kennedy is handling the negotiations as the President's personal representative. Consequently, questions concerning this issue should be addressed to the White House press office, which alone has authority to respond to such inquiries."

The last month of the negotiations was a hectic time for Anthony Jurich. Japanese textile industry leaders were trying every avenue possible to avoid more stringent restrictions than those they had already accepted, but at every turn they encountered Jurich, who was steadfastly unwilling to deviate from the Kennedy proposals and insisted that an agreement must be reached before October 15. By October 11, Tanaka, with the support of important segments of the Japanese business community who wanted more than anything else to avoid American quotas on other Japanese goods, announced that he was going to negotiate a government-to-government agreement with the United States even if he did not have the support of the textile industry. That decision was formally ratified by the Japanese cabinet October 12. Almost simultaneously, Nixon told a press conference, that the United States would take unilateral action "against Japan and other textile-exporting nations if no agreement is reached or significant progress made by Friday," that is, October 15.

The stage was now set for Kennedy to fly to Japan on October 13 to sign the agreement Tanaka and Jurich had reached. The last step in the forced settlement agreed to by Kennedy and Tanaka was about to be taken. Tanaka played his part well; now was the time for Kennedy to provide him with some face-saving concessions. The beginning date of the restrictions was advanced from July 1 to October 1; the restrictions were to last three years, but the automatic two-year extension in the original Kennedy proposals was eliminated. Then Kennedy gave Tanaka an unexpected gift: the United States would not apply to textile imports under the agreement the 10 percent surcharge on all imports that the President had announced August 15. After they shook hands on the settlement, Tanaka drew his hand across his stomach indicating that he had just committed political hari-kari. Kennedy quickly picked up on the gesture and told Tanaka that the agreement was good for both countries, and that rather than committing political suicide, Tanaka was on his way to becoming prime minister.

The agreement that Jurich hammered out with his Japanese counterparts was now ready for formal signature. Kennedy was to sign for the United States and Tanaka for Japan. However, just before the ceremony began, the Japanese deputy foreign minister told Kennedy that five textual changes had been made in the agreement, but they did not affect its substance. Kennedy asked the State Department interpreter who accompanied him in place of

Chester Ito, the interpreter he normally used in his negotiations with the Japanese, what the changes said. He was assured that they were just what the Japanese said they were: word changes and nothing more. Kennedy was not convinced, and when his interpreter insisted that they were just word changes, Kennedy dismissed him and asked his staff to find Ito. When Ito read the changes, he confirmed Kennedy's fears that they did make substantive changes in the agreement.

Kennedy did not argue the point further with Tanaka or the deputy foreign minister; rather, he phoned Sato. Sato heard him out and then promised that there would be no substantive changes in the Kennedy-Tanaka agreement. Kennedy agreed to Sato's request that the deputy foreign minister be saved from embarrassment by finding a way to change the text that did not affect the substance of the agreement. When those changes were made, Kennedy took the document to the deputy foreign minister and said, as he recalled, "Here are some changes. They are not ones you suggested, but they are minor changes that will not change the substance of the agreement." The deputy foreign minister nodded his head, but

Kennedy knew from his experience in Japan that he probably meant that he had heard Kennedy, not that he agreed with him. Kennedy did not ask what the nod meant, but he waved the document in the air, announcing that an agreement was reached. He then walked to the other end of the table and laid the agreement before Tanaka. Tanaka, faced with a *fait accompli*, took up his pen and signed.

Once the Japanese agreed to a government-to-government pact, the other three exporting countries quickly agreed to a settlement. The textile issue may have been laid to rest for the time being, but the larger issue of free trade versus protectionism was left unresolved and continues to affect American relations with the four Asian textile exporters some sixteen years later. Paradoxically, Japanese textile exports to the United States soon ceased to be a major factor in American-Japanese trade, as automobiles, television sets, electronics, and a host of high-quality, low-priced goods soon found an expanding market in the United States.

Whatever one thinks of the merits of the final settlement or the wisdom of President Nixon making agreement on textiles a special case to be pursued regardless of other foreign policy interests, Nixon's description of Kennedy's performance as a "masterful job of negotiation" has stood the test of time. Kennedy knew he could address the textile issue only after he had established a relationship of trust and confidence with his negotiating partners. That relationship was created by quiet diplomacy free from the spotlight of the daily press; hence he refused to talk to the press about the progress of the negotiations, even when his negotiating partners used that weapon against him. He also understood that Sato, Fukuda, and Tanaka would be unable to resist pressure from the Japanese textile industry unless the United States's threat of unilateral action was clear and credible. To achieve that goal, he insisted on and received unequivocal support from the President, which made it possible for him to confine the negotiations to channels he could control. Once these conditions were established, Tanaka could effectively play out the "kabuki" scenario that he and Kennedy had agreed to at Williamsburg. "Thus Kennedy succeeded with an approach similar to the one with which diplomatic 'superstar' Henry Kissinger had badly failed—using strong pressure to cut a deal with the Japanese leadership over the heads of the Japanese (and American) bureaucracy," wrote I. M. Destler in his book *The Textile Wrangle*. Kennedy had some advantages that previous American negotiators lacked: "a strong counterpart similarly set on agreement, the post-August 15 political climate, the back-burner threat to Okinawa ratification in the Senate, and, of course, the final ultimatum." No doubt those advantages helped him succeed where others failed. But after all, it was his handling of the negotiations that made the American ultimatum credible and created the climate in which Tanaka could conclude a government-to-government agreement despite the determined and continued opposition of the Japanese textile industry.

Early in the fall of 1971, after the successful conclusion of the textile negotiations, Nixon asked Kennedy to become the United States's permanent representative on the council of the North Atlantic Treaty Organization (NATO). The post had been vacant since the summer of 1971, when the former ambassador, Robert Ellsworth, resigned. Kennedy was willing to take the appointment, but only if it did not require that he resign as ambassador-at-large and thus lose his position as a cabinet member. He spelled out his reasons in a memorandum to the President:

> Peter Flanigan recently conveyed to me your interest in my taking the position as Ambassador to NATO. I have given much thought to this possible assignment and feel that I could be most effective for you in that position only if I maintain my present title and Cabinet rank and, consequently, serve in effect as Acting Ambassador to NATO until you have completed your trip to the Soviet Union in the spring. This then would be a special assignment for a specific purpose and a temporary period.
>
> It seems to me that such an arrangement has certain definite advantages. Most important, it would indicate the priority you attach to NATO affairs throughout this period in which I would act as your personal representative to that organization. In addition, it could have beneficial repercussions on the Hill and perhaps serve to dampen some of the

difficulties we are experiencing with Congress on the troop level and troop support issues.

If, on the other hand, you have me in mind as a permanent replacement for Bob Ellsworth rather than as a temporary trouble shooter in that position, then I would view the assignment in a different light. From my experience with NATO, the Ambassadors have a cozy club passing back and forth positions sent to them by someone in their various governments. I do not see how my own background and experience would be of any material advantage in performing the customary duties and responsibilities of the Ambassador to NATO. There are numerous individuals who are certainly as well or better qualified than I am to hold that post.

In subsequent discussions with Henry Kissinger, Kennedy suggested that any announcement of his appointment as ambassador to NATO include a clear statement that the appointment was intended to underline the importance the President placed on American participation in NATO and his intention to strengthen American and European economic ties. He also asked, since he was to have general responsibility for American economic involvement in Europe, that the American ambassadors to the European Economic Community (EEC) and the Organization for Economic Cooperation and Development (OECD) clear their statements through him so that the President's economic policies were reflected accurately to the Europeans. Kennedy wanted a deputy ambassador and an economic minister appointed so that his office could pay attention to the full scope of economic and political issues within NATO. These recommendations, as well as the conditions spelled out in his memorandum to the President, became the basis of his appointment as ambassador to NATO; they also propelled him into a protracted struggle with the State Department over the structure and scope of his assignment.

Ambassadors are appointed by the President with the advice and consent of the Senate, but they report to the President through the Secretary of State. If Kennedy were appointed ambassador to

*David and Lenora Kennedy in front
of ambassador's house in Brussels*

NATO and simultaneously returned his status as ambassador-at-large and as a member of the cabinet, he would become the second-ranking officer in the State Department and thus would have a unique position in the department hierarchy. Secretary of State William Rogers, with whom Kennedy had a good personal relationship, raised vigorous objections to the Kennedy appointment under the conditions the President had specified. He was concerned that he would have a subordinate who had direct access to the President and who would not fit neatly into the department's organization structure. He told Kennedy that the Senate would never approve his appointment to the two posts, since it was illegal for him to draw two salaries. He argued that there was no budgetary provision for a deputy ambassador, and expressed concern that Kennedy's plans to retain his apartment in Washington and continue to serve as ambassador-at-large would make him a part-time ambassador to NATO.

Kennedy met Rogers's objections one by one. He would not draw two salaries; therefore, there were no legal barriers to his appointment. Further, the White House had learned that the Senate had no objections to his holding the combined offices. He assured Rogers that he would not be a part-time ambassador; on the contrary, his position in the cabinet would increase the prestige of the

305

NATO appointment and make him more effective. When the State Department continued to raise objections, Kennedy refused to go ahead with confirmation hearings until the issues were settled. Indeed, as Kennedy's aide, Rex Beach, told Alexander Haig, Kissinger's deputy in the White House, that "the way things were going, Kennedy was not sure this assignment was for him." That information moved Haig to ask that Kennedy "not do anything and that they would get it settled." Beach believed that as a result of this conversation that Haig "seemed to be genuinely concerned that Kennedy would call the whole thing off."

Haig judged Kennedy's mood correctly, for as the deadlock continued and rumors about the controversy drifted back from NATO headquarters in Brussels, Kennedy drafted a letter of resignation to the President, stating that if the issues could not be settled, the President should, in the best interests of the administration, withdraw his nomination. In the end, Kennedy won his battle to retain his position as ambassador-at-large as well as his membership in the cabinet, thus becoming the first person to hold those positions simultaneously. Given his unique position, there were no precedents to guide the State Department in deciding where he fit in the department hierarchy. It recognized that only the Secretary of State outranked Kennedy, and, therefore, for protocol purposes he was the second-ranking officer in the department. But that did not make Kennedy second in the chain of command, since he did not want any administrative responsibilities, and he told Rogers that he would never serve as acting secretary in Rogers's absence.

The President could assure that Kennedy would serve in both positions, but Kennedy was unable to avoid involvement in the continuing conflict between the State Department and the National Security Council, under Kissinger, for control of U.S. foreign policy. Kennedy's appointment, coming as it did from the White House with Kissinger's approval, aroused substantial State Department opposition, including petty harassments. Kennedy hoped to have Anthony Jurich appointed as deputy ambassador to NATO, but the department objected, and Kennedy never overcame that resistance. He was constantly reminded that financial support for his ambassador-at-large activities would be limited, and further, there would be virtually no support from the NATO budget for non-NATO activities in Europe. These reminders were accompanied by efforts to reduce his staff in Washington, and, finally, in a classic display of bureaucratic disapproval he was told that his ambassador-at-large office space would be needed for a new Under Secretary of State. Even more disturbing to Kennedy was the delay in replacing the ambassador to the EEC, even after the department was directed to do so by the President. All of these incidents reinforced Kennedy's concern that the effectiveness of the administration's foreign policy was being undermined by the "continual and consistent opposition from the Department of State." Consequently, he urged the President to look carefully at the leadership of the department, since that leadership would be "crucial to the effectiveness of your foreign policy in both a political and economic sense and, consequently, to your ability to accomplish the masterful objectives of your Administration."

Kennedy's decision to divide his time between Washington and Brussels involved substantial traveling and at times a hectic schedule. Generally, Lenora traveled with him, but often he had to leave her in either Washington or Brussels as special assignments took him one place or the other. Thanksgiving Day 1972 found David in Washington and Lenora in Brussels. The Secret Service officers assigned to NATO were facing Thanksgiving without their families, so Lenora invited them to dinner at her home. The size of the party was enlarged and the place changed when the Lewis and Gail Burnham family and other members of the branch of the Mormon church in Brussels, thinking that Lenora would be alone on Thanksgiving, invited her to spend the day with them. When they found that she had invited guests to her home, they suggested they combine the parties at the Burnham home. The invitation was accepted, and both Leonora and the Secret Service officers spent the day surrounded by a family, even though it was not their own. David also had anticipated a lonely Thanksgiving dinner at his hotel, until his lifelong friends Bill and Alice Marriott learned he was in town and insisted that he spend the day with their family at their farm in Virginia.

Fears that he would not be in Brussels long enough or often enough to carry out his duties as ambassador proved to be groundless, for Brussels became his base of operations. He attended regularly the weekly meetings of the NATO ambassadorial council as well as the weekly informal luncheons hosted in turn by each member of the council. In addition to his duties at NATO, he monitored important economic developments affecting American interests in the EEC, the OECD, and under the General Agreement on Tariffs and Trade (GATT). He retained the staff that joined him when he became ambassador-at-large, but they remained in Washington. His principal aide in Brussels was George Vest until Vest was appointed as the United States representative to the Multilateral Preparatory Talks, preparing the agenda for the Helsinki conference of 1974. Vest was replaced by Eugene McAuliffe, an aide to General Andrew J. Goodpaster, Supreme Allied Commander in Europe. Sidney Jones, an economist, became Kennedy's chief economic advisor and traveled with him in his visits to the EEC, OECD, and GATT. Unhappily, Kennedy had to ask for the recall of the ambassador to the EEC, who became dissatisfied with Nixon's economic policies and was expressing his disagreement in public.

A wide range of topics came across Kennedy's desk in his assignment to NATO. The most persistent issues were financial. Many in Congress believed that the United States was carrying a disproportionate share of NATO defense costs, which meant continuing discussion among NATO ambassadors on the level of support each nation should bear. Financial issues also surfaced in discussions over standardization of NATO equipment. There were many reasons why standardization made sense militarily: lower costs, interchangeable equipment, more efficient training, and a more effective supply system. But there was also the economic question, since the country that produced the standardized weapons system would benefit economically from that decision. Therefore, each country sought to persuade the military and political leaders in NATO that the weapons produced in their country ought to be the standard weapon for all NATO forces.

In addition to these persistent problems, Kennedy and his staff dealt with many issues that arise because NATO is more than a mutual defense pact; it is an integrated military organization. Consequently it is responsible for a substantial infrastructure that includes transportation systems, supply depots, hospitals, and military bases. Its experts consult on health care, air quality, road hazards, food and agriculture, and ocean shipping, among many others. These negotiations are further complicated by the fact that military and civilian personnel of every member nation are involved. Of course, Kennedy was not involved directly in all these issues, but when a question made its way through the bureaucracy to the ambassadorial level, he had to be prepared to present the American case persuasively.

Richard Nixon's overwhelming victory in the November 1972 election was followed by the unique and surprising request for all cabinet and sub-cabinet political appointees to submit resignations. There was considerable speculation in the press about the reasons for this request, but for David Kennedy, it provided the occasion to leave government. He sent his letter of resignation, but told the President that he did not want to be reappointed even if that was the President's intent. He was now sixty-seven, two years past the retirement age he had set for himself, and he wanted to return to private life.

Kennedy made his decision to leave the Nixon administration knowing that during those four years of service his advice to the President reflected his strongest economic and political convictions. He was pleased when his advice was accepted, disappointed when it was rejected. But in fighting both losing and winning battles, his fundamental assumption was that the President had the right to determine policy. In Kennedy's view, cabinet members should give the President the best advice they could, but if that advice was not accepted, they should support the President's decisions or resign. Guided by that conception, Kennedy gave Nixon his loyal support. That loyalty was not totally one-sided. Although Nixon had released Kennedy as Secretary of the Treasury, he ultimately supported Kennedy in his battle with the State Department over the terms of his appointments as ambassador-at-large and ambassador to NATO. Furthermore, in the textile negotiations the President made it clear to all departments that Kennedy was in charge and that he would brook no interference with Kennedy's conduct of the negotiations.

Kennedy gave his loyalty to one of the most complex men to hold the office of president. There was the public Nixon: a president with a fundamental grasp of world politics and a determination to carry out a coherent foreign policy; a president who surprised both his supporters and his detractors in his bold bid to change the nature of Chinese-American relations after twenty-nine years of conflict; a president who was at, or near, the center of American politics for thirty-five years; a president whose public conduct of his office was well within the limits fixed by past presidents; and finally, a president who for many symbolized the hope that the size and scope of the federal government could be contained after forty-five years of expansion and that fiscal responsibility might once again be enthroned in Washington. This was the Nixon that Kennedy agreed to serve as Secretary of the Treasury.

A side of Nixon that Kennedy did not see was the Nixon revealed by the Watergate tapes: a president who in an inner circle talked of high policy and low politics in the imagery of the locker room and the language of the barracks, and a president whose quest for power took him beyond the limits of the law. Kennedy saw none of this. Their relationship from the beginning was based on the position each of them had in the government, and that linkage remained the basis of their relationship throughout Kennedy's tenure. Professional and official, then, are the adjectives that best describe Kennedy's relations with Nixon. Within that context there was no place for the easy informality that prevailed in the President's inner circle. Kennedy later recalled that in his meetings with the President, "I never heard the language that they have on the tapes, and in no case did he shout or fuss at me." In the same vein, Charls Walker, who witnessed many of the meetings between Kennedy and Nixon, noted: "I can say this categorically, that I was never at a meeting with the President and Kennedy . . . when the President expressed any disfavor with what Kennedy was doing."

Although Kennedy did not experience the side of Nixon revealed by the Watergate tapes, he did come to see more clearly Nixon the politician, who subordinated the fight against inflation to the need to win elections—a ranking of priorities reflected in Kennedy's resignation as Secretary of the Treasury. In addition, there was the canny political analyst who was able to anticipate and understand the problems faced by other politicians because he could put himself in their place. In his discussions of other political leaders, Kennedy recalled that Nixon "was very analytical. He'd unravel before you what they were thinking and say, 'If I were in their position, this is the way I'd be going.' . . . He looked upon himself as a master politician. There was no question about that."

Kennedy found that Nixon also saw himself as president of the leading industrial and military power in the world. That is, he was not content to respond to the initiatives of other nations; rather, he sought to strengthen the ability of the United States to exercise the maximum influence in world affairs. "In many cases where I attended state dinners and meetings with heads of state of other countries," Kennedy remembered, "there's no question but what he was not just responding to them, but he was outlining a philosophy or a doctrine." In the years after he left government, Kennedy came to believe that Nixon's book *Leaders* provided the deepest insight into the Nixon he knew. Nixon's assessment of the leaders discussed in the book reveals both the explicit criteria and the inarticulate assumptions he used in judging others, and, in the process, he reveals much about himself.

Kennedy quickly discovered that Nixon's administrative style focused decision making within a circle of his closest advisors. The cabinet did not meet on a regular basis. When it did meet, discussions were dominated by the President and there was little give and take over policy matters. The ability of cabinet members to command the President's undivided attention depended on their access to him. The Secretaries of State, Treasury, and Defense, along with the Attorney General, have an advantage in getting access to the President because of the saliency of the issues with which they deal. Kennedy tried to exploit that advantage by taking to the President only those issues that only the President could resolve. Further, he came to realize that when political issues were involved, access to Nixon was most readily available. Hence, during the textile negotiations, when Nixon had a vital interest in fulfilling a campaign pledge, Kennedy found no difficulty in seeing him.

Yet, there were occasions when the President disappointed Kennedy. When the International Monetary Fund meetings were held in Washington in September 1969, Nixon was expected to give a welcoming address as the head of state. "The President left the door open until the very last minute, and then he told me to give his welcoming address and I did," Kennedy recalled. "It was not well received, because I was pinch hitting for the President of the United States, and it was a letdown to the governors and the others." There was also an undercurrent of disappointment in Kennedy's reaction to Nixon's request that he not speak in opposition to the Family Assistance Plan at the Camp David meeting, a request that exposed him to a rebuff from his closest colleagues. But those disappointments were minor compared to his chagrin at the President's decision to inflate the economy in the fall of 1970, thus making Kennedy's two-year effort to control inflation a futile gesture. Finally, there was disappointment in the selection of his successor. He advised Nixon against making John Connally the Secretary of the Treasury, and that advice was coolly ignored.

In March 1973 Kennedy left the service of his country. He was toasted at a farewell ceremony at the NATO council, where Secretary General Joseph Luns spoke of his service, and sent on his way with a tribute paid to him by the Belgium ambassador to NATO, Andre de Staercke, the senior member of the council:

> Our American Colleague has stayed with us long enough for us to regret his departure but not long enough for us to profit fully from his experience nor to reap the benefits of his talent.
>
> Ephemeral or absent, this seems to be for some years past, the fate of the United States Permanent Representatives to NATO. So much so that we ask ourselves, with melancholy, Lamartine's immortal question: "So always toward new shores driven away / Shall we never be able . . . to cast anchor for a single day?"

Around this table, David Kennedy was a good partner. We shall remember him, with that childlike appearance his clear blue eyes give him and which his white hair is unable to belie; we shall remember him as, bending forward slightly, he followed the Atlantic controversy intently. . . . He spoke little, he spoke softly, but he spoke well. In a few words, he expressed what he had to express with that empiricism of a man whose experience of life dictates the necessary phrases and not the superfluous statements. May I also say that, behind the prestige of a career pursued without aging and heaped with honors, one feels the beating of a warm heart and often moved. In sympathy, David Kennedy understood all the languages in the Council, all the positions of his partners and was able, on many occasions, as in Ezekiel's vision, to wrap a human aspect around the skeleton of his instructions. It will be understandable that we see with sorrow a colleague leaving us who was not only among us but was one of us.

Kennedy's departure from government was accompanied by a gift from President Nixon of the chair Kennedy occupied at cabinet meetings and a word of appreciation:

Dear David,

The Cabinet table of this Administration has seen some of the country's great leaders around it, but few of the men in those chairs could match your record of dedicated, devoted public service. You have handled as wide-ranging a group of assignments as anyone has ever been asked to undertake, and without exception each of these responsibilities was discharged with consummate skill.

As a token of my deep admiration and enduring appreciation for your contributions to our Nation's well-being, I want you to have the Cabinet chair you occupied with such distinction. Needless to say, this chair comes to you with my warmest personal regards.

Sincerely,
/s/Richard Nixon

18

THE KENNEDY STYLE

Over a lifetime, individuals and families develop a life-style that is a complex mosaic of recurring patterns. Some patterns are consciously chosen and deliberately reinforced; others emerge unbidden out of the give and take of daily life. A life-style implies the inclusion of some things and the exclusion of others; none can be so open as to justify all kinds of behavior and the acceptance of all possible values. Those who place a high value on honesty cannot simultaneously make a place for a consistent pattern of pretense. Broad generalizations about life-styles, if they do not become static stereotypes, can then be useful ways of thinking about ourselves and others. Hidden in those generalizations—when they do not become stereotypes—are as many variations as in a Mozart concerto. Those variations emerge from the interaction of three themes: personal qualities and characteristics, values, and the environment or situation in which the individual or family has its existence.

A newspaper reporter writing under space constraints might describe the Kennedy style as being that of a soft-spoken, well-to-do, conservative banker; a dedicated public servant, Mormon in his religious persuasion, Republican in his politics, and devoted to his family. None of that would be untrue, but it conceals more than it reveals, for in that generalization there is little of the complex person that is David Matthew Kennedy, none of the variations that would give life and vigor to the generalization, and none

314

of the highways and byways that led from Randolph, Utah, to Chicago, Washington, and other capitals of the world.

The Kennedy style has at its core those personal qualities that emerged from his childhood and youth in Randolph and Riverdale. His boyhood was a curious mixture of the carefree days of youth and adult responsibility. At eleven his father treated him as an adult when he left him in Ogden for the summer to care for his mother. That experience, perhaps subconsciously, helped him define himself in adult terms for the rest of his life. Flowing from that early sense of being an adult was a calm self-assurance that gave him confidence to take on a series of ever enlarging responsibilities. When the question of Walter Cummings's retirement came before the Continental' board of directors, Kennedy assured the board that he would not have accepted the appointment as president if he did not think himself competent to be chairman. The corollary of that self-assurance was his willingness to accept responsibility for the acts of his subordinates. When John Ehrlichman wanted to fire Charls Walker for allegedly taking a position different from that of President Nixon on the reduction of the depletion allowance on gas and oil exploration, Kennedy bluntly told him, "You can fire me, but you can't fire Charls Walker."

There is in Kennedy a strong streak of loyalty. The highest expression of loyalty is fidelity to the marriage bond, and while Kennedy's loyalty centered in the first instance on those vows, many others were drawn into its circle. He was loyal to Randolph, the place of his birth; and out of loyalty to his grandfather Kennedy, he would have moved to Randolph as a young man to take over the bank, even though he preferred another occupation and another place to live. He was loyal to his subordinates at the bank and at the Treasury, and extended that loyalty to Richard Nixon. Kennedy left the Nixon administration before Watergate and thus saw that national tragedy from a distance and learned of a side of Nixon that was never part of their relationship. It would be tempting, therefore, for him to distance himself from Nixon and see in his own departure from the administration a reflection of the political arrogance and paranoia that led to Watergate. Kennedy has not taken that easy route, but has left the final judgment to history.

315

His deepest professional loyalty was to Continental, which continued in the years after he left the bank. But that loyalty was yoked to a deep sense of disappointment when the bank, during the energy boom of the late 1970s and early 1980s, failed to maintain the equilibrium between growth and liquidity that was the hallmark of his tenure there. The deepest disappointment was that the chairman of Continental, Roger Anderson, and the president, John Perkins, were his protégés. In the years after Kennedy left the bank, the energy division's confidence in the future of the petroleum industry led the bank to lend money through the Penn Square Bank of Oklahoma City for oil and gas exploration on questionable assets and to people whose vision outran reality. When energy prices began to fall in 1981, Penn Square failed, and that failure set off a chain of events that ended with the government stepping in to save Continental from closure. Kennedy anxiously watched as Continental's clients, many of long standing, began to close or reduce their accounts at the bank. At several points in those years he could have sold his stock in Continental, but his sense of loyalty, coupled with a hope that the bank could survive despite its losses, led him to hold on to his Continental stock until the government bailout made it practically worthless. In the end, the basis of what Kennedy hoped would be a substantial estate built around Continental stock vanished in the hubris of growth that transformed many Continental executives from bankers into money salesmen.

Although Kennedy's sense of loyalty was strong, there was at times a tension between that sense of loyalty and his own vigorous independence of mind. He was, therefore, most comfortable in those situations in which he was able to exercise his own judgment with a minimum of supervision. As chairman at Continental, he unilaterally negotiated the merger with City National Bank, asking and receiving from the board a blank check to conduct the negotiations as he thought best. He decided against the advice of his senior vice-presidents, to push Continental into a rapid overseas expansion solely on the basis of his judgment that it would be in the bank's best interest. Appointment as Secretary of the Treasury brought its own set of rewards, but he had to surrender the independence of action he enjoyed at the bank. Although as Secretary he was free to manage the internal affairs of the department, substantive decisions had to be cleared with other departments, pushed through the maze of the White House staff, and receive presidential approval before any action was taken. The textile negotiations gave him an opportunity to take control of the situation with the firm backing of the President and to conduct the negotiations with a freedom he never enjoyed as Secretary of the Treasury.

Finally, the personal characteristic that forms the basis of the Kennedy style is that bundle of qualities which define a gentleman. He was approachable without being a hail-fellow-well-met; he was reserved without being austere; he was kind without being indulgent; he was soft-spoken without being diffident; and he was honest, even when there was advantage in obscuring the truth. His honesty was taken by the Washington press corps for political naiveté and did much to shape his public image during his tenure as Secretary of the Treasury. That trait got him into political trouble even when his aides foresaw the problem and tried to steer him past the pitfall. At a congressional hearing when the unemployment rate was 4 percent, he was asked if he would accept that rate as necessary in the fight against inflation. Murray Weidenbaum, who accompanied him to the hearing, passed him a note that suggested that he "fudge" the answer. Ignoring the note, Kennedy told the Senate committee that he was prepared to accept a 4 percent unemployment rate if that were necessary to bring down inflation. Such candor brought down on him the scorn of the committee members for his callous disregard for those out of work. On the way back to the office, as Weidenbaum recalled, he asked the secretary why he had not "fudged" the answer. "You know me, Murray," Kennedy said, "I don't fudge."

If Kennedy's personal characteristics make him a gentleman, they do not make him unique. Gentlemen are found in every walk of life. Personal characteristics, then, are just the starting point; only when they are linked to an explicit set of values do they begin to define a life-style. Kennedy's hierarchy of values began with a deep commitment to his extended family as well as to Lenora and their children. He left his family home when he was a young man, but he never left the family circle. His involvement in the lives of his parents and brothers continued until their deaths. In his letters home he spoke to the details of their lives, and he early assumed the role of family counselor and guide. Vacation time meant a drive across the country to renew family ties and introduce his own family to the scenes of his youth. He spoke at the funerals of both his mother and his father, a fitting recognition that he knew and understood them better than anyone else, either in or out of the family.

The core of Kennedy's devotion to his family is his love affair with Lenora, which began in their youth and continues unabated. Some marriages succeed because husbands and wives are alike in temperament; David and Lenora's succeeded because their differences gave zest and color to the tapestry of their marriage. David is rational, methodical, reserved, task oriented, and conscious of time; Lenora is intuitive, spontaneous, gregarious, patient, and oblivious of time constraints. They learned to live with those differences (not without friction) because they became unimportant in the context of their shared experiences. They lived in genteel poverty during the Great Depression while David was in school, they raised a family of four girls in whom they found joy, and they shared the satisfaction and fulfillment of church service. Moreover, they nursed each other through serious illnesses. That experience as no other sharpens the sense of loving and being loved that can enrich even the happiest marriage.

If adjusting to new circumstances and accepting new challenges has been David's strength, Lenora's has been in continuing to be herself despite the changes in David's career. Even though his increasing income made them well-to-do, if not wealthy, Lenora had no need for conspicuous consumption. She admitted to a fellow guest who admired her gown at a party while David was Secretary of the Treasury that she made it by remodeling a pantsuit. Her confession made the society pages of the Washington press when the confidence was told to a reporter. If Lenora had a moment of doubt about her ability to cope with a change in David's career, it was some trepidation about entering the protocol-dominated life during his assignment as ambassador to NATO. But there, too, she found that being herself was all that was needed to make her place in that diplomatic circle secure. When it was her turn to host the weekly luncheon of the wives of the ambassadors, at which it was customary for the hostess to provide a small gift for each guest, Lenora surprised and pleased her guests with wild flowers from Utah, dried and encased in brass and glass.

David tried as much as possible, at the bank and in the government, to have Lenora travel with him as he expanded the bank's operations and attended international conferences. Still there were times when she had to remain at home. She did not like the separation, but it was not her nature to complain about being left behind, and she had more than enough demands on her time to keep busy during his absences. More difficult were the personal attacks that Wright Patman launched against David during the first months of his tenure as Secretary of the Treasury. In a moment of frustration, Lenora wrote Patman a letter expressing her bitterness at his treatment of her husband. The next day, to David's surprise, he learned that a television station had arranged to interview her. Knowing her feelings about Patman and afraid that she might share those views publicly, he sent his press officer out to monitor the interview. When his press officer came back, he told David that they ought to substitute Lenora for David in television interviews, for when the subject of Patman was raised, she blandly said that he looked like a nice grandfatherly type. When David got home, he asked her about the letter, only to find that her mailbox was the wastebasket.

Lenora brought to their marriage a winsome disposition with a willingness to see the best in others, which led some to see "sweet Lenora" without discovering the strengths that sustained and protected her marriage and family. In a subtle but profound way, she learned to live a full and productive life without having to be in full control of events and people who could affect her life. Thus it was to Lenora that David sent their daughter Carol for advice when divorce disrupted her life and left her uncertain about which way to turn. "You know, you ought to talk to your mother," he told her, "because your mother has great wisdom and thought,

319

The Kennedy family: Front, from left, Patricia K. Campbell, Barbara K. Law, Carol K. David, Marilyn K. Taylor. Back, from left, Lewis Campbell, Carl Law, David Kennedy, Lenora Bingham Kennedy, Ben Davis, Verl Taylor

more than I have, and she is able to cope with life." Over the course of six decades of marriage, David has depended on Lenora's ability to cope with life. The depth of that dependence was never more evident than in the days following Lenora's open-heart surgery. In those hours when he could do nothing but wait and pray, when his energy, determination, and ability to control events were for naught, his anxiety spoke more loudly than words: what he found impossible to face was life without Lenora.

The stability of David and Lenora's marriage created a home in which their four daughters could grow up with a sense of security and support. The professional recognitions that came to David seemed to them the natural reward for his ability, but they were never overawed by them. They continued to see him primarily in the role of the patriarchal father, less concerned with the daily details of their lives than was Lenora, but their ever-present source of spiritual guidance and sound counsel. The deference they paid him was based not on his domination of their lives but on their respect for his strength of character, on his forceful personality, and on their admiration of his experience and knowledge. He is a man, Barbara wrote in a tribute to her father, "who has never lost the common touch" and who "possesses . . . qualities that endear him to his children and make them want to pattern their lives after his example." As the Kennedy daughters became adults, married, and had families of their own, they kept close ties to their parents; David was wont to introduce each of them as "my favorite daughter," but those family ties did not mean that he was consulted and his approval sought on every decision affecting their families. He remained a wise counselor, but he never became the object of a "cult of the personality" in the family.

If concern for family was foremost among the values that define the Kennedy style, his commitment to The Church of Jesus Christ of Latter-day Saints was so inexorably intertwined with his family that it is impossible to separate them. It is possible to know much about David Kennedy without knowing that he is a Latter-day Saint, but it is impossible to understand him without taking his religious faith into consideration. He defined himself in categories derived from the basic teachings of the Church: God the Father as the creator of earth and the father of each person's spirit; His Son Jesus Christ, who was crucified and who three days later rose from the tomb, as the Immortal Messiah; and the restoration of the gospel of Jesus Christ through the prophet Joseph Smith, beginning with the prophet's vision of the Father and the Son and followed by his translation of the Book of Mormon from gold plates that an angel named Moroni delivered into his hands.

Kennedy's understanding of that faith had its beginnings in his parents' home, it was expanded by his missionary service in England and service later as a bishop, and it was made more profound by a series of personal spiritual experiences. The promise of his faith that family ties could endure across the eternities enriched

Mormon church president Spencer W. Kimball and his wife, Camilla, with Lenora and David Kennedy at the Church's Washington D.C. Temple

his unfeigned love for Lenora and the children. Indeed, his love for his family and his faith became so closely interwoven that, while they can be separated analytically, much of their deeper meaning is lost in doing so. His lifelong commitment to his religious beliefs explains why he could leave a bride of two months to serve as a missionary in England for two years, and it makes understandable the hours he was willing to give in church service as a bishop and as a counselor in the Chicago Stake presidency. And at a time when he was ready to retire from public life, it called him to the task of assuring that the message of the restoration was heard worldwide.

Kennedy's commitment to his faith was profound, but he did not flaunt it in public. His children learned of his faith by the example he set for them in his church service, his respect for church leaders, and the integrity of his life. As awkward as it sometimes was, he observed the Church's teachings against the use of alcohol without making others feel uncomfortable in the presence of his abstention. His faith was the perspective through which he saw the world, not an inflexible guide in every concrete situation. When his friend and fellow cabinet member, George Romney, came to him with the suggestion that they jointly inform President Nixon that as Mormons they could not work on Sunday in violation of the Sabbath, Kennedy declined, for he knew there would be times when as Secretary of the Treasury he would have to help "pull the ox from the mire."

Mormons are sometimes accused of being clannish and of promoting each other's careers whenever possible. That charge cannot be laid at Kennedy's door. None of his closest associates at the bank or at the Treasury were Mormons; they were chosen because of their professional ability without regard to religious affiliation. On the other hand, he made no studied effort to distance himself from Mormon colleagues. While he was ambassador to NATO, one of his principal aides was an able economist, Sidney Jones, who was also a Mormon. At the bank there were Mormon officers but none among the senior vice-presidents of the bank.

The Kennedy style is reflected not only in his family life and his religious faith, but also in a circle of friends drawn largely from the Mormon communities in Washington and Chicago. Some of their friends in Washington, like J. Willard and Alice Marriott, and Ernest and Alice Wilkinson, they had known at Weber College; but most of their Washington friends they did not know until they met them in the Washington Stake. All of them were young, ambitious, yet a bit fearful so far from home and searching for someone with whom they could share not only their hopes but also their fears. The experience of leaving old friends for new was repeated when the Kennedys moved to Chicago. There, too, the Mormon community made it easy for them to create a new circle of friends whose support eased the transition.

Beyond this core of friends drawn from the Mormon community, Kennedy's expanding professional eminence and his increasing responsibilities at the bank drew the Kennedys into an ever-widening circle of professional and social acquaintances. Some of these, like Hank Knight, certainly became friends in every sense of the word, but for the most part David's relationships with his professional associates did not involve the network of social and personal relationships that normally are associated with friendship. Indeed, the priority that he gave to his family and the life-style that flowed from his religious faith tended to keep his professional and personal life separated. The same pattern characterized his relationships with his colleagues at the Treasury Department. And in both cases that separation was reflected in David and Lenora's preference for fulfilling his representational responsibilities at the bank and as Secretary of the Treasury by entertaining their guests at the various clubs to which they belonged rather than at home.

A close friend with whom Kennedy shared a love for fishing and horses entered his life as a customer of the bank. Glenn Nielson, the founder of Husky Oil, became dissatisfied with the New York bank that had financed his company's exploration efforts and came to Chicago looking for a new bank. He settled on Continental in the first instance because the bank was able to satisfy his financial concerns. But he was also impressed with a bank that numbered among its customers some of the largest corporations in the country and yet treated a relatively small oil company with genuine

David Kennedy with long-time friends Glenn and Olive Nielson

interest, including an introduction to the chairman of the board; at other banks he never made it past a senior vice-president. Nielson did not come to Continental because the chairman was a Mormon; he did not know Kennedy, even by reputation. He was searching for a bank that understood the problems of a small but growing oil company. At Continental he not only found the bank he was looking for but also the beginning of a lasting friendship with its chairman.

Soon after Nielson knew that in Kennedy he had found not only a banker but a friend, he invited Kennedy to his ranch in Wyoming for some fishing and horseback riding. When he issued the invitation he was not sure of Kennedy's skills, either as a fisherman or a horseman, but as he watched Kennedy mount his horse, he knew he was not dealing with a tenderfoot, and he was to learn that Kennedy approached fly fishing with the same single-minded passion he brought to every task. They had been fishing for some time and became separated when Nielson, who was nearing the limit of twelve fish, thought that he ought to see how his guest was doing. His guest, he found, was doing just fine. He not only had his limit but was still pulling them in. When Nielson expressed some concern that they were over their limit, Kennedy said that if they would just fry up a batch for lunch, there would be no problem. That fishing trip was the first of many that Nielson and Kennedy shared on the streams of Wyoming. Nielson would later regale Kennedy's associates at the bank with stories of his banker who found it impossible to count past twelve while fishing. He found in Kennedy not only a banker and a fishing companion, but also an advisor on whom he could count for impartial advice on his management of Husky Oil. Consequently, when Kennedy became a director of the company, Nielson learned to call on Kennedy at the end of the discussion because, as he remembered, "he had a way of summing up and pulling things together . . . in such a way that it was pretty hard to take exception to his conclusions." Furthermore, Nielson found that in addition to Kennedy's judgment being sound, it was impartial. "The thing that was so different with Dave, you never felt that his judgment

325

or what he was saying was influenced by whether it was going to do something for his bank or himself."

Kennedy's character and the values that dominated his life are two of the four cornerstones of the Kennedy style. They are the keys to his personal life, but they do not fully reveal his approach to the challenging tasks he faced at the bank, as Secretary of the Treasury, and as ambassador-at-large. His first administrative experiences were as a bishop and as a counselor in a stake presidency. Leaders in voluntary organizations like churches, where sanctions such as dismissal and reduction in rank or pay are not available, learn that persuasion, encouragement, and praise, along with delegation of responsibility, are indispensable to successful leadership. Kennedy remembered those lessons when he rose to the top leadership positions in the bank. If there was one hallmark to his administration of the bank, it was that he picked able people and then gave them the authority and responsibility they required to do their job. An important part of that process was his willingness to recognize his own limitations. He became the chairman of a large commercial bank without ever having been a commercial banker; he recognized that limitation and, without losing control, shared decision-making authority with the senior officials. The same ability to attract superb associates and a willingness to delegate responsibility characterized his tenure at Treasury. Donald Webster, his administrative assistant, said one day, "Mr. Kennedy, I'm making a lot of decisions for you." Kennedy responded, "That's OK, just bring me the hot ones." Thus, the trust Kennedy invested in his staff created the same creative administrative environment in the department as had existed in the bank.

While Kennedy's management style remained the same, Washington was not Chicago. In Chicago Kennedy was responsible only to a board of directors; in Washington the decisions he reached as Secretary of the Treasury were just the beginning of the decision-making process, not the end. Decisions had to be fought through the opposition of other departments, cleared with the White House staff, approved by the President, and explained to Congress. Often the links in that decision-making chain were manned by people who lacked the necessary financial and economic background to assess the importance or consequences of the Treasury's recommendation, or, like John Ehrlichman, thought only how the decision might affect the next election. Furthermore, neither he nor H. R. Haldeman appreciated the respect that Kennedy enjoyed with his counterparts in the major nations of the world, or that his presence gave the United States added weight in international financial and monetary conferences. In terms of economic and financial competence, Ehrlichman's emergence as the President's principal assistant for domestic affairs was a classic case of pigeons—or some might say vultures—watching eagles. But Washington is a city where politics, not economics, is the deciding factor.

If Kennedy's success in Chicago was based on his ability to recruit and manage a superb staff, his ability to do the same in Washington was not the standard by which he was judged. A reporter complained to Charls Walker that Kennedy seemed content as Secretary of the Treasury to supervise a first-rate staff. Walker asked the reporter who he thought recruited that staff. Did he think it appeared out of plain air? But his retort was brushed aside because the reporter was interested in image, not substance. Washington is a city where image is based on power, and power is seen as access to and influence with the President, as the ability to dominate the headlines, and as success in winning interdepartmental battles. That image is by and large the creation of the Washington press corps' assessment of each cabinet member's success or failure in the continuing struggle for power. But images do not just happen; they have to be created and nurtured by a constant struggle to assure access to the President, which necessarily involves a continuing tension with members of the White House staff who are engaged in their own pursuit of power. But, above all, the press must be wooed and won, so that every success is highlighted and every failure minimized.

Kennedy was unwilling to play the Washington game. He did not like dealing with the press and left much of it to other Treasury officials. He disliked testifying before congressional committees, and at first let Walker and Paul Volcker carry that burden. He soon learned that congressional committees were not satisfied with anyone but the secretary, and he had to put aside his distaste for the experience and make the mandatory trips to the Hill. He had little need to see his name in print; therefore he did not insist on being the sole spokesman for the administration's economic policies and shared that role with his friend and colleague, Paul McCracken. In a city where the importance of a cabinet member is judged partly by how late he works, Kennedy kept to his long established practice of leaving his office most days between 5:30 and 6:00 P.M. He learned from experience that he could do more work early each morning in the quiet of his study than he could lingering in his office at the end of the day. Nor were the Kennedys swept up in the social life of Washington beyond that in which they were naturally involved. That social life was demanding enough; when they found an evening free, they were happy to spend it at home with each other.

In retrospect, the assessment of the contemporary press on Kennedy's performance as Secretary of the Treasury seems shallow and shortsighted. His access to the President may have become more difficult after his first year in office, but we now know that Haldeman and Ehrlichman were consciously limiting access to Nixon to enhance their own power. Yet even they could not isolate the Secretary of the Treasury from the President, and while on some issues they might ask for a memorandum, whenever Kennedy pushed the issue he got his appointment with the President. Kennedy was criticized for his lack of political sensitivity in pushing the fight against inflation in the face of a modest rise in unemployment, but who now would argue that inflation was not indeed the major economic danger facing the nation? The press thought of him as a commercial banker, ignoring the years he spent at the Federal Reserve learning from Marriner Eccles how to use monetary policy to manage the nation's economy. They thought of him as mild mannered, not knowing of his refusal to bow to Ehrlichman's pressure to fire Walker or that the President left the tough decision on Penn Central in his hands, and that, against strong pressure from Arthur Burns and the financial community, he let the company fail. Kennedy and Walker may have underestimated the political opposition to the renewal of the income tax surcharge, but certainly David Broder's charge that Kennedy approached the task with political naiveté was ill judged.

The contemporary press assessments of Kennedy's performance, obsessed as they were with the question of power and which perspective did not range beyond the next six months, mistook Kennedy's concern about inflation as the reflex reaction of a conservative commercial banker. Their economic perspective was still influenced, as was that of most of Americans, by the fear of mass unemployment inherited from the depression years. It would take the experience of the next decade with its double-digit inflation to convince the American public, and the press, that inflation could be just as devastating as recessions or even depressions. Kennedy and his colleagues, Paul McCracken and Robert Mayo, fought a losing battle because in the end elections were more likely to be lost because of recession than inflation. Unemployment is a visible evil, while inflation is a hidden tax whose worst effects take time to become evident.

Had Kennedy's first goal been to stay in office, then his neglect of his public image and his concentration on the fight against inflation would certainly have been political errors. But if retention of office meant he had to "fudge" his answers before congressional committees, or play court to the press to assure a favorable public image, or engage in political fighting with the White House staff or other departments, or push for economic and financial policies that he believed unsound for political gain, or subordinate his long-established personal life-style to the lure of office, then the price was too high regardless of the political costs. In the end, politics became more important than economics, style more important than substance, and Kennedy gave way to John Connally, whose aggressive personality, ambition, and political shrewdness were attractive to a White House that was already looking forward to the 1972 election.

The last cornerstone of the Kennedy style is an appreciation, understanding, and acceptance of a variety of cultural differences. The development of his cultural horizons involved a twofold process. The first was learning to accept and respect the difference between Mormon culture and the larger American scene; the second, to understand American culture in its larger world setting. He began life in Randolph among a large extended family on both his mother and father's sides, many of whom were indifferent to church teachings and discipline. He became aware at an early age, therefore, that differences with the Mormon culture itself had to be respected. Yet the strongest influences in his early life, both within his parents' families and in the communities in which he lived, were those that flowed from the Church and its loyal adherents.

The move to Washington, paradoxically, simultaneously strengthened Kennedy's ties to the Mormon community and awakened his appreciation for the diversity and richness of American culture. There was in Washington not only a sharp contrast between urban and rural America, and between east and west, but most noticeably between black and white America. His colleagues at the Federal Reserve Board, who came from all parts of the country, shared some of his values, rejected others, and found some simply quaint. Kennedy responded to that experience not by withdrawing even deeper into the Mormon community but by trying to come to grips with the challenge of living, and serving, in a large cosmopolitan city. Thus, when it became evident that his plans to return to Utah after completing his legal education were unrealistic, he was able to make a home for his family far away from Utah and explore the substantial opportunities that living in Washington afforded.

The move to Chicago sharpened the Kennedys' appreciation for their ties to the Mormon community as well as their respect for and understanding of the extended American society. Kennedy's career at the bank heightened his awareness that integrity, loyalty, dedication, and compassion—values that he treasured from his Mormon inheritance—were shared by colleagues. In that context, there was mutual respect for the differences in values and lifestyles that divided them, but those differences did not undermine their ability to work together effectively and efficiently. Beyond his professional life, he and Lenora encouraged their children to take full part in social and extracurricular activities in school, unafraid that the values they were taught at home would be eroded or attenuated by exposure to friends coming from different backgrounds. His intense involvement in Chicago civic affairs was recognized and valued by the Chicago religious community. He was honored by the Jewish and Protestant communities and became the first non-Catholic to receive the St. Vincent de Paul award of DePaul University for "service to God through the needs of men."

Kennedy's twenty-three years in Chicago were important not only in the development of his understanding of his Mormon heritage within the context of the larger American society, but also because they marked a major step in the expansion of his appreciation of the American experience in its relationship with other cultures of the world. His realization that the rest of the world was different from the United States had its origin in his missionary experience in England. His travel abroad on bank business reawakened that early experience and expanded it beyond the English-speaking world.

Every American businessman who wishes to do business abroad must eventually come to grips with the way that business affairs are conducted in other countries. Kennedy understood that reality, but his search for understanding went beyond what was needed to manipulate the system to his own advantage. He wanted to understand not just how but why business practices in the various countries were different from those he knew as an American. In his search for understanding, he was an attentive student, willing to learn from mentors in each country. His grasp of the subtle ways Japanese did business and of the mores and folkways of Japanese bureaucracy was due to the instructions he accepted from his friends in the Japanese business community. Those instructions not only benefited Continental but also paid a rich reward in his conduct of the textile negotiations with a Japanese government reluctant to reduce its textile exports to the United States.

Although Kennedy never forgot that at Continental his first task was to represent the interests of the bank, and as Secretary of the Treasury those of the nation, he understood that agreements of lasting value were pacts from which all parties benefited. His constant search, therefore, whether asking for permission to open a branch of the bank or concluding an international agreement, was for a solution that would be for the benefit of all. Further-more, he recognized that a healthy world economy required that the underdeveloped countries must make real progress toward economic growth and stability. As Secretary of the Treasury he paid greater attention to the problems of underdeveloped countries than did most of his predecessors, and after leaving government he continued to argue the cause of the developing nations with friends in government and the financial community.

Kennedy's interest in international, economic, and political questions led him to accept the invitation of Brigham Young University to create the David M. Kennedy Center for International Studies. At its inception, the center received a generous endowment from a trust created by Glenn Nielson and his wife, Olive, for the support of projects sponsored by the Church. Soon after the center was named for Kennedy, the Neilsons recommended that a substantial portion of the trust be designated as an endowment to provide a permanent source of funds for the purposes of the center. With its financial base secure, the center was assigned the responsibility of coordinating all of BYU's international activities, including the study-abroad centers in London and Vienna; fostering research in a broad range of international affairs; supervising area study programs; conducting seminars and symposiums on international topics; sponsoring an exchange of American and foreign scholars; and contributing to scholarship through its publication program.

Kennedy's expanding cultural horizons have taken him from a view of the world as seen from the vantage point of a small rural Mormon village to that of a world traveler who has seen and come to appreciate the rich cultural differences in both his own nation and the world. In that journey of the world, he has been guided by a sure sense of self-identity that has its origins in family, faith, and friends. Knowing who he is has given him the confidence to accept others without feeling the need to make concessions in his life-style to win acceptance. At the same time, that clear self-identity has made it easier for others to accept him, for it has provided an unambiguous basis for their relationship. Consequently, his daughter Patricia observed that while her father over the course of his lifetime has developed a world view, he has not become a worldly individual. That characterization succinctly sums up the essence of the Kennedy style: the ability to reach out with understanding and sympathy to a wide range of peoples and cultures without losing touch with his roots in Randolph and the values of his Mormon heritage.

19

AMBASSADOR TO THE WORLD

For a year following his resignation from his ambassadorial posts, Kennedy pursued the life of a private citizen. He and Lenora returned to Chicago to their comfortable home in Northfield, where they resumed their work in the Church and David quickly became busy with personal business concerns and continued public service.

He became a founding member and chairman of the United States of America–Republic of China (USA–ROC) Economic Council, an organization created to promote trade and good will between Taiwan and the United States. On December 12, 1986, the ROC awarded Kennedy the Order of Brilliant Star, an honor similar to knighthood in England and one of the highest awards of the ROC. It was given in recognition of Kennedy's efforts to strengthen relations between the two governments. He was also an honorary member of the International Finance Committee, composed of representatives of the fifty largest banks in the United States and the fifty largest banks in the rest of the world, plus representatives of central banks and finance ministries throughout the world. He and Lenora made frequent trips to Utah, where two of their children, Marilyn and Patricia, lived. It was during one such a visit that Marilyn received a telephone call from N. Eldon Tanner of the Church's First Presidency, asking if she knew where to get in touch with her father. "Yes," she replied, "he's standing right here."

President Tanner, always one to come to the point, asked how soon Kennedy could arrange to meet with him. Kennedy, never one to put things off, said he could be there in twenty to thirty minutes. In that meeting, President Tanner explained the plans that he and Harold B. Lee (president of the Church until his death in December 1973) had discussed for appointing a special representative to assist the First Presidency in three areas: first, in getting the Church recognized in countries where it did not yet have missionaries; second, in helping to solve visa and other problems in countries where the Church was already established; and third, in dealing with government agencies in Washington. The appointment had been postponed because of President Lee's death, but President Tanner said that the new president, Spencer W. Kimball, was now ready to move ahead. Kennedy made some suggestions about how the special representative might serve the Church, then named some of the people he thought might be called to serve in that position. President Tanner listened to him patiently; but, in the end, he said that President Kimball wanted Kennedy to be the first special representative of the First Presidency.

The tasks that President Tanner thought the special representative should undertake did not come as a surprise to Kennedy. Over the years the two of them had discussed problems the Church was having in getting legal recognition in some countries and the visa problems it was having in others. Kennedy had already been of considerable assistance in the case of two missionaries jailed in Thailand for photographing each other while sitting on the head of a large statue of Buddha. During his trip to Southeast Asia, after his appointment as ambassador-at-large, he had arranged for the mission president, Miller Shurtleff, a longtime friend, to meet with the American ambassador to Thailand, Leonard Unger. As a result of that meeting and Kennedy's continued interest in the fate of the missionaries and the future of the Church's Thai Mission, Unger took a special interest in the case and was able to help reduce pressure to expel all Mormon missionaries from the country.

Kennedy was familiar with the problems that the special representative might encounter, but he was not sure that he should undertake the task or just how the position might fit into the organizational structure of the Church. Any doubts that he should

accept the invitation to serve were resolved the following morning, when President Kimball personally called him to serve. Kennedy
had turned down the presidency of the Federal Reserve Bank of
Chicago and placed conditions on his appointment as ambassador
to NATO, but he was not prepared to refuse this call or place conditions on his acceptance, for it came from the one man on earth
he was prepared to acknowledge as the prophet of God.

Kennedy found himself appointed to a position that had no
clearly defined duties. What the position would become and how
it would fit into the Church's organization would emerge gradually. He decided from the beginning that to be effective, he needed
very little staff support beyond that provided since 1982 his superb
secretary, Marlys Brown, for as he envisioned this new assignment, it required his experience and personal attention rather than
substantial staff support. Nor did he think it required a large budget; he did not need a salary, and he was given an office in the
Church Administration Building at 47 East South Temple in Salt
Lake City. Since the assignment would require considerable travel,
Kennedy's request that Lenora be permitted to accompany him
whenever possible was granted. The First Presidency also suggested
that he keep some of his outside interests, including his chairmanship of the USA–ROC Economic Council, as well as his involvement with the International Monetary Fund, the World Bank, and
the International Finance Committee.

After his appointment was announced in April 1974, Kennedy
was frequently asked by Church officials for help with a variety of
problems related to missionary work. Since he did not believe it
was his responsibility to determine which of the many pressing
problems he should address first, he put the matter to the First
Presidency. The result was a decision that all assignments would
come from the First Presidency and that he would report on the
fulfillment of those assignments to that same body. As is the case
with most organizational innovations, the import of that decision
was not clearly understood by other church officers who wanted
or needed his help. But an unequivocal reminder by President
Kimball of Kennedy's responsibility to the First Presidency fixed

clearly the relationship of the special representative to the other organizations of the Church.[1]

Organizational innovations sometimes fail, not because of the abilities of the people involved, but because the environment and circumstances are not conducive to change. Kennedy was fortunate to assume his new role in the Church during the presidency of Spencer W. Kimball. Succession to the presidency of the Church passes to the senior member of the Quorum of the Twelve Apostles on the death of the president. Thus, in his seventy-ninth year, Kimball became the twelfth president of the Church after Harold B. Lee's death. President Kimball was known throughout the Church for his fearless defense of the faith, for his carefully crafted sermons, for his compassion for those struggling with their faith, and for his tireless efforts to improve the lot of the American Indians in the Intermountain West.

President Kimball quickly established the agenda of his presidency at the general conference of the Church in April 1974. He beseeched Latter-day Saints to "lengthen their stride," particularly in support of the Church's missionary work. The Church, he proclaimed, must not only redouble its efforts in countries where missionary work was underway but must also prepare to expand that effort worldwide. In subsequent messages he would gradually but surely transform the way the Latter-day Saints thought about the Church. The persecutions Mormons had suffered in the early days of the Church in Ohio, Missouri, and Illinois, had driven them westward to Utah and tended to make them look inward and for those of other faiths to think of the Church in restricted geographical terms. It was first viewed as a Utah church, and then, as it spread into the surrounding states, it became known as a western church. Finally, after World War II, it became an American church. For President Kimball those geographical definitions were too narrowly drawn. In his view there was only one geographical designation for the Church, and that was a worldwide church, and he was determined to make that vision a reality.

The questions President Kimball asked were not about limitations but about possibilities. In which countries are there no missionaries? What is the possibility of sending missionaries to those

Gerald Ford and David M. Kennedy at Brigham Young University, 1987

countries? Are the obstacles legal or religious? Have we sought permission for our missionaries to enter those countries? Why are we having difficulty in getting visas for our missionaries? What can be done to solve those problems? Does missionary work have to be done in the traditional way with two missionary companions going from door to door to find those willing to listen to a more extended explanation of the restoration? As he searched for answers to these questions, it became clear that behind his sense of urgency was the faith of a shepherd who was anxious for the welfare of his flock. His concern was not only for those safely within the fold but also for those whose lives needed yet to be enriched by the message of the truth he could bring them.

President Kimball's challenge to the Saints for a renewed effort to expand the missionary work created the environment in which David Kennedy could successfully fulfill the tasks expected of him. He, of course, brought one unique qualification to his calling: his extensive network of friends, acquaintances, and colleagues throughout the world. There was hardly a country where he did not know the principal political and financial leaders. He was known to them for his honesty, forthrightness, intelligence, and decency. These relationships predisposed them to help him, and thus the Church, as far as the constraints of their own social and political systems would permit.

Kennedy brought to his task this rich network of associations and an understanding that an effective diplomat was one who could speak for the Church, yet who at the same time was dispensable. While it may seem a paradox for a diplomat to have the power to speak authoritatively and yet be dispensable, that paradox is at the heart of classic diplomacy. Kennedy recognized the value in having a spokesman for the Church other than the president, declaring, "The danger . . . is that the President is right on the firing line, and everything he says is taken as coming from a prophet of the Lord. But what I say can always change. I'm dispensable. But he's not."

That understanding of the role of the diplomat led to a division of labor between President Kimball and his ambassador-at-large. At the beginning of their relationship, President Kimball confessed to Kennedy that he found talking to government leaders and heads of state the most difficult part of his service as president. He feared that he might say something that would hinder rather than help the Church. Kennedy suggested that President Kimball speak of religion, home, the family, and moral values, those issues he felt most at home with and that were closest to his heart, and leave the political issues to Kennedy. If there were then objections, or if Kennedy stumbled, the Church would not necessarily be committed.

Good diplomats must possess the ability to communicate across cultural boundaries. As a result of his experience at the bank and in government, Kennedy had acquired that skill. His sensitivity to his own and other cultures permitted him to see the difference between the essential truths of the gospel and his own American culture. He knew that distinction would not be evident to many outside the United States who saw the Church as essentially an American institution. Nor, he knew, would many within the Church be aware of their own failure to draw that distinction. The goal of the missionary effort, he thought, was not to make the people in other countries "all over in the image of a Utah Mormon, but rather in the image of a son or daughter of God, a Christian, a believer, a liver of the truth. Then we've accomplished what the Savior wants."

The distinction between the fundamental truths of the gospel and the distinctive and valued features of American society involve profound political issues. Kennedy found that some journalists tried to trap church leaders into admitting that the value Mormons place on political freedom was contradictory to the Church's desire to expand its missionary effort worldwide, particularly into Eastern European countries. In one instance a Japanese journalist relentlessly pressed this question on President Kimball, refusing to accept the President's reply as a responsive answer to his question. Kennedy knew the reporter from other visits to Japan, and requested the President's permission to intervene. Then, calling the reporter by name, he pointed out that indeed Mormons prized political freedom, but they also believed, as the Church's twelfth Article of Faith states, in being "subject to kings, presidents, rulers, and magistrates and in honoring, obeying, and sustaining the law." The essential thing, Kennedy reminded the reporter, is that the Church could enter and prosper in any country that will "permit us to offer our sacraments, . . . permit us in our homes to have our family organization and live within our religious pattern. Then we can get along." If we are allowed those freedoms, Kennedy emphasized, then our presence in any country "doesn't mean that we are doing anything inconsistent with our general beliefs."

The issue that the Japanese reporter raised was one that Kennedy had considered carefully. He valued the political and economic freedoms that were an essential part of American society, yet he came to realize that the central issue was not which economic and political system he preferred as an individual. Rather, it was to define what restrictions on individual freedom would make it impossible for the Church to exist as an institution or prevent its members from following its fundamental precepts. Put this way, Kennedy came to the conclusion that "so long as the government permits me to attend church, so long as it permits me to get on my knees in prayer, so long as it permits me to be baptized for the remission of sins, so long as it permits me to partake the sacrament of the Lord's Supper, and to obey the commandments of the Lord, so long as the government does not force me to commit crime, so long as I am not required to live separately from my wife and children, I can live as a Latter-day Saint within that political system."

Kennedy's careful and subtle distinctions between the kind of government he or others might prefer and the relationship of the Church to governments that did not meet those standards was not always understood. He underlined that point to a *Time* reporter who pressed him on the implications for the standards and practices of the Church as it became a worldwide institution: "Our belief in Christ is secure and sincere. He's the Son of God, the Savior of the world. The question of baptism by immersion for the remission of sins, the laying on of hands, priesthood, those things, will not or cannot change. Moral values will always be there. The question of what happens in your work and whether you are regulated as to whether you can travel here or whether you can travel there, what you can do with respect to your desires to study this, that or the other, where you might be put in a field that you don't want, or you might have to have military service forced upon you, those kinds of things you can live with and still be a Christian. You can still be a son or daughter of God living his commandments."

Kennedy's views on the relationship between the various governments of the world and the Church flowed not just from his own experience and study; he could also see no other position to take if President Kimball's urgent, relentless desire to expand the missionary effort of the Church into new countries was to succeed. "Brother David, are we doing all that we can to get into these lands?" was the President's constant question. If there was the slightest chance, he wanted to explore that possibility and was willing to adjust the traditional way missionary work was done to meet the exigencies of the moment. When it became apparent that there was a difference between being legally recognized as a religious institution in a country and obtaining permission to proselyte for new members, President Kimball approved sending missionary couples who would represent the Church and answer the

Paul Volker, chairman of the Federal Reserve, and David Kennedy

questions of those who voluntarily sought information about the Church. When dark suits and white shirts made the missionaries unduly conspicuous, President Kimball authorized dress that was more in keeping with local customs. As urgently as he desired to spread the gospel, the President instructed Kennedy always to enter by "the front door." If entrance was to be by the front door, then the laws regarding religious freedom and the activities of churches had to be understood and respected. Where those laws permitted the Church to establish its presence, however limited that was, it was enough for President Kimball to pull out his atlas and discuss with "Brother David" how soon that presence could be achieved.

It was against this background of President Kimball's urgent desire to expand the scope of the Church that Kennedy's skills came into play. An understanding of peoples and cultures, a network of contacts, and the backing of the president of the Church were just the beginning; Kennedy started from scratch to create a process for achieving the goals the First Presidency set for him. In the beginning, a monthly meeting was scheduled with the First Presidency, but as his work developed, that meeting became submerged in the frequent meetings he had with President Kimball, who asked him to keep the other members of the First Presidency briefed on the things the two of them discussed. Despite being responsible solely to the First Presidency, Kennedy did not operate in isolation from the other units of the Church involved in missionary work. He had frequent discussions with Bernard P. Brockbank and other General Authorities who succeeded Brockbank as president of the Church's International Mission. In those meetings they discussed a wide variety of topics—substantive and organizational—dealing with missionary work. Kennedy also became a member of the International Affairs Committee, which considered many of the issues related to his responsibilities.

No issue has demanded more of Kennedy's time than the task of expanding missionary work into new areas. That expansion became the highest priority for him precisely because it was President Kimball's first priority. When Kennedy and the President first began to consider which countries might be likely targets for expanding the missionary effort, President Kimball did not have a fixed list of countries to which he wanted to send Kennedy. His process was to examine the countries one by one, exploring with Kennedy the possibilities each offered.

In those early discussions in 1974, as they studied together the large atlas that the President kept in his office, Kennedy placed his hand over sub-Saharan Africa. That gesture eliminated most of the African continent from consideration because, he argued, the Church could not operate without local leadership, and exclusion of blacks from the priesthood precluded the development of that essential leadership. Kennedy took his hand away from the map of sub-Saharan Africa on June 8, 1978, when President Kimball announced to the world that he had received a revelation confirming "that the long-promised day has come when every faithful, worthy man in the Church may receive the holy priesthood . . . without regard to race or color." On returning from the temple where he shared that revelation with the Quorum of the Twelve Apostles, President Kimball met with Kennedy and told him that he knew Kennedy would be pleased with the announcement.

In addition to sub-Saharan Africa, there were other parts of the world where the chances of the Church's gaining recognition or receiving permission for missionary work appeared marginal. Religious freedom was restricted in some countries, mostly in the Muslim world, because of the influence of the dominant religion. Governmental restrictions in other countries, mainly in Eastern Europe, likewise made them unlikely targets for missionary work. Still, there were countries where the Church was not yet established to which Kennedy could turn his attention. Before he could begin his work, the Church faced a policy decision regarding the approach to missionary activity. Some countries under consideration drew a clear distinction between simple legal recognition of the Church (that is, recognition of the right to worship) on the one hand and the right to actively proselyte on the other. In several countries the first right was extended but the second right was denied. Traditionally, the missionary system of the Mormon church has been based on tracting—that is, missionaries going from door to door offering free tracts, explaining the origins and theology of the Church, and inviting people to attend church meetings. Given the scarcity of resources in time, money, and manpower, there seemed to be good reasons for concentrating efforts on those countries where missionaries were free to proselyte. But President Kimball's vision of a worldwide church in response to the Savior's commandment to teach the gospel to every nation, kindred, tongue, and people was not bound by the way in which missionary work had traditionally been done. He envisaged new ways of reaching the peoples of the world that would take into account the legal restrictions on traditional proselyting methods. At President Kimball's direction, then, Kennedy began a series of visits to countries where there were problems gaining recognition or where recognition had never been sought.

In each country Kennedy visited, he began as near to the top of the governmental hierarchy as he could. In Greece, where the Church had sought for several years to gain legal recognition as "a house of prayer," he found that the application was buried in the lower levels of the bureaucracy. His first step was to use his contacts at the American embassy and with the Greek government to arrange an appointment with His Beatitude Seraphim, Archbishop of Athens and All Greece, whose influence was crucial in getting final approval for the Church to be recognized as a house of prayer. He pointed out to His Beatitude that the Greek Orthodox Church had full freedom of religion in the United States, that in 1953 the Greek government had honored President David O. McKay for the aid that the Church sent to Greece after a devastating earthquake, and that the Church was fully recognized by other countries of Western Europe.

In many countries Kennedy would first see the minister of finance, not because he had the authority to grant legal status to the Church, but because he knew the minister and could ask him to introduce Kennedy to those who had such authority. Once Kennedy gained an appointment with the minister whose jurisdiction included religious matters, his two goals were to explain the purpose of the Church and to commit the Church to obey the law. Since the countries that required Kennedy's intervention were those where freedom of religion was either restricted or carefully regulated, the reputation of the Church for aggressively proselytizing new members was often raised as an objection to granting legal recognition. In those cases, Kennedy assured government officials that the Church understood that limitation and was ready to abide by the law. In other countries where there were objections to non-nationals serving as church leaders, Kennedy explained the organization of the Church and its reliance on an unpaid lay leadership drawn from the local members. There were ancient tales of Mormons and polygamy to put to rest, objections to be answered regarding recognition of a church with only a few scattered members, and assurances to be given that the Church believed in obeying and sustaining the law in every country where it was established.

Kennedy used every relevant argument possible in his effort to convince reluctant government officials to grant recognition. In Greece and in the Eastern European countries he visited, he called attention to the fact that the Church was a respected religious body in the United States and pointed out that its members held responsible positions in the federal government and were leaders in American business and educational communities. In some countries, government officials asked his advice on international financial matters or his aid in solving this or that problem with the United States. He willingly responded to those requests, knowing that he could contribute to both his country and his church by doing so. He was realist enough to understand that there were limitations on how far his personal efforts could reach in helping the Church in some countries. He knew that regardless of the good will shown by his friends and associates, there were social, political, and religious constraints that no amount of good will could overcome. But to the extent that his contacts and personal representations could advance the cause of the Church, he was willing to use every possible means to accomplish that task.

During the first two years following his appointment, Kennedy visited Lebanon, Greece, Portugal, Thailand, India, Pakistan, Yugoslavia, the Philippines, Hungary, Poland, the German Democratic Republic, Iran, and Egypt. He returned to Greece several times before the Church was granted recognition as a "house of prayer." Despite

David Kennedy and Yugoslavian basketball star Kresimir Cosic

his frequent contacts with the minister of finance during his tenure as Secretary of the Treasury, the task in Yugoslavia proved to be more difficult than expected. The Yugoslavian government was reluctant to give approval for missionaries to enter the country and to recognize the Church as a legal religious institution, although there were Yugoslavian members of the Church. Kresimir Cosic—a national basketball star, who constantly amazed American basketball fans with his skills when he played for Brigham Young University—was a Latter-day Saint, but even his fame and position as coach of the Yugoslavian national basketball team did not speed recognition of the Church through the labyrinth of the Yugoslavian bureaucracy. In Iran the groundwork for recognition had already been laid by the establishment of a branch, composed mainly of Americans working in Tehran. In addition, Loren C. Dunn, a president of the Church's First Council of the Seventy, had explored the legal steps necessary for the Church to gain recognition in Iran before Kennedy's first visit there in late 1974. Following Kennedy's visit, Dean Farnsworth, a BYU faculty member, was chosen to preside over the Iran Tehran Mission. After his arrival in 1975, Farnsworth spent much of his time working for legal recognition of the Church. It was granted November 11, 1977, but hopes of expansion were swept away in 1979 by the revolution that made any chance for religious freedom and church growth impossible.

In some countries where Kennedy was successful in obtaining recognition for the Church, that step permitted the Church to open a mission, call missionaries, and begin proselyting openly for new members. In others, recognition gave the Church legal status as a religious institution, but missionary work was limited to explaining the gospel to those who voluntarily came to the Church. Portugal is the most striking example of the first case, Poland of the second.

If a revolution washed away whatever hopes the Church had in Iran, a revolution opened the door in Portugal. The Portuguese revolution had its roots in the economic and political unrest resulting from Portugal's protracted effort to maintain its colonial empire in Africa, largely in what is now Angola. The costs of that effort proved too high and the Portuguese armed forces overthrew the

Lisbon government in a coup d'état. It was not apparent in the first months of the revolution what economic and social policies the new government would adopt. But clearly the revolution meant a sharp decline in the influence by the Catholic church, which was a mainstay of the previous regime. Given these far-reaching changes in Portuguese society, early in 1974 Kennedy suggested to President Kimball that Portugal offered a good chance for the Church to expand into a new country. The President took up his suggestion and, following an area conference in Stockholm, Sweden, in August 1974, sent Kennedy to Lisbon to begin the process of obtaining recognition.

Contrary to Kennedy's experience in most countries, he had only limited contacts with the leaders of the Portuguese government, since they were new men thrust into power by the revolution. He did, however, have a good relationship with Mario Soares, the foreign minister. With help from the American embassy, he was able to arrange meetings with Soares, the minister of finance, and the minister of justice. The meetings with both Soares and the minister of finance, Silva Lopes, were marked by conversations that alternated between problems of international finance and politics and the desire of the Church for recognition in Portugal. Soares was looking forward to a trip to the United States and wanted to talk about developments in Portugal, including Portuguese membership in NATO and the renegotiation of American bases in Portugal's Azores islands, while Kennedy wanted to talk about the Church. They compromised. Kennedy listened to the foreign minister's concerns about Portuguese-American relations and promised to convey those concerns to the Secretary of State on his return to the United States. In return, Soares listened to Kennedy's hopes for permission to open a mission in Portugal and, while noting that granting such permission was beyond his jurisdiction, promised to speak to the minister of justice, a boyhood friend with whom he was dining that very evening. The meetings with Lopes followed the same pattern with the same results. Kennedy would undertake to discuss Portugal's economic problems with the Secretary of the Treasury, and Lopes expressed his support for Kennedy's mission and offered what help he could.

Kennedy approached the crucial meeting with the minister of justice, Salgado Zenha, with some trepidation, but his worries were soon dissolved by the courtesy with which he was received and the cordiality of the visit. He was happy to learn that Zenha knew about the Church, and because of his visits to the United States, the word *Mormon* was not offensive to him or entirely new. But what really gave Kennedy hope was Zenha's belief that the freedom of religion he had observed in the United States should be introduced into Portugal. Kennedy could not let such a favorable moment pass. "That's precisely what I'd like you to do in our behalf," he said. "Our church would like to become established in Portugal. We seek the privilege of having your people hear about our faith and our way of life."

Kennedy went to Portugal knowing that he would be dealing with a government that had come to power through a coup d'état and had then imposed martial law. As he listened to Zenha express support for freedom of religion, it occurred to him that martial law gave the minister the power to rule by decree. Emboldened by his faith in his mission, he made a suggestion to Zenha: "Since this is a military government, you can simply order it. You have the power to do so right now." Zenha responded to Kennedy's directness with decisiveness and assured him that as of that date the Church was a legally recognized religious body in Portugal. Kennedy did not let the matter drop there, for he knew from his experience in negotiating for the bank that privileges unfounded in law could be as easily withdrawn as they were given. He had one more suggestion: Would it not be wise to extend to all churches the same recognition as the minister was giving to the Mormon church? Zenha agreed and was as good as his word, for in November 1974 the new parliament adopted a statute assuring freedom of religion in Portugal.

Thus, far more easily than Kennedy ever expected, the door was opened to missionary work in Portugal. But he also knew it was a fragile opportunity that could be destroyed by a careless or thoughtless act. In the report of his visit to the First Presidency, he suggested that missionary work be centered in Lisbon until a congregation of sufficient size and vigor developed, rather than sending missionaries throughout the country with the resulting scattered membership in small and weak congregations. He also cautioned against attaching Portugal to the Spanish mission because of the longstanding conflict between the two countries. Portugal was dedicated for missionary work by Thomas S. Monson, then a member of the Quorum of the Twelve Apostles, and the Portuguese Mission was established in November 1974 by missionaries, led by William Grant Bangerter, transferred from Brazil. Both Bangerter, who became an Assistant to the Quorum of the Twelve Apostles in 1975, and his wife, Geraldine, spoke excellent Portuguese. Among the missionaries transferred to Portugal was Kennedy's grandson, David Law, who served as interpreter for his grandfather during a January 1975 visit.

The political changes that took place in Portugal as a result of the revolution eased Kennedy's task of gaining recognition for the Church. On the other hand, the political changes that occurred in Poland after World War II made it more difficult to establish the Church there. Yet Kennedy believed that, of all the Eastern European countries, Poland and Yugoslavia offered the best chances for the establishment of the Church. There were a few Latter-day Saints in Poland who were visited from time to time by church leaders from the German Democratic Republic, but there were no organized branches or regularly held church services. Hence, in September 1975 he went to Warsaw to begin the process of gaining formal recognition.

During his visit Kennedy met with a variety of financial officials and central bankers. Only after those courtesy calls were made did he meet with Kazimierz Kakol, minister of religion, and Tadeusz Dusik, director of Protestant affairs. In that meeting, Kennedy explained the assignment given him by the First Presidency, which led to a general discussion of the place of religion and churches in Poland. Since Kennedy was not yet ready to enter formal negotiations for recognition, he expressed to Kakol his appreciation for the courtesies extended and expressed hope that they could meet again during future visits.

On the whole, Kennedy was encouraged by his first visit to Poland, and in May 1976 he returned to renew discussions with Kakol. This time they moved from the general to the specific. Kakol wanted to know more about the Church—its theology, structure, and governance. He also wanted to know how many members the Church had in Poland. Kennedy was specific in describing the origin, beliefs, and structure of the Church, but since the Church did not have an accurate record of church membership in Poland and because he sensed that size might be a factor in getting recognition, he avoided giving an exact number for church members in Poland. Further, he wanted Poland to recognize the Church on the basis of its worldwide membership and not just because there were a few members in Poland. He then moved to the heart of his visit and asked what the Church would have to do to gain official recognition. Kakol was reassuring about the possibility, but he then laid out the bureaucratic procedure for gaining that recognition and cautioned Kennedy that, even after recognition, the Church would have to keep in close touch with the ministry.

Now that Kennedy had put the Polish government on official notice that the purpose of his visits was to gain recognition for the Church, he prepared a detailed statement to present to Kakol on his next visit in November. The statement included information about the Church's teachings and organization, its position on crucial moral issues, its belief in the separation of church and state as expressed in the twelfth Article of Faith, the role of the president of the Church, the recognition of the Church in other countries, and statistics on church membership worldwide. By the time of his third visit, he had established cordial relations with Kakol, who invited him to spend a day or two sightseeing in Poland as a guest of the Polish government. Kennedy reciprocated by inviting the minister to visit the Church's headquarters in Salt Lake City.

Despite the cordial personal relations that Kennedy established with Kakol, there was silence from the ministry of religion on the request for official recognition. In February 1977 Kennedy wrote to Kakol asking what progress had been made in processing the Church's request but received no answer. In May of that year, accompanied by Lenora, Kennedy traveled to Japan to attend meetings of the International Monetary Conference. They planned to visit Korea at the end of the meetings in Japan, but Kennedy was unable to get the Polish issue off his mind. In a moment of inspiration he decided that rather than go to Korea, they would go to Poland. He wired Kakol, reported his tentative itinerary, and asked for an appointment. By the time Kakol wired back fixing the date of the appointment, David and Lenora, with the help of the American embassy, had their visas—with the customary twenty-dollar visa fee waived compliments of the Polish government.

When Kennedy arrived in Warsaw at 8:00 P.M. on May 25, after a long and tiring flight from Tokyo with a stopover in Copenhagen, he thought he would have the next day to prepare the document he was to present to Kakol. He found instead that the meeting was scheduled for 8:00 A.M. the next morning. Working through most of the night, with the help of the Church's attorney and an interpreter, he put together the formal request for recognition, along with supporting documents. The American embassy photocopied the documents, and he arrived just in time for the scheduled appointment.

Kakol was not surprised that Kennedy was in Warsaw to talk about recognition for the Church, and he had a surprise of his own. "When I got your cable, I thought you would be wanting to talk about recognition for the Mormon church," Kennedy recalled the minister telling him. "I pulled all of our information together, and we have done quite a bit of checking." Then Kakol went to his desk and with a smile handed Kennedy a neatly bound folder containing a document. Although Kennedy could not read Polish, he recognized the name of the Church and surmised that it was a statement granting recognition. Even though the statement was unsigned, Kennedy told Kakol that it was an eventful day for the Church to gain recognition for the first time in an Eastern European country. "When it is signed," Kennedy said, "we will have to have a celebration because this is a historic moment." Kakol made history by taking up his pen and signing the document then and there.

Legal recognition gave the Church the right to own property, to conduct worship services, and to distribute literature and explain the tenets of the Church to those who voluntarily asked for information. It did not include the right to proselyte because, as Kakol explained to Kennedy, that would invade the freedom of the people. On this basis the Church established a small visitors center manned by missionaries—usually a married couple—who spoke Polish where Sunday services were held, and church literature was available.

President Kimball was delighted with this historic first and began to make plans to dedicate Poland for the teaching of the gospel. At first he was concerned that a formal dedication might offend the Polish government and reverse the progress already made. But Kennedy assured him that the Polish government would welcome him as president of the Church and that the dedication services could be held if they were unobtrusive and dignified.

President Kimball, accompanied by his wife, Camilla; his secretary, D. Arthur Haycock; his doctor, Ernest L. Wilkinson, Jr.; and Kennedy and Lenora, arrived in Warsaw on August 22, 1977, to dedicate Poland for missionary work. The trip to Poland came near the end of a trip that had already taken President Kimball to Switzerland, Austria, Italy, and England. His schedule in each of those countries had been demanding, and he had become ill in London. He nonetheless insisted on going to Warsaw; but as soon as he arrived Wilkinson ordered him to bed, where Kennedy found him barely two hours before they were scheduled to host a formal dinner to which they had invited Kakol and members of his staff. Kennedy suggested to President Kimball that he not attend the dinner, but stay in bed and rest. The President resisted and asked only for a blessing. Kennedy asked Haycock to assist him, and the two of them, with Kennedy acting as spokesman, gave President Kimball the blessing he desired. By the time Kennedy arrived at the dinner to greet the guests, after having stopped by his own room to get Lenora, the President and his wife were already there. At President Kimball's request, Kennedy greeted the guests and acted as host. Following the meal, Kakol offered a toast in which he spoke of the common concerns that made it possible for the

Mormon church officials in Polana, 1977. President Spencer W. Kimball and his wife, Camilla, are in center of picture, with David and Lenora Kennedy

Polish government to recognize the Church, regardless of the differences they might have. President Kimball responded to that toast with an appreciation for Poland and the Polish people, in particular his admiration of their respect and love for family and hearth.

At 7:00 A.M. on August 24, 1977, a small group of Latter-day Saints, led by President Kimball, met in a secluded spot in the Ogrod Saski park to dedicate Poland for missionary work. The services were simple: a word of welcome from Kennedy, whom President Kimball asked to conduct the services, followed by the group singing quietly one verse of the hymn "We Thank Thee, O God, for a Prophet," and an opening prayer by Haycock. Matthew Ciembronowicz, an old friend of Kennedy's from Chicago, who, with his wife Marion, was representing the Church in Poland, bore his testimony, and then President Kimball dedicated Poland for missionary work. His prayer was an expression of love and appreciation for "the good people who live here. We have known of the terrible loss of life and extreme suffering endured under the destruction of war." He appealed to the Lord to "sanctify this land and cause that the leaders therein may be committed to making of

354

this a great land with great leadership and great opportunities for the people who have suffered so much." In his prayer of dedication, President Kimball asked for assistance to "display our gratitude to the leadership of this nation for their understanding and willingness to cooperate with us and permit us to make a contribution toward the lives of men and women and purposes in their families, with strong family relationships and loyal citizens which may result from the service that we shall render."

President Kimball asked a special blessing on the fathers and mothers of Poland and on the Polish nation: "Now, Father, we pray that thou will bless these fathers and mothers in this nation, that they may bring up their children in righteousness, that they may train aright and bless the children that they may grow up to be honorable, peaceful, loving parents themselves, so that the generations may bring to Thee, their Lord, great satisfaction in the development of the souls of men. We pray that no wickedness or combination of evils could possibly raise up against this nation and that they may be delivered from the hands of wicked assassins and from all their enemies and evil deeds of enemies may be confounded to the end that this people may live in peace and comfort and happiness and that they may hear the word of the Lord with gratitude."

President Kimball invoked the blessings of the Lord on those who received his servants: "Let Thy peace, Thy salvation be . . . upon that people." And in closing he asked "that our efforts toward blessing the people of this land may cause them to be righteous and to love Thee, our God. . . . We ask these blessings and dedicate this land by the authority of the Holy Priesthood which we hold that it may go forward and move intensely in the interest of bringing the people to the Gospel program."

That simple service and a prophet's prayer marked the successful end of David Kennedy's efforts to gain recognition of the Church in Poland. Yet it was just the beginning of the struggle to maintain a viable presence of the Church in that troubled land. Forbidden by the law to send missionaries door to door, the Church has had to be content for several years with missionary couples in

Warsaw to staff the modest visitors center that the recognition agreement permitted the Church to maintain. The Church, with no paid clergy, must rely on local lay leadership to supervise its daily activities, to conduct Sabbath services, and to maintain church discipline. This reliance on lay leadership has substantial advantages when there is a body of experienced members from which to choose leaders and where communications between the central organization and local leaders are easily maintained. In Poland, however, where there were few Latter-day Saints, and none with experience in church leadership, those chosen to lead the local branches have not always understood the organization of the Church, its programs, or its theology. In at least one instance, Kennedy had the unpleasant chore of releasing a local church leader who found it difficult to accept that decision and who appealed to the government authorities for support. Kennedy anticipated that possibility and forewarned Kakol's office so that the charges of the disgruntled member were discounted before they were made.

Despite these and other difficulties, the Church continues to maintain its existence in Poland. A series of missionary couples has been willing to accept the isolation and the often difficult living conditions to keep the visitors center open for those who, in one way or another, hear about the Church and are attracted by its message. The establishment of the Church in Poland and its gradual growth is a tribute to the vision of President Kimball that the Church's mission must be pursued in every nation where the slightest possibility for spreading the gospel exists. Kennedy's contribution to the fulfillment of that vision was possible because he approached his task with patience and an understanding for the cultural and political constraints he would encounter. It was also possible because of his faith that what a prophet of God envisioned could be achieved.

In addition to his visits to the nations of the world, Kennedy sought out the embassies of the various countries in Washington, D.C., where the Church was doing missionary work. He knew that the ambassadors assigned to Washington and their staffs were often much better informed about the Church than were the officials in foreign capitals. In many instances, they knew prominent Mormons personally and were therefore able to give their governments assurances about the Church's reputation for obeying the law, as well as confirm the respect that the Church commanded in the United States. Many of the Church's visa problems could be solved through those embassies, making it unnecessary to undertake lengthy and costly trips.

Another function that gradually emerged in the evolution of Kennedy's assignment as the special representative of the First Presidency was the hosting of foreign dignitaries. As he visited around the world and in Washington, he regularly invited influential people to visit Salt Lake City and to meet with church officials. He knew that many visitors to the United States saw New York, Washington, Chicago, and Disneyland without stopping in Utah. It was important for those who had the power to affect the work of the

David M. Kennedy with Queen Sirikit of Thailand, right, and her daughter

Church in other lands to see the Mormon people on their home ground and to talk face to face with church leaders. Kennedy issued far more invitations than were accepted, but many official visitors responded to his hope that he would have the pleasure of welcoming them in Salt Lake City. Ambassadors from Greece, the German Democratic Republic, Turkey, Egypt, and other countries have met with church leaders, seen the beauty of the Wasatch Mountains, wondered at the salinity of the Great Salt Lake, and enjoyed a concert by the Tabernacle Choir.

A particularly enjoyable occasion for Kennedy was the opportunity to welcome Queen Sirikit of Thailand to Salt Lake City. Relations between the Church and Thailand were uneasy because the incident of missionaries having their pictures taken atop a Buddha had become a *cause célèbre* in Thailand. Since that episode, negotiations with the Thai government were near the top of Kennedy's agenda as the Thais found one reason or another not to issue a visa or to delay its approval. The visit of Sirikit was a sincere effort by the Church to demonstrate to the Thai government that the

Utah Governor Scott Matheson, Queen Sirikit of Thailand, Gordon B. Hinckley, Princess of Thailand, David M. Kennedy, Mark E. Petersen, Mrs. Scott Matheson

Buddha incident was an unintentional departure from its willingness to obey the law and respect the customs and religions of its
people. During her stay in Salt Lake City, Kennedy was able to
introduce her to the First Presidency and other General Authorities, show her the temple grounds and the beauties of the city,
explain more fully the programs of the Church, and wish her god-
speed on her return.

Visits from officials from other parts of the world were reminders that the Church is under constant scrutiny, particularly in those
countries where there is a general suspicion about religious organizations and certainly about one that is usually identified as an
American church. The scope of that scrutiny was brought home to
Kennedy when two journalists from the German Democratic Republic (GDR) visited BYU in Provo and the Church Administration Building in Salt Lake City. With the two journalists was a representative
of the GDR embassy in Washington and a representative of the
United States Department of State. The meeting, which included
Thomas S. Monson and a fellow member of the Quorum of the
Twelve Apostles, James E. Faust, was at first a general discussion
of their impressions of the university and their tour of the United
States. Monson, who frequently traveled to the GDR, described the
way the Church operated there, particularly its dependence on
local German leadership and the good relations the Church had
with the GDR government. But the group's visit was more than a
courtesy call. The real reason for their visit was to discuss the way
the Church made decisions affecting its presence in the GDR and
to assure themselves that the Church was purely a religious body.
Monson pointed to a picture of President Kimball and said that
only the president of the Church spoke for the Church as a whole.
What others said included counsel and advice worthy of thoughtful consideration by the members, but only pronouncements of
the First Presidency were official church policy. Kennedy picked
up on the point Monson made and explained that when Mormons
spoke on political matters, they were speaking for themselves, not
the Church. "You know how to run your own government better
than we do," he told them, and he stressed that the Church was
not in the GDR in order to give advice to the government. "Our

members may well have positions, but that's up to them individually. When a member speaks, he's speaking for himself, not for the Church, and you are not to confuse it with the Mormon view." Kennedy reminded his visitors that they would most surely misread the position of the Church if they took too seriously statements made by individual members, regardless of the forum in which they spoke.

Kennedy not only saw the usefulness of inviting visitors to Church headquarters, but also the role that BYU could play in providing occasions for influential visitors from abroad to visit Utah and to see the Church firsthand. When those visitors came from countries outside Eastern Europe, the university was anxious to cooperate, but when Kennedy proposed that an Eastern European poet be invited to speak at the university, there was some initial reluctance. Kennedy understood the source of this reluctance and moved to still any criticism the university might encounter with a letter from President Kimball authorizing such a visit. He followed the same procedure when he asked the university to invite Kakol to visit church headquarters in November 1981. Kakol's call was followed later by a visit by Dusik to the university and to church headquarters. Not only did Dusik come to BYU, but he shared a family home evening in the home of Spencer and Dorothea Condie, who were called to preside over the Austria Vienna Mission, which also included Poland and other Eastern European countries. After an evening of music, scripture study, and prayer, Dusik told the Condies that they had "a holy family."

In addition to asking the university to host foreign dignitaries, Kennedy realized that many members of the BYU faculty, with their areas of expertise, could be useful in helping him to understand the cultural, political, and religious conditions in countries where his experience was limited. As Kennedy turned to the university for help, a key role was played by Spencer J. Palmer, a Korean scholar and a former mission president in Korea. Palmer, a professor of comparative religion, was excited by President Kimball's vision of a worldwide church and eager to assist Kennedy by organizing briefings, writing memoranda, and supervising research that would contribute to the successful fulfillment of

Kennedy's mission. The two of them developed a close working relationship that generated a flood of ideas about the way the university might be used as the missionary effort expanded in an increasing number of countries. A relationship that began with informal discussions and briefings was a crucial element that led to the creation of the David M. Kennedy Center for International Studies, which among other functions serves as a liaison between the university and the Church on international issues.

While his three principal duties—visiting countries outside the United States, contacting embassies in Washington, and hosting foreign dignitaries—took up most of Kennedy's time, a variety of other tasks were thrust on him. He briefed mission presidents who were going to the countries where the Church had to be particularly careful about political or religious sensitivities. As the Church began holding area conferences around the world, Kennedy traveled with President Kimball to introduce him to the heads of state and to political leaders in the countries within the scope of each conference. On particularly sensitive occasions, notably the dedication of the Orson Hyde Memorial Park in Jerusalem, Kennedy was asked by the First Presidency to review the talks given by the General Authorities to ensure that they did not inadvertently touch the raw nerves of either the Muslims or the Jews.[2] There were also fires to be put out, as when a mission president in an Eastern European country ordered a large number of tracts from a local printer. When the printer as required by the law reported the order to the government, the government officials wanted to know why a church with only a handful of members needed so many copies of a tract if it was not intending to proselyte aggressively for new members. Kennedy rushed into the breach to assure the government that the printing request was a mistake and that the Church was indeed abiding by his previous commitment and would do so in the future. An equally challenging but far more pleasant assignment was the commission to negotiate the purchase of additional land for the Church's temple in Tokyo. Kennedy arrived in Tokyo armed with full authority to commit the Church to the purchase of the land if the price, which was expected to be high, fell within the limits the First Presidency had fixed. He returned to Salt Lake

Officials of the Republic of China on Taiwan visit Mormon church leaders. Left to right, Y. S. Sun, minister of economics; David M. Kennedy; Vice Premier Chiang Chingkuo; Spencer W. Kimball; Yu Kuo-hwa, president of the Central Bank of China

City pleased with the results, for not only had he bought the property—a purchase he long believed necessary—but the price was substantially lower than anticipated, owing to the easing of the real estate market in Tokyo.

The demands on Kennedy's time and energy were compounded by the need to deal with "amateur diplomats," church members who were sure that they had just the contacts needed to open the door for the Church in any and all countries. Often these were well-meaning but naive friends of General Authorities who used that friendship to offer their services or to suggest that their so-called influential contacts could help the Church. Sometimes they came to the Church with hidden agendas, as did one person whose concealed purpose was to advance his business of selling arms around the world. In moments of frustration, after listening to people who did not have an adequate background in the foreign country involved or who did not know of the approaches the Church was quietly taking, Kennedy often resented the time he spent with

David M. Kennedy greets President Ronald Reagan

"mother's little helpers," as he ruefully called them. Yet each one had to be heard out in the off chance that they could be of some real help to the Church and because so many of them came motivated only by a desire to help the Church that it would have been unnecessarily churlish to dismiss them out of hand.

David Kennedy began his service as the special representative of the First Presidency with a question about how that position would fit into the ongoing structure of the Church. In his years of service the question has become, What will the future bring? There is no question that he has performed a valuable service, but recognition of that fact raises the issue whether it was the position or Kennedy's unique experience and skills that made the difference. Has the experience resulted in the position being institutionalized so that Kennedy's departure will be followed by a new appointment to the position? Certainly there are countries where his name, reputation, and stature have made the difference. That point was underlined when an application to transfer the responsibility of the Church's affairs from one missionary couple to their replacement in an Eastern European country was disapproved because it was not signed by David Kennedy. The Israelites in Egypt experienced persecution when a pharaoh rose up who knew not Joseph. Will the Mormons in Eastern Europe lose recognition when Kennedy is no longer here to plead their cause?

Kennedy is sensitive to such issues and realizes the extent to which the position has become an extension of his own personality. At the same time, he recognizes that the world is too large to be the responsibility of any one man. Some of the tasks he has performed could be done by others. The recurring visa problems might be assigned to a group of area experts, he believes, who could over time develop the kind of relationships with embassies in Washington and consulates in other cities, even with the foreign ministries in the host countries, that would make solution of visa problems easier. The key to the success of such area experts would be for the Church to look on them as diplomats assigned to an area over an extended period of time. Kennedy's experience has convinced him that to be successful, diplomats cannot be short-timers; they must have time to build contacts, cement relationships, and develop a keen understanding of the cultural patterns of their assigned areas.

But if some aspects of the special representative's position could be institutionalized, there are others that would be more difficult, if not impossible, to specify with any precision in a job description. Kennedy has become aware during the evolution of his assignment how much his success and effectiveness were determined by the way President Kimball viewed his job, and by the access he had to the President. Kennedy's position outside the normal structure of church organization eliminated any organizational tension that might have existed had he simultaneously held a position among the General Authorities. The success of his replacement will be determined, he believes, by the extent to which the president of the Church wants to use the special representative. Some presidents, he recognizes, might feel comfortable performing many of the functions he has undertaken and thus feel less of a need for the special representative. Should the position of special representative be continued, its usefulness to the Church will also depend on the experience and contacts of the person appointed and by the way the position fits into the organization of the Church, including other assignments the special representative might carry.

The end of David Matthew Kennedy's service to his profession, his community, his country, and his Church cannot be told. Even as this last note is being written, he may be on a plane headed for Eastern Europe, the Middle East, the Far East, Africa, or South America—solving one more visa problem, explaining one more time to reluctant government officials that the Church believes in obeying and sustaining the law, or attending one more area conference where he will arrange for the leaders of the Church to meet the leading government officials. Or he may be in Salt Lake City meeting with the ambassadors from several Middle Eastern countries who are in Utah for a conference, or talking to mission presidents who will be going to countries where the relations of the Church and the government are sensitive and delicate, or discussing the international thrust of the Church with members of the International Affairs Committee, or dictating to his secretary a letter of appreciation to a friend from abroad who has interceded on behalf of a missionary needing help. He may at times remember wistfully his plans for the cottage in Huntsville, but he also remembers that the call to serve the Church came from a prophet of God and that long ago in the fields of Randolph his father answered his question about the purpose of life simply and succinctly: "I'll tell you what the purpose of your life is. It's very simple. Then you won't have to worry about it. You think about it and that'll be it. Your purpose in life is to serve God and your fellowmen, period. That's it. That's all you have to remember." Kennedy has never forgotten, and now past eighty, that fatherly counsel still guides his life.

SOURCES AND NOTES

SHORTENED TITLES

Works and collections cited numerous times throughout this section have been shortened as follows:

Continental Illinois: Continental Illinois National Bank and Trust Company.

Kennedy Oral History: David M. Kennedy Oral History, Interviews by Gordon Irving, 1981–85, 3 vols., typescript, The James Moyle Oral History Program, Archives, Historical Department of The Church of Jesus Christ of Latter-day Saints, Salt Lake City, Utah.

Kennedy Papers: David M. Kennedy Papers, David M. Kennedy Center for International Studies, Brigham Young University, Provo, Utah.

LDS Archives: Archives, Historical Department of The Church of Jesus Christ of Latter-day Saints, Salt Lake City, Utah.

Lee Library: Harold B. Lee Library, Brigham Young University, Provo, Utah.

GENERAL

An excellent source on the life of David Matthew Kennedy is the Kennedy Oral History. In addition to providing background material, this three-volume work is a guide to other sources of data.

The Kennedy Papers are the best source for detailed, specific information on Kennedy's professional career. In addition, they lead to other sources that, along with the Kennedy Papers, have been used to document and verify Kennedy's recollections and those of others interviewees. The papers provide a chronology of Kennedy's years at Continental Illinois and in government service. They include his extensive correspondence in those years, and they are particularly detailed for his tenure at the Treasury. The voluminous subject-matter files cover all of the major events during his professional career. Requests for permission to use the Kennedy Papers should be directed to Spencer J. Palmer, Associate Director, David M. Kennedy Center for International Studies, Brigham Young University, Provo, Utah 84602.

A longer transcript of this biography with detailed documentation is in the Kennedy Papers and is available for review by scholars and other interested individuals.

This effort would not have been accomplished without the many hours of interview sessions. David and Lenora Kennedy graciously consented to ten transcribed interviews by the author and others; other brief contacts for clarification or confirmation purposes are too numerous to mention. The genealogical data on the Kennedy and Bingham families was provided by the Kennedy and Bingham families. The transcriptions of some fifty other interviews are in the Kennedy Papers.

Finally, the newspaper stories on Kennedy and events that he has been involved with are voluminous. Only the name of the paper and the date of issue cited from are included herein. Again, more detailed notes containing specific references are included with the typescript of this volume in the Kennedy Papers.

CHAPTER 1

Volume 1 of the Kennedy Oral History is the best source of information on Kennedy's early years in Randolph. Interviews with Kennedy and others were also helpful.

Steven L. Thomson, Jane D. Digerness, and Mar Jean S. Thomson, *Randolph—A Look Back* (Randolph, Utah: By the Authors, 1981), combines a history of the early years of Randolph with selected biographical sketches of some of the families and individuals who played an important role in the development of the town. Also useful are an incomplete file of the *Rich County News,* found on microfilm at the Lee Library; Paul J. Kennedy, "James D. Kennedy Family History," 1983; and interviews with Gladys Kennedy Groll (Randolph, Utah, November 1983); and Mable Kennedy Richey and Ruth James, (Ogden, Utah, October 1984).

Other sources include James B. Allen and Glen M. Leonard, *The Story of the Latter-day Saints* (Salt Lake City: Deseret Book, 1976); Andrew Jensen, *Encyclopedic History of The Church of Jesus Christ of Latter-day Saints* (Salt Lake City: Deseret News, 1941); John Snowball, "Early Days of Rich County," Special Collections, Lee Library; Dale J. Stevens et al., *Utah Weather Guide* (West Jordan, Utah: Society for Applied Climatology, 1983); "Minutes—General, 1910–1913," Argyle Ward, Woodruff Stake, February 9, 1913, LDS Archives; Wilford Woodruff, "Official Declaration–1." Doctrine and Covenants (Salt Lake City: The Church of Jesus Christ of Latter-day Saints, 1981); Richard D. Poll et al., *Utah's History* (Provo, Utah: Brigham Young University Press, 1978); Gustive O. Larson, *The "Americanization" of Utah for Statehood* (San Marino, California: Huntington Library, 1971); and *Secretary of State, Utah State Election Papers,* Microfilm, Lee Library.

Notes for Chapter 1

1. Although Bear Lake Valley is north of Randolph and nearly the same elevation, the lake makes the climate more temperate there than in the Bear River Valley. John Snowball, an early settler, recorded, "Bear Lake valley was our Egypt where we went to get our wheat and potatoes." (Snowball, "Early Days of Rich County," p. 6.)

2. Family traditions differ on the reasons for the Kennedys' decision to immigrate to the United States. In a family history, a grandson of John Kennedy Jr. wrote: "The reason for the family leaving Scotland is obscure but some clues may be found in the stories told by grandfather to my father as they worked together on various projects on the homestead. Apparently it was a family decision to make the move and although the Mormon Church was very active in proselyting throughout the British Isles and encouraging movement to Utah at that time, I believe the move was entirely a family decision and not connected in any way with the Church." (Paul J. Kennedy, "James D. Kennedy Family History," p. 10.) However, I draw a different conclusion. In view of the family's conversion to Mormonism and the saliency of the doctrine of the gathering, it is difficult to conclude that the decision to immigrate to the United States was completely divorced from any connection with the Church.

3. In the mid-forties, at the urging of G. Willard Peart, who was in charge of a public works project and who was also bishop of the Randolph Ward, George agreed to become the foreman on the project because, as Peart told him, you are the only one who can get the men to work. David Kennedy visited the project and remarked to a cousin who was working on it that it was going well as a private venture. "It looks as if you were working for yourself," he said. His cousin ruefully replied, "Your dad's over there." (Kennedy Oral History, 1:17.)

4. Indicative of the neglect of the Church's central rites is the fact that when George's brother-in-law, William Johnson, was called to be Sunday School superintendent at nineteen, he had not been baptized. His future father-in-law, Bishop John Kennedy Jr., cut a hole in the ice of a nearby pond and baptized him. (Thomson, Digerness, and Thomson, *Randolph—A Look Back,* p. 326.) "Most of the settlers had joined the Mormon church, not because they were intensely religious or supportive of the religion but I think they all or most all of them believed their children should have some kind of religious training and since the Mormon religion was actively pushed and available they accepted it. Very few of the Kennedys were very religious." (Paul J. Kennedy, "James D. Kennedy Family History," p. 20.) Gladys Kennedy Groll agrees with that assessment.

5. John Snowball ("Early Days of Rich County," pp. 4–5) blames the conflict on "three apostate Mormons" elected to the school board.

369

6. Although George's purchases and sales of farm land are fully recorded in the Rich County Recorder's Office, there is no record of his having purchased a home in Randolph. The home was probably built on land owned by his father, which accounts for the absence of a recorded deed.

CHAPTER 2

Volume 1 of the Kennedy Oral History, interviews with David and Lenora Kennedy, and the Kennedy Papers are the chief sources of information. An interview with Marlon Schade (Provo, Utah, November 1983) provides valuable information on David's years in Ogden and Riverdale. Also helpful are the Riverdale Ward Historical Record, LDS Archives; and *Acorn,* 1929, the yearbook of Weber College.

Notes for Chapter 2

1. Some sources assign this event to 1914, when David was nine, but his diary, the sequence of his school attendance in Ogden, and his own recollection fix the date as the summer of 1916. (Cf. Thomson, Digerness, and Thomson, *Randolph—A Look Back,* p. 240.)

2. Schade remembered that David was the mainstay in helping his father on the chicken farm: "Ivan and Melvin, his brothers, they were not the industrious kids that David was. David always assumed his responsibilities."

3. Marlon Schade recalled, "David always wanted to give the speeches, and I was always tagging along pulling his coattail saying, let's go someplace else. But he'd always deliver them, and then we'd go."

4. Wilkinson was the president of Brigham Young University, 1951–71.

5. Schade said, "I think she was a little hard to get. I think that was one thing that interested David is that she gave him just a little bit of a rough time."

6. Schade's recollection of the trip differs in detail from that of David and Lenora, but they agree on the essential elements.

7. Despite Jacobs's enthusiasm for David's mission, he did not write to David while he was in England. (See David to Lenora, December 15, 1927, Documents, Mission to England, Kennedy Papers.)

CHAPTER 3

In addition to volume 1 of the Kennedy Oral History and interviews with David and Lenora, typed excerpts from David's letters to Lenora and her letters to him while he was in England provide a weekly, sometimes daily, documentation of his mission. The excerpts are in the Kennedy Papers. Other sources helpful in providing a historical setting are Allen and Leonard, *The Story of the Latter-day Saints*; Richard L. Evans, *A Century of Mormonism in Great Britain* (Salt Lake City: Deseret News, 1937); Richard S. Van Wagoner and Stephen

Walker, *A Book of Mormons* (Salt Lake City: Signature Books, 1982); William Manchester, *The Last Lion: Visions of Glory 1874–1932* (Boston: Little, Brown & Co., 1983); *Millennial Star*, January 20, 1927; Jean Paulsen, *Ken Garff: A Biography* (Salt Lake City: Kendall Day Garff, 1983); and an interview with Kendall Garff, Salt Lake City, December 1983.

Notes for Chapter 3

1. David deplored the loss of local leadership resulting from immigration because it weakened the Church in England. (Kennedy Oral History, 1:55; David to Lenora, March 29, 1927, Documents, Mission to England, Kennedy Papers.)

2. David's moments of discouragement were less frequent during the last year of his mission. There were despondent moments, but they usually came when he was in poor health. (See David to Lenora, May 27, 1927, Documents, Mission to England, Kennedy Papers.)

CHAPTER 4

Volume 1 of the Kennedy Oral History, interviews with David and Lenora, and documents in the Kennedy Papers provide the basic information. Sources are the interview with Marlon Schade; Neal Lambert, "Some Thoughts on Mormon Literature and the Mormon Sense of Sacred Space," in *Proceedings of the Symposia of the Association for Mormon Letters* (1978–79); *Acorn*, 1929, Weber College; and George Santayana, "Sonnet III," *Poems* (Charles Scribner's Sons: New York, 1935). The contemporary flavor of David's first years in Washington, D.C., is obtained from the letters he sent his parents. Those letters and other documents used as supporting evidence are in the Kennedy Papers.

In addition, many interviews were conducted with people who lived in Washington, D.C., during those years, including Milton A. Barlow (Chevy Chase, Maryland, October 1984), W. Victor and Eleanor Bartholomew (Salem, Utah, October 1984), Samuel R. Carpenter (Salt Lake City, July 1984), Byron F. Dixon (Arlington, Virginia, October 1984), Lawson Hamblin (Wildwood, Utah, September 1984), William Haslam (Provo, Utah, July 1984), Rosel H. Hyde (Washington, D.C., October 1984), George Y. Jarvis (Sandy, Utah, October 1984), Steven Kennedy (Ogden, Utah, December 1983), Miller F. Shurtleff (McLean, Virginia, October 1984, and Provo, Utah, June 1986), Jesse R. Smith (Washington, D.C., October 1984), Albert Swenson (Provo, Utah, September 1984), Florian Thayne (Washington, D.C., October 1984), and Alan Young (Salt Lake City, October 1984).

Additional information was gleaned from Frank W. Fox, *J. Reuben Clark: The Public Years* (Provo, Utah: Brigham Young University Press and Deseret Book, 1980); Allen and Leonard, *The Story of the Latter-day Saints; 1985 Church Almanac* (Salt Lake City: Deseret News, 1984); The Edgar Brossard Oral History, Interviews by Davis Bitton, 1973, typescript, The James Moyle Oral History Program, LDS Archives; Robert O'Brien, *Marriott: The J. Willard Marriott Story* (Salt Lake City: Deseret Book, 1977); Mary L. Bradford, "From

Colony to Community: The Washington, D.C., Saints," *Ensign*, August 1974; and D. Michael Quinn, *J. Reuben Clark: The Church Years* (Provo, Utah: Brigham Young University Press, 1983).

Notes for Chapter 4

1. Kennedy remembered Randolph as "our home, I had a happy childhood and I liked the place. I still like it. I've always claimed Randolph as my home, even when we were in Washington all those years, or Chicago, or Europe. When people asked me where I was born or where my home was, I'd say, Randolph, Utah." (Kennedy Oral History, 1:11–12.)

2. Brossard was a member of the Tariff Commission from 1925 to 1959 and served as chairman in 1935 and from 1953 to 1959.

CHAPTER 5

The impressions of family life in Kennedy's home are drawn from volume 1 of the Kennedy Oral History, interviews with David and Lenora Kennedy, and interviews with Marilyn Kennedy Taylor (Salt Lake City, July 1984), Barbara Kennedy Law (Salt Lake City, November 1983), Carol Kennedy Davis (Salt Lake City, November 1983), Patricia Kennedy Campbell (Ogden, Utah, December 1983), and Steven Kennedy (Ogden, Utah, December 1983). Additional information is found in Kennedy's letters to members of his family and in other documents in the Kennedy Papers.

The following sources provide helpful information on the Church in Washington: Edgar Brossard Oral History; Manuscript History of the Church, Capitol Ward [not paginated], LDS Archives; "Genealogical Reports, Form E," 1941, Capitol Ward, Washington Stake, LDS Archives; and Manuscript History of the Church, Washington Stake, 2 vols. [not paginated], LDS Archives. Additional information on the Church was acquired from interviews with Samuel Carpenter, Jesse R. Smith, Florian Thayne, Victor Bartholomew, Alan Young, and Albert Swenson.

Notes for Chapter 5

1. Samuel Carpenter, a close friend, said Kennedy was more devoted to his family than any other man he knew.

2. Kennedy wrote: "Washington is surely a beautiful city. We like it fine. The only thing we do not like about it is the fact that about two-thirds of the population is made up of Negros." (David Kennedy to Melvin and Helen Kennedy, October 14, 1929, Letters to Family, Washington—1929–46, Kennedy Papers.)

CHAPTER 6

Volume 1 of the Kennedy Oral History, interviews with David Kennedy, and documents in the Kennedy Papers provide the basic data. Additional sources are Public Law 43, December 23, 1913, *United States Statutes at Large* (Washington, D.C.: GPO, 1915); Harold Barger, *The Management of Money: A Survey of American Experience* (Chicago: Rand McNally, 1964), which contains a good overview of the Federal Reserve system; Marriner S. Eccles, *Beckoning Frontiers: Public and Personal Recollections*, ed. Sidney Hyman (New York: Alfred A. Knopf, 1951); Board of Governors of Federal Reserve System, *Federal Reserve Bulletin*, December 1937; Arthur M. Schlesinger Jr., *The Age of Roosevelt*, vol. 2 of *The Coming of the New Deal* (Boston: Houghton Mifflin, 1959), one of the best studies of this period of the New Deal; Studs Terkel, *Hard Times* (New York: Pantheon Books, 1970); Dean L. May, "Sources of Marriner S. Eccles' Economic Thought," *Journal of Mormon History*, 1976, and *From New Deal to New Economics: The American Liberal Response to the Recession of 1937* (New York: Garland Publishing, 1981); Arch O. Egbert, "Marriner S. Eccles and the Banking Act of 1935" (Ph.D. diss., Brigham Young University, 1967); E. A. Goldenweiser, *Monetary Management* (New York: McGraw-Hill, 1949), and *American Monetary Policy* (New York: McGraw-Hill, 1951); John Morton Blum, *Roosevelt and Morgenthau: A Revision and Condensation of: From the Morgenthau Diaries* (Boston: Houghton Mifflin, 1970); Marriner S. Eccles Papers, Special Collections, Marriott Library, University of Utah, Salt Lake City; and Lawrence S. Ritter and William L. Silber, *Principles of Money, Banking, and Financial Markets*, 2nd ed. (New York: Basic Books, 1977).

Notes for Chapter 6

1. David M. Kennedy's Personnel File, Washington—1929–46, Kennedy Papers, does not give the date he was made Eccles's administrative assistant. However, the file does contain a job description, dated October 27, 1942, that shows him as assistant chief of the Government Securities Section. The next job description, dated May 6, 1943, lists duties both as an administrative assistant to the chairman and as assistant chief of the Government Securities Section. I assume, therefore, that his appointment as administrative assistant occurred early in 1943.

2. Eccles reproduced part of the memo in *Beckoning Frontiers: Public and Personal Recollections*, pp. 340–41. He reports (p. 343) that he took the memo to the White House, and, "as usual, that harassed and overburdened man, on hearing my report of what had happened, took the necessary steps to soothe the bruises on all sides."

CHAPTER 7

Volume 1 of the Kennedy Oral History, documents from the Kennedy Papers, and interviews with David Kennedy were used. Other interviews used as sources were with John Perkins (Provo, Utah, February 1985), Herbert Prochnow (Chicago, March 1985), Owen West (Chicago, March 1985), John K. Edmunds (Salt Lake City, December 1983), and Carol Kennedy Davis.

Additional information has been obtained from Hays Gorey, "The Bank That Made a U-Turn on LaSalle Street," *Fortune*, March 1966; "A Pictorial Visit to—Continental Illinois National Bank," *Finance*, February 28, 1949; A. E. Holmans, "The Eisenhower Administration and the Recession, 1953–55," *Oxford Economic Papers*, New Series, February 1958; Gary W. Reichard, *The Reaffirmation of Republicanism* (Knoxville: University of Tennessee Press, 1975); *United States Monetary Policy: Recent Thinking and Experience, Hearings before a Subcommittee on Economic Stabilization of the Joint Committee on the Economic Report*, 83rd Congress, 2nd session, 1954; Treasury Department, *Annual Report of the Secretary of the Treasury on the State of Finances, For the Fiscal Year Ended June 30, 1955; Federal Economic Policy*, 4th ed. (Washington, D.C.: Congressional Quarterly, 1969); Seymour E. Harris, *The Economics of the Political Parties* (New York: Macmillan, 1962); William R. Willoughby, *The St. Lawrence Waterway: A Study of Politics and Diplomacy* (Madison: University of Wisconsin Press, 1961); House of Representatives, *St. Lawrence Seaway, Hearings before the Committee on Public Works*, 83rd Congress, 1st session, 1953; *Congressional Record*, 83rd Congress, 2nd session; Public Law 358–201, May 13, 1954, *United States Statutes at Large* (Washington, D.C.: GPO, 1955); and U.S. Department of Transportation, *1968 Annual Report, Saint Lawrence Seaway Development Corporation* (Washington, D.C.: U.S. Department of Transportation, May 15, 1969).

Notes for Chapter 7

1. Kennedy's affection for Knight is evident throughout the Kennedy Oral History. See particularly 1:159–61.

2. The exact point at which this substitution was made is obscure since the hearings at which Kennedy testified were not published. The debates on the St. Lawrence Seaway bill in the House on May 6, 1954, which is after Kennedy remembers testifying, show that the original bill provided that "in order to finance its activities, the Corporation is authorized and empowered to issue to the Secretary of the Treasury, from time to time and to have outstanding at any one time in an amount not exceeding $105 million, its notes, debentures, bonds or other obligations." That provision had been replaced with an amendment striking out the words "notes, debentures, bonds or other obligations" wherever they occurred in the bill and substituting "revenue bonds." (May 6, 1954, *Congressional Record*, 83rd Congress, 2nd session, 100:6137.) The statute was adopted as amended in the committee. (*United States Statutes at Large*, 68:94–95.) Although this evidence is circumstantial, it is fully consistent with Kennedy's recollections and reflects his proposal that the Seaway bonds be purchased by the Treasury rather than sold to the public.

CHAPTER 8

Volume 1 of the Kennedy Oral History, interviews with David Kennedy, and documents from the Kennedy Papers provide most of the source material.

One document that provides an excellent outline of Kennedy's years as chairman of Continental Illinois is "The Kennedy Years at Continental Bank," Summer 1977, Bank Archives, Continental Illinois National Bank and Trust Company, Chicago. A copy is now in the Kennedy Papers. Also crucial to an understanding of Kennedy's leadership and achievements at Continental are the insightful recollections of Donald Graham (Chicago, May 1985) and Tilden Cummings (Chicago, May 1985). Another useful source dealing with Kennedy's years at Continental Illinois is *Columns*, the house organ of the bank. Some copies of *Columns* are found in *Columns* Magazine, Bank Materials (#1), Kennedy Papers. Helpful interviews were conducted with Robert Mayo (Chicago, February 1985) and John K. Edmunds. Other sources include Hays Gorey, "The Bank That Made a U-Turn on LaSalle Street"; David M. Kennedy, "Personal Integrity," *Ensign*, December 1979; and Doctrine and Covenants.

Notes for Chapter 8

1. Kennedy Oral History, 1:140. The entry creates the impression that Kennedy's influence with Cummings on loan decisions came before his fourteen months at the Treasury, but my conversations with Kennedy confirmed the context found here.

2. Kennedy Oral History, 1:139. This entry suggests that Kennedy became secretary of the board before his fourteen months at the Treasury, but Drew's retirement in 1955 makes clear that Kennedy's appointment did not occur until after he rejoined the bank.

3. "I interviewed each one, and they each pledged to me whatever help they could. And it was a real change and a surprise to me that they became very aggressive bankers." (Kennedy Oral History, 1:176.)

4. Tilden was no relation to Walter, and he took pains to make that fact known.

5. A memorandum of conversation of this meeting prepared by Alfred Cowles (December 16, 1957, Retirement of Walter Cummings, Bank Materials [#1], Kennedy Papers) implies that only the second alternative was presented to Cummings, but that is clearly in error since the statement read to Cummings by William Mitchell is explicit in outlining the two alternatives. (Statement by William Mitchell to Walter Cummings in early December 1957, Retirement of Walter Cummings, Bank Materials [#1], Kennedy Papers.)

6. See Kennedy's account of this period in "Personal Integrity." He does not identify Cummings by name, but it is clear from his reference to his discussions with John Edmunds that he is referring to the retirement of Cummings.

CHAPTER 9

Volume 1 of the Kennedy Oral History and the extensive documentation in from the Kennedy Papers, particularly Kennedy's "Notes" on the merger, are valuable. Interviews with Tilden Cummings and Donald Graham are also helpful in detailing the merger process and its problems.

Other sources used are Hays Gorey, "The Bank That Made a U-Turn on LaSalle Street"; *Chicago Daily Tribune*, December 15, 1960; Statement by Donald M. Graham, House of Representatives, *To Amend the Bank Merger Act of 1960*, Hearings before the Subcommittee on Domestic Finance of the Committee on Banking and Currency, 89th Congress, 1st session, 1965; *United States Code*, 1982, Title 15; George Bookman, "Loevinger vs. Big Business," *Fortune*, January 1962; *Chicago Daily News*, August 30, 1961; U.S. v. Philadelphia National Bank et al., 374 U.S. 321, 83 S. Ct. 1715 (1963); U.S. v. First National Bank & Trust Co. of Lexington et al., 376 S. Ct. 1033 (1964); U.S. v. Manufacturers Hanover Trust Co., 240 F. Supp. 867 (U.S. District Court, S. D. New York, 1965); and *Wall Street Journal*, February 8, 1966.

Notes for Chapter 9

1. Section 1 of the Sherman Act forbids actions that would involve a restraint of trade (*United States Code*, 1982, Title 15, 1). Section 7 of the Sherman Act as amended in 1950 prohibits behavior that would "lessen competition, or to tend to create a monopoly" (*United States Code*, 1982, Title 15, 18).

CHAPTER 10

The basic references for the story of Continental's expansion overseas are volume 1 of the Kennedy Oral History; documents from the Kennedy Papers; Hays Gorey, "The Bank That Made a U-Turn on LaSalle Street"; *Chicago Daily Tribune*, March 2, 1962; Ritter and Silber, *Principles of Money, Banking, and Financial Markets*; and interviews with David Kennedy and Donald Graham. Particularly helpful were interviews with Roger Anderson (Chicago, March 1985) and Alfred Miossi (Chicago, March and May 1985). The Kennedy Oral History and interviews with David Kennedy are valuable in developing the Sindona issue. Other helpful material includes Gordon Thomas and Max Morganwitts, *Pontiff* (Garden City, New York: Doubleday, 1983); Joan Edelman Spero, *The Failure of the Franklin National Bank: Challenge to the International Banking System* (New York: Columbia University Press, 1980); Luigi DiFonzo, *St. Peter's Banker* (New York: Franklin Watts, 1983); Sanford Rose, "What Really Went Wrong at Franklin National," *Fortune*, October 1974; *New York Times*, March 23, 1986; Dan Cordtz, "What's Behind the Sindona Invasion," *Fortune*, August 1973.

Notes for Chapter 10

1. Alfred Miossi agrees with this assessment.

2. In the hurly-burly of the postwar years in Milan, Michele Sindona became the "city's leading property tax expert; he seemed to know a hundred different ways to avoid duty on all kinds of speculation and development deals." (Gordon Thomas and Max Morganwitts, *Pontiff*, p. 144.)

3. Kennedy did not receive a salary as a director of Fasco, but all of his travel and other expenses were paid into an account that he hoped to use in a joint venture with Sindona. (Salt Lake City, June 1985.)

4. Joan Edelman Spero, *The Failure of Franklin National Bank: Challenge to the International Banking System*. This book, the best work on the subject of Franklin's failure, has a careful analysis of the national and international factors as well as the management failures that led to the crisis at Franklin. While the author makes clear the relationship between Kennedy and Sindona, the book is free from the conspiratorial tone that is the most salient characteristic of the book by Luigi DiFonzo, *St. Peter's Banker*.

All accounts of Sindona's activities in the United States mention his close ties to Kennedy. DiFonzo strongly suggests that Kennedy intervened with the American regulatory authorities, particularly James Smith, Comptroller of the Currency, to persuade them not to force Sindona to sell his stock in Franklin National Bank. DiFonzo argues that Sindona intended from the beginning to loot the assets of the bank to shore up his teetering Italian financial empire. Spero's book, Kennedy's recollections, and other sources suggest that Sindona knew his affairs in Italy were on the verge of collapse and that he wanted to make the United States the center of his financial activities, using Franklin as a base of operations. This second theory does not deny that Sindona did in fact divert some of Franklin's assets to his Italian venture, but it assumes that Sindona had a vested interest in seeing Franklin remain solvent since without Franklin, his plan to build a financial empire in the United States as he had done in Italy was hopeless. If this second theory is accepted, then what happened at Franklin was the result of an initial mistake on Sindona's part in buying a weak bank. Then when it became apparent that drastic measures were needed to save it from bankruptcy, his ego led him and the bank officers first into gambles on the foreign exchange markets and, when those gambles failed, into deception, fraud, and thievery.

5. Gleason was characterized as "a good public-relations man and a smooth and persuasive talker." (Sanford Rose, "What Really Went Wrong at Franklin National.")

6. There was considerable ambiguity surrounding the extent to which Sindona really controlled Franklin. Under the then-existing law, any corporation that owned 25 percent of a bank was deemed to have control. The question whether Fasco International, with 21.6 percent of Franklin National's stock, came under the law—thus under the supervision of the Federal Reserve system—was posed but never decided. The Federal Reserve Board, which had responsibility for determining the issue, was uncertain just how the law applied

to Sindona through Fasco International, and while there were continued requests for information, a decision was delayed until the issue became moot. (Spero, *The Failure of Franklin National Bank,* pp. 57–60.)

7. Kennedy, in fact, already had authority to vote Sindona's control of Fasco International. The voting trust granted him in the Franklin crisis was made irrevocable so he could deal with the problem without a veto from Sindona.

8. Following his June 1980 prison sentence in the United States, Sindona was extradited to Italy in September 1984. In Italy he was convicted of fraud and sentenced to twelve years in prison. He was also tried and convicted of contracting the 1979 killing of Giorgio Ambrosoli, who had been in charge of liquidating Sindona's Italian empire. On March 18, 1986, Sindona was sentenced to life imprisonment for contracting Ambrosoli's death. Four days after being sentenced, Sindona died of cyanide poisoning. Suicide was suspected, as Sindona had attempted to take his own life following his 1980 conviction. (Wolfgang Saxon, "At the Center of Scandals," *New York Times,* March 23, 1986, p. 44.)

CHAPTER 11

Key sources include volume 1 of the Kennedy Oral History, documents from the Kennedy Papers, interviews with David Kennedy, and interviews with Donald Graham and Tilden Cummings. Other sources are Public Law 87–624, August 31, 1962, *United States Statutes at Large* (Washington, D.C.: GPO, 1963); Hays Gorey, "The Bank That Made a U-Turn on LaSalle Street"; Public Law 511–240, May 9, 1956, *United States Statutes at Large* (Washington, D.C.: GPO, 1957); *Behind That Quiet Facade...* (Chicago: Continental Illinois Corporation, 1982); and Norman C. Miller, "Tino's Bottomless Tanks of Oil," *Saturday Evening Post,* April 25, 1964.

Notes for Chapter 11

1. The organizational changes in Continental during the period Kennedy was chairman can be traced in the annual reports of the bank. A comparison between the organization described in the "1961 Annual Report to Shareholders" with that described in the "1968 Annual Report to the Shareholders" makes clear the organizational changes that occurred in those eight years.

2. "In the recent banking difficulties of Continental Illinois, this credit card business was sold to Chemical Bank of New York at a very substantial profit, which outweighed all the losses of the initial period. So over the years this became a very profitable operation." (Kennedy Oral History, 1:253.)

CHAPTER 12

Volume 1 of the Kennedy Oral History, interviews with David Kennedy, and documents in the Kennedy Papers have been used. Interviews with Barbara

Kennedy Law, Marilyn Kennedy Taylor, Carol Kennedy Davis, Patricia Kennedy Campbell, and John K. Edmunds contain a wealth of information on the Chicago years, as does volume 2 of the John K. Edmunds Oral History, Interviews by Gordon Irving, 1979-82, 4 vols., typescript, The James Moyle Oral History Program, LDS Archives. Also helpful are interviews with Owen West, Willard Barton (Chicago, March 1985), and Craig Carpenter (Chicago, March 1985), and the Manuscript History of the Church, Chicago Stake, 2 vols. [not paginated], LDS Archives.

Notes for Chapter 12

1. "Lenora was taking care of me at home at that moment, and every day Hank Knight would call or come out and see me, never missed a single day, not even Saturday or Sunday." (Kennedy Oral History, 1:143).

CHAPTER 13

Volume 1 of the Kennedy Oral History, interviews with David Kennedy, and documents in the Kennedy Papers serve as important sources. Interviews with Gary H. Raddon (Chicago, March 1985), Robert Mayo (Chicago, February and May 1985), and other bank officers are also helpful.

Other sources include Edward Banfield, *Political Influence* (New York: Free Press, 1961); Alfred Balk, "Chicago's Bi-Party Boss," *Nation*, July 1, 1961; Bill Gleason, *Daley of Chicago* (New York: Simon and Schuster, 1970); David Halberstam, "Daley of Chicago," *Harpers*, August 1968; Charles J. Lewis and Ralph Whitehead Jr., "The New Kennedy in Washington: Mayor Daley's Banker," *Commweal*, January 10, 1969; Mike Royko, *Boss* (New York: E. P. Dutton, 1971); *Chicago's American*, March 17 and June 15, 1966; Clark Kissinger and Paul Booth, "[Welcome to Chicago]: Meet the Men Who Own It," *Ramparts*, September 7, 1969; Richard N. Gardner, ed., *Blueprint for Peace* (New York: McGraw-Hill, 1966); and *Report of the President's Commission on Budget Concepts* (Washington, D.C.: GPO, 1967).

CHAPTER 14

Volume 2 of the Kennedy Oral History, interviews with David and Lenora Kennedy, and documents in the Kennedy Papers are important sources for this chapter. Interviews with Charls Walker (Washington, D.C., May 1985) and Robert Mayo provided key information. Other sources are *Washington Post*, November 28 and December 12, 1968, April 30, May 13 and 14, and June 4, 18, and 22, 1969; Rowland Evans and Robert Novak, *Nixon in the White House: The Frustration of Power* (New York: Random House, 1971); *New York Times*, December 12, 1968, January 17 and 21, April 30, and June 4, 1969; *Times* (London), December 12, 1968; *Wall Street Journal*, December 12, 1968, and April 30, 1969; *Congressional Record*, 91st Congress, 1st session; Joint Economic Committee, *The 1969 Economic Report of the President, Hearings on the 1969 Economic Report of the President*, 91st Congress, 1st session, 1969;

Committee on Banking and Currency, *Investigation of Increase in Prime Interest Rate*, 91st Congress, 1st session, 1969; and *Chicago Tribune*, May 17, 1969.

Although not specifically cited, Richard Nixon, *The Memoirs of Richard Nixon* (New York: Grosset & Dunlap, 1978); Henry Kissinger, *White House Years* (Boston: Little, Brown & Co., 1979); and John Ehrlichman, *Witness to Power: The Nixon Years* (New York: Simon and Schuster, 1982) are useful in acquiring a sense of the Nixon administration and some details of its policies.

Notes for Chapter 14

1. Nixon was referring to political jokes about not counting Republican votes in Cook County.

2. Before the confirmation vote, Gore made a speech in which he explained his objections to the original proposal and outlined the changes that Kennedy had agreed to make in order to satisfy those objections. (January 20, 1969, *Congressional Record*, 91st Congress, 1st session, 115:1293–94.)

CHAPTER 15

Volume 2 of the Kennedy Oral History and interviews with David Kennedy are key sources. Documents from the Kennedy Papers provide much of the detail of the events covered. Essential are the interviews with Charls Walker, Robert Mayo, Donald Webster (Washington, D.C., August 1985), and Paul Volcker (Washington, D.C., August 1985). Also helpful are interviews with Patricia Kennedy Campbell, Barbara Kennedy Law, Sidney L. Jones (Washington, D.C., May 1985), and Mary Harris (Provo, Utah, July 1985).

Other sources include *Wall Street Journal*, May 27, 1969; Treasury Department, *Annual Report of the Secretary of the Treasury on the State of the Finances for the Fiscal Year Ended June 30, 1969*; Office of the Federal Register, *United States Government Organization Manual, 1969–70*; Joseph R. Daughen and Peter Binzen, *The Wreck of the Penn Central* (Boston: Little, Brown & Co., 1971); Public Law 774–932, September 8, 1950, *United States Statutes at Large* (Washington, D.C.: GPO, 1951); Robert Solomon, *The International Monetary System 1945–1981* (New York: Harper & Row, 1982); Robert Warren Stevens, *A Primer on The Dollar in the World Economy* (New York: Random House, 1972); Richard N. Gardner, ed., *Blueprint for Peace; Congressional Record*, 91st Congress, 2nd session; and Public Law 91–14, May 23, 1969, *United States Statutes at Large* (Washington, D.C.: GPO, 1970).

Note for Chapter 15

1. Dorothy Andrews Elston became Dorothy Andrews Kabis in September 1970 when she married Walter Kabis.

CHAPTER 16

Important sources for this chapter are the second volume of the Kennedy Oral History, interviews with David Kennedy, and documents from the Kennedy Papers. Interviews with the following provided good background material, as well as specific recollections of individual events: Charls Walker (Washington, D.C., May and August 1985), Paul Volcker, Murray Weidenbaum (Provo, Utah, August 1985), and Robert Mayo.

Other important sources are "Exclusive Interview With Treasury Secretary Kennedy, 'We Must Get Inflation Under Control,' " *U.S. News & World Report*, May 5, 1969; Neil De Marchi, "The First Nixon Administration: Prelude to Controls," *Exhortation and Controls: The Search for a Wage-Price Policy, 1945-1971*, ed. Craufurd D. Goodwin (Washington, D.C.: Brookings Institution, 1975); *Wall Street Journal*, June 11, 1969, and October 6, 1969; Joint Economic Committee, *The 1969 Economic Report of the President, Hearings before the Joint Economic Committee*, 91st Congress, 1st session, 1969; Richard Nixon, "Special Message to Congress on Fiscal Policy," *Public Papers of the Presidents of the United States, 1969* (Washington, D.C.: GPO, 1971); Richard Nixon, "Special Message to the Congress on Reform of the Federal Tax System," *Public Papers of the Presidents, 1969; Congressional Record*, 91st Congress, 1st session; Senate, *Proposed Extension of the Surcharge and Repeal of the Investment Tax Credit. Hearings before the Committee on Finance on HR. 12290*, 91st Congress, 1st session, 1969; *Washington Post*, June 11, 12, and 15, and July 11 and 31, 1969; Public Law 91–53, August 7, 1969, *United States Statutes at Large* (Washington, D.C.: GPO, 1970); House Committee on Banking and Currency, *Investigation of Increase in Prime Interest Rate. Hearings Before the Committee on Banking and Currency*, 91st Congress, 1st session, 1969; A. James Reichley, *Conservatives in an Age of Change* (Washington, D.C.: Brookings Institution, 1981); *Chicago Tribune*, January 12, 1971; *New York Times*, December 13, 1970; Arthur F. Burns, *Reflections of an Economic Policy Maker* (Washington, D.C.: American Enterprise Institute for Public Policy Research, 1978); Joint Economic Committee, *Report on the January 1970 Economic Report of the President*, 91st Congress, 2nd session, 1970; Joint Economic Committee, *Changing National Priorities. Hearings before the Subcommittee on Economy in Government*, 91st Congress, 2nd session, 1970; Richard Nixon, "Address to the Nation on Economic Policy and Productivity," *Public Papers of the Presidents of the United States, 1970* (Washington, D.C.: GPO, 1971); and Richard Nixon, "Statement on Signing Bill Extending the Defense Production Act," *Public Papers of the Presidents, 1970*.

CHAPTER 17

Volume 2 of the Kennedy Oral History, interviews with David Kennedy, and documents from the Kennedy Papers provide a substantial part of the source material for this chapter. Donald Webster, Charls Walker, and Anthony

Jurich (Washington, D.C., August 1985) provided helpful interviews and Richard Nixon, *Leaders* (New York: Warner Books, 1982), was used.

The single most significant source on the textile negotiations and Kennedy's role in the final agreement is I. M. Destler, Haruhiro Fukui, and Hideo Sato, *The Textile Wrangle: Conflict in Japanese-American Relations, 1969–1971* (Ithaca: Cornell University Press, 1979). Other useful sources are Public Law 77-354, December 18, 1941, *United States Statutes at Large* (Washington, D.C.: GPO, 1942); Richard Nixon, "Imposition of Supplemental Duty for Balance of Payments Purposes," Proclamation 4074, *Weekly Compilation of Presidential Documents* (Washington, D.C.: GPO, 1971); *New York Times*, September 25, and October 13, 1971. For background information on the change in the United States's relations with the People's Republic of China and the economic measures taken in August 1971, see Richard Nixon, *The Memoirs of Richard Nixon*, and Henry Kissinger, *White House Years.*

Notes for Chapter 17

1. "Moreover, he was enormously respected in Japan as a man of stature and decency, and the President continued to think highly of him despite his decision to replace him at the Treasury." (Destler, Fukui, and Sato, *The Textile Wrangle: Conflict in Japanese-American Relations, 1969–1971*, p. 280.)

2. Kennedy remembered that his efforts were often frustrating because American officials were telling their foreign counterparts, "Alex Johnson went through this. Ambassador Kennedy is going through this. He has to. The President has told him to. You listen to him, but you don't have to make any agreements. It's all political." (Kennedy Oral History, 2:148.)

CHAPTER 18

Obviously, a chapter on David Kennedy's style and human characteristics relies on all the data. Again, the Kennedy Oral History is important, as are the interviews with David and Lenora Kennedy. Other interviews specifically used herein are Charls Walker, Murray Weidenbaum, Mary Harris, Carol Kennedy Davis, Glenn Nielson (Provo, Utah, August 1985), J. R. "Jack" Simplot (Boise, Idaho, August 1985), Donald Webster, Sidney L. Jones, and Patricia Kennedy Campbell. Although not specifically cited, all of the interviews contributed important information crucial to this chapter. Also helpful are *Wall Street Journal*, May 27, 1969, and Edwin O. Haroldsen, "Two Latter-day Saints in U.S. Cabinet Posts: David M. Kennedy," *Improvement Era*, February 1969. Mark Singer, *Funny Money*, (New York: Alfred Knopf, 1985), and Steven R. Strahler, "Anderson's rise and fall: An inquiry into why the best and brightest failed," *Crain's Chicago Business*, January 14, 1985, are two good sources dealing with the decline of Continental Illinois.

CHAPTER 19

The first two chapters of volume 3 of the Kennedy Oral History, interviews with David Kennedy, and documents in the Kennedy Papers are key sources. Another important source is the "Palmer Files" in the Kennedy Papers. This material was gathered by Spencer J. Palmer in the preparation of his book *The Expanding Church* (Salt Lake City: Deseret Book, 1978). Interviews used as sources herein are Miller Shurtleff, David P. Farnsworth (Provo, Utah, May 1986), and Spencer J. Condie (Vienna, Austria, October 1985). The Doctrine and Covenants is also a source.

Notes for Chapter 19

1. "President Kimball notified them in one of their temple meetings of the assignment and of the fact that I'd be reporting directly to the First Presidency. But despite that, a number of the Twelve would have some problem they'd been working on and wanted to turn it over to me and have me do this, that or the other. So a second time he told them I was reporting to him, because I told him about this. He said, well, let me handle that." (Kennedy Oral History, 3:8.)

2. The procedure worked with all but Elder LeGrand Richards. He told Kennedy that he had never written a talk in his life and he was not about to start. (Kennedy Oral History, 3:30.)

INDEX

Abs, Hermann, 167
Accident, car, DMK involved in, 32, 370, n. 6
Adams, Orval, 206
Administrative assistant, DMK named, 373, n. 1
Ads, DMK sells, 29
Agnew, Spiro, 269
Agreement: government-to-government, 294; textile. *See* Textile agreement
Aid to Families with Dependent Children, 275
Aides of DMK, 249
Aishton, Richard, 129, 140
Alberti, Blanch, 87
Alcohol, not allowed in bank, 131
Allen, Lyndon K. "Mort," 272
Ambassador-at-large: DMK appointed, 288; DMK resigns as, 312–13
American Bankers Association, 217
Amer, Abdel Hakim, 167
Anderson, Arch, 105
Anderson, Robert B., 227, 234
Anderson, Roger: appointed to international division, 160; education of, 161; searches for bank site, 162; announces DMK

in Japan, 164; as business leader, 184; as chairman of Continental, 316
Argyle, Utah, 3, 5
Arthur Anderson, accounting firm, 146, 147
Ashley, Thomas L., 156
Awards presented to DMK, 218–19

Balance of payments, international economic challenge of, 258–59
Banco Privata Finanziaria, 169–70
Banfield, Edward, 211–12
Bangerter, Geraldine, 350
Bangerter, William Grant, 350
Bank Holding Company Act, 184
Bank Merger Act of 1960, 151, 154, 155
Bankers, aggressiveness of, 375, n. 3
Banking, DMK considers, as a career, 106
Banking Act of 1935, 96–97
Barr, Joseph, 175, 222, 234, 236
Beach, Paul R., 249, 291, 306
Bear River Valley: history of, 1–2; winters in the, 7–8; climate of, 369, n. 1
Beggs, James, 256
Bennett, Wallace, 348
Benson, Ezra Taft, 84